MYRTLE HILL received a doctorate in history from Queen's University Belfast, where she is Director of the Centre for Women's Studies. She is co-author of *Evangelical Protestantism in Ulster Society, 1740–1890* (Routledge, 1992) and of *Women in Ireland: Image and Experience, c.1880–1920* (Blackstaff Press, 1999). She has published many articles on Irish, social, religious and women's history.

D1605713

WOMEN
IN IRELAND

A century of change

MYRTLE HILL

THE
BLACKSTAFF
PRESS

BELFAST

Frontispiece

Lady Augusta Caroline Dillon from
Clonbrook House in County Galway
pictured with her daughters Edith and Ethel
at their presentation to society in London, *c.* 1900

COURTESY NATIONAL LIBRARY OF IRELAND

First published in 2003 by
Blackstaff Press Limited
4c Heron Wharf, Sydenham Business Park
Belfast BT3 9LE, Northern Ireland

Printed in Ireland by Betaprint

A CIP catalogue record of this book
is available from the British Library

ISBN 0-85640-740-2

www.blackstaffpress.com

For my daughters
Catherine and Joanne
and for Rebecca

For sisters
Bobbie, Liz and Dorothy

And for
Eilish, Eleanor, Hazel, Hilary, Michelle and Sally
in appreciation of the walks and talks, love and laughter,
of our 'women's weekends'

Contents

ACKNOWLEDGEMENTS   ix
ABBREVIATIONS   x
INTRODUCTION   1

1 Into the new century   14

2 Emerging identities   51

3 War and welfare in a divided island   88

4 Challenging the state(s) we're in   137

5 Towards the millennium   186

CONCLUSION   240
NOTES   247
BIBLIOGRAPHY   276
INDEX   305

Acknowledgements

I owe thanks to many people who have helped, formally and informally, in researching and writing this book. Staff at various libraries and institutions have generously and efficiently given of their time and expertise. I would particularly like to thank the staff of Cork Public Museum, the National Library of Ireland, Trinity College Dublin and the Special Collections library of Queen's University Belfast. I made extensive use of both the Irish and Political Collections of the Linen Hall Library, where Yvonne Murphy was especially helpful. I am grateful to the Deputy Keeper of Records at the Public Record Office of Northern Ireland for granting me permission to publish material, and to Michael Duffin, for permission to quote from Emma Duffin's diaries. The Trustees of the Ulster Folk and Transport Museum, Cork Public Museum and the National Library of Ireland helped me to locate and granted permission to reproduce photographic images, as did Paul Kavanagh, Allan Leonard, Sean McCarthy and Lesley Doyle. Yvonne Murphy similarly helped with reproductions from the Troubled Images and the Victor Patterson collections at the Linen Hall Library. Margaret Curran and Jacqueline O'Donnell kindly granted me permission to quote from their poetry.

As the bibliography indicates, I owe a vast debt to those who have explored, analysed and discussed the experiences of Irish women throughout the course of the twentieth century. I hope this book contributes to the process of knowledge-making and to the stimulating debates that it has set in motion. Thanks are due to those who read parts of the manuscript at different stages: Eilish Rooney, Jennifer Fitzgerald, John Lynch, Linda Edgerton Walker and Margaret Ward. I am most grateful for the advice and information they shared with me. And to Reg for digging out some illuminating bits of information which have been incorporated into the text and for ensuring there were lovely meals after long days at the word processor.

Anne Tannahill, Wendy Dunbar, Patsy Horton, Bronagh McVeigh and all at Blackstaff Press provided expertise at the various stages of production and encouragement when deadlines loomed, while Hilary Bell offered love and support in addition to employing her rigorous editorial skills well above and beyond the call of duty – thank you all.

Abbreviations

ADAPT	Association for Deserted and Alone Parents
AIM	Action, Information, Motivation
ARP	Air-raid precautions
ATS	Auxiliary Territorial Service
CAP	Contraception Action Programme
CHERISH	Children Have Every Right in Society Here
CSJ	Campaign for Social Justice
CSW	Council for the Status of Women
DUP	Democratic Unionist Party
EEC	European Economic Community
EOC	Equal Opportunities Commission
EU	European Union
FANY	First Aid Nursing Yeomanry
HCL	Homeless Citizens' League
IAW	International Alliance of Women
ICA	Irish Countrywomen's Association
ICTU	Irish Congress of Trade Unions
IHA	Irish Housewives' Association
IPP	Irish Parliamentary Party
IRA	Irish Republican Army
IRB	Irish Republican Brotherhood
ITGWU	Irish Transport and General Workers' Union
IWFL	Irish Women's Franchise League
IWLM	Irish Women's Liberation Movement
IWSF	Irish Women's Suffrage Federation
IWSL	Irish Women's Suffrage League
IWSLGA	Irish Women's Suffrage and Local Government Association
IWU	Irishwomen United
IWWU	Irish Women's Workers Union
LOT	Lesbians Organising Together
MLA	Member of Local Assembly
NHS	National Health Service
NIAC	Northern Ireland Abortion Campaign
NICRA	Northern Ireland Civil Rights Association
NIFPA	Northern Ireland Family Planning Association
NIWC	Northern Ireland Women's Coalition
NIWRM	Northern Ireland Women's Rights Movement
PD	People's Democracy

PR	Proportional Representation
PUP	Progressive Unionist Party
QAINS	Queen Alexandra Imperial Nursing Service
RAC	Relatives' Action Committee
RTÉ	Radio Telefís Éireann
RUC	Royal Ulster Constabulary
SDLP	Social Democratic and Labour Party
SPUC	Society for the Protection of the Unborn Child
UDA	Ulster Defence Association
UDR	Ulster Defence Regiment
UI	United Irishwomen
UUC	Ulster Unionist Council
UUP	Ulster Unionist Party
UVF	Ulster Volunteer Force
UWC	Ulster Workers' Council
UWUC	Ulster Women's Unionist Council
VADs	Voluntary Auxiliary Detachment Nurses
WAAC	Women's Army Auxiliary Corps
WAAF	Women's Auxiliary Air Force
WNHA	Women's National Health Association
WPA	Women's Political Association
WRAF	Women's Royal Air Force
WRNS	Women's Royal Naval Service
WSPU	Women's Social and Political Union

This mother proudly displays her baby and the goose she has
fattened to sell at Dundalk market in the early 1950s.

Problems, perspectives and possibilities

Without a knowledge of our past, we are always having to begin again.[1]

Reflecting on women's experience over the course of one hundred years has proved a major personal and academic challenge. While it is not difficult to view the first fifty years of the twentieth century as a historical era, the next five decades, encompassing my own life span, have been more problematic. My professional training as a historian has left me in no doubt that an objective history is neither possible nor desirable, but to research and write a historical narrative so 'close to home' has been a challenging task. My background, interests and priorities have helped to shape this work – my experiences and memories mingle with those of sisters, friends and colleagues – sometimes meeting, often contrasting. However, finding a 'voice' which crosses generations, acknowledges diversity and yet pinpoints important landmarks, is no easy matter. We are, after all, never *just* women, but have other, and sometimes more important, aspects to our identity. Moreover, we prioritise these in different ways, at different times. This is particularly, but not uniquely, reflected in the emergence of second-wave feminism in the north of Ireland, when nationalist/unionist/feminist agendas coincided – and sometimes conflicted. While the constitutional debate continues, the first generation of second-wave feminists has now reached maturity, and its impact on the prospects of the young women who will shape and be shaped

by the events of the twenty-first century has yet to be assessed. The possibility of these young women achieving their personal, political and economic potential on an island still divided by politics, religion, class and
culture, as well as gender, has perhaps been enhanced by equality legislation
and the advances made by the women's movement.

The main purpose of this book is to contribute to the recovery of Irish
women's experiences in a century that witnessed two world wars, recurring
social and political disruption, and an economic context that has altered the
nature of their involvement in the labour market. Family structures, employment patterns, attitudes to religion and to sexuality, and women's participation in both the cultural and political sphere, have all undergone significant
shifts. From the early suffrage campaigns through to the challenges to constitutional constraints on individual sexual rights, women have been found
on both the conservative and the radical wings of debate. Their voices have
been heard on national and international stages – speaking out from the
European Commission in Brussels, the Dáil and the Seanad in Dublin, the
House of Commons in London, or on the steps of Parliament Buildings at
Stormont in Belfast. Their support – active or passive – has been critical to
those engaged in the violent assertion of their political views in the
Northern conflict, and their strength has sustained family life in the strife-
torn communities of Belfast, Derry and elsewhere. Some aspects of both
individual and collective female experience have been recorded, assessed
and analysed, but many stories remain untold and no overview of women's
myriad responses to the challenges and changes of the century is currently
available. It is vitally important to the continuing progress of women that
these issues are addressed.

Between 1900 and the year 2000, change took place at an unprecedent-
ed rate. While the exploration of space became a reality, back on earth war
on a worldwide scale provided a sombre background to the sophisticated
advances of science and technology. The ability to clone human and animal
life, to intervene in the production of the human embryo and to replace
vital organs in the human body would have been considered as nothing
short of miraculous in 1900. Both the working and domestic environments,
transformed by sleek electronic equipment and the silicon chip, would also
have appeared alien to men and women for whom the first petrol-powered
cars, the wireless telegraph, the telephone and the cinema were massively
expanding the potential of transport, communication and leisure activities.

There is no doubt that the generation of women entering maturity as the
twentieth century closed inhabited a different world from that of their
female predecessors, who witnessed the death of Queen Victoria and the

There's room for both baby and toddler in this
elegant, turn-of-the-century baby carriage.

onset of the Home Rule crisis. How much of the change, however, has been
fundamental, and how much superficial or illusory? What difference does it
make to women living in Ireland that during the course of the century they
gained the right to vote and to be elected as public representatives at
parliamentary level? That the patterns of employment were transformed by
both economic and technological developments? That medicine, science
and technology developed the capacity to control the processes of human
reproduction? And so on.

Some dimensions of these changes are measurable. For example, an Irish
woman born in 1900 could not expect to live beyond her mid-fifties, her
chances of marriage would be considerably less than those of her counterparts in England, Scotland or Wales, and she was likely to join hundreds
of thousands of her contemporaries in seeking her fortune in Britain or on
the far side of the Atlantic Ocean. The average family had 7 children, and
150 of every 1,000 babies (15 per cent) died before reaching their first
birthday, and the risks were even greater for urban dwellers. In sharp contrast, Irish women born at the end of the century can expect a lifespan of
around eighty years, infant mortality rates have fallen to around 5.5 per cent,
family units are smaller, and the number of single-parent families has
dramatically increased.

Useful as they may be in facilitating generalisations, the problem with statistics is that they relate to some elusive 'average' woman, and are less representative once variables such as class, background and geographical location are brought into play. While such figures help us to chart long-term shifts in social life and provide a useful measuring stick, to talk, for example, of an average life expectancy is to ignore the mass of evidence detailing how life can be curtailed by a range of socio-economic, environmental and genetic factors. It is worth noting, however, that the degree of social difference would be much less at the end of the century than at the beginning. By the year 1999, few of even the most geographically isolated rural areas would have been untouched by the approach of modernity: television, radio and the worldwide web having transformed communications. Moreover, the greater centralisation of government and a blanket of social services have resulted in a much higher degree of uniformity in living standards throughout Ireland. In addition, membership of the European Union (EU) has ensured that the rights of Irish men, women and children are enshrined in and determined by a process that extends beyond national boundaries – both physical and symbolic.

The range of opportunities open to late twentieth-century Irish women would have been unimaginable in the early 1900s. Though illiteracy may still exist in remote areas or amongst some Travelling peoples, girls in the twenty-first century are generally achieving much higher results than boys at primary and secondary levels. Indeed, the relatively poor academic performance of boys has become a major concern of successive governments, with the results of the eleven-plus examinations, held in the North, skewed in their favour until a public outcry ended the practice in the 1990s. At tertiary level, the first nine female graduates receiving their degrees from the Royal University of Ireland in 1884, were paving the way to a situation where, by the year 2000, women not only numerically outnumbered male students in Irish universities, but were beginning to overtake them in terms of achieving higher levels in their degree results. A less positive aspect comes to light, however, when we examine the disciplines studied by each sex. Women remain overrepresented in the arts and social sciences, while men dominate the 'hard' sciences, medicine and technology. Specialising in these latter areas tends to lead to better rewards in terms of finance and status in the labour market, which accounts for only one of a number of factors working against women's ambitions once they enter employment.

Nonetheless, women have statistically made significant gains in employment in the course of the century, though there are regional differences, and the opportunities for working women in the north-east of the island have always followed a different pattern from the rest of Ireland. While the issue of working mothers remained contentious throughout the century, the greatest contrast with the early 1900s was in the large number of married women in employment by the year 2000. But, even at the century's end, and despite three decades of preventative legislation, women still suffer discrimination in the workplace and are most likely to be overrepresented in part-time, low-paid jobs. The 'significant minority' of women who make it to the top of their chosen field – and it is a growing minority – all too often do so at considerable cost to their personal lives. A combination of economic shifts, civil disruption in the North, and the influence of the European single market ensured that employment opportunites for women in Ireland underwent substantial change, particularly in the Republic, where the newly vibrant economy of the 1990s became known as the Celtic Tiger.[2]

In Ireland, historically, religion has always been important to individuals and to communities. The solace and the strictures of the Catholic and Protestant Churches helped shape the lives of Irish men and women, in many cases determining their behaviour, their interaction with others and their views of the world around them. For the first seventy years of the twentieth century this particularly impacted on matters of sexuality. While the major denominations strove to influence sexual behaviour, the close relationship between Church and state in the South served to reinforce the power of the Catholic hierarchy, which was seemingly 'preoccupied with the sinfulness of sex, with its dangers outside of marriage, and with the need to subordinate it within marriage to procreative ends'.[3] Bridie Quinn-Conroy, growing up in the west of Ireland, remembered:

> To say we were 'led and said' by religion is an understatement. Everything done or said was overshadowed by religion. We were afraid of what the priests would say. We were afraid of what our parents would say. We were afraid God would punish us. So we let the time for change pass us by and we let the time for discussion elapse.[4]

The perusal of a variety of sources suggests, however, that, at least until the 1960s, religion in the South was a source of power and affirmation for many women, who were in turn ardent promoters of the faith. But by the year 2000, a realignment of the relationship between Church, state and civil society indicated that the Church's authority, particularly on sexual matters, was gradually diminishing, and that a gulf was beginning to emerge between formal religious practice and the activities of everyday life.

In the north of Ireland religious identity was central to the conflict that erupted in the late 1960s and which would dominate life there until the end of the century and beyond. The political stalemate preceding the First World War resulted in the founding of 'a Protestant state for a Protestant people' in 1921, characterised by discriminatory practices against the large Catholic minority. The treatment of minority ethnic or religious groups is problematic in many regimes, as witnessed in several areas of Eastern and Central Europe throughout the twentieth century. Northern Ireland's situation is not therefore unique, though it often appears so to its beleaguered inhabitants. The 1960s civil rights movement, which, in line with American and European campaigns called for substantial reforms in the institutions of government, became a major politicising force for many women, who responded with shock to the brutality of state-backed authorities. Throughout the following decades, a minority of women became involved in active resistance to British rule, or, less often, in support of militant loyalism. Whether through active resistance or passive acceptance, women played a role in the construction and changing nature of unionism, nationalism and pacifism in these years. However, for the majority of women living in troubled areas of the North, like most of their counterparts in other countries enduring civil disruption, holding together families and communities in the face of the persistent practical hardships generated by conflict was the major priority.

Women's activism had been one of the driving forces behind change in all of these areas, from the early campaigns for suffrage, through to demands for greater personal and sexual freedom, and equality of treatment, participation and representation in all spheres of public life. And, despite the limitations, there were some remarkable achievements. In 1900 women's official political participation was confined to the offices of local government as Poor Law officers or in public posts such as factory inspectors, and their work in these areas was highly significant in bringing a female dimension to the society they served. Participation in local government was also important in the longer term as a stepping stone to power at a national level, and as an indicator of female talent and abilities. Though slow to respond to demands for women's suffrage, governments were eventually forced to acknowledge their contribution both before and during the First World War and, indeed, in the Irish Free State, during the War of Independence. By the century's end, the Republic had fourteen female TDs (Teachta Dála) sitting in the Dáil, and had elected two female presidents. In the North representation at national level was a much more complicated affair. During the period of Direct Rule, the Northern State was governed by a female British Prime Minister (Margaret Thatcher) and administered by a female Secretary of State (Mo Mowlam).

Perhaps one of the most significant developments of the twentieth century was the collective experience of women in their local communities. In the last decades of the century, a number of groups brought together women for a variety of purposes – educational, environmental, political and social. These organisations not only raised women's consciousness about their positions and opportunities, and enhanced their personal experience, they also provided innovative and supportive forums for those wishing to participate or intervene more directly in the affairs of their locality. Providing training, solidarity and access to funding for programmes of action which raise the profile of women and increase the visibility of *their* concerns and aspirations, women's community groups look likely to prove the most effective agents of the voluntary sector. It could be argued that these alternative female structures have to some extent replaced the solidarity of the tight-knit neighbourhoods of the past.

By the year 2000 women were also much more likely than before to be visible in cultural arenas. For example, the conservative, Catholic ethos of the Free State effectively removed women from competitive athletic sports for around thirty years after its founding. Pope Pius XI had, after all, decreed in 1929 that in athletics and gymnastic exercises 'special precaution must be taken in regard to Christian modesty in the case of girls, inasmuch as it is extremely unbecoming for them to display themselves before the public gaze'.[5] Even when such strictures were removed, it took Irish sportswomen some time to regain the ground lost over several decades, and it was not until the 1970s that they were represented in any kind of strength at the Olympic Games, and the 1990s before medals were brought home. Northern Ireland's sportswomen were not constrained to the same extent, and medals were won as early as the 1940s.

While social convention and cultural constraints also considerably restricted women's activities within the world of art and literature, even a cursory glance at the most prominent examples suggests that there was much hidden talent and unrecognised potential. For instance, women were major contributors to the Arts and Crafts exhibitions that helped focus public attention on Ireland's celtic heritage in the early twentieth century, producing work of outstanding quality in textiles, metal and glass.[6] They were also significant as patrons of the visual arts. Although not admitted to the Royal Hibernian Academy until the 1920s, many female artists donated their work to Hugh Lane in support of his attempts to establish a permanent Gallery of Modern Art in Dublin. Painters Evie Hone and Mainie Jellett are credited with introducing modernist art, particulary cubism, to Ireland in the 1930s. Art historian Brian Kennedy notes that 'women, both artists and non-artists, played an important role in creating the first Living

Art Exhibition' in the 1940s.[7] Women were also active in all areas of the flourishing artistic scene of the 1960s – a consequence of new economic prosperity – and they centrally contributed to debates during the seventies and eighties 'about what art is and what it might be'.[8] A 1986 Dublin exhibition of women's art from the eighteenth to the twentieth century, which featured around 270 artists, reflected the growing acceptance of their work. As Joan Fowler commented:

> If at the turn of the twentieth century women artists were, with very few exceptions, regarded as little more than happy amateurs, the closing decades of the century indicate a substantial increase in the numbers of professional women artists who regularly exhibit their work.[9]

A critical dimension of the second-wave feminist movement was the emphasis placed on the need to rewrite and reread Ireland, in order to combat what Eavan Boland has called the 'disproportionate silence' of women. In 1985, when the Northern Ireland Women's Rights Movement (NIWRM) published an anthology of women's writing to mark its tenth anniversary, editor Ruth Hooley noted that although they were writing in a decade which saw the setting-up and expansion of women-only publishing presses throughout the world, the number of published women in the North was minimal.[10] Moreover, on this issue at least, the border was meaningless, with women's writings equally dismissed North and South. As Catherine Byron pointed out in the late 1980s:

> Looked at from England there seems to be more heated discussion about whether the Northern poets have an unfair advantage in publication and publicity over those in the south, than concern about the fifty percent of the population on both sides of the border that still hardly has a poetic voice at all.[11]

Medbh McGuckian was the only woman amongst the ten poets featured in Paul Muldoon's *Faber Book of Contemporary Irish Poetry*, published in 1986. In her autobiography, writer Nuala O'Faolain, discussing her interview with Seamus Deane on RTÉ's *Bookline* on the publication of his three-volume *Field Day Anthology of Irish Writing* in 1991, described how she could not find in herself 'an unemotional response to its omission of women's testimony'.[12] The eagerly awaited volumes IV and V in this important series, devoted to women's writing and traditions and commissioned after considerable debate, were eventually published in September 2002.[13] It is difficult not to agree with the comment that 'until comparatively recent times, Ireland was a text written by men'.[14] As in so many other areas of life,

Two sisters, the Misses Martin, work on the magnificently colourful mosaic roof of the Baptistery in St Anne's Cathedral, Belfast, 1927.

the major focus of public literary debate reflected political, not gender, sensibilities.

Another critical area of women's writing was the uncovering, assessment and analysis of women's historical experience – as Mary Cullen remarked, 'current changes in women's history did not just happen. They grew direct-ly from the contemporary feminist movement.'[15] The first major pioneering work on Irish women's history was a 1978 publication edited by Margaret MacCurtain and Donncha Ó Corráin: *Women in Irish Society: The Historical Dimension.*[16] This book set the agenda and the standard and has been fol-lowed by a plethora of studies which have collectively mounted a challenge to traditional images, concepts and notions about women's place, aspirations and experiences. There is little doubt that women's history, which has drawn attention to the value of unconventional sources and innovative method-ologies such as discourse analysis, has brought about a fundamental shift in the ways in which we think about the past. Like all disciplines, it is still evolving and has developed its own areas of concern. Writing in 1997, Mary Daly commented that,

> until recently, Irish women's history has usually been analyzed from a per-spective that has led to an excessive emphasis on the uniqueness of the Irish experience, and to an underestimation of the important contribution of Irish women.[17]

However, as she suggests, the more recent advent of comparative studies and works which contextualise the Irish experience reflect the growing sophis-tication of the discipline. There are, of course, gaps and, more seriously, there is a danger that feminist historians are too often tempted to impose their own values, attitudes and feelings on lives lived differently. The focus of historians in general is to a large extent determined by the agendas and priorities of the age in which they write – in the case of the twentieth cen-tury, nationalism and feminism. While this focus has produced a great many valuable texts, it has perhaps resulted in an unbalanced historiography, one that favours the champions of 'popular' causes. Salma Leydesdorff, discussing the issue of identification with historical subjects, urges us to reintroduce into the picture 'those elements which conjure up unpleasant feelings and are therefore in danger of being forgotten or omitted'.[18] Such a project would focus on the difficulties and contradictions as well as the triumphs of women, placing them firmly within the context of their own times. Our dependence on accessible source material is one of the reasons for this his-toriographical emphasis, and one which is often reflected in this current work. But more recent publications are helping to rectify a situation where

domesticity and powerlessness were seen as synonymous and where unionism was often dismissed as deviant, a political conviction that could not be
sustained in the long term. The more general shift from the concept of a
'master narrative' to recognition of the significance of localised studies has
also been important to the evolution of women's history. More latterly, creative writing classes and local community projects are contributing to the
expanding archive for future historians seeking to locate the 'ordinary' Irish
woman.

That women's history is increasingly taught not only in women's studies
and other university courses, but also in schools and colleges, is recognition
of its growing acceptance. One ongoing, and crucial, debate is around
whether by treating women as a separate and distinctive category feminist
historians are in fact contributing to and reinforcing women's marginalisation. However, a fully integrated, inclusive history remains an aspiration, and
in the meantime there is still some way to go in actually *finding* the women
of the past.

A serious concern among feminist theorists of the 1990s has been the
tendency of some writers to discuss women as a homogenous group – a
dangerous and unsustainable position. Women's experiences are determined
by a range of circumstances – geographical location, social status, personality, age, and sexual orientation. Whether they are married, single, mothers,
paid employees or creative artists (or any combinations of these) is also relevant.

Moreover, changes taking place over the lifetime of an individual, both
contextual and personal, can also alter or influence lifestyle and experience.
For example, born at the midway point of the twentieth century, I have
been daughter, sister, wife, mother, aunt and grandmother, and have experienced life as a schoolgirl, office worker, housewife, childminder, student and
academic. I have moved from embracing religious evangelicalism to a position of agnosticism, from a conservative and materialistic to a feminist outlook. The lives of most women reveal similarly shifting perspectives.
Furthermore, Lynne Segal argues that shifts and changes also occur collectively: 'Women's lives, like men's, are constantly changing . . . indeed,
women's lives have changed much faster than men's throughout this century.'[19] Segal's concern is that twentieth-century feminism has made women
into 'collective victims', and does not take into account 'uneven and contradictory advances in women's lives and aspirations, nor the hierarchies and
divisions between women'. In relation to twentieth-century Irish women,
the barriers that divided, as well as the experiences that united, them
became all too obvious in the course of researching and writing this book,

defying any attempt at a simplistic analytical overview, and pointing instead to the multifaceted nature of women's lives past and present.

What follows makes no claim to be a comprehensive study, but is rather an attempt to trace the major shifts and developments in women's experience over the course of a century of turbulent economic, social and political change. Chapter 1 concerns the difficult task of scene-setting. Its purpose is to outline some of the diversity of female experience at the opening of the century and the major factors that helped determine the shape of women's lives: living and housing standards, family life, and educational and working opportunities are all considered.

Chapter 2 covers the same time period, but narrows the focus to explore and assess the activities and experiences of particular individuals and groups of women who attempted to influence the wider political agenda. Their commitment to the political ideals of suffrage, nationalism, unionism or republicanism drew them into the world of public debate, as did their experience of war and rebellion. More has been written of these women than of others, though they represented only a small élite of Irish women in this period. Their impact on history, however, has been disproportionate, a reflection of contemporary political events and concerns. Moreover, although they were unrepresentative of society at large, and were often unsuccessful in their endeavours, they would be of considerable significance to future generations, as role models and upholders of radical traditions.

Chapter 3 discusses the emergence of new jurisdictions and their impact on the political, economic and social life of women. During much of the 1920s and 1930s women were much more restricted in the degree to which they could participate in public life than in previous decades, but the conservatism which confined so many to family life in Ireland, reflected the experience of women across Western Europe. The Second World War affected North and South in different ways, as did the post-war emphasis on restructuring and revitalising the nation-states.

Chapter 4, opening with the 'swinging' sixties, looks at the impact of international trends in a decade that marked the beginning of a period when institutional authority of all kinds faced a range of challenges. Women, through a variety of forums, mounted individual and collective intellectual and physical campaigns against the culture which constrained their activities and narrowed their opportunities. But, change would be slow. Travel writer Dervla Murphy reflected in the mid-1970s that it was

> hard to believe – especially after a period abroad – that in Ireland we are still arguing about legalising the sale of contraceptives. I remember arriving

home from Baltistan last year and feeling that I'd come from the Third World to some dotty Fourth World consisting only of Ireland.[20]

The start of the conflict in the North ensured that the women's movement there was itself divided, and divided also from the broader context of the 'fight for rights' on the rest of the island.

In Chapter 5 women's position in terms of health, living standards and participation in employment and politics is again addressed and their achievements and failures discussed. As the century drew to a close, at least some of the differences between North and South narrowed, with the Southern standard of living beginning to catch up, and, in many respects, exceed, that in the North.[21]

Throughout the century, women's progress has been unsteady, with advances and setbacks, and periods of optimism swiftly followed by despair. What remains clear, however, is that women were, in the main, neither silent nor passive observers of the world they inhabited, but played their part in determining its direction. The intention of this work is to make visible the hopes, dreams and fears of those women whose experiences shaped the present, and of those who will help to mould the future. It is about thirty years since Elizabeth Janeway commented that, 'Like their personal lives, women's history is fragmented, interrupted; a shadow history of human beings whose existence has been shaped by the efforts and demands of others.[22] It is the task of today's historians to overturn that legacy, and this book aims to make a contribution to that agenda, with its gaps, omissions and questions suggesting the extent to which further research is necessary.

Into the new century

Women are the basis of a nation's wealth.
On them practically depends the efficiency
and welfare of the race.[1]

On a day of brilliant sunshine in the spring of 1900, the 81-year-old Queen of the British Empire landed in Kingstown at the beginning of a three-week visit to her Irish subjects. Her reception, reported the *Irish Times* on 5 April 1900, was 'magnificent', a 'triumphal pageant' amidst 'scenes of wonderful enthusiasm'. The streets of Dublin were heavily and colourfully decorated; flags waved from a number of buildings, and enthusiasts such as the 'female apostles' of the 'Ragged Mission' exhibited the colours of the Union Jack 'on their bosoms'. The *Irish News and Belfast Morning News*, however, claimed that Victoria's spirited welcoming had been ensured by the importation into the city of 'contingents of loyalists' from Belfast and elsewhere, and that the majority of Dublin's citizens, enjoying a day's holiday, were merely 'curious' about the royal visitor. In a tone markedly different from his colleague on the *Irish Times*, the *Irish News* reporter praised the 'civil, courteous and respectful' reception given by nationalists to a woman who, in the view of many, symbolised centuries of oppression.[2] Other nationalists voiced their anger. Many believed that the Queen's visit was timed 'to bolster the reserve of Irish soldiers who were in Her Majesty's service in the Boer War'.[3] Maud Gonne, their most ardent spokeswoman,

Judging by their empty baskets, these three cockle-pickers are just
about to begin work along the shoreline, c. 1890–1910.

demanded that she return to her own land. In an article entitled 'The
Famine Queen', which was suppressed when it first appeared in the *United
Irishman* during the Queen's visit, Gonne went on to argue:

> Every eviction during sixty-three years has been carried out in Victoria's
> name, and if there is a Justice in Heaven the shame of those poor Irish emi-
> grant girls whose very innocence renders them an easy prey and who have
> been overcome in the terrible struggle for existence on a foreign shore, will
> fall on this woman.[4]

When Victoria died less than a year later, on 22 January 1901, there was
remarkably little mourning outside of the north-east of the island. Indeed,
a vote of condolence was initially rejected by Dublin Corporation, and only
passed with abstentions. And many would have shared the Countess of
Fingall's feeling that 'with her death a chapter had ended'.[5]

With 1900 declared a Holy Year by Pope Leo XIII, the opening hours of
the twentieth century had been marked by phenomenally large attendances
at midnight mass throughout the country. And in Belfast the streets were
'thronged with people' as Protestants went to watch-night services.[6] On
New Year's Day in Dublin, in contrast to the extravagant celebrations
greeting the year 2001, there appears to have been little public fanfare. Most

businesses remained open, and Dubliners shopped unhindered by parades or other festivities. The *Irish Times* went so far as to suggest that 'New Year's Day runs a close chance of becoming extinct altogether'.[7] Nonetheless, most people recognised that Ireland was entering a new era in national life, her constitutional relationship with Britain the subject of intense parliamentary debate. Victoria confessed in her diary that on this first day of the new century she was 'full of anxiety and fear of what may be before us'.[8] With the Boer War, infirmity and old age uppermost in her mind, it is unlikely that she was referring in any way to the position of women. While a small number of middle-class, well-educated young women were claiming the right to fully participate in public life, most of those lower down the social scale were too preoccupied with the trials and small triumphs of daily life and labour, to speculate on the future prospects of Irish womanhood.

THE HOME ENVIRONMENT

However they celebrated (or not) the coming of the new century, the everyday experience of women in Ireland, as elsewhere, was largely determined by their social class, geographical location and wider economic factors. In 1911 Ireland was still very much a rural country, with only about a third of the population living in towns. Belfast and Dublin were the main urban centres, though the two cities were quite distinctive in character. Belfast, with a population of 386,947 in that year, was a fast-growing industrial centre, while Dublin's slightly smaller population reflected the lowest average rate of urban growth on the island. Cork, Galway, Limerick and Waterford were, like Dublin, commercial cities, but Ireland as a whole was still 'a rural area studded by a network of small agricultural service towns'.[9] The land problems that had dominated the previous century were well on the way to resolution and the rural community, which was studied by social anthropologists Conrad M. Arensberg and Solon T. Kimball in the 1930s, was now emerging, with the prevailing ethos of rural conservatism ensuring that urban life exercised only a minimal influence on 'the governing values' of Irish society as a whole.[10]

Wealthy home-owners of the upper echelons of society were taking up residence in handsome, leafy suburbs, beyond the centres of commercial and industrial activity, and like the owners of country houses and prosperous farms, their comfortable lifestyle was facilitated by a retinue of servants. Indeed, the number of domestic employees gave a clearer indication of a family's social status than traditional class categories, which do not adequately reflect the full range and diversity of economic status experienced by Irish men and women in this period. On average, the mistress of a large country house employed a staff of around fourteen, while the wife of a High Court judge could expect to have six servants to do her bidding. A cook, a maid and a nurse was a common combination for 'comfortable' families, but for many lower down the social scale the presence of one servant was sufficient to ensure an air of respectability.[11] Although servants required to be overseen and given daily orders, the engagement diaries of the women of the household would have been filled with a round of social or domestic engagements, varying according to the season and their place in the social hierarchy. For the social élite, the Anglo-Irish, these would have included garden parties, games of tennis, croquet or bridge, local visits and dinner parties. A good deal of time would have been spent with family or relatives in England, enjoying 'the season' in London, and foreign travel was increasingly seen as an essential 'finishing touch' to a young woman's and young man's education. Emma and Ruth Duffin from Belfast, for example, enjoyed trips to France, Germany and Switzerland, and spent a good deal of time in London.[12] For the wives and families of ambassadors, diplomats and army officers, travel was a way of life, albeit involving less choice of destination. Nora Robertson's childhood residences depended upon her father's military career, and so she lived in army quarters in Athlone, Fermoy, Clonmel and Cork, was educated at Heathfield in England, and spent time in India as a teenager.[13]

Belfast, with its bustling mills and busy shipyard, provided employment opportunities for both men and women, but religious identity could play a major part in determining working experiences and standards of living. Henry Patterson argues that there was 'a predominantly Protestant elite in the Belfast working class',[14] so that the good standard housing noted by factory inspector Hilda Martindale in 1911 accommodated a mainly Protestant skilled workforce. Saidie Patterson's description of the house in Woodvale Street in which she was born in 1906 is probably typical of such a home. She remembered that it was

> one of a street of red-brick terrace houses two rooms downstairs and two or three above; no bathroom, a tiny scullery at the back, with its single cold water tap. Cooking was done on the open fire or on the gas ring.[15]

John Lynch comments that a range of styles and rents were available for different groups of workers. In 1901, for example, 'only 0.4 per cent of Belfast's population were living in a single room; 29.1 per cent of Belfast families in four-roomed houses, 59.4 per cent in dwellings of five rooms or more'. Lynch also demonstrates, however, that the situation was much worse in the heavily populated western areas of the city and in older districts, where 'as late as 1898, 29 per cent of the city's houses lacked a separate rear entry'.[16] And though the unskilled labour force included both Protestants and Catholics, Jonathan Bardon points out that 'Catholics tended to live in the more dilapidated houses . . . and only one Catholic household in sixteen had a fixed bath, compared with one in six in Protestant households'.[17] Despite the advances made when a Housing Act of December 1908 gave local authorities the power to build houses and to establish funds to support home construction, the number of families living in one room in Belfast actually increased between 1911 and 1926.[18] The continuing expansion of the population, economic inflation and religious sectarianism combined to increase both social and financial difficulties for the city's poor and to widen the gap between their experience and that of the suburban middle classes.

Just over one hundred miles to the south of Belfast, the streets of Dublin presented a very different façade. With no strong industrial base, the capital city offered little in the way of skilled employment, and its slow-growing economy was visibly reflected in housing conditions. The large Georgian terraces, which were formerly the opulent, comfortable homes of the gentry, were now divided into cramped tenement accommodation for over 21,000 families. In the worst localities there were

> as many as a hundred persons in a single house. Here it was common to find fifteen to twenty persons in one room and eight sleeping in a bed. Some rooms were found to be less than six feet by four and labelled 'styes' and 'coffins' by witnesses.[19]

The weekly rent for a single room was around three shillings, and at a time when unskilled labourers earned between 15s 3d and one pound a week, this was a significant outlay. Moreover, a high proportion of tenement dwellers were irregularly if at all employed, with a disproportionate number of families headed by women whose earning capacity was even more curtailed than that of men.[20] In such circumstances life was a constant struggle for survival, with mothers in particular adopting a range of strategies as the family grew or moved on. Second-hand clothing was probably the norm, and visits to the pawnshop, 'the economic powerhouse of the neighbourhood',[21] a regular feature of life. In the early decades of the century, for example, Chrissie Hawkins pawned her wedding ring to buy breakfast the day after she was married. Cash could also be earned by walking out to the surrounding countryside to pick cabbages or potatoes; Ellen Preston, mother of twelve children, was one of those who carried out trading of all kinds. She remembered:

Oh there was loads of street traders. All had large families. Times were very hard then, it was very, very, poor. I started selling when I was about 12. Then I got married when I was 19 and the children started coming along and I was selling fruit and flowers off me pram. The men, there was no work for them and the women traders, they *had* to go out, they held the families together. Every day I pushed me pram, *every day*. Some days were miserable with the rain beating off me. If you got five shillings from the pram in them days that'd get you loads of bread and butter and milk. You were just making ends meet . . . but we reared our families.[22]

Feeding the family was the first priority; Maggie Byrne recalled:

Some days we didn't really have a meal, maybe just bread and butter. On a bad day she'd (mother) get a half dozen of eggs and that'd have to do for the father, mother and four children. A boiled egg for dinner – and that would be it![23]

Although some people managed better than others, the most vulnerable succumbed to constant ill health and an early death. Perhaps the most striking and measurable result of poverty, overcrowding and malnutrition in Dublin, was one of the highest infant mortality rates in Western Europe.

There were other dangers to life in these run-down and crowded Dublin dwellings. In 1902 a three-storey tenement on Townsend Street suddenly gave way and buried two families. Eleven years later, the complete and sudden collapse of two tenement houses on Church Street killed seven and injured many others. Such tragedies at least drew public attention to what the press claimed to be a national scandal, resulting in calls for action on the part of government. However, even new public housing schemes were based on the concept of communal dwelling. A project begun in 1905 provided 460 tenements between Montgomery Street and Purdon Street, with single rooms let to widows and families with two children or less, and two-roomed dwellings occupied by those with larger families.[24]

An example of philanthropic intervention was provided by the young women of Alexandra College, Dublin, who in 1912 purchased several tenement dwellings and rented them out after renovation. In return for a moderate rent, tenants were expected to pay promptly and to keep their rooms clean and in good order. The establishment of a library, a club for factory girls, a holiday fund and the setting up of sewing and singing classes, reflected the middle-class desire to 'improve' several aspects of working-class life. For parents, one of the most popular activities, especially on cold, wet afternoons, was a children's playroom supervised by students.[25] Despite such endeavours, an official inquiry in 1914 reported that 28,000 Dubliners were living in houses that were considered 'unfit for human habitation', and, largely as a result of the unsettled nature of early twentieth-century Irish political life, poor conditions prevailed until well into the 1940s. In some cases they even got worse.

Living conditions throughout the countryside varied considerably. Molly, one of fourteen children, described her County Galway home in the early years of the century:

> We lived in a cottage – it was my grandfather's small farm. There were three rooms, one to one side and one to the other. The kitchen was in the middle. There was a place above the two side rooms, and you had to have steps to get up there. Three or four of the boys used to sleep up there. There were three girls in the bed, myself and two of my sisters. Then there would be smaller ones in cots, and beds here and there. It was very crowded. We couldn't all have a meal at the same time. My mother and father would have theirs first, and two of us would sit with them.[26]

Despite overcrowding, this home compared favourably to slum housing in Roscrea, County Tipperary, which was considered to be typical of many Irish small towns. In 1911 a rural district council clerk described habitations where there was

> no pure air, no clean light, no adequate arrangement for the separation of the sexes, no sanitary convenience of any kind, no drainage. Darkness, damp-ness, dirt and dust . . . everywhere, all creating a feeling of despondency and despair.[27]

Conditions were believed to be improving, however, with some sources claiming in the early years of the century that around 70 per cent of the rural population lived in houses categorised by officials as 'good farm-houses' or better.[28] By 1920 the British government had spent over £9 million building 47,966 labourers' cottages, 40 per cent of which were sit-uated in Munster, 36 per cent in Leinster, 19 per cent in Ulster and 5 per cent in Connacht.[29] Even on the Great Blasket, Ireland's westernmost island off the Kerry coast, the Congested Districts Board had initiated change, funding the building of a road and five new cement-built houses with slate roofs. While these residences stood in stark contrast to the older homes, built of stone mortared with mud and washed with white or yellow lime, visitors noted that the old-style furnishings remained. The kitchen, the heart of the home, contained a settle, which provided seating in the daytime and could be used as a bed at night, a large table, a dresser and a few chairs.[30] The island was nonetheless in decline; by 1953, when it was abandoned, the 160 inhabitants had been reduced to a mere 20.

In less isolated areas the process of modernisation was well under way. The railway network linking town and country altered the relationship between farmer and shopkeeper, and opened up new leisure and shopping activities for men and women alike. In Cork, for example, an electric tramway system, which was introduced in 1898 with six suburban lines, took over from hackney carriages, and with fares ranging from one penny to threepence, and trams running every ten to twelve minutes, travel to or across towns was cheap and fast.[31] The wider world was also becoming more accessible, with Marconi's wireless telegraph opening for transatlantic press telegrams at Clifden in County Galway in October 1907, while, just two years later, the first aeroplane flight on Irish soil took place near Hillsborough, County Down. As journalist Mary Kenny has commented, for many, the beginning of the twentieth century was 'seen as a time brimming with promise, tumultuous with change, disturbance, invention, speed and globalisation'.[32]

DAILY LIFE

The home – wherever it was situated – was considered to be the woman's domain, and early twentieth-century discourse increasingly confined her within its boundaries, proclaiming that both personal fulfilment and social status would naturally accompany marriage and motherhood. While late twentieth-century feminists regarded the notion of 'separate spheres' as limiting and damaging, there is little doubt that most women of the earlier period perceived it differently. Marriage was the ultimate goal of most young women, and in rural areas, where possession of land and property was a high priority, the matchmaker still had a role to play in ensuring that a union was satisfactory to the families of both bride and groom. A series of Land Acts, beginning with the Wyndham Act of 1903 which facilitated tenant purchase, created a class of small farm proprietors which formed a conservative core in Irish society and strongly supported property rights.[33] As a result, the 'widest social gap in rural Ireland was that between the farmer and the landless labourer, and marriage rarely, if ever, bridged that gap'.[34] Expectations were likely to be different in urban areas, where the skills necessary for a well-paid job might be more attractive to a potential partner. But for all the emphasis on the desirability of the married state, most brides reached the altar in blissful ignorance of the details of wifely duty. Even as late as 1940, Sarah Hartney, a former domestic servant, remembered that 'When you got married you were innocent and you knew nothing, marriage was very unknown. It was a kind of mystery to you. There was no one to tell you the facts of life and girlfriends wouldn't talk. We went like lambs to the slaughter'.[35]

Despite widespread naivety around sexual matters, the major and expected consequence of marriage was, of course, motherhood, and this status was endowed with saint-like qualities. Nora Tynan O'Mahony, writing for the Catholic magazine, *Irish Monthly*, in 1913 described

> a mother's influence, a mother's dignity . . . [as] very sacred and holy; hardly less so, one might say without irreverence, than that of the priesthood itself . . . Who can measure her power and her influence for good in the world? The good wife and mother is the best guardian not only of the physical health and comfort of her husband and sons, but of their virtue and spiritual welfare as well.[36]

While secular ideology similarly reinforced the notion of the strong Irish mother, transmitter of the faith and moral guide to her children, this did not always reflect the actuality of everyday experience. Over one-third of married women in 1911 (36 per cent) had seven children or more, and when recurring pregnancies were accompanied by poverty and hardship, premature ageing was a more likely result than spiritual elevation. Middle-class women like Cecily Grehan may have been able to hire a nurse to attend her during her pregnancy and the birth of her child in the 1920s, but the cost of such care at £16 per month was well beyond the reach of most.[37] Saidie Patterson's mother, for example, was unable to find even the 3s 6d necessary for a doctor's visit, and died in childbirth.[38] A growing minority would have attended maternity hospitals, where they would have experienced increasing medical intervention in the process of delivery (see Table 1.1). Despite the Midwives (Ireland) Act of 1918, many poorer women still availed themselves of the services of an unqualified, but usually experienced handywoman, who would provide assistance for a few shillings, or, in some cases, a baby Power's whiskey.[39] Whether from professionals or amateurs, the medical advice given to all new mothers was that they take nine full days' bed rest following the birth 'to allow internal organs to resume their normal position'.[40] Although this was impracticable for the poorest field or factory workers, Catriona Clear claims that women themselves colluded in the long lying-in period, as 'it was the only rest most of them got in their lives'.[41]

In the early decades of the century childbirth was a risky business for both mother and baby, with geographical location and social class again being major determinants. Prenatal and infant care were major concerns in many Western European countries in this period and Ireland was no exception. In fact, Irish infant mortality rates as a whole were fairly low by European

TABLE 1.1

Increased intervention in deliveries in the Rotunda Lying-In Hospital, Dublin, 1909–29

	DELIVERIES	INDUCTION (%)	FORCEPS (%)	CAESAREAN SECTION (%)
1909	2,060	0.8	3.9	0.05
1929	17,224	6.4	7.9	2.50

Tony Farmar, *Holles Street 1894–1994: The National Maternity Hospital: A Centenary History* (Dublin, 1994), p. 50

standards, but babies born in urban areas were almost twice as vulnerable as those born in the countryside: 150 and 74 infant deaths per 1,000 live births respectively,[42] and, as Table 1.2 indicates, a baby born into the family of a labourer was 17 times more likely to die within a year than the child of a professional household.[43] Much human heartache, pain and despair lie behind these stark statistics. A growing body of health visitors and voluntary workers visited the poor to offer both verbal and practical assistance. From around 1908, the Women's National Health Association (WHNA), under the energetic though often eccentric leadership of Lady Aberdeen, wife of the Viceroy of Ireland, operated mother and baby clubs in Dublin and Belfast.

For isolated island families such as the one below, the visit of an itinerant nurse could make a considerable difference to the health and well-being of young children. Arranmore Island, County Donegal, c. 1906–14.

TABLE 1.2

Average death rates for Irish children under 5 by class
(per 10,000 live births), 1913–15

CLASS	DESCRIPTION	DEATHS
1	Professional	7
2	Middle, Business	22
3	Skilled Artisan and Small Shopkeeper	49
4	General Service	98
5	Labourers	120

Tony Farmar, *Holles Street 1894–1994: The National Maternity Hospital: A Centenary History*
(Dublin, 1994), p. 62

At these centres, babies were weighed, doctors were on hand to provide medical advice, and nurses visited homes to ensure that their strictures on feeding and hygiene regimes were heeded.[44] Probably the most effective aspect of the work of this association was the provision of free or cheap pasteurised milk, with infant mortality rates showing a drop in areas where it was introduced. Intervention, however well meant, was not, of course, always welcome. The secretary of the Mullingar branch of the WHNA noted 'a natural prejudice of the poor afflicted against a person invading their homes'.[45]

The minutes of the Cork Child Welfare League, established in 1918, provide further insight into the attitudes and activities of such philanthropic bodies. The league distributed tickets for milk and food amongst the needy. Recipients had to be approved by the committee and certified by the doctor, and provision was only to be given free 'in cases of extreme poverty'. For example, Baby Coffey (four and a half months), one of a family of eight and visibly 'wasting', was granted a daily quart of milk free of charge for a month. For a family whose income was one pound a week from the father's gardening occupation, this may indeed have made a difference to the child's chances of survival. Mrs Healy, whose husband was a soldier fighting in France, with four children, two of whom were reported to be very run down after a bout of influenza, had to pay threepence for her daily quart of milk, since she was in receipt of £1 12s 6d separation allowance. There is no doubt that this type of assistance helped to alleviate the distress of at least some of the most needy children, but as Dr E. Webb indicated in a report on maternity and child welfare in Dublin in 1917, there was a clear need for the co-ordination of the efforts of state and voluntary agencies.[46]

Despite the problems surrounding motherhood, those without children – around 7 per cent of married women – were regarded as objects of pity or derision by their neighbours. Amongst those knitting socks for a Needlework Guild in West Cork at the turn of the century, for example, Mary Spillane's work stood out as being particularly soft and well shaped, a result of washing the wool before she began to knit. This, however, brought little praise from the rest of the knitting circle:

> 'Och! She have the time!' the others say. Mary has no children; her neigh-bours pity her and secretly despise her. She is sad and a little furtive, as if she were under the shadow of God's wrath, or had been 'overlooked' by a witch.[47]

More seriously, children were seen to be important in securing a wife's place in the home; widows who were childless might well find themselves with-out a claim to their husband's farm, homeless and vulnerable.[48] With wid-ows outnumbering widowers by two to one in the 1926 census, this was a significant factor in the lives of many women. Moreover, the 1901 census recorded that only half as many widows as widowers had remarried during the previous year, and this, together with women's greater life expectancy, meant that a substantial number of bereaved wives lived out their final years in the workhouse.[49] Only widows with two or more dependent children were granted other types of relief. Maisie Barry, whose husband died of consumption ten years after their marriage, recalled how she coped when she was left with seven children and no money. Living in a Cork tenement, in one room with a leaking roof, she regularly relied on help from her neighbours. When she applied for home assistance she was granted ten shillings a week, barely enough to cover the rent. The family's circumstances only improved when the eldest girl reached the age of ten and was deemed old enough to look after the younger children, leaving Maisie 'free to char for a few shillings a week in a big house in Montenotte'.[50]

There had been enormous advances in children's education since the introduction of the national system of schooling in 1831. Though there was some regional diversity, overall levels of illiteracy had dropped from 54 per cent to 14 per cent in the second half of the nineteenth century and the gap between male and female attendance had also been greatly reduced.[51] Changes in the curriculum in the early 1900s put greater emphasis on voca-tional education, with all aspects of domestic economy deemed essential training for girls. It is likely, however, that most schoolgirls would have already been familiar with a range of domestic chores. Children, particular-ly of large families, would have been expected to lend a hand about the

home or farm as soon as they were able. Florence Mary McDowell recalled
that in the late 1890s all farm children learned to milk when they were six
years old,[52] and Kathleen Sheehan, born in County Cavan in 1894, the oldest of a family of nine, remembers how she managed to fit her schooling in
around a range of household tasks:

> Before school, we carried the water from the spring well. Turf had to be
> brought from the bog, cows brought from one place to another and so on,
> and then run all the way to school. I learned to do most things at an early
> age. I milked the cows and made butter, made bread in the pot oven with
> hot coals on the lid. I made 'boxty' and potato cakes for the tea, while my
> mother was helping with work in the fields.[53]

Urban children, too, had many tasks to perform, running to local shops for
messages, washing the yard, or whitening the step. For the oldest daughter
in a family, domestic tasks may well have taken priority over schooling; all
too often the need to tend to sick parents or siblings, or to bring income
into the household, brought school-days to an early, sometimes abrupt, end.
In 1901 the legal age to start work was raised from eight to thirteen, but a
parliamentary report into the number of children street-traders in Dublin,
Cork and Belfast in the following year revealed that problems remained.[54]
While there was little work for children under fourteen in Cork or Dublin,
girls between the ages of twelve and fourteen regularly worked as 'half-
timers' in the mills and factories of Belfast, where they worked alternate
days from 6 a.m. until 6 p.m., with two hours for dinner, and on alternate
Saturdays from 6 a.m. to midday. On the days they were not working they
went to school from 10 a.m. to 3 p.m. By 1907, 3,000 half-timers in Belfast
were earning around 3s 6d a week, money which went straight to their
mothers, with a little pocket money given in return. This system, which
obviously supplemented many family incomes, remained common until
after the First World War.

Such daily toil was a far cry from the experiences of the daughters of
more prosperous families, who would have been educated by a governess,
usually more concerned with the social rather than the academic success of
her student. Some attended young ladies' seminaries, where they attained a
similarly patchy and inadequate education. Girls, after all, were usually seen
as appendages of either father or brother – the prospectus of Miss Hardy's
School on the outskirts of Belfast (later to become Richmond Lodge
School for Girls) described the establishment as 'a school of boys and their
sisters'.[55] Increasing numbers of middle-class parents, however, acknowledged that their daughters would not always succeed in finding a husband

to support them and would have to earn an independent living. They there-fore sent them to schools such as Alexandra College in Dublin, Victoria College in Belfast, or one of the many convents which were also now offer-ing a full academic curriculum. The nationalist Hanna Sheehy Skeffington, who was educated at the Dominican Convent in Eccles Street, Dublin, felt that the nuns there had equipped her well for life, instilling in her 'great independence of thought and action'.[56] The Duffin sisters attended Ladies Cheltenham College in England, painter Grace Gifford, who was later to marry republican James Plunkett, polished her talent at the Dublin Metropolitan School of Art,[57] and a small minority gained a university degree – an opportunity made possible by the passage of the University (Ireland) Act of 1879, which created the Royal University of Ireland as the grant-awarding body for the Queen's Colleges of Belfast, Cork and Galway. Many of these higher education students were able to carry out a large pro-portion of their studies at women's colleges until a further University Act of 1908 decreed that full attendance at the reconstituted Queen's universities was compulsory. Intellectual middle-class women also began to build their own support networks; the Irish Association of Women Graduates and Candidate Graduates, for example, was formed in March 1902, with Alice Oldham serving as first president and Mary Hayden as vice-president. Networks like this helped to counter the resistance to female higher educa-tion amongst both the wider population and male academics. W.B. Yeats had voiced a common concern in 1889:

> What poor delusiveness is all this 'higher education of women'? Men have set up a great mill called examinations, to destroy the imagination. Why should women go through it, circumstance does not drive *them*. They come out with no repose, no peacefulness, their mind no longer quiet gardens full of secluded paths and umbrage-circled nooks, but loud as chaffering market places.[58]

While Yeats's romantic stance echoed Victorian feminine ideals, the Catholic Church took a more pragmatic view, strongly opposing the emergence of the 'modern woman', who threatened the 'old order', forcing men to marry 'useless and hopeless' women, rather than good housewives educated in cooking, laundry and needlework.[59] They were right to be worried. Many from this first generation of female graduates would go on to mount a con-siderable challenge to the status quo.

Whether their mothers were rich or poor, children were only welcomed when born within a union legalised by marriage. In a country which placed a high value on chastity and self-restraint, illegitimacy was socially

Women in academia

Although in the early years of the century women had the right to sit examinations and be awarded degrees, arrangements for their third-level teaching were *ad hoc*. Alexandra College in Dublin invited fellows from University College Dublin to repeat lectures for their female students, an expensive and unsatisfactory arrangement. The three Queen's Colleges in Belfast, Cork and Galway admitted women to their honours lectures, although members of the Catholic hierarchy often opposed their attendance. The situation was resolved by the Universities (Ireland) Act of 1908 which obliged all students to attend the university where they wished to qualify for their degree. The presence of small numbers of women in the lecture theatres was treated with a good deal of humour by male undergraduates, as the following extract from the magazine of Queen's College Belfast in 1905 illustrates:

> There are probably few Queensmen who are not familiar with those stately rooms opening on to the corridors which are sacred to the study of the arts, under whose majestic portals I now propose to pass, and make the acquaintance of those interesting beings who frequent them.
>
> The front seats are usually occupied by a few members of the fair sex, whose elegant blouses of diverse brilliant colours contrast well with the more sombre attire of the male students.
>
> These damsels are almost invariably late for lectures, and usually come quietly sauntering into the room at about five minutes past the hour.
>
> Sometimes, indeed, wonderful to relate, two or three of them actually manage to get in in time; but as the ladies always seem to consider that they must occupy the same seats, this very often complicates matters.
>
> The late comers in due course arrive, and as they are of course precluded from stepping over the forms by reason of their dresses, the few early arrivals have to march out into the middle of the floor in order that their long expected sisters may pass along to their accustomed places.
>
> But let us now return to the artsmen; what shall we say of them?
>
> The freshman, too, is extremely shy, and is rarely seen in the company of the other sex; in fact, when the other day the ladies commenced to sit in the second and third benches, he in terror retreated to the back of the room, so we must implore these fair daughters of Eve not to encroach any further on the seats of their fellow students, or the poor wretches will be compelled to sit on the stove!
>
> *Queen's College Belfast*, vols 5–7, 1905–7

unacceptable. However, in the absence of reliable, accessible and affordable contraceptive methods, the heartbreak of unplanned pregnancies must have marred many a young life. The Catholic Church maintained that illegitimacy rates were low because of the shame and humiliation with which such a condition was associated. The Reverend James Cassidy, writing in 1924, claimed that

> Whenever a child is born out of wedlock, so shocked is the public sense by the very unusual occurrence, that it brands with an irreparable stigma and, to a large extent, excommunicates the woman guilty of the crime.[60]

Social exclusion was certainly common; Margaret Byrne remembers a young pregnant woman being thrown out of her home in the Liberties in Dublin, and a woman from east Belfast tells of her grandmother leaving the city to have her baby in Glasgow, never to return.[61] As Mona Hearn points out, young serving women who were particularly vulnerable to sexual exploitation, would lose both home and job on becoming pregnant.[62]

It is likely that in many cases couples – Catholic and Protestant – legitimated their expected child by marriage, either through preference or under pressure from family and Church, passing off the 'early' birth as premature. Illegitimate children were also frequently brought up by their grandmother or other family member, or in the workhouse or other charitable institution. Both public and private bodies aimed to separate young mothers expecting their first illegitimate child – their 'one misfortune' – from the influence of more experienced inmates in these homes. Limerick workhouse kept such women under the care of a Sister of Mercy; after the birth most were then placed in service. The tragic experience of Hannah Kavanagh, a twenty-year-old domestic servant from Cloughjordan in Tipperary, was by no means unique. Having borne a child to a man who had promised to marry her, Hannah was charged with infanticide on 22 September 1900 when her baby's body was found drowned near Pigeon-House Fort in Dublin. Despite excellent references from her employer, this 'sad and sordid story of a woman's undoing' ended with Hannah's conviction.[63] A perusal of early twentieth-century newspapers uncovers many such reports, but although infanticide was a capital offence in this period, most sentences were, in fact, commuted to terms of imprisonment. While serving a sentence in a women's prison in England in 1918, republican Countess Markievicz found herself in the company of 'a gang of murderesses'. She commented that 'some were bad', but went on to condemn the circumstances that had led them to Aylesbury: 'most were foolish working girls who had got into trouble and had killed their little babies because life with them was impossible: because they had no way of earning a living, nowhere to go and nothing to eat.'[64]

More common acts of violence reported by newspapers, however, were directed at women, sometimes by fathers or brothers, though more usually by husbands. In January 1900 the *Irish News and Belfast Morning News* noted several assaults; one man was brought to court for repeatedly 'jumping on his wife', and Liz Steiner-Scott suggests that almost daily reports of abuses of women could be read in the *Irish Times* or the *Cork Examiner*. The middle-class young women of Alexandra College were made graphically aware of the harsh realities of some marriages by the activities of the slum children for whom they provided playgroups:

> The little girls sat by the fire rapturously nursing the dolls, while their broth-
> ers more often gave the dolls very rough treatment. One urchin was seen to
> snatch a doll from his sister, and after threatening it to 'remember now that
> I'm your husband,' then proceeded to enforce his marital rights by knock-
> ing its head violently and repeatedly against the door-post.[65]

There was nothing new in such brutal 'domestic' behaviour, and it was not confined to the working classes. In February 1919 the *Irish Citizen*, calling for more women on the bench, referred to the case of a soldier who was given six months in prison for almost beating his wife to death with a poker: 'She was still in hospital by the time the case went to court.'[66] Steiner-Scott points to 1,012 appeals by men convicted of beating their wives, mothers and sisters lodged before the Lord Lieutenant of Ireland between 1853 and 1920, as evidence of a much larger problem. In examining why this issue did not provoke a public reaction for so long, she suggests, among other factors, that the harsh reality did not fit the popular myth that Irish men were 'kind and chivalrous towards women'.[67] The Catholic Church's emphasis on the need for girls to be disciplined was perhaps also pertinent; in 1925 Bishop O'Doherty of Galway advised fathers: 'If your girls do not obey you, if they are not in at the hours appointed, lay the lash on their backs. That was the good old system, that should be the system today.'[68]

The ideological emphasis on marriage and motherhood, which was so dominant throughout Western Europe in this period, has led to historical neglect of the situation of single women. This is especially interesting in Ireland, where an unusually high proportion of women remained unmar-ried – largely a result of post-Famine inheritance patterns which saw the growth of the stem family stystem, where only one son inherited control of the family holding. In contrast to the pre-Famine period when all sons inherited part of the family wealth, in post-Famine Ireland other siblings were left with the choice of remaining at home as unpaid servants or leaving to seek employment elsewhere. The number of eligible marriage partners was thus greatly reduced and, with the nuptials of inheriting sons often postponed until the head of the household was ready to relinquish control to the next generation, Robert Kennedy argues that, 'the stem family system was and is the essential social institution which motivated and permitted individuals to remain permanently single, or to marry at a relatively late age'.[69] This is borne out by the 1901 census, which recorded that over half of those women aged between 25 and 34 were unmarried, a significantly higher proportion than in England and Wales (see Table 1.3). Other, more international factors could also have an impact on a woman's marriage prospects. Helga Gore-Knapp explained the difficulties from the perspective of the Protestant middle-class in early twentieth-century Cork: 'There weren't many eligible men when I was growing up because they were killed in the Great War.'[70] Single life for some could be fulfilling, for example, when writer Edith Somerville inherited the family home at Castle Townshend in County Cork,

> She set about reorganising the garden, renovating the house, running the demesne farm, introducing Friesian cattle, buying, training and selling horses in America, designing and supervising the building of a cottage, caring for Violet Martin after her riding accident, becoming MFH [Master of Foxhounds] of the West Carbery Hunt and writing lots of letters to her brother.[71]

TABLE 1.3

Percentage of single people among persons aged 25–34 years

	MALES		FEMALES	
	IRELAND	ENGLAND & WALES	IRELAND	ENGLAND & WALES
1901	72	36	53	34
1911	74	38	56	36

Robert E. Kennedy, Jr., *The Irish: Emigration, Marriage, and Fertility* (London, 1973), p. 143

Engagement in charity work was a time-consuming and rewarding occupation for single women; while some may have been mostly concerned with imposing their own particular values on the poor, many middle-class women worked for social justice through a range of philanthropic endeavours.[72] For poorer women, however, choices were often limited to the less attractive options of housekeeping or childminding for other family members. One woman recalled that, following the death of their mother, her father and uncle refused to let their sister socialise for fear that she might meet an eligible man, 'locking her in her bedroom when any of their friends came to the house, afraid of having to look for a good house-keeper'.[73] There are many accounts, both real and fictional, of the lonely and isolated existence of single women, struggling to maintain a façade of dignity whilst living in near pauperism.[74]

The partnership between Edith Somerville and Martin Ross (Violet Martin) was particularly close. Though they never explicitly described their relationship as lesbian, they did regard themselves as married, and the intimate nature of their bond was clearly expressed by Somerville in her 1917 recollection of their first meeting in the late 1880s:

> it was . . . though we knew it only dimly, the beginning, for us, of a new era. For most boys and girls the varying, yet invariable, flirtations, and emot-ional episodes of youth, are resolved and composed by marriage. To Martin and me was opened another way, and the flowering of both our lives was when we met each other.[75]

At a time when it was impossible to openly discuss female sexual identity in even a general way, it is difficult to estimate the extent to which lesbian-ism was a common experience among Irish women. Some of the literature of the period does, however, hint at such relationships and suggests that a minority of women (and men) engaged in same-sex relationships that they felt they could not publicly acknowledge.[76]

One option taken up by a rising number of Catholic women in late nineteenth- and early twentieth-century Ireland was to marry into a life of full-time service to the Church. By 1901, around 8,000 female religious, representing an increasingly influential Catholic middle-class culture, embraced both the restrictions and the opportunities of convent life.[77] Although confined by the discipline and regulations of the various religious orders, nuns played a vital role in society more generally, responding posi-tively to the educational and welfare needs of the secular world. On a per-sonal level, spiritual fulfilment and the prospect of a communal life of shared values, purpose and commitment would have been further enhanced by family pride in what was regarded as a prestigious vocation. Although those who could not afford the required dowry to become a choir sister norm-ally undertook the more lowly tasks in the day-to-day life of the convent, recent research has revealed how 'respectable young girls' without financial means were also recruited to work as nuns in America.[78] As Sue Ellen Hoy notes, many of these novices would have received a sound convent education, and this initiative enabled them to follow their vocation in American schools, hospitals and orphanages. Travelling in groups, with a sense of purpose and mission, the experiences of these women represent a relatively unexplored aspect of emigration patterns.

Migration was more usually an enterprise taken up by individuals and, with an annual average of around 14,400 women leaving Ireland between 1901 and 1911, was one that had a significant impact on Irish society.[79] Emigration was a common feature of European life, but Ireland was unusual in that, at certain periods, women emigrants significantly outnumbered men. Reflecting the limited opportunities for marriage or employment at home, most were young and single. *Bean na hÉireann*, the progressive journal of the republican women's organisation Cumann na mBan, was clear about the causes of this outflow of women, particularly from rural areas:

> The Irish girl flees the country because she knows that if she remains she will have to work as hard as any man; that she will have no gaiety in her free hours and that she will become an old woman before she is thirty.[80]

How to keep its young people was to be a recurring problem for successive Irish governments.

Until the 1920s, America was the most usual destination for Irish women, though Australia and Canada were also popular. Many travelled a much shorter distance to England, Wales or Scotland. In 1901, for example, there were estimated to be over 426,500 Irish-born people living in England and Wales. Although these numbers were actually beginning to decline, between 1891 and 1921 more Irish females than males emigrated from Ireland to Britain.[81] Most of the Irish who journeyed 'across the water' found work in industrial cities, usually as servants or in textile mills. Teachers and nurses also found that both pay and opportunities were better in other parts of the British Isles. Leaving behind all that was familiar was not easy, of course, particularly for young women in the throes of adolescence. In Liam O'Flaherty's *Going into Exile*, Mary Feeney, on the eve of her departure for America, is beset by fears and longings:

> Unlike her brother, she did not think of the work she was going to do or the money that she was going to earn. Other things troubled her, things of which she was half-ashamed, half-afraid, thoughts of love and of foreign men and of clothes and of houses where there were more than three rooms and where people ate meat every day.[82]

For the more adventurous, the attractions of America were at least as strong, if not stronger, than the disadvantages of remaining in Ireland. In the

industrial cities of the New World the gap between male and female earnings was significantly less than in Ireland and marriage there was a more
attainable ambition. But, although more than 14 per cent of Irish-
Americans in 1900 were classified as lower middle class, there was no guarantee that working life on the other side of the Atlantic would be greatly
different from that in Ireland.[83] Kerby Miller notes that Irish-born females
in America were largely concentrated in 'domestic service, laundry work
and the least well-paid branches of the textile industry',[84] the same areas
of employment which they would have taken up had they remained at
home, albeit at a higher rate of pay. Moreover, it seems that Irish immigrants
usually married and took as their partners men from the Irish-American
community whom they met at social occasions such as weddings or wakes.
Often their husbands would be from the same city or area that they themselves had left behind, and, with this common background, it is perhaps
unsurprising that Irish immigrants maintained the high marital fertility rates
of their homeland. Nonetheless, despite these qualifications, America did
seem to offer better opportunities for subsequent generations to move up
the social ladder. Lawrence McCaffrey suggests that in the early twentieth
century,

> changes in American culture and technology . . . added new vocations. The
> daughters and granddaughters of maids and scrubwomen became secre-
> taries, telephone operators, nurses and teachers in the rapidly developing
> public school system.[85]

Many suffered homesickness, and some returned, often with the means to
secure marriage. It was reported that in Carna, County Galway, returning emigrant women brought dowries of between £50 and £300,
in Roscommon between £50 and £200.[86] A Mayo man, talking to
John Millington Synge in 1905, described the advent of the 'self-dowered
returner':

> All the girls in this place are going out to America when they are about sev-
> enteen years old . . . then they work there for six years or more, till they grow
> wearied of that fixed kind of life, with the early rising and the working late,
> and they do come home with a little stocking of fortune with them, and
> they do be tempting the boys with their chains and their rings, till they get
> a husband and settle down in this place. Such a lot of them is coming now
> there is hardly a marriage made in the place that the woman hasn't been in
> America.[87]

Those who did live out their lives in the United States usually maintained strong links with the family at home, frequently sending a ticket for a younger sibling to make the journey. Most also sent regular postal orders, which for many rural Irish families were 'essential to the continued payment of rent and shop debts and to the maintenance of the old people'.[88] In West Cork, for example, it has been suggested that American money made it possible 'to maintain an otherwise hopeless position on uneconomic holdings, and to persist in an irrational, if understandable, resistance to emigration'.[89] Whether in the form of cash or the eagerly awaited 'parcel', practical assistance from departed relatives could make a real difference to life in homes where utilisation of everyday materials was the major housekeeping principle. While the rich were tucked up in cool linen sheets, flour bags were the most usual substitute for sheets and pillowcases for the poor: these were unstitched and the trademarks bleached out; four made a sheet, two a long bolster, and one a pillowcase.[90]

Battling against dirt was a constant struggle for the women of the family. An annual event in many homes was the burning of the old straw (along with the bedbugs) which filled the palliasses, 'and for two or three weeks you had a nice fluffy bed'. In Belfast Gusty Spence, who would later rise to prominence as the leader of a loyalist paramilitary group, recalled bedposts being set in Cherry Blossom polish tin lids filled with paraffin oil to prevent the bugs from climbing up.[91] In the Dublin tenements, despite appalling conditions and in contrast to the comments of visiting officials, oral accounts insist that the constant scrubbing and cleaning of communal areas such as stairs and landings maintained a minimum of respectability.[92] Nora Connolly O'Brien, recalling the one tenement room in which she and her family lived at the beginning of the century, paid particular tribute to her mother's housekeeping:

> The bare boards which mother used to scrub upon the floor; the strip of lino between the two beds; the trundle bed in which I slept and which was pushed underneath by day; the water carried in a bucket from the yard; the fireplace on which much of our cooking was done with the aid of a gas-ring; all the ingenuity she put into making a single room look like a cheerful home.[93]

The 'wee palaces' of the Belfast streets reflected a similar desire to present a respectable façade to neighbours and provide a cosy retreat for the family. For women everywhere, the Monday wash took up a full day of boiling, bleaching and starching. Molly, from County Galway, recalls how she hated returning from school to her home on wash day: 'There would be a big bath of clothes and two buckets, one each side. We'd have to take them down to the river to rinse the clothes, then bring them back up again and hang them on lines or hedges to dry.'[94]

Those in officialdom, however, were generally unimpressed by Irish standards of housewifery. In the early years of the century the newly established Department of Agriculture and Technical Instruction took steps to improve 'knowledge and skill' in domestic economy by employing itinerant teachers to work in rural areas. Florence Irwin was one such employee, travelling around the towns and villages of County Down between 1905 and 1913, giving classes in cookery, laundry work and dressmaking.[95] Equipped with a Mistress American stove, she spent from six to eight weeks in each location, working in local barns or halls. Irwin found that she frequently had to exercise her ingenuity when met with a scarcity of equipment in country kitchens – on one occasion being presented with a large flowerpot and a sawn-off piece of window pole with which to mix the ingredients for a beef-steak pie.[96] It proved difficult to introduce innovation in rural areas, particularly in terms of diet, where bacon and cabbage, along with the ubiquitous potato, were the staple dish. When a student of Elizabeth Bloxham presented her brother with a nicely dressed salad, he refused to touch it, commenting that 'It might be all right if it was boiled.'[97]

The introduction of itinerant teachers was only one of several initiatives designed to improve life in country areas through promoting education into how families could help themselves. The United Irishwomen, formed in the first decade of the century by Anita Lett, the English-born vice-president of the Wexford Farmers' Association, gave lectures on cattle testing for diseases such as brucellosis, and on cheese-making, horticulture and fruit-growing, and provided demonstrations in hygiene and health care. The group also turned its attention to the provision of funeral cars in poor areas, and the training of nurses to operate in the countryside. Although this organisation was upper class in origin, its leaders tried hard to make it more democratic, forming branches in every parish in the country with a subscription rate of sixpence. Apart from introducing educational activities, Lett was anxious to brighten up rural life, the dullness of which, she argued, often led to 'alcoholism, vagrancy, and . . . an end in the asylum'.[98] One of the first activities of the United Irishwomen was a Flower and Industrial Show held in Bree, County Wexford, in 1910, which became an annual event. Building on the work of the late nineteenth-century Co-operative Movement, the United Irishwomen (UI) which became the Irish Countrywomen's Association (ICA) in 1935, was the precursor of the modern-day Women's Institute. Lady Aberdeen's WHNA probably drew in greater numbers – it had a membership of 18,000 by 1910 – and education in housework was deemed to be a critical element in its primary campaign, which was to reduce Ireland's high rate of mortality from tuberculosis. For its part, the Congested Districts Board encouraged cleanliness by awarding prizes to 'tidy' and 'healthy' householders.[99]

Self-help was also deemed to be a more appropriate response to poverty than the giving of charity, which, it was believed, would only encourage idleness and apathy. As a tenement dweller remarked of the attitude of the St Vincent de Paul Society, 'If you had furniture in the place they'd say you didn't need help. You had to have nothing in your room before you'd get help from them.'[100] Most of the charitable institutions that had flourished during the nineteenth century, and there were a great many, operated on similar principles. Alison Jordan considers that this approach was partly responsible for the long-lasting success of the Workshops for the Blind. The recipients of this charity were taught a range of skills, which helped them to become self-sufficient. Moreover, they were 'clearly innocent of blame for their condition, they bore no responsibility for their disability and so were truly worthy of the help given to them'.[101]

Diane Urquhart argues that the admission of women to the administrative structure of the Poor Law in 1896 enabled the 'formalisation' of much female philanthropic work.[102] And indeed this measure, which granted suitably qualified Irish women the same rights in municipal government as their Scottish and English counterparts, was important in bringing about reform in workhouse management.[103] Poor Law work fell into what were seen as 'natural' gendered divisions. Thus, male guardians were responsible for finance and maintenance, while women's duties included the appointment of nurses and domestics, matters of hygiene, midwifery, illegitimacy, and the care of 'boarded-out' or fostered children. This last duty was felt to be within women's sphere to the extent that ladies' boarding-out committees were the only all-female permanent committees in the Poor Law structure. Women themselves believed this work to be the most fulfilling of tasks. Mrs Pim of Lisburn Poor Law Union, said of her late colleague, Louise Stannus, that 'her greatest happiness was found in working for the welfare of the children, and she greatly valued the opportunities which her Membership of the Board gave her . . . the duties of her office [were] a labour of love'.[104] It was, of course, only middle-class women who had the time and resources to devote to such work, and though they were always in a minority on the boards as a whole, their input was influential in the period preceding the establishment of the welfare state.

Religion was a major motivating factor behind the public service or philanthropic work of many middle- and upper-class women, and it is important to acknowledge the central role it played in their lives. The chapel, church or meeting-house was the forum for a host of social activities in every locality and, as recent research has demonstrated, its family and congregational networks could play an important part in political, social and charitable life.[105] For members of Protestant denominations, Sundays were days set apart and usually remembered as a series of sermons and meetings, when play was forbidden and best clothes worn with care and pride. For Catholics, confession, novenas, benedictions, retreats, stations of the cross, holy days and fast days were an integral part of daily life. The institutions and rituals of religion had much to offer the poor, in terms of both physical and spiritual sustenance, and, not least, entertainment and excitement. As Sean Connolly points out, occasions such as Patterns combined ceremonial and festive elements. The Pattern held at Ballyheigue (near Kerry) on 8 September, for example, involved walking round the holy well three times saying the rosary, attending open-air mass, and surveying the wares of a range of stallholders.[106] Sunday school excursions to seaside resorts often represented the only escape from the city for children and their parents, and the celebrations of Easter and Christmas were a welcome break in the mundane routines of many lives.

Holidays were a rare luxury for the poor, though for the working-classes day trips by train to the growing number of seaside resorts were now possible. Philanthropists believed that breaks from urban squalor could be both morally and physically beneficial, and charitable organisations were formed to this end. The Belfast Girls' Club Union, founded in 1904, offered 'educational, recreational and holiday facilities for [the] working girls' of the Falls Road and the Shankill Road,[107] and the Bangor Homes of Rest provided refuge to those confined for most of the year to city factories and slums.[108] The extent to which these institutions fulfilled their founders' aims of spiritually uplifting their working-class charges is difficult to estimate. What is clear, however, is that changes in transport were significant in enabling people to travel to venues beyond the areas in which they lived and worked. Cheap excursion tickets encouraged weekend trips to the zoo, the seaside or countryside, while tramways, up and running in Belfast, Dublin and Cork by 1872, and electrified in the early twentieth century, greatly facilitated local travel.

When not travelling abroad, much of the leisure time of the social élite revolved around yachting, racing and hunting. Irish women excelled at golf, winning the British Ladies Open Championship in 1899, 1900, 1902 and 1903.[109] Selective rounds of social visits, punctuated by balls and dances, provided young women with time on their hands with opportunities to show off the latest fashions and keep in touch with events. The aristocratic wives of Lord Lieutenants became involved in a supportive role in their husbands' careers. As noted earlier, women were also very much at the heart of the Celtic Revival, making an important contribution to the cultural renaissance in literature, drama, music and the arts. Lady Dudley, Lady Londonderry, Lady Cadogan and Lady Aberdeen all encouraged local arts and crafts, with Lady Aberdeen particularly active as president of the Irish Industries Association.[110] Other women were active in the Gaelic League, teaching Irish language and dance, or in the productions of the Abbey Theatre or the Ulster Literary Theatre (established 1902).[111] Ellen Duncan, curator of the Hugh Lane Municipal Art Gallery, was secretary of the Dublin United Arts Club, and artist Sarah Purser and playwright Lady Gregory played hostess for local and visiting intellectuals at Dublin literary gatherings.[112] Women therefore fulfilled a range of important functions in the world of higher culture – whether as patrons, contributors or participants.

There were many types of entertainment which did not rely on lavish expenditure, charity or ideological approval. A proliferation of cycling clubs demonstrated the popularity of a machine that could quickly transport young couples to a romantic day in the country. During the 1930s, Tish

Entertainment

The first cinema to open in Ireland was the Volta, in Abbey Street, Dublin, and this new craze, which brought the romance and glamour of Hollywood to Irish towns and villages, took off rapidly. By 1914, there were twenty-seven picture houses in Dublin alone. A few pence or two stone jars would gain admission to 'Wee Joe's', otherwise known as the Shankill Picturedrome, on the west Belfast road, and in country towns such as Dungannon, County Tyrone, local people flocked to see the western romance, *The General's Daughter*. There was also no shortage of live shows. Newspaper advertisements testify to the wide range of entertainment on offer in Belfast during the first Easter of the new century: the Empire featured musical comedians and Princess Pauline, comedienne and dancer; the Grand Opera House was staging the *Mikado*, and Cinderella was showing in the Theatre Royal. On the stage of the more bawdy Alhambra, Cissie Arria demonstrated her skill at clog, tap-boot and skipping-rope dances.

Gavan enjoyed many Sunday mornings exploring the countryside around Cork, and when she and her boyfriend 'became serious', they swapped their two bicycles for a tandem.[113] Tenement families enjoyed regular 'hooleys'. Wakes and weddings, the departure or return of emigrants, hiring fairs and harvest homes were all occasions of sociability, merriment, music and dancing. In rural areas, 'crossroads' dancing was common on summer Sunday evenings. At Biddy Doyle's corner in the townland of Ballyvally, County Down, for example, hundreds of young people, accompanied by mouth organ, melodeon or fiddle, enjoyed these get-togethers until in 1923 the local priest decided that the parochial hall was a more suitable venue.[114] With one shilling admission charge, this local dance was just one of a growing number of affordable commercial enterprises.

Drinking, however, was perhaps the most traditional leisuretime activity, and one in which all classes engaged. Among the wealthy, 'Champagne was almost invariably given for a dinner party', with port, sweet sherry and claret accompanying the dessert.[115] This type of consumption rarely caused public comment; the attention of temperance reformers was almost completely directed at the poor, with 'the national curse of Ireland' blamed for all manner of domestic distress and public disorder. Drunkenness amongst women was seen as particularly offensive, a moral misdemeanour which, trade unionist Delia Larkin argued, threatened family life, '(causing neglect of) the children, and branding the future generation with ill health, disease, and [an] inherited taste for intoxicating drink'.[116] Although some reformers fully understood the dreadful conditions in which the poorest of these women lived, exaggerated reports of female drunkenness were a regular feature of temperance literature.[117] Most commentators conclude that drunkenness was actually in decline in the early twentieth century, part of a wider reform of manners and adaptation to a busy working life. Also relevant were legislative measures aimed at decreasing the opportunities for excessive drinking. The Intoxicating Liquors (Ireland) Act of July 1902 reduced the number of public houses and introduced 10.30 p.m. closing, and a Bill banning Sunday opening was passed on 29 November 1906.

The greatest health hazard facing men and women was tuberculosis – 'the white plague'; death rates from which were rising rapidly among the 15–25 age group (more than 11,500 deaths a year), at a time when deaths from other diseases were in decline.[118] According to John Lynch, there was considerable local variation in these as in other statistics, with particularly high death rates in Belfast, for example, where the hot and humid conditions of the linen mills helped the spread of tuberculosis.[119] At the beginning of the century only two sanatoria – Crooksling in County Wicklow and

Heatherside in County Cork – had been built by local authorities. Sufferers therefore had little option but to enter the local fever hospitals, from which they (rightly) feared they were unlikely to emerge alive. It was in this context that Lady Aberdeen established the WHNA in 1907 and launched a crusade to tackle the problem. An intensive educational campaign, involving travelling exhibitions with lectures, lantern slides and music reached into the most isolated rural areas, bringing both entertainment and enlightenment. Sanatoria were also built, and in recognition of her work, the countess was made an honorary member of the British Medical Association – the first woman to be so honoured. She was also awarded the Médaille d'Honneur by the Medical Society of France, and elected president of the Royal Institute of Public Health in Dublin in 1911.[120] Such honours were in stark contrast to the insults heaped upon her head by Irish nationalists such as Alice Milligan and her friend 'Barbara', who claimed that the Irish poor 'won't stand patronising, meddling in their private affairs, or bullying them over their dirty houses, or bad ventilation'.[121] Although tuberculosis was no respecter of social class, those with the means at their disposal could travel abroad to climates that would facilitate their recovery. Hanna Sheehy Skeffington, for example, travelled to the Rhineland when at the age of eighteen she was diagnosed with incipient tuberculosis.[122] Those who had witnessed the disease taking hold were all too aware of its horror, captured here in a contemporary account:

> There is a shortness of breath, pains in the breast, profuse sweats during sleep, spitting of blood and matter. Shivers succeeded by hot fits, with flushing of the face and burning of the hands and feet, and, in the last stages of the illness, a diarrhoea that helps to waste what little remains of flesh and strength.[123]

Between 1905 and 1918 better economic and social conditions, improving standards of domestic hygiene, and public recognition of the dangers of infection, combined to reduce the annual number of deaths from tuberculosis by about a quarter. Workers in some occupations, were, however, particularly vulnerable. There is plenty of evidence, for example, that mill girls were especially prone to illness – the hot and humid conditions which were ideal for the production of linen were also highly conducive to the spread of infection. As one worker commented, 'We came out of the factory soaked to the skin and covered with a layer of white fluff – sure candidates for "pucey chest" and other lung complaints.'[124] Regulations to control the amount of humidity permissible were introduced in 1903, 1905 and 1914, but in densely populated urban areas, disease amongst mill girls was all too common.

More generally, statistics clearly show that urban life carried greater health risks than rural life, and that there was a direct link between poverty, poor housing and bad health. It is therefore not surprising that Dublin had the highest overall death rate of any city in the British Isles. But it has also been suggested that the subordination of the Irish female to the male in almost all aspects of life also affected mortality trends. While females everywhere have a biological advantage that ensures them a longer life span, it would seem that in Ireland this extra life expectancy was considerably less than in other comparable regions (see Table 1.4).[125]

TABLE 1.4

Excess years of female over male life expectancy

	IRELAND	AMERICA	ENGLAND & WALES
1900–2	0.3	2.9	3.9
1910–12	0.5	3.4	3.9

Robert E. Kennedy, Jr., *The Irish: Emigration, Marriage, and Fertility* (London, 1973), p. 55

There is certainly plenty of anecdotal evidence that the woman of the household fed her husband and sons first, and that she was most likely to do without when times were hard. According to Robert Kennedy, the high maternal mortality rate and the large number of healthy young women who left the country each year complicate the issue, but he agrees that the statistics reflect the low status of Irish women within their community. For those who did live into old age, the Liberal government's introduction of the old age pension at the rate of five shillings per week, first paid to people over seventy on 1 January 1909, was an important, often life-saving, bonus. The introduction of the 1911 Health Insurance Act was also significant; by April 1913, 700,000, or 15.9 per cent of the population were insured, and thus entitled to sickness, maternity and disability benefits.[126]

WORK

It should already be clear that, despite traditional ideology, many women had to engage in some kind of paid labour, whether to supplement other income, or to fully support the family. As we have seen, wages for outworkers or homeworkers such as Saidie Patterson's mother were abysmally low, and yet their work was essential in the textile industry of Belfast or the shirt factories of Derry. Mary Daly notes that 18,000 factory workers and 80,000 outworkers were employed in Derry and Donegal in 1902, and that 80 per cent of this workforce was female.[127] In the early twentieth century, outworkers were also common in the North's 'Linen triangle' area, around Lurgan, Portadown and Dromore, with children again frequently kept from school to lend a hand with the various processes of linen production.[128] While this type of work paid less than employment carried out in a mill or factory, those working away from home had to fit domestic tasks and the care of children into a more rigid schedule. The imposition of fines for lateness, the unhealthy working conditions in linen mills and frequent accidents caused by unprotected machinery or a moment's inattention have been the focus of much comment by historians. However, more recent research, particularly that using oral accounts, has demonstrated the diversity of the experiences of spinners, weavers and dressmakers, and the camaraderie which developed within the workforce:

> Oh, it was great. We used to sing, you know, maybe one woulda started and the rest woulda joined in, and we used to sing maybe for a whole day we'da sung, you know. Probably then the next day it was all talkin' and some days it was quieter than others. Aye, we used to have good fun in the mill.[129]

Belfast workers were also considered to be in a much better financial situation than those elsewhere. *A Report on the Cost of Living of the Working Classes*, published in 1908, suggested that the availability of work for both men and women in the north-east (because of the combination of linen and shipbuilding), accounted for 'the general prosperity of the working classes'. However, as John Gray comments,

> low wages were not mentioned [in the report] ... Such conclusions begged the question as to whether women and children worked in the mills to raise family income to a 'high' level, or out of a dire necessity stemming from the extraordinarily low rates of pay for male unskilled labour.[130]

The rest of Ireland lacked a strong industrial base, though women could find work in small scale woollen mills, clothing, textile, biscuit or baking factories. Conditions of work varied from place to place. Those employed in Jacob's Biscuit Factory were perhaps fortunate in their paternalistic employers, who were from an old Quaker family:

> a doctor and a dentist were in attendance at the factory, and the workers had a very good canteen and recreational facilities. There was a roof garden on top of the factory for workers' use. Beds for convalescent workers were retained in a convalescent home.[131]

However, as Maura Cronin noted in her study of work and workers in Cork city and county, 'paternalism, female labour and low wages went hand in hand'.[132]

TABLE 1.5

Representation of women within occupational classes, 1911 (%)

Professional	26.6
Domestic	84.9
Commercial	8.8
Agricultural	7.6
Industrial	29.1
Indefinite or non-productive	68.7

Extracted from Joanna Bourke, *Husbandry to Housewifery: Women, Economic Change and Housework in Ireland, 1890–1914* (Oxford, 1993), p. 32

TABLE 1.6

Regional variations in occupational profile of
Irish urban female labour force, 1911 (%)

	MANUFACTURE	DOMESTIC	DEALING	CLERICAL	PROFESSIONAL	OTHER
Belfast	73	14	5	4	4	
Cork	29	37	19	3	10	2
Derry	59	27	5	3	5	1
Dublin	32	39	1	4	10	1

Extracted from Mary E. Daly, *Women and Work in Ireland* (Dundalk, 1997), pp. 34–5

As can be seen from Tables 1.5 and 1.6, in areas where manufacturing was weak, domestic service was correspondingly stronger; it was thus more important in Dublin and Cork than in Derry. Many daughters of small farmers or estate workers made the transition to paid work via the local Big House, and it was considered by the authorities that the provision of bed and board made this a particularly suitable occupation for former incumbents of orphanages and industrial schools.[133] The working experience of servants varied significantly; they could be affectionately and respectfully treated as faithful family retainers or they could find their living areas consisting of no more than 'cupboards and black holes'.[134] One woman from County Limerick recalled, 'We suffered nothing but hardship, working long hours with poor diet. I remember working on a farm where the mistress was so mean she would save the left-overs for us. I was so hungry that I ran away.'[135] Servants had little free time, but, on the other hand, all personal expenses were met and wages could therefore be sent home to support other family members, or put aside towards setting up one's own home. Most female servants were young and unmarried and were regarded as making particularly good wives, though the contrast between their own homes and those of their wealthy employers may well have caused resentment. The decline in the numbers of domestic servants in the first quarter of the twentieth century can be explained by a combination of increased emigration, the growth of alternative employment opportunities, and changing attitudes towards what were seen as dependent and inferior roles.

An increasingly more attractive area of employment for young women was in the growing retail trade, as shopworkers in cities or country towns, or catering for summer visitors in seaside resorts such as Bangor, Bundoran, Newcastle and Portrush, made popular by the railway network. Married women could also supplement the family income by taking in lodgers and providing bed and breakfast. Those living close to fishing areas, like Ardglass in County Down, could find employment in net-making and transporting fish to market; the herring industry also recruited young women from Donegal and Scotland.[136]

Many women were still engaged in traditional agricultural activities in Ireland – around 13.7 per cent, according to the 1911 census – though, overall, numbers were declining.[137] This area of work had undergone significant change over the course of the nineteenth century. The onset of creameries and the mechanised milking of cows, for example, had brought about women's removal from much of the productive work of the dairy farm. However, the 1911 census record of 4,000 female agricultural labourers did not include the work of wives or female relatives, who would have assisted with a range of tasks both inside and outside the farmhouse. It has now been accepted by economic historians that the keeping of livestock by women, whether poultry, pigs or goats, was for many not just pin money but an important addition to the family income. Kitty Matthews's mother in the townland of Leitrim in the Mourne country of County Down made use of such resources:

> She kept a lot of turkeys coming up to Christmas, and when the turkeys were fat and ready to sell they were brought to the market in Rathfriland. The money that was made from the turkeys she took to Thompson's the drapers, and she bought all the clothes for us girls, and the boys for the springtime. Socks and jackets and jerseys and things for school. And she would have also got together all the ingredients for the Christmas cake and the pudding.[138]

That women working on farms gained little if any reward or recognition for their contribution was graphically reflected in the fact that they were not counted in the statistical returns. Moreover, the socialist leader James Connolly claimed that the Irish farming woman was treated by both peasants and clergy as a mere 'tool with which to work the farm'. He went on:

> She has toiled on the farms from her earliest childhood, attaining usually to the age of ripe womanhood without ever being vouchsafed the right to claim as her own a single penny of the money earned by her labour, and knowing that all her toil and privation would not earn her the right to the farm which would go without question to the most worthless member of the family, if that member chanced to be the eldest son.[139]

It is also difficult to assess women's involvement in other types of intermittent or casual labour, whether as washerwomen, charwomen, childminders, street-traders, cabbage-, potato- or fruit-pickers.

Perhaps one of the most contentious and marginalised ways of earning a living was through the sale of sexual favours, and here numbers are almost impossible to calculate. Many women engaging in prostitution would do so part-time or intermittently; even for full-time workers, this was unlikely to be a long-term occupation. Most prostitutes were aged between twenty and thirty; women older than this, often forced out of brothels and onto the streets, were more vulnerable to arrest.[140] Campaigns against prostitution usually focused on the larger towns and cities, and on the threats posed to public morality and public health. The Monto area of Dublin, for example, was frequently cited as 'one of the most dreadful dens of immorality in Europe'.[141] As Mary Corbally's account indicates, the highly publicised views of moral reformers were a far cry from the experience of the tenement community:

> I don't feel any shame in coming from the Monto, but the reputation was there cause of the girls. In them years they was called 'unfortunate girls'. We never heard the word 'whores', never heard 'prostitute'. Very rarely you'd hear of a brothel, it was a 'kip' and the madams we called them kip-keepers. But the girls were very good, they were generous. They were very fond of kids. If you went for a message for them you'd get thruppence or sixpence. If they seen a kid running around in his bare feet they'd bring him into Brett's and by him a pair of runners . . . the girls were generous.[142]

Public accounts also fail to note the diversity of living and working standards amongst 'the girls'. While many operated from dark lanes or down basement steps, dressed only in a raincoat, those from a smarter part of town, 'wore evening dress, and each month a special costumier visited the street to make sure they were in fashion'.[143]

At the other end of the social scale, young women were entering the workforce in increasing numbers, many of them benefiting from the opening of clerical posts to women in an expanding service sector. The Post Office was regarded as the 'official pioneer' of women's employment, offering positions as telegraph operators or behind the counter to intelligent, educated working-class women. The first civil service typist took up her post in the Department of Agriculture and Technical Instruction in 1901, while the Guinness Brewery held its first examinations for four lady clerkships in June 1906. By 1914 almost 8,000 women were employed as clerks, the fastest-growing area of female employment in the twentieth century.[144]

Nursing and teaching were regarded as 'natural' spheres for women, and in these, as in other areas, women's remuneration and working conditions were often insecure and unsatisfactory. In 1900, for example, 55 per cent of all teachers were women, earning 80 per cent of the male wage. However, only 28 per cent of school principals were women, and in every case these were in small schools where they were in fact the only teacher.[145] An important factor in determining experience and progress in these female-dominated professions was the strong influence exerted by religious bodies. The personal lives of both teachers and nurses were under constant scrutiny and, as Mary Daly notes, nuns often monopolised the senior positions of hospital matron or secondary school principal within the Catholic community. In schools, even those educated to degree level could find themselves replaced by unqualified, thus cheaper, female candidates,[146] and despite women's dominance in the field of nursing, in 1911 there were only 33 qualified female medical doctors and 68 female medical students. It is interesting to note that a significant percentage of women doctors in this period practised their skills not in Ireland but on the mission field – a reflection, perhaps, of the limitations placed on their progress at home, on the strength of religious influence, or of the personal impulse to 'serve'.[147]

Women had little impact on the other major professions: the 1911 census recorded only one female architect (and she may have been an architect's assistant), and there were no female lawyers at this time. In 1919 the women's suffrage newspaper, the *Irish Citizen*, argued that such a situation in the legal world had serious consequences for all women:

> Recently in the Dublin Courts the foreman of a jury declared that the list of criminal offences was very light, there being only one 'light' offence on the calendar, 'that of indecent assault upon a child'. Imagine the mind of a man who describes such an offence as trivial. Unfortunately, this mentality is by no means uncommon both in juries and on the bench. We believe that men as a rule are disposed to be over lenient to such offences, which to

women are far more revolting than attacks upon property. It is but another instance of the need of women lawyers, women jurors, women on the bench.[148]

While it would be a long time before professional bodies could be persuaded to fully engage with the issue of equality for their women members, the process of unionisation within the broader labour movement had the potential at least to improve working conditions. This process, however, was to prove slow and cumbersome, for, despite the reality of women's experience, female employment was viewed by society at large as a temporary condition, preceding marriage, or supplementing the earnings of a husband. Their work was regarded as unskilled, and the large pool of available labour also served to keep wages low and jobs insecure. These factors also delayed their effective unionisation. Although there was some trade-union activity among female linen workers in Belfast in the last decade of the nineteenth century, this, like the early unions of unskilled male labour, was relatively short-lived.[149] In 1906 a group of Belfast spinners demonstrated that it was possible to strike – and have their demands met (in this case an extra shilling a week) – without unionisation, particularly when supported by workers in other mills,[150] but it was nonetheless becoming obvious that organised solidarity produced better results.

Traditional trade unions, representing the skilled male workforce, were generally reluctant to admit women. One of the first to do so was the Drapers' Assistants Association, founded in 1901, which had a female membership of 1,400 by 1914.[151] Since drapers' assistants at this time underwent a long apprenticeship, were closely supervised and disciplined and lived in, usually over, the shop – with fire hazards resulting in numerous deaths – there were many difficulties faced by both male and female workers which trade-union membership could help alleviate.

Women also responded to the more militant union activity generated by Jim Larkin and James Connolly. During the Belfast strike of 1907, 1,000 women walked out of Gallaher's tobacco factory after the owner sacked 7 of their number for attending a meeting held by Larkin during the previous lunch break. They were also active against blacklegs, on one occasion stripping a woman van driver and rolling her in a puddle.[152] The Textile Workers' Union, formed by Connolly during the Belfast mill workers' strike of 1911, had a membership of around 300 women, the majority from the Catholic Falls Road area, while Mary Galway headed up the predominantly Protestant Textile Operatives' Union.[153] Larkin was the first president of the Irish Women Workers' Union (IWWU), founded in 1911, and his

Members of the IWWU join male trade unionists from the Irish
Transport and General Workers' Union (ITGWU) on the steps
of Dublin's Liberty Hall, the headquarters of the ITGWU,
during a period marked by bitter disputes, c. 1911–14

sister Delia was its first secretary. This all-female union represented women
from a wide range of occupations, such as confectionery makers, waitresses,
laundry workers and flower-sellers.

Employers too, however, were flexing their muscles during this period,
and in 1913 workers in Dublin were told to choose between union membership or their jobs. There followed a nine-month lockout, a period of
hunger and struggle, punctuated by violence. Women union members suffered alongside their male colleagues in the battle for the rights of labour,
and wives and children were profoundly affected by the prolonged lack of
income. British trade unionists gave generously to funds to feed the Dublin
poor, and the IWWU organised a soup kitchen and Delia Larkin instigated
a Save the Kiddies project, which planned to house the children of strikers
with sympathetic British supporters. This latter initiative was greeted with
horror by the Catholic hierarchy, who feared Protestant influence on the
children of their flock. The 1913 lockout was a harsh and bitter dispute,

Case against working mothers

The case against the employment of married women was argued not only by men – leading women trade unionists also expressed their opposition. Delia Larkin, secretary of the Irish Women Workers' Union, was among those who argued that the solution to poverty was a fair 'family wage' paid to the male breadwinner:

> What a crime this system of married women going out to work is. It is a crime against the woman herself, against the husband and against the children . . . [It] has a bad effect on the whole community of workers; it keeps women's wages at a starvation rate, men's wages low and is the means of making drunkards of both men and women. The woman goes out to work the same as the husband and works as many hours. There is no home life for them, and no meals are prepared. Therefore the temptation to indulge in strong drink is very strong.
> A married woman's duty is not to help the sweater [the sweatshop employer] and [the] publican, but to look after her home and those who live there. This can only be done when the men's wages are of such as standard as will enable them to live in decent houses and provide in a right manner for their wives and children.

Irish Worker, 8 March 1913

which could claim no real victors and which left the Irish labour movement in disarray.[154] Not all women joined unions or took part in strikes, of course; for many, family considerations came first and some at least must have faced pressure not to add to everyday hardships.[155] Recent research has also indicated that class-consciousness and the individual's relationship with the local community were important in helping to determine different attitudes to strikes and labour relations.[156]

Although the significance of the IWWU can be overestimated in terms of the overall trade-union movement, it is worthy of further comment, given that it was intricately involved in the wider cultural and political movements which were transforming Irish society in this period. Leading members and supporters of the union, such as Countess Markievicz, Hanna Sheehy Skeffington, Louie Bennett, Helena Moloney and Helen Chenevix, espoused the causes of suffragism, nationalism or socialism, their participation in the passionate debates of the early twentieth century a reflection of their desire to make women's voices heard and their citizenship a reality.

2

Emerging identities

Our desire to have a voice in directing the affairs of Ireland is not based on the failure of men to do so properly, but is the inherent right of women as loyal citizens and intelligent human souls.[1]

A great deal has been written on the public activism of Irish women in the late nineteenth and early twentieth centuries. In the decades during which Ireland suffered civil disruption, world war and dramatic constitutional change, a minority of women, proactive and vocal, made their own impact on history. While women had participated in public campaigns, both political and social, in previous periods, their activities during the years 1880–1920 were particularly noteworthy. The causes to which they gave their time, energy, support and commitment, were diverse and sometimes conflicting, and would affect the lives of future generations of Irish women. But these were also years of sweeping change – cultural, legal and constitutional – on the broader canvas of Western Europe, and it is important to view developments in Ireland within this context. National conflicts and debates took place against a backdrop of shifting ideologies, processes and policies which helped determine the shape of the new century. The interaction of local and global influences gave rise to situations which were by no means unique, but which nonetheless in many aspects were particular to the island of Ireland.

During this period of controversy, debate and the passionate pursuit of ideals, there was considerable overlap between the various strands of female activism. The same names recurred within suffrage, pacifist, trade-union and nationalist or unionist societies, and while it can be difficult to separate these strands of allegiance, it should be remembered that on frequent occasions individual women did not themselves do so. For many, one cause was intricately bound up with the other, with individual rights and freedoms seen as an integral part of wider constitutional or ideological issues, and vice versa. Writing in 1913, Countess Markievicz claimed that the three great movements in contemporary Ireland – the national movement, the women's movement and the labour movement – were 'all fighting the same fight, for the extension of human liberty'.[2] However, while historians have also been keen to focus on these particular linkages, it was clear that some women at the time perceived that political progress could be best achieved by maintaining and indeed strengthening the Union with Britain. Feminists were no more immune from the consequences of conflicting political loyalties than any other grouping.

SUFFRAGE

The suffrage campaign in Ireland, north and south, has been the subject of much feminist historical analysis. Developments on the island to a large extent paralleled those in Britain, with small groups emerging firstly in the urban centres of Belfast and Dublin,[3] then proliferating at an increasing rate as the debate became more public and contentious. The range of societies in existence at the beginning of the twentieth century reflected the diversity of women's voices seeking the common goal of the parliamentary franchise: the Irish Women's Suffrage and Local Government Association (IWSLGA), the Munster Women's Franchise League, the Conservative and Unionist Women's Franchise Association, the Church League for Women's Suffrage, the Irish Catholic Women's Suffrage Society. As well as 'special interest' groups, some individual societies embraced a broad range of political opinion. As Marie A. Johnson, of the Ulster Women's Suffrage Centre commented:

> We had Unionists like Dr. Bell, Nationalists like Winifred Carney and the Misses Boylan, Liberals: Mrs Bennett, Mrs Russell, Mrs McCracken, me Labour, and so was Mrs Adamson; Mrs Kavanagh was Sinn Féin. It was doubly hard on the Liberal women, for our actions were directed against the Asquith government.[4]

While the hopes of suffragists ebbed and flowed in line with broader parliamentary developments, there was no doubt that Asquith's administration

Suffrage activism

Elizabeth Hutchinson remembers that when her mother joined the Belfast branch of the suffragette movement in 1910, they were often visited by members of the Women's Social and Political Union:

> In Donegall Place in Belfast there was a very fashionable cake shop and tea room called the Carlton. Their trademark was a cardboard cake box in black and white stripes, it was excellent for carrying cakes and also a good camouflage for carrying firelighters. When one of these visitors stayed with us we always had cake for tea. My mother and two other members of the committee were put under police surveillance. The two other ladies took delight in embarrassing their detectives, they would go in to town to one of the large stores and make a beeline for the underwear/corset department or go to the ladies' rest room and read a book for about an hour. Another trick was to get hold of a young assistant and say that they thought that there was a man following them and she would very likely get them out by the back door. If my father and mother were going to the theatre or the opera house my father booked two seats in one row and one in the row behind for the detective. On cold wet nights the man on duty was very often invited in for a cup of tea and a sandwich. This consideration paid off as one night one of the men told my father that the house was going to be raided that night. When the police arrived there was no sign of a visitor and certainly no sign of a Carlton cake box and we didn't get so many cakes for a long time.

Elizabeth Hutchinson, 'Reminiscence', unpublished manuscript, in possession of author

proved a major disappointment. Liberalism in Ireland had already been critically fractured over the question of Home Rule – a measure of independence for Ireland involving the setting up of a separate Irish parliament – which was vehemently opposed by the Ulster Unionist Party (UUP) for giving away too much, and by radical nationalists for proposing too little. But, whatever their views on other aspects of the Irish constitution, no mainstream political party, with the exception of the small but growing Labour Party, supported the women's campaign. Although individual men proved willing to align themselves with the suffrage movement, wider party considerations generally predominated in public debates. For example, the Irish Parliamentary Party (IPP), committed to constitutional separation from Britain and in 1912 holding the balance of power at Westminster, felt it necessary 'in the interests of Home Rule to save the Liberal Ministry from the disruptive effects of women's suffrage', and in that year voted decisively (71 votes to 5) not to include female suffrage in its Home Rule Bill.[5] Similarly, the Unionist camp was unwilling to be deflected from the critical constitutional question, or even to devote parliamentary time to discussion of the issue.

There had been some movement in terms of female representation at local government level. From 1896 women with certain property qualifications had been eligible to stand for election as Poor Law Guardians, and within three years eighty-five women had taken up this position, suggesting that a reservoir of talent and ability was ready to be tapped. The 1898 Local Government (Ireland) Act gave women the municipal franchise and by 1911 they were able to serve on county councils and boroughs. Welcome as this was, Rosemary Cullen Owens has observed that it was not an advance to be cheered, so much as Ireland 'catching up' with legislation already enacted in Britain. Therefore, although progress was undoubtedly being made in the political realm, it seemed that 'the more power connected with the office, the longer it was withheld from women'.[6]

In 1903 growing impatience and a rising sense of frustration with this situation in Britain was reflected in the formation in Manchester of the Women's Social and Political Union (WSPU), a group prepared to resort to unconstitutional and even militant action to bring their cause to the forefront of the public arena. Five years later, inspired by this example, Hanna Sheehy Skeffington and Margaret Cousins formed the Irish Women's Franchise League (IWFL) with the aim of having a 'votes for women' clause introduced into the Home Rule Bill then making its way through parliament. Within four years, the league could boast a membership of 1,000. Although the IWFL stressed its independence from the organisation of the English militants, the two groups were mutually supportive. The WSPU, recognising the importance of the support of the Irish lobby, visited Ireland on a regular basis, often accompanied by or sharing the platform with leading members of the IWFL.

As the number of suffrage groups and societies proliferated, Lisburn Suffrage Society seems to have been responsible for initial moves to form an umbrella association to co-ordinate activities, and in 1911 the Irish Women's Suffrage Federation (IWSF) was founded by Dubliners Louie Bennett and Helen Chenevix. By July 1913 twenty societies had become affiliated. Interestingly, around 70 per cent of affiliated societies were fronted by the Northern Committee of the IWSF, reflecting the strength of the suffrage movement in the province of Ulster.[7] Overall statistics for suffrage activity are difficult to ascertain, however, as an editorial in the *Irish Citizen* was quick to point out:

> The mere question of numbers is immaterial . . . great questions are never

decided by a counting of heads ... but by the force of the spirit of right and justice which makes a handful of determined souls carry along with them a host of the merely ignorant and undecided, of the selfish and the cynical.[8]

A majority of these determined souls in the suffrage campaign were from middle-class backgrounds, and many of those involved were, like Skeffington, among that generation of articulate, motivated young women who had benefited from widening educational opportunities only to discover that their ambitions to fully participate in social and political life were severely curtailed. Thus, on joining the IWSLGA, Skeffington remarked, 'I was then an undergraduate, and was amazed and disgusted to learn that I was classed among criminals, infants and lunatics – in fact that my status as a woman was worse than any of these.'[9] Contemporary sources demonstrate the extent to which this shared sense of outrage was a critical motivating factor. With middle-class males increasingly broadening their participation in the political world, it is perhaps not altogether surprising that the more progressive of their female relatives also demanded a share in power. For many – perhaps a majority of the more articulate – the argument was one of equity in terms of gender: votes for women on the same terms as for men – that is, with a property qualification. The 'suffrage catechism', published in the *Irish Citizen* on 10 May 1913, clearly stated that the demand for the vote was not for every woman, 'because every man has not got a vote. Men have to qualify for the vote in certain ways ... what we ask is that women who qualify in the same way should have the same right to vote'.[10] Not all suffragists agreed with this stance, however, and a significant number of activists lobbied for a broader, more inclusive, extension of the franchise. Marion Duggan of the IWFL felt that it was essential to organise working-class women in the battle for the vote; only then, she argued, would their claims for better wages and conditions be addressed. This was seen to be a particularly important issue in Belfast, where 'without political power to enforce their economic necessities, the sweated women workers of [the city] are virtually powerless to secure the legislative changes which they demand'.[11] It is not surprising, therefore, that the Northern Committee was concerned to reach out to working women, adopting the tactics of a generation of evangelical preachers by holding lunch-hour meetings at factory and mill gates, and proclaiming their message from street corners.

Class was only one of the issues dividing suffragists; within wider society objections to women attaining the vote focused on gender difference. The articulate, assertive suffrage campaigner must have been anathema to those already horrified by the boldness of modern womanhood:

Suffrage militancy in Belfast

As this *Irish Citizen* report suggests, militant action in 1914 by Dorothy Evans and Madge Muir, members of the English-based Women's Social and Political Union, caused a stir both within suffrage circles and the wider community.

Belfast is still in the midst of a genuine revolution. Whatever may be said by Liberals and their Irish allies about 'bluff' with regard to the Ulster Militants who acknowledge the lead of Sir Edward Carson, there is no bluff about the women militants who have hoisted in Belfast the banner of the W.S.P.U. While we remain unchanged in the opinion (also expressed this week by Mr. T. M. Healy) that the work of organising Ireland on the suffrage question ought to be left to the Irish Suffrage Societies, militant and non-militant; we cannot refrain from noting the inconsistency of the Government's attitude, which has been disclosed at close quarters by their arrest of Miss Dorothy Evans and other militants in Ulster.

Miss Evans last week made an effective protest against the injustice of arresting her while Sir Edward Carson was left at liberty. In consequence, bail was refused on her next remand, and she and Miss Muir at once entered on the Hunger and Thirst Strike, which led to their release, in a shockingly debilitated state from the poisoning which this protest induces, on Sunday, after four days without touching food or water. They were not, we gather, deprived of any of the usual privileges of a bail prisoner while on hunger strike; the reform, we may assume, that the amendment in this respect of Irish officialdom is permanent and not accidental. (It will be remembered that the first Irish Hunger-strikers in Mountjoy were deprived of these privileges, but they were not taken away from Mrs. Sheehy-Skeffington on her last hunger strike, also as a bail prisoner.) Meantime, the imprisonment of Miss Evans and Miss Muir, and the threats of conspiracy charges made against their friends in Belfast, do not appear to have had any effect in stopping the militant campaign there. On the contrary, another mansion, valued at £10,000, has been burned, glass has been broken in the Unionist headquarters, and Bangor Railway Station has been attacked. When will the Government learn in the case of women, as it apparently has learned in the case of Ulster men, the futility of coercion, and the need for applying fundamental remedies to the grievances which lead to these violent methods? – in this case, Votes for Women. Miss Evans and Miss Muir were too ill to appear in Court on Tuesday, and their case was adjourned for a week. The savage sentence of two months' imprisonment on Miss Mabel Small, for breaking a window in the Unionist headquarters, has excited much unfavourable comment even in non-suffragist areas in Belfast.

Irish Citizen, 18 April 1914

> The mannish cut of the modern woman's scanty garments, the short skirts, the liberal display of ankle, the often bared throat and neck (even in the street), the jaunty set of her hat jammed down to one side and completely covering her hair and her eyes – it may be convenient and comfortable, but it certainly is not womanly or dignified or nice.[12]

For its part, the Catholic Church expressed the view that, 'allowing women the right of suffrage is incompatible with the catholic ideal of the unity of domestic life'.[13] While representatives of the conservative and conventional voiced their opinions in journals and periodicals, the majority of people viewed the campaign as peripheral, either to everyday life or the political agenda. Unfortunately for the suffragists, so too, did Ireland's politicians.

By the summer of 1912, the attitudes of the various political parties were clear, with the defeat of compromise Conciliation Bills clearly reflecting their opposition to the issue of women's franchise. Feeling that they had exhausted every other avenue, the leaders of the IWFL made the decision to engage in more public militant action – after all, if northern unionists were prepared to resort to violent methods to demand changes to the Home Rule legislation which had now gone through the various stages of parliamentary procedure, why should suffragists not do the same?[14] Some members of the league had served terms of imprisonment as a result of stone-throwing activities in London as early as 1910,[15] but 13 June 1912 saw the first arrests of suffragists in Ireland, for breaking windows. Not surprisingly, given the intention to gain as much publicity as possible, all of the eight accused refused the option of a forty-shilling fine, choosing the alternative of a prison sentence.[16]

The scene was thus set for open hostility between suffragists and their opponents, with militant activism introducing another element of division and disagreement within the feminist movement. Several individuals, as well as a number of societies, voiced their disapproval of militancy, and there was some shifting of allegiance between militant and non-militant groupings.[17] While Skeffington insisted that the oppressed should use whatever means were available to them, Bennett argued that 'no real victory has ever been gained by force or coercion'.[18] The issue was further confused by the dramatic militancy of English suffragists in Ireland, who not only acted without consulting their Irish sisters, but also alienated a significant portion of wider nationalist opinion with their assertion that there should be no Home Rule without votes for women. In July 1912, during a prime ministerial visit to Dublin, Asquith was attacked by three members of the WSPU, who also tried to set fire to the Theatre Royal. Following their arrest, the two English women went on hunger strike, and were subsequently force-fed, the only two convicted of suffrage militancy in Ireland to suffer this brutal treatment, though a total of twelve engaged in hunger strikes. As Skeffington later remarked, 'Hunger strike was then a new weapon – had we but known we were the pioneers in a long line.'[19]

Militant action undoubtedly raised the temperature and heightened tension, both among suffragists and in the public debate on their activities. Onlookers who had been merely curious were now more likely to be hostile. Skeffington recalled a meeting in Limerick where she was confronted by an angry mob. As she made her escape, 'the women – they are swift actionists – tore my hat from my head. An elderly "bum" thrust a dirty face close to me and shouted beerily: "Are ye a suff?" I said, "Yes", whereupon he spat copiously into my face.'[20] Militancy could have other negative consequences: on her release from Mountjoy, Skeffington received notice of dismissal from her part-time teaching post at Rathmines College of Commerce; Georgina Manning, another Dublin teacher, suffered the same fate. On the other hand, the committee of Belfast Technical College permitted suffrage prisoner Mabel Small to keep her post, as she had undertaken only to be involved in militant action during school holidays.[21]

But while militancy was divisive, the ideological clash with nationalism was probably of greater significance. The fear that inclusion of suffrage in the already contentious and difficult parliamentary debates would irretrievably damage the passage of Home Rule has already been noted, and within mainstream unionism the suffrage issue was generally regarded as an irrelevance. However, a mass meeting of suffragists held in Dublin in June 1912 to demand the inclusion of votes for women in the Home Rule Bill indicated that not all unionist women agreed. Mrs M.E. Cope, from Armagh Suffrage Society, sent a forceful message to the organisers:

> I write from the purely Unionist point of view. But it seems to me imperative that all women, of whatever political party, should now stand for a great principle – the principle that no democratic Government can be considered complete which ignores not only a class but a whole sex. It is because I know we are one in standing for this that I would gladly have joined you on your platform tonight.[22]

At the same time, within the nationalist community, those revolutionaries following an extra-parliamentary agenda similarly felt that the 'women' issue would detract from the major aim of independence. They deplored the Irish suffragist links with British societies and their attempts to influence a British, therefore alien, government. For politicised Irish women, the tensions between the two movements could create both ideological and practical difficulties. But as Cliona Murphy suggests, 'Irish suffragists were not the only ones to experience this tug of loyalties between nationalism and feminism'.[23] Within nationalism generally, a fairly traditional perception of gender roles prevailed, with women's major contribution seen to be in the private domain, sustaining and nurturing family life and thus perpetuating the race. Feminism, on the other hand, transcended national boundaries, challenged the separation of private and public spheres, and sought women's freedom of choice in matters such as birth control, education and employment. Murphy argues that contemporary observers in many parts of Europe thought that support for such issues undermined the state and, as a result, were hostile to national aspirations. Women pursuing both nationalist and feminist ambitions therefore experienced significant tension in the expression and pursuit of their goals.

In Ireland in the pre-war period of growing nationalist fervour, it is perhaps not surprising that some women shifted their allegiance. In May 1914 Mary MacSwiney, a former member of Munster Suffrage Society, argued that 'Ireland had the question of national sovereignty to settle and to oppose the government now would, in effect, mean to oppose Home Rule'.[24] However, a majority of those women for whom national identity came first, and who were unwilling to compromise in the battle against British rule, found little outlet for their political energies in the male-dominated nationalist organisations of the day. Women's involvement in the Celtic Revival has already been mentioned, and it was against the background of growing nationalist political campaigns, both constitutional and militant, that Inghinidhe na hÉireann (Daughters of Ireland) was founded in October 1900. The twenty-nine women attending the first meeting elected Maud Gonne as president and dedicated themselves to the 're-establishment of the complete independence of Ireland'. Much of their work was educational, with a strong focus on the Irish language and on Irish literature, history, music and art. They also supported and helped to popularise Irish manufacture, reflecting their commitment to discouraging all things English – which were defined as 'low', 'vulgar', and antipathetic to the 'artistic taste and refinement of the Irish people'.[25] All members were required to be Irish or of Irish descent, and a belief in the necessity of violence to aid the cause was clearly expressed: 'A movement that stops short of shedding blood, and therefore forbids you to make the last sacrifice – that of your life – cannot be taken very seriously, and must end in contempt and ridicule.'[26] But although members of the Belfast branch, for example, received instruction on the cleaning and loading of weapons, Diane Urquhart argues that such radical nationalism was too nonconformist to attract widespread popular support.[27] The society's journal, *Bean na hÉireann*, edited by Helena Moloney, advocated 'militancy, separatism and feminism'; however, an editorial reflected the commonly held view among many nationalist feminists that suffragism was not just a deflection, but a betrayal: 'The feminist cause in Ireland is best served by ignoring England and English politicians . . . At all events, women should first set their own house in order.'[28] As Margaret Ward comments, to ignore Westminster was rather difficult when it was the forum where suffrage Bills were being debated.[29] Some individuals did manage to straddle both the suffrage and nationalist camps, but this became much harder to achieve as the constitutional crisis deepened. It was more usual for opinion to polarise, particularly when both nationalists and unionists formed armed movements in support of their respective causes.

It was in response to this fast-changing situation that Cumann na mBan, a new all-female nationalist organisation, was formed in Dublin on 5 May 1914. Largely led by relatives of leading Irish Volunteers, it was seen as an auxiliary to the male movement. In her opening address, Agnes O'Farrelly made it clear that the women of Cumann na mBan were to play a supportive role in advancing the 'cause of Irish liberty', particularly by helping to arm the men: 'each rifle we put in their hands will represent to us a bolt fastened behind the door of some Irish home to keep out the hostile stranger. Each cartridge will be a watchdog to fight for the sanctity of the hearth.'[30] One hundred women attended the first meeting of this organisation, which was to play a significant role in nationalist politics, although until the Anglo-Irish Treaty split of the 1920s that role would be largely supportive. The Irish Citizen Army, initially formed to protect striking workers during the Dublin lockout of 1913, was much more likely to offer women immediate involvement in all the activities of the organisation, including military training. Cumann na mBan's prioritising of nationalism over suffragism, however, given women's lack of equality of status within the nationalist movement, inevitably engendered suspicion and conflict between it and the wider feminist groupings.

From within the unionist tradition, also, women came forward to lay claim to their heritage and their identity, participating in the political, religious and cultural debates critical to the growing constitutional crisis of this period. Irish women had been active in support of the Union before the twentieth century, but by 1911 the progress of the Home Rule legislation, coinciding with the crescendo of suffrage activity, combined to empower political activists of all shades. Many women in the north-east concentrated their energies on the Ulster Women's Unionist Council (UWUC), formed in that year with upper-class leadership, but set to become 'the largest female political organisation in Ireland'. This was a highly effective grouping, linking together a range of unionist opinion and engaging in intensive propaganda campaigns.[31] For example, in June 1911, Mrs Wetherall of Ballycastle, County Antrim, and Miss Johnson of Londonderry, were sent to conduct an anti-Home Rule campaign in the south of England at the request of South Berkshire Conservative Association.[32] In November it was announced that twelve workers had been sent to England and Scotland, and that Mrs Sinclair of Strabane, County Tyrone, who was going to conduct a campaign in Cambridgeshire, proposed to bring with her a conjurer and entertainer 'as the means of securing an audience amongst the working classes'.[33] A delegation from the British Women's Amalgamated Unionist and Tariff Association, arriving to study the Home Rule issue, were not to be subjected to any enormous public displays – in case of rioting; instead they 'should be sent first to the North West of Ulster to see the condition of affairs in a Nationalist district, and should then be brought to the loyal districts in the East to contrast the prosperity and industry which prevailed there'.[34]

That the contrast between social conditions in east and north-west Ulster was a result of religious allegiance rather than economic or environmental issues was a recurring theme in the loyalist discourse of the period. UUP leader James Craig referred to the UWUC as 'the motherhood of Ulster', and as Lurgan Women's Unionist Association warned, Home Rule would threaten the sanctity of the Protestant home:

> If our homes are not sacred from the priest under the existing laws, what can we expect from a priest-governed Ireland ... [L]et each woman in Ulster do a woman's part to stem the tide of Home Rule ... The union ... meant everything to them – their civil and religious liberty [and] their homes and children ... [T]he home was a woman's first consideration ... [I]n the event of Home Rule being granted, the sanctity and happiness of home life in Ulster would be permanently destroyed.[35]

These kinds of tensions between the two major religious communities had been considerably heightened in 1907 by the publication of *Ne temere,* the papal decree which attempted to ensure that Catholics marrying Protestants would bring up their children in the Catholic faith.

Unionist women were also involved at a more populist level in working-class Protestant culture, participating from around 1887 in a short-lived association of loyal Orangewomen. Revived at the end of 1911, within 8 years this organisation had 12 female lodges, 10 of which, based in Belfast, had a membership of over 1,000. During the Twelfth celebrations of July 1912, the *Belfast Evening Telegraph* recorded the public tribute to the women's progress made by the Orange Grand Master of Londonderry:

> What that meant to Protestantism no one could estimate, because they all knew that the hand that rocked the cradle ruled the world. So they said to their Orange sister: – 'Go on and God be with you in your splendid work for the truth and home and freedom.'[36]

Women outside their local church in Strabane sign a declaration in support of the union between Britain and Ireland, 1912.

Perhaps the greatest public display of unionist commitment to the existing constitution was the signing of the Solemn League and Covenant on 28 September 1912 by 218,206 men, some of them symbolically writing their names in blood. Women showed their solidarity by signing a supplementary declaration of support: after marching in procession to church services, a total of 234,046 women signed in Protestant parochial halls.

The UUP was emphatic that Home Rule took priority over any other political issue. However, there was a brief flurry of excitement among suffragettes in September 1913 when a letter from Dawson Bates, secretary of the Ulster Unionist Council (UUC), to Mr. Hamill, secretary of the UWUC, was published in the press. The letter indicated that the UUC's plans for a provisional government in the north-east would include granting the franchise to women. This revelation was greeted with some surprise by the officials of the UWUC. Indeed, Dowager Marchioness of Dufferin and Ava wrote to her friend:

Ulster women in defence of the Union

The Ulster Women's Unionist Council co-ordinated women's opposition to the proposals for Home Rule under discussion in the Westminster parliament. This excerpt from the petition of 1912 highlights the issues the UWUC felt directly affected women.

> Serious dangers would arise to our social and domestic liberties from intrusting legislative functions to a body of which a large permanent majority would be under ecclesiastical control.
>
> No legislative safeguards would avail to protect us against such dangers, as the Roman Catholic Church refuses to recognise the binding effect of any agreements which curtail her prerogatives and claims an uncontrolled jurisdiction in the provinces of education and the marriage laws, a claim which has been recognised in practice by the Irish Parliamentary Party.
>
> The late iniquitous enforcement of the Ne Temere Decree – a Decree which specifically affects the women of Ireland – and the slavish acquiescence of the Irish Nationalist Members of Parliament in its operation, demonstrate that in an Irish Parliament the natural instincts of humanity would be of no avail as against the dictates of the Roman Church.
>
> The dominating power of ecclesiastics over education in Ireland, which is already excessive, would be largely increased and schools and colleges under the control of religious orders would be state-favoured institutions under an Irish Parliament.
>
> There would be no prospect of beneficent legislation to ameliorate the conditions of life of unprotected women engaged in industrial work in many conventual institutions, as the Irish Nationalist Members of Parliament steadfastly oppose any such legislation. No valid reason has been advanced for depriving Irish women of the rights and privileges which they now enjoy.
>
> We therefore pray the honourable Commons of the United Kingdom of Great Britain and Ireland in Parliament assembled to reject any legislative proposals to disintegrate the United Kingdom and expose us to the disastrous consequences of such disintegration.

Petition, 1912, Minute Books of the Ulster Women's Unionist Council, PRONI D/1098/1/1

There is a great deal of feeling about Mr. Bates's letter, and the suffragettes are triumphant. Others wrote to suggest that we 'veto' the resolution. So I came to the conclusion that it would be best entirely to ignore the suffrage part of the letter.[37]

It proved to be a wise decision. In the spring of 1914, in response to WSPU demands that he clarify his position, Unionist leader Sir Edward Carson asserted that he 'had never agreed with the suffrage movement'. Nor could he make such a demand on his party as they were divided on the subject.[38]

The reaction of the WSPU, which had established a branch in Belfast, was perhaps also predictable. While Belfast, in particular, had already witnessed suffrage militancy, the small, dedicated group of WSPU members declared war on Carson and made Ulster the focus for a series of incendiary attacks on private property. Dorothy Evans and Madge Muir were arrested following the burning of Abbeylands House in Whiteabbey and the breaking of windows in Castle House, Lisburn, both in County Antrim. Although Muir defiantly cried 'No Surrender!' on her arrest, such actions were counterproductive.[39] The growing hostility of the public may have been related to the passing of the Malicious Injuries (Ireland) Act, which meant that payment for damage to private property resulting from such attacks was taken from public rates. County Antrim paid a total of £92,000 in damages for property destroyed by suffragettes, and consequently a threepenny levy in the pound was applied to the county's rates.[40] Suffragettes, however, felt that such dramatic actions were necessary if their cause was to make an impact at a time when the spectre of civil war loomed close, and significant numbers of women, as well as men, were physically demonstrating their commitment to more traditional political allegiances.[41]

By early 1914, around 3,000 women had enlisted in the unionist Ulster Volunteer Force (UVF), training in the signalling section, as ambulance and dispatch riders, postal workers, typists and intelligence workers. Women on both sides of the political divide were also involved in more unconventional activities in support of their political interests. Among the wealthy Anglo-Irish supporters of republicanism were Mary Spring Rice, daughter of Lord Monteagle, and Molly Childers, who took part in a major gun running exercise, helping to bring in 1,500 rifles and 45,000 rounds of ammunition from Germany in July 1914. Rice's account of this adventure aboard the 28-ton yacht *Asgard* conveys the excitement and the tension, the apprehensions and the discomfort of the crew, as they sailed into Howth, County Dublin, with Mary's red skirt signalling their co-conspirators at the harbour.[42] Loyalist women were also engaged in unloading weapons and ferrying them to safe houses during the loyalist gun-running at Larne, County Antrim, just three months earlier.[43] Indeed, former unionist supporter and ardent suffragist Mrs L.A.M. Priestly McCracken denounced the

> ethical and moral distinctions which unionist women made in supporting
> the militancy of their own party through the arming of the Ulster Volunteer

Force, whilst opposing that of suffragettes, as nothing short of 'nauseating'.[44]

1914–1918: WAR

When Britain declared war on Germany in August 1914, Ireland was already engulfed in an atmosphere of tense expectation in which violent protest and popular militarism were common. Responses to the new situation, however, differed among societies and individuals. An Emergency Council of Suffragists, formed in Dublin in 1914, aimed to enable and encourage women to retain their identity as suffragists while engaging in war relief works, a compromise of priorities which was firmly rejected by the IWSL. Some members of the IWSF who did go down this route later changed their minds, and from early 1915 re-engaged in the suffrage activities which they had initially suspended. Louie Bennett continued her opposition to militarism in all its forms and called for international solidarity, arguing that 'Suffragists of every country must face the fact that militancy is now the most dangerous foe of women's suffrage, and of all that women's suffrage stands for.'[45] But once war had broken out, international co-operation was difficult to maintain. While three Irish women had been present at the Budapest Congress organised by the International Women's Suffrage Alliance in 1913, travel restrictions prevented their participation in the 1915 Hague Conference, which resulted in the formation of the International Committee of Women for Permanent Peace. When this body called for representatives from national committees, Irish women responded with two distinct lines of approach. Skeffington was to the fore of those linking the call for women's full citizenship to the cause of Irish freedom, and strongly lobbied for the recognition of the rights of small nations. Peace from this perspective, had to be accompanied by justice. As Skeffington explained:

> If I saw the hope of Ireland being freed for ever from British rule by a swift uprising, I would consider Irishmen justified resorting to arms in order that we might be free. I should still be radically opposed to war and militarism. This is of course my personal view and in no way represents the League. But I hold no such hopes. I think that freedom for small nations lies in Justice by Arbitration and there is one of my strongest motives in standing for Peace.[46]

Bennett, on the other hand, represented a pacifism that refused to be confined within national boundaries or compromised by nationalist ideology, and these conflicting views reflected the dilemma of feminists across Europe and America. But feminists debated the intricacies of their positions on the morality of war against a backdrop of patriotic fervour, which ensured that the voices of those urging pacifism, on both national and international platforms, were marginalised and rendered irrelevant.

In most local suffrage societies in Ireland war relief took precedence over all other activities, as women considered the best ways in which they could help the war effort. In wider society, too, traditional middle-class activism was redirected to focus on the needs of the battalions of soldiers making their way to the Front. Lady Clonbrock, for example, used her influence as president of Galway County Temperance Association to purchase an ambulance for use in France;[47] so too did the United Irishwomen's branch of the Red Cross in County Wexford. The women of Killyleagh, County Down, raised funds by organising fêtes and fairs, concerts, football and rugby matches.[48] In Omagh, County Tyrone, the normal work of the WNHA took a back seat while its members busied themselves picking sphagnum moss for their local hospital war supply depot.[49] The moss, after being soaked in garlic oil, was used as an antiseptic dressing on the battlefields, and its use is thought to be one of the reasons for the low rate of infection among British soldiers compared to those of other armies. The UWUC, already well prepared for civil war, adapted their plans and strategies to deal with the new situation; £1440 was raised for financing and equipping a hospital in Pau in south-west France, originally established by the Tyrone Nursing Corps. Although the hospital was under French military control, it was managed by a Miss Sinclair, assisted by a Miss Ballantine, both from Strabane. Members of the South Belfast Ulster Women's Association were amongst those who fund-raised for the Ulster Women's Gift Fund, which by November 1918 had collected a total of almost £191,500.[50]

The pupils of Alexandra College founded a War Guild, established a hostel for around fifteen Belgian refugees, and in 1915 opened a War Club to provide a meeting place for women left on their own while their sons, brothers, or husbands were fighting overseas. Typically, these middle-class girls focused on providing opportunities for self-improvement, with classes in cooking, exercise, sewing, music and health care. As the war progressed they also opened a hostel for young country girls, who had come to the city seeking work in munitions factories; their aim was 'to provide a physically wholesome and morally safe abode for the working girls of the poorest classes'.[51] It seems that the war extended the opportunities for middle-class women to exert power and influence over working-class women.[52]

More generally, wives and mothers played an important role in the government's recruitment drive, their persuasive powers recognised by the local press, which urged them to use their influence in the home on behalf of the Crown forces:

> Do you realise that the one word 'Go' from *you* may send another man to fight for Ireland? ...When the war is over and your husband or son is asked, 'What did you do in the Great War?' is he to hang his head because *you* would not let him go?[53]

Not all women were willing to succumb to such pressure. Belfast woman Winifred Campbell recalled how her father, a dispatch clerk in an export firm, enlisted despite the disapproval of his wife, who firmly believed he should stay home to do his bit to defend Ireland from the threat of Home Rule. Recruitment from Ulster certainly declined in the aftermath of the 1916 Easter Rising, when the argument that young unionist men were needed 'to hold the fort' appeared more compelling. Some on the nationalist side were also reluctant to support the British effort. A fund-raising fête planned by the UI at Cappagh, County Waterford, for example, met with initial hostility as this organisation was 'looked upon as one of John Bull's pocket perquisites'.[54] Keith Jeffery insists, however, that initial support for the war was a shared experience in Ireland, with only a 'tiny, eccentric collection of irreconcilables dissent[ing] from the majority'. Among the complex set of reasons given for such support, he includes financial considerations, quoting, for example, the experience of Wexford labourer James English who found that, 'with separation allowances, he and his family were 154 per cent better off once he was soldiering'.[55] Catholic religious periodicals of the period were full of obituaries and requests for prayers for frontline soldiers, calling attention to the sacrifice made by 'Irish Tommies', so long ignored in subsequent nationalist and unionist histories.[56]

Opportunities also existed for women to engage directly in the war effort, both at home and overseas. For many, the most obvious way to help was in the traditional role of nursing and there were plenty in need of their care. Both old and new organisations recruited staff to meet the growing demand, with nurses from the various units entering the war at different stages. Women of the Queen Alexandra Imperial Nursing Service (QAINS), founded in 1902, landed in France in August 1914 as part of the British Expeditionary Force, and tended to the wounded on the front. Doctor's daughter Rosabelle Osborne, from County Donegal, joined QAINS as a sister in 1903, became a matron in 1911, and was one of the first to go overseas following the outbreak of war. During the course of the next five years she served in France, Egypt, Malta, Salonika and the Black Sea. By 1917 she was matron-in-chief at Salonika, in control of 26 hospitals and a field ambulance and had lost 15 members of her staff to climate and disease.

However, she recalled that

> in spite of malaria and dysentery, mud and mosquitoes and many other discomforts, there was a special fascination about active service in Macedonia. The beautiful mountains, wild and rugged country with exquisite sunsets and a wonderful variety of wild flowers were among the many compensations.[57]

Recognition of Rosabelle's wartime efforts came in the form of five mentions in dispatches, a CBE and Royal Red Cross and decoration by the French government.

The mainly upper-class First Aid Nursing Yeomanry (FANY), formed in 1907 after the Boer War, was the first women's voluntary corp in Britain. The volunteers, who had to be expert horsewomen and own their own mount, were trained in first aid and in 1914 became a unit of the Belgian military, administering hospitals and providing convoys. Later in the war its ambulance drivers became the first female motor division in the British army. The Voluntary Auxiliary Detachment nurses (VADs) also predated the war. Formed throughout Great Britain in 1909, over 4,500 Irish women served as VADs at home and abroad between 1914 and 1918. Belfast-born Emma Duffin served as a VAD nurse in front-line hospitals in France and Egypt, and her diaries record the experience of wartime Christmas duty:

> Christmas day was a very strenuous day for everybody. The captain was very musical and trained a choir of orderlies and MO's (medical officers) and they went all round the wards singing carols, to the great delight of all the patients . . . We had great difficulty in persuading the men that beds must be made and the tent tidied even if it was Christmas day, especially as we were to be visited by a General and the Matron-in-Chief. However, we at last got things spick and span, attired each of them in a clean shirt and gave them a rose for their buttonholes and made them look quite smart.[58]

As the war progressed women were increasingly organised into auxiliary uniformed services. One of the earliest was the Women's Legion, formed by Lady Londonderry in 1915 as a pioneer corps to enrol and train women for army work. The work carried out by women in the legion was at first very traditional, with cooks and kitchen staff supplied for the army, followed by all classes of domestic workers, with the Women's Legion Motor Drivers formed in 1916. Lady Londonderry's traditional views on womanhood come through very strongly in her speeches and writings. In one early lecture she stressed that the audience should not go away with 'the idea that we had in mind the creation of a militant force of warlike Amazons capable

Nursing during the First World War

Born into a middle-class merchant family, Emma Duffin enlisted as a Voluntary Auxiliary Detachment nurse during the First World War and served in front-line hospitals in northern France and Egypt. Here she describes her work – and her feelings – on Christmas Day 1919:

> I thought of the only other Christmas I had ever spent away from home, in Germany. We had visited a hospital there too and sung German carols outside the wards and I wondered if they had done it this year and if they had their Christmas trees as usual ... It seemed impossible when we thought of all the dreadful things they had done but they had been very good to me and I felt sorry that we could never meet on friendly terms again.
>
> I thought of the patients I had seen that evening when I went in to help. I had found them singing hymns and it had given me a lump in my throat to see some of them so terribly ill and worn singing 'Abide with me' and 'Onward Christian Soldiers', and 'Peace on Earth Goodwill to Men'. We were all singing it and no doubt the Germans were doing the same and what a farce it would seem to an outsider and what hypocrites we ought to appear and yet I know we weren't all hypocrites and all the Germans weren't, though I felt a good many must be. It was impossible to understand and reconcile. What fools we all were. I gave it up as a bad job and went to sleep.

Emma Duffin, Nursing Diaries, PRONI, D/2109

of fighting side by side with men in the fighting-line. Our object was to organise the women of the country to take the place of men required for active service.' She stressed too that the women engaged in this work were not 'unfeminine' or unattractive or 'those of masculine build', but 'lovely girls' who benefited from 'the effect of the regular work and wearing sensible clothes and thick shoes'.[59] Her defensive attitude says a lot about popular perceptions and fears. There were many other opportunities for women to don uniform and take up various male activities – or more traditional activities, but in a thoroughly different venue and context. The Women's Army Auxiliary Corps (WAAC) was formed in December 1916, and despite the intentions of the authorities, remained a mostly lower-class organisation. The Women's Royal Naval Service (WRNS, or more popularly known as Wrens), one of the most favoured of the female uniformed services, was formed a year later, providing opportunities for both overseas and local work. The Women's Royal Air Force (WRAF) came into being in the last year of the war.

For those who remained at home, civilian life was considerably disrupted. Winifred Campbell recalled the hardships in a family accustomed to the regular wage of a white-collar worker:

> The army allowance was barely adequate and soldiers' wives were hard pressed to cope. There were plenty of voluntary committees, sewing circles and the like, all working to provide comforts for the troops but very little practical help for their families. The factories and foundries were flourishing and there was plenty of money to be made by those who stayed at home, but we had quite a struggle and the comparison made mother resentful. Nevertheless, she refused to ask for or accept anything that savoured of charity.[60]

Shortage of manpower was also problematic in the countryside. During the war some of the branches of the United Irishwomen in County Wexford, notably Foynes, Laurencetown and Bree, undertook co-operative wheat schemes. A woman, in her nineties when she was interviewed by Sarah McNamara, recalled:

> We used to take shares. I think a share was 5/-. Then we rented a field and paid to have it tilled and sown, and harvested, of course, though we all took a hand at this. When the harvest was won, enough wheat was sold to pay the expenses and the rest of it was divided among the share-holders, in proportion to the shares they had. We used to grow wheat for two years, and then let the field down to grass, and with the money we got for this, take another field and begin again. The flour was very bad sometimes, and we were glad to have our own wheat and get it milled for ourselves.[61]

Upper-class women also found scope for their talents. They were needed, for example, to replace their husbands on charitable and other committees, to chair meetings and make speeches. Elizabeth, Countess of Fingall, attended classes in Dublin 'to learn how to do these things properly'.[62]

Although the absence of conscription in Ireland meant less pressure for women to take over men's jobs than those in Britain, the war did provide new working opportunities for civilian women, particularly in the linen industry, which, already growing before 1914, underwent rapid expansion. This was a direct result of 'the increased demand for linen goods for military purposes, notably tents, haversacks, hospital equipment and aeroplane fabric, which more than offset the losses in overseas markets'. Employment in this sector rose from 76,000 in 1912 to 90,000 during the war.[63] Agriculture and shipbuilding also enjoyed new prosperity in the war years, and the production of armaments offered many women new working opportunities in factories. Their financial contribution to the household was also significant. Florence Ross, working in a Dublin shell factory, earned an average of 50 shillings a week, a huge increase on the 2 shillings weekly wage of her previous employment, even when wartime inflation is taken into account.[64] In Belfast, Elizabeth McCullough's mother left school in 1914, and 'instead of pursuing the usual [middle-class] female skills of the time – needlework, watercolour painting, piano playing – she went off to work on a conveyer belt, making shellcases in Mackie's Foundry'.[65] The women in Mackie's worked a 36-hour week in two shifts – from 8 a.m. until 2.30 p.m. and from 2.30 to 8 p.m., and, as this composition shows, many felt that they were making an important contribution to the war:

> Mackie's Girls are full of glee
> All as busy as a bee
> Coming in at nine or three
> Keen as ever they can be,
> Interested in all they see
> Each one gladly knows that she
> Something does for her country.

Some munitions workers, however, were aware of the more sombre aspect of their employment: 'Midst the laughter and the singing I often wonder why am I with others engaged in this awful occupation. To see a row of shells, so innocent looking, yet made for a specific and terrible purpose . . .'[66]

There were, of course, many who suffered personal tragedy, with the deaths of husbands, sons, fathers, lovers and brothers regularly reported. The towns and villages of Ulster were particularly hard hit by the Battle of the Somme on 1 July 1916, and the Dublin Fusiliers and Munster Fusiliers were decimated at Verdun and Gallipoli. A Lurgan Orangeman claimed that there was 'hardly a house in Hill Street in which at least one member of the family has not been killed or wounded',[67] and Enid Starkie from Dublin noted that, 'there was scarcely a family around us who had not lost someone'.[68] Although the overall impact was less dramatic, women too died in the course of duty, as evidenced by the eighteen sisters and staff nurses of QAINS remembered in St Anne's Cathedral, Belfast.

For some others, however, death in this period came as a result of war, not with Germany, but with Britain. One soldier, returning wounded from France to his home in Dublin, found himself by the deathbed of his wife, mortally wounded on Easter Monday, 24 April 1916, during the briefer, more localised, conflict that was to change Ireland's history.[69]

Members of Cumann na mBan and the Irish Citizens' Army, who had taken part in the Easter Rising of 1916, pose in a Dublin garden, summer 1916.

1916: REBELLION

The armed rising of 1916 took most people by surprise. Day-trippers to the seaside, racegoers at Fairyhouse, and those simply enjoying a warm and pleasant bank holiday in the streets of Dublin, suddenly found themselves in the midst of rumour, confusion and chaos. The insurrection, which began with the declaration of an independent Irish Republic, was largely planned and carried out by men: around 1,558 members of the Irish Volunteer Force led by Patrick Pearse, together with James Connolly's Irish Citizen Army. But women also participated; Margaret Ward estimates about 30 female members of the Irish Citizen Army and 60 women from Cumann na mBan took part,[70] though Ruth Taillon claims that these figures do not take account of those who slipped away before the surrender and were not therefore included in official tallies.[71]

Women were particularly important during the early phase, when divisions in the Volunteer leadership meant that plans went awry and movements were uncertain. With many of the male leaders under police surveillance, women played a crucial role in passing messages and information even before the rebellion began. Min Ryan, Bridget Foley and Lily O'Brennan were among these women couriers, while others busied themselves gathering supplies of ammunition and first-aid materials. The tasks carried out varied in terms of importance: Lily O'Brennan purchased tricolour bunting to be made into flags, and Kathleen Clarke was entrusted with important Irish Republican Brotherhood (IRB) plans and detailed information on personnel.[72] With thousands of Irish men also fighting for the British in Europe, many families found their loyalties split and their young men liable to a range of pressures. Patricia Lynch recalled that,

> a girl living near the North Wall, has one brother fighting at the front, another in the Irish Volunteers. The latter, when the revolution started, went off without being aware of what was on hand. Before he reached his destination he met a friend, who told him that ammunition was being served out, and that fighting was going to commence. He returned home, and in order to protect his family from any unpleasant consequences, gave himself up to the police at once. His sister has heard nothing of him since. She is afraid that he may be taken to England and forced to join the army.[73]

When the fighting broke out, around thirty-four women were present in the republican headquarters in Dublin's General Post Office, mostly organising food and stores. It would seem that the role of Cumann na mBan was largely supportive, mainly consisting of cooking and nursing. Women in the ICA were more likely to be directly involved in military activities. The best-known of these, Countess Markievicz, second-in-command at St Stephen's Green, spoke of 'tackling any sniper who was objectionable',[74] but as one observer commented, she was by no means alone: 'These women could throw hand grenades, they understood the use of bombs; in fact, they seemed to understand as much about the business of warfare as men.'[75] Most Volunteers welcomed the contributions made by women, the major exception being Eamon de Valera, who refused to have any females under his command at Boland's mill.[76] While stating at the time that they constituted a possible encumbrance, de Valera's later assertion that women were 'at once the boldest and most unmanageable of revolutionaries', suggests that issues of control might have been uppermost in his mind.

There is no doubt that women rebels were able to make use of traditional gender assumptions in carrying out their activities. They could usually depend upon male perceptions of their femininity, on popular notions of female respectability and modesty, to protect them. A British soldier, for example, provided an escort for Julia Grenan and Elizabeth O'Farrell through the dangerous streets of the city, unaware that they had ammunition and food for the rebels packed around their bodies.[77] However, with martial law declared on 25 April, those most centrally involved were put at considerable risk. Margaretta Keogh of Cumann na mBan was killed in the South Dublin Union while helping a wounded Volunteer, and young

Glasgow schoolteacher Margaret Skinnider, sniping from the roof of the College of Surgeons, was shot by a British soldier and badly injured.[78] Women suspects were vulnerable to acts of brutality, and were frequently subjected to strip-searching, harassment and arrest. Chris Caffrey was attacked by a crowd hostile to the rebels, and on another occasion was taken into a room where he was stripped and searched by soldiers.[79] During the course of the Rising around seventy-seven women were arrested and taken into custody.

Civilian life in Dublin was considerably disrupted during this Easter week. For those living in areas known to be rebel strongholds, the risks were great. Eighteen-year-old Molly Baker, from Stoneybatter in the heart of Dublin, remembered:

> In 1916 you didn't go near a window. You dare not open a door. You'd pull the blinds and get inside. When there was a curfew everyone was in fear. There was a terrific lot of shooting. You could be knocked up at night and your house ransacked . . . we'd hear rumours of people being shot at night and things taken from their homes and people being taken out, even women.[80]

Fires raged in many areas, whole streets were demolished by British shells and mortars, and accidental killings of men, women and children were commonplace. A serving maid was shot dead as she looked out of a window; twenty-eight children were amongst those who lost their lives.[81] In all, 426 people were killed, of whom 230 were civilians, and 3,000 injured in this one week. Many Dublin citizens lost their furniture to barricades and suffered acute food shortages, though the general confusion provided ample opportunities for some to augment family provisions. One reporter recorded looting on the Thursday of that Easter week:

> The gutted condition of Knowle's shop (fruit and vegetables) explains the crowds of women and girls from Longford Street and Mercer Street and adjacent lanes, carrying home orange boxes with fruit, potatoes, bananas, apples, etc. etc. Boys in the raided (Knowle's) shop 'lifting' all they can, in spite of the bullets going past, and even occasional rushes across the street with their plunder. By back ways, down to Exchequer Street, but stopped there by military on duty there, lined across the street with rifles ready – apparently to prevent pillage of shops. Back up to head of Grafton Street by lanes at rear. The French sweet shop next to the raided Noblett's has also been looted. At the back of Knowle's vegetable shop are stores, and here an army of slum girls and women were hurrying away with bundles of stuff, while scores of women were meeting them on their way to the source of

supply. No interference with this industry.[82]

Nuala O'Faolain's grandmother from north Dublin declared that her main memory of 1916 was that 'we got vegetables in 1916 that we never got before or since!'[83] In old age Máire Comerford recalled her fascination with seeing the flag of the Irish Republic flying for the first time and recounted, 'Funny flashbacks . . . like the red plush three-piece suite, sitting incongruously outside a shop window, where someone had been interrupted in the act of looting it.'[84]

The Rising was doomed to failure, however, and with much of the city in flames the decision to surrender was taken by the republican leaders on Saturday. Elizabeth O'Farrell, carrying a white flag, delivered the unconditional surrender to the British commandants, and twenty-two women marched alongside the defeated men, refusing to evade the consequences of their actions. With 179 buildings totally destroyed and over 5,000 families made homeless, it is perhaps unsurprising that the Dublin crowd was mostly hostile to the insurgents. Women in receipt of separation allowances while their husbands served in the war against Germany were among those loud in their denunciations, and some of these were suspected of informing on the rebels.[85] Less cynically, support from those so recently bereaved at Gallipoli was hardly likely to be forthcoming. Constance Markievicz, viewed as an eccentric by many, was a particular target of hostile criticism. The daughter of the Provost of Trinity College Dublin watched the surrender from the college windows with horror, focusing particularly on the rebel aristocrat:

> The one woman amongst them of high birth – and therefore the most depraved – surrendered at Stephen's Green – where she had been since Monday – mostly in the College of Surgeons. She came out and having kissed her pistol publicly handed it up to the soldiers and was taken into custody in the courtyard. Here 50 men were lying dead – separated from her only by one wall. She showed the most callous indifference. Lighting cigarettes and strutting about, as conceited as an old draggle tailed peacock; she seemed to anticipate no disagreeable consequences of her shameful and silly conduct . . .[86]

Louise Ryan has argued that the mockery of Markievicz by the popular press, as both a woman and an aristocrat, completely undermined not only her personal contribution, but the serious nature of the rebellion itself.[87] The countess's sex was also significant in the immediate aftermath of Easter week, providing the rationale for commuting her death sentence to one of life imprisonment.

Much has been written about the swift change of opinion among Dubliners following the execution of fifteen rebel leaders by the British army. The dead were almost immediately hailed as heroes; facing the firing squad with dignity, they were quickly accorded the status of martyrdom. The women with whom they were associated also provoked popular sympathy. An aura of romance surrounded Grace Gifford, married to Joseph Plunkett just ten minutes before his execution. Kathleen Clarke, taken to see her husband Tom, the first signatory to the 1916 proclamation and who was to be shot at dawn, was also a tragic figure. The last revolutionary to be shot was James Connolly, who was an important figure in socialist and trade-union circles. Connolly had been wounded during the fighting and his daughter Nora, who accompanied her mother to Dublin Castle on the eve of his execution, gave a moving account of the last meeting of her parents:

> The officer . . . told us we had only five minutes more. Mother was nearly overcome. We had to give her water. My father tried to clasp her in his arms but he could barely lift his head and arms from the bed. 'Time is up,' the officer said. My father turned to say goodbye to me. I could not speak. He said, 'Go to your mother.'
> I tried to bring her away. I could not move her. She stood as if turned to stone. The nurse came forward and helped her away. I ran back and kissed my father again; then the door shut and we saw him no more.
> . . . We went to Castle in the morning to ask for my father's body. They would not give it to us. A kind nurse managed to get a lock of my father's hair which she gave to my mother.
> That was all we have of him now.[88]

Seventy-seven women were among the 3,000 taken prisoner immediately after the Rising, and with many of them listening to the firing squads from their prison cells, the hardening of their republican convictions is not unsurprising. Bridget Foley recorded how the women prisoners started a branch of the Gaelic League and held lessons in Irish language and dancing. Eventually released after three months, because of the confused details of her case, she later asserted:

> I am glad now, I always did feel glad, that I was one of the women chosen to even do a very slight deed for my country's cause, and I pray to our Holy martyrs, who trusted us with so much, that in the next great struggle, which, please God, will not be long, they will pray that the women of Ireland will take the greater the noble part, in our march to Freedom.[89]

This identification with the executed leaders of the Rising was common among republican women, and explained much of their later struggle against compromise in the ongoing constitutional crisis. Their strong convictions proved particularly important in holding the republican movement together in the immediate aftermath of the Rising, when many of the male leaders were either dead or imprisoned. Financial support for those suffering as a result of their relatives' activities was provided by IRB funds, overseen and distributed by Kathleen Clarke. Masses for the souls of the dead heroes reminded the public of their unselfish sacrifice, and several women, including Min Ryan, Nora Connolly and Nellie Gifford crossed the Atlantic to keep Irish-America informed of events. Hanna Sheehy Skeffington, whose husband Francis had been murdered by British soldiers during the Rising, also undertook a lecture tour of the United States, taking the opportunity to publicly denounce British militarism.[90]

The efforts of these women did much to revitalise Irish nationalist feeling, so that returning prisoners found themselves welcomed as heroes by the Dublin crowds just months after the events for which they had been reviled. Attempts by the British to introduce conscription into Ireland in 1917 helped to further unify and consolidate nationalist opinion. At this stage, the need for more soldiers for the final push against German forces seemed to the British government to be worth the risk of a violent reaction in Ireland. But a one-day strike against this move, called by the Irish Trades Union Congress on 23 April, demonstrated the degree of opposition which existed outside Ulster. Since conscription would depend upon the availability of women to take over male civilian jobs, the support of women was crucial. Cumann na mBan and the IWWU played an important role in co-ordinating their resistance. Bearing flags proclaiming 'Women Won't Blackleg', thousands of women signed a pledge promising 'not to fill the places of men deprived of their work through enforced military service'.[91] By 1918 a newly vibrant Irish nationalism was claiming the Easter Rising as a 'triumph of failure', for which Sinn Féin as the prominent nationalist party was granted most of the credit. While this view did not reflect reality, it did win popular support. Republicanism had thus firmly supplanted constitutional nationalism, and women were among the most ardent and active supporters of this realignment in the first election campaign of post-war Ireland.

THE AFTERMATH

With the ending of war in Europe in 1918, the attention of the British government once more turned to the Irish constitutional dilemma. Much had changed in four years; over 49,000 Irish men had died in the Allied cause, and survivors of the Western Front returned to a country in which

A song for Cumann na mBan, June 1916

Air 'The Men of the West'

When you honour, in song and in story,
The fighters who shouldered a gun,
And recked not tho' death's sting should reach them
If so Ireland's freedom was won;
Forget not the women of Erin,
Who stood without terror or dread,
Beside those who battled for freedom,
mid shell fire and deluge of lead

Chorus
Then here's to the women of Ireland.
Who bravely faced death in the van,
Old Ireland is proud of her daughters,
Hurrah for the Cumann na mBan!

Our tricolour flag flew to Heaven,
Proclaiming o'er old Dublin town,
That men of the nation, then wakened,
Would die 'ere the flag would come down.
And into our ranks came the colleens,
Like the women of Limerick of old,
And their smiles made our weakest a hero –
Write their fame, boys, in letters of gold

Chorus

Tho' our fight in the old G.P.O., boys,
Came to grief as its flames touched the sky,
We lit there a light that will blaze boys,
Till the power of the Saxon shall die.
And cherish for ever the glory,
While the pages of our records you scan,
Of those valiant daughters of Erin –
Hurrah for the Cumann na mBan!

Cork Public Museum, AQNO 1974:58/48

Home Rule had been bypassed, to be replaced by a more radical republi-canism, pledged to honour the proclamation of 1916. Meantime, in the North, war had served to deepen unionists' sense of integration with the British Empire, while the Rising reinforced an already vehement distrust of Irish nationalism. This was despite the fact that of the 170,000 Irish men who enlisted, about half were from outside of Ulster. That Catholics accounted for around half of the 40,000 to 50,000 Irish men killed in the war has only been very recently publicly acknowledged.[92] War against a common enemy had not, therefore, brought orange and green to a closer understanding of each other's positions, as John Redmond had hoped it would.[93] Instead, the suspended Home Rule clauses were subject once more to intensive scrutiny and heated debate.

While women throughout the island had made important and varied contributions to the European war effort, their exclusion from decision- or policy-making when hostilities ended ensured that, in the main, their daily lives were not fundamentally altered by the experience.[94] The granting of the vote to women over thirty in February 1918 was welcomed, however, and political parties both large and small were quick to recognise the vital nature of women's support, both as voters and as party workers.

In the North, the social interaction of unionist women of all classes had been significantly reinforced by fund-raising and other war work, and as Diane Urquhart indicates, this communications network had important political implications in strengthening unionist solidarity.[95] An effective local power base for female unionist leadership was established in The Ark, Lady Londonderry's weekly political club held at her home in Mountstewart, County Down, which provided regular opportunities to exchange and influence opinion; and at a more popular level, female Orange Lodges were given representation on the UWUC in 1920.[96] The UWUC leadership also worked closely with the UUC, which, anxious to secure the continuing active co-operation of newly enfranchised women, conceded them twelve seats on their council. The results of the 1918 election, with the UUP winning 25 seats and 5 going to Independent Unionists, guaranteed their continuing predominance in the north-east.

Sinn Féin nominated two women as candidates in the 1918 election: Countess Markievicz and Winifred Carney. In Dublin, old differences were forgotten as the IWFL and Cumann na mBan rallied in support of Markievicz, ensuring personal success in an election which swept Sinn Féin to victory with 73 seats (65 per cent), compared to the 6 retained by the IPP. Carney was less fortunate in Belfast. As Margaret Ward points out, although supported by a few prominent men and women, Carney was marginalised by the press, isolated among UUP and IPP supporters, and undermined by poor organisation in the local party.[97] Winning only 395 votes, she lost her deposit, declaring with some bitterness,

> I had neither personation agents, committee rooms, canvassers or vehicles, and as these are the chief agents in an election, it was amazing to me to find that 395 people went to the ballot on their own initiative, without any persuasion. The organisation in Belfast could have been much, much, better.[98]

Markievicz, on the other hand, as Minister for Labour, became the first woman elected to a cabinet post, albeit in a party which, refusing to take its seats in Westminster, set up an alternative Irish parliament. The members of this new Dáil were, however, soon 'on the run', as it, together with Sinn Féin, the Gaelic League and Cumann na mBan were proclaimed illegal by a British government struggling to retain control of a fast-changing situation. In the event, the Government of Ireland Bill of December 1920 allowed for the creation of two new states in the following year – 6 counties in the new Northern Ireland, and 26 counties in the South – each with a Home Rule executive and parliament. Irish Republican Army (IRA) militant resistance, however, ensured that the situation in the South rapidly disintegrated into a bitter war between republican and Crown forces.

1919–22:
THE WAR OF INDEPENDENCE

Women's role in the militant republican campaigns of the early twentieth century has lately been the subject of much feminist analysis. Both as nationalists and as women, their actions, images and representations have come under close scrutiny,[99] confirming that, in Ireland as elsewhere, 'war is a highly gendered experience which is both informed by and informs constructions of masculinity and femininity'.[100] This needs to be borne in mind when assessing both secondary and primary material of the period. Histories of violence, whether by or against women, produce particular kinds of discourse, with marginalised and stereotypical heroines and victims portrayed as no more than a backdrop to heroic masculine militarism. The deeds of women, like those of men, require more contextualised treatment.

In the War of Independence (also known as the Anglo-Irish War) a relatively small number of women played key roles in support of the IRA campaign. Siobhán Lankford is perhaps typical of these; as a postal official in

Women march in 1920 in protest at the killings of nationalists by British forces during the War of Independence.

Mallow, County Cork, Lankford was well placed to access vital information for the rebels. She claims to have been a trained and experienced IRA officer even before the outbreak of the 1919 hostilities, and, 'to the exclusion of all other parties to be THE officer who placed at the disposal of GHQ details of the Secret British Military Plans and Preparations for the enforcement of Conscription on the signing overnight of a British Order in Council'. There were other high profile female activists, but many more women hid, nursed, fed and cared for, republican activists. No doubt, in many cases these would be relatives – husbands, fathers, brothers and sons. In both town and countryside, the provision of 'safe houses', to conceal men, weaponry or uniforms, was particularly important. A leading republican later noted that the home of Sheila and Nora Wallace in the Cork area, was practically a brigade headquarters from 1917 onwards:

> Over a period of intensive struggle, bitter fighting, the deaths of two senior officers and many junior officers, changes in command and personnel . . . [they] had taken upon themselves, with great courage and tenacity, a multitude of daring duties.[101]

Published and unpublished memoirs and diaries, official documents and personal letters record a wealth of similar activities and the diversity of duties carried out by women, without which the IRA units could not have operated. While many of these activities were confined to the domestic setting, they were nonetheless risky, with raids and searches becoming increasingly commonplace. From March 1920 the dangers intensified as the Special Constabulary (the Black and Tans), a new force sent by the British to support the Royal Irish Constabulary, gained a reputation for brutality. Houses, sometimes whole streets, were burned down, and though incidents of sexual violence are difficult to verify, there is plenty of evidence of humiliating assaults: 'The going was tough on the female sex . . . To intensify the reign of terror, swoops were made at night, entries were forced into their homes, and the women's hair cut off in a brutal fashion as well as suffering other indignities and insults.'[102] From the unionist perspective, however, the Black and Tans were 'wonderful in their bravery', risking their lives in defence of 'Loyalist and English interests'.[103] While the historiography of the period reflects these opposing views, a *Report of the Labour Commission to Ireland* in 1920 concluded:

> Unfortunately, in their work of hunting down people, the agents of the British Government often act in a way which is terrifying to women . . . This rough and brutal treatment is by no means the worst that is to be said against men in the service of the British Crown. It is, however, extremely difficult to obtain direct evidence of incidents affecting females, for the women of Ireland are reticent on such subjects.[104]

Both the wording and tone of this piece of officialdom leave little doubt that uncontrolled brutality was common, and that the only apparently acceptable 'proof' depended on women coming forward with information and thus placing themselves in greater danger.

In the wider context of international peace-building, in which Irish women continued to lobby for Irish self-determination, support was sought for the ending of a range of injustices. In Zurich in May 1919 an 'Appeal on behalf of Ireland' was sent to the Women's International League for Peace and Freedom (formerly the International Congress of Women for Peace and Freedom). Later in the same year the 'Principal Women's Associations of Ireland' demanded the establishment of a Committee of Inquiry into the conditions of Irish political prisoners. America was also visited by peace activists, who urged that the Irish question be considered as one of morality rather than politics, and by members of Cumann na mBan whose stance was rather different. Mary MacSwiney was instructed to assure Americans that 'the women of Ireland are standing with the soldiers and that "no surrender" is the watchword'.[105]

A total of 50 women were imprisoned in Ireland during this period of warfare; they ranged from a 14-year-old girl to two elderly sisters aged 70 and 80, and their sentences were usually short.[106] The wives of imprisoned men also found life difficult. Máire Comerford, in Galway to distribute relief, found 'women whose husbands were in jail or fighting and they would have a house full of kids and no income at all. And many of them were in the Republican tradition long enough to be at feud with the parish priest, to have been denounced off the altar . . .'[107]

Young women who courted soldiers or policemen were liable to 'punishment' from republicans, with the forcible cutting of hair again considered an effective deterrent.[108] Women who were loyal to the Crown, or at least opposed to the militant activities of republicans, also experienced danger and hardship. Seventy-year-old Mrs Lindsay, who ordered her coachman to drive to Ballincollig barracks to warn the authorities of a possible ambush at Dripsey, was kidnapped and shot dead.[109] Florrie Dreaper, who also informed the authorities about an imminent ambush, had her house burned down while she and her dog sat in a steel water tank until they were eventually rescued.[110] Throughout the countryside, houses belonging to families with known, or suspected, loyalist sympathies were reduced to smouldering rubble. The smart French school in Bray, County Wicklow, attended by Molly Skine, 'was full of girls in tears because their homes had been burnt.'[111] And as happens in all warfare, many who were caught up in events were completely uninvolved. In Cork, for example, Margaret O'Donovan's entrance into the world was more than usually dramatic, as she later explained:

> I was born on the 4th of June 1921. The night I was born a bullet came through the window, fired by the Black and Tans. I got pneumonia at a day old and my mother's hair turned white overnight from the shock of the bullet.[112]

Less fortunate was young bride-to-be Jeannie Boyle, who was trampled to death at Dublin's Croke Park when Black and Tans raided a Gaelic football match on 21 November 1920. This day, which became known as Bloody Sunday, had begun with the killing of alleged English agents by the IRA. Boyle's death was one of twelve resulting from the Black and Tans indiscriminate act of revenge; sixty people were wounded.[113]

Although the IRA's campaign was mostly concentrated in the twenty-six counties, the Catholic minority in the North was particularly vulnerable to the reaction of Ulster unionism. Jonathan Bardon notes that in the summer of 1920 an estimated 10,000 Catholic men and 1,000 Catholic women were expelled from their jobs in the shipyards and the Sirocco works, Mackie's,

McLaughlin and Harvey's, Musgrave's and Combe Barbour's. The end of the post-war boom and the onset of economic depression meant that very few recovered their positions.[114] And although Catholics made up only 24 per cent of Belfast's population, they amounted to 58 per cent of the 455 people killed in the city between July 1920 and June 1922.[115] By the time the British offered a truce in July 1921, both sides in the conflict had suffered military and propaganda losses, but it was the bitterness and mutual suspicion of this transitional period that would prove most difficult to overcome. Outbreaks of sectarian violence and evictions from homes and jobs reinforced existing political and religious divisions and threatened the validity of any negotiated settlement.

For those most vehemently committed to ideals of 1916, the Treaty eventually agreed between the British government and representatives of the republican movement was anathema. While the proposed new 'Free State' would be self-governing, the retention of a British Governor-General, the requirement for the new body to take an oath of loyalty to the Crown, and recognition of the existence of Northern Ireland as a separate state, were bitter pills for idealists to swallow. Countess Markievicz put it succinctly: 'I have seen the star and I am not going to follow a flashing will o' the wisp.'[116] Supporters of the Treaty argued that this 'modified dominion status' was the best that could be hoped for, and that, as Michael Collins told Kathleen Clarke, 'once everything promised in the Treaty is got . . . then we will work through it to complete freedom'.[117]

During the heated debates on the Treaty, as has so often been remarked, the voices of women were particularly loud in denunciation of the proposed legislation. Four of the six female members of the Second Dáil (which had been elected in May 1921) had lost male relatives during the past years of war: Mary MacSwiney's brother Terence had died on hunger strike in a British jail; Kate O'Callaghan's husband Michael had been murdered by Black and Tans; Kathleen Clarke had also lost her husband, and Margaret Pearse her sons. All these women wore black throughout the debates and repeatedly made reference to the sacrifice that had been made. Margaret Pearse asserted that while she feared the Black and Tans, it was not so much as she feared this Treaty 'because I feel in my heart [if I accepted that Treaty] that the ghosts of my sons would haunt me'; she then broke down and sobbed.[118] Accused by their opponents of playing on emotion by 'rattling the bones of the dead' and drawing on their 'unique qualifications of mother or wife', they argued that they not only represented those who were gone, but 'the wives of Ireland'. Analysis of the discourse both at the time and in most historical accounts reveals the gendered nature of the debate, with the

Constance Markievicz played a central role in the Irish nationalist movement of the twentieth century. A member of Maud Gonne's Inghinidh na h'Éireann, she went on in 1909 to found Fianna Éireann, served as second-in-command in the Irish Citizen Army during the 1916 Easter Rising and in 1918, as a Sinn Féin candidate, was the first woman to be elected to the British parliament.

arguments of the women in the Dáil dismissed as due to bitterness or mental instability caused by 'the terrible experience' they had gone through. All six women vehemently denied this interpretation, and most, like Mary MacSwiney, had already demonstrated their commitment to the cause of the Republic. In rhetoric worthy of Pearse, she warned that:

> [England] cannot win this battle, for if she exterminates the men, the women will take their place, and if she exterminates the women, the children are rising fast; and if she exterminates the men, women and children of this generation, the blades of grass, dyed with their blood, will rise, like the dragon's teeth of old, into armed men and the fight will begin in the next generation.[119]

On 7 January 1922 the Treaty was accepted by the Dáil by a vote of 64 to 57.

One of the earliest issues facing the Dáil following the vote on the Treaty was a demand for the immediate extension of the franchise to all women over the age of twenty-one. Having 'fully participated in all the dangers of war', women regarded the continued restrictions of their rights of citizenship as unacceptable. As Kate O'Callaghan commented, if, as Arthur Griffith had claimed, 95 per cent of Irish women fully supported the Treaty, then their ability to vote 'would strengthen, not weaken, the case for ratification'.[120] Opposition was fierce, however, with many convinced that a majority of young women supported the radical republican stance and, in the event, Griffith would go no further than promising full enfranchisement after the election which would ratify the Treaty.

All six women deputies had opposed acceptance of the Treaty, and just over a month later their stance was overwhelmingly endorsed by 419 votes to 63 at a Cumann na mBan convention. Old friends parted bitterly, as pro-Treaty women, mostly related to ministers of the new government, formed their own group, Cumann na Saoirse (Society of Freedom). Mostly middle class and certainly not militarily active, Margaret Ward states that the new organisation 'looked with horror and distaste on the wild women of Cumann na mBan'.[121]

With the Irish Free State formally established on 6 December 1922, the scene was set for the long-awaited withdrawal of the British army. However, the outbreak of civil war between those accepting and those rejecting the new constitutional arrangements, guaranteed that conflict, violence and disruption did not end with their departure. The newly created provincial government in the North was also vulnerable to attack from both sides of its border, and as attempts to compromise over border issues came to nothing, relations between Dublin and Belfast rapidly deteriorated. In this situation, the vulnerability of religious minorities on either side of the border was reflected in the movement of the population. The number of Protestants in the 26 counties declined sharply, falling from 327,000 to 221,000 between 1911 and 1926. Catholics in the North, regarded collectively and individually as hostile to the unionist regime, were subject to measures ranging from employment discrimination to reprisals and attacks. Many thousands fled to the Free State. Although the outbreak of civil war in the South eased pressure in the North, leading to 'the descent of a fragile peace', it also completed 'the sense of isolation and despondency' felt by a nationalist minority demoralised by sectarian warfare.[122]

Men and women in both parts of Ireland thus lived out their daily lives against a backdrop of militarist activity and social disruption. This in itself,

of course, was not unique in a period during which the drawing or redrawing of borders and the creation of new states was common. During 1918
alone, some half a dozen new countries emerged throughout Europe,[123] and
in Ireland, as in other disputed territories, the new arrangements may have
redirected local conflict but ultimately they 'failed to resolve the antago-
nisms that engendered it'.[124]

The first two decades of the twentieth century witnessed tumultuous
change on the island of Ireland, during which a particularly vibrant brand
of feminist political activism made important though diverse contributions.
As Mary Daly has observed, this was all the more remarkable for taking
place in a country that was largely Catholic and agricultural.[125] While suffragist, nationalist, unionist and pacifist women represented only a small
minority and their words and actions were all too often drowned in the
stridency of the male-dominated constitutional debates, they were nonetheless destined to inspire future generations of women.

3
War and welfare in a divided island

The State recognises that by her life
within the home, woman gives to the State
a support without which the common good
cannot be achieved.[1]

By 1922, on paper at least, two separate constitutional entities had been established on the island of Ireland. The citizens of each new state, however, responded with, at best, reluctant acceptance rather than celebration, and governments began the task of consolidation against a background of violent disruption. Northern Ireland was vulnerable to hostility from republicans both outside and within its border, and the suspicion with which its new political leaders regarded the minority Catholic population ensured that discrimination and sectarianism filtered through all levels of Northern Irish society. The politicians of the new Free State, Saorstát na hÉireann, welcoming the break with British rule but also under attack from dissidents from within, sought to assert their authority over the populace and to stabilise the political situation. With the exception of the more determined females, the militaristic nature of society in these years militated against women's involvement in party politics. Most 'ordinary' women got on with the task of raising their families and finding work, either in Ireland or overseas. The creation of the border, however, was not only a territorial division, but as time went on, reinforced political, cultural and religious boundaries, and, for many, became the symbol of a fragmented nation.

For the women of the UWUC, as with their male counterparts in the UUC, the new constitutional arrangements were little more than an unhappy compromise. While the Union with Britain had been maintained for the six counties, much concern was expressed about the isolation of fellow unionists in the Ulster counties of Monaghan, Cavan and Donegal, now located within the Free State. Indeed, a plan to evacuate the women and children from the three border counties had been drawn up in 1916, but this came to nothing, and there were several resignations from the UWUC in protest at the 'abandonment' of their religious compatriots.[2] The main priority, however, was the consolidation and maintenance of unionist power in the newly created state, and all resources were utilised to this end. In the early months of 1921 the women of the UWUC prepared for Northern Ireland's first election, encouraging the registration of women voters and holding classes to instruct them on the working of the system of Proportional Representation (PR) which was to be used.[3] (The Irish Women's Civic Federation carried out similar work in Cavan, Monaghan and Donegal.[4])

Women on the nationalist side were also involved in supporting their political representatives, though the constitutional parties did not actively seek their participation to anything like the same extent. Cumann na mBan carried out propaganda and electioneering work for Sinn Féin, but Diane Urquhart suggests that this body, like others in Northern nationalism, suffered 'disillusion, apathy and discord' in the inter-war period.[5] The Ladies' Auxiliary of the Ancient Order of Hibernians was probably the most popular female nationalist organisation in the North during these years. Established in 1910, the Hibernians underwent something of a revival in Ulster in the 1920s, with a total of 296 branches established by 1923, 42 of which were Ladies Auxiliaries. At first mainly concerned to defend Catholic interests, and thus encouraging charitable and 'rescue' work, the organisation's attitude to women underwent a significant shift after they attained the vote. The *Hibernian Journal* declared in September 1919 that:

> Women are now admitted into practically all the professions; they have a voice in the country, too long denied them; their administrative ability, as well as their aptitude to learn, were amply demonstrated during the war. There is no reason why their power for good in the Hibernian movement should not be availed of to the utmost.[6]

Largely working class in composition, and relying heavily on family networks, this organisation provided visible and enthusiastic support to constitutional nationalist Joseph Devlin.[7] In the event, Sinn Féin and the Nationalist Party won 6 seats apiece, the UUP, 40 seats. However, the decision of the Nationalist Party and Sinn Féin not to recognise or participate in the Northern state resulted in a lack of structures and organisation at both local and national levels, militating against the politicisation of women and reinforcing nationalist inability to dent the strength of unionism. Cumann na mBan, meanwhile, found itself outlawed by the Northern Ireland parliament, along with the IRA and Fianna Fáil on 23 May 1922.

The vulnerability of the new state was one reason given for the UWUC's promotion of male, rather than female, candidates for election. The minutes noted that:

> The essential thing in the first parliament was to preserve the safety of the unionist cause, that much organisation and construction work would be necessary for which perhaps women had not the necessary experience, and except in the case of outstanding qualifications, men candidates were preferable.[8]

Not all women agreed with this prioritising. Belfast Women's Advisory Council and Belfast Women's Citizens' Union both called for women candidates to deal with issues such as Poor Law reform, education, moral reform, child welfare, and other areas where women's input was felt to be particularly appropriate.[9] Conservatism was inherent within unionism, however, and most women voters probably followed family loyalties in their choice of candidate, strongly influenced by the political allegiances of husbands and fathers. Nonetheless, the sense of pride many women felt in being able to publicly participate in political decision-making should not be underestimated. Winifred Campbell noticed that her mother 'never went [to vote] until the late afternoon, holding onto her little bit of power as long as possible. When at last she decided to go and although the polling station was only two streets away, she travelled in the largest, grandest car the Unionist Party could provide.'[10]

Two women were among the forty unionists returned on 24 May 1921, taking their seats at the opening of the Northern Ireland parliament in Belfast City Hall on 22 June.[11] Each the widow of a former UUP MP and both active members of the UWUC, Julia McMordie and Dehra Chichester had sound unionist credentials. McMordie, vice-president of the UWUC, had been the first woman member of Belfast Corporation and an alderman.[12] In her maiden speech she demonstrated a concern for women's participation in at least one area of public life. Calling for the number of women police officers to be doubled – there were only 2 in the Belfast force of 3,000 – she also argued for equal allowances and pensions:

> I do not see why women should serve without any hope of a pension any more than men should, I have never been one who thought that a woman who did the same work as a man should get the same pay – I am very modest in that respect – but I do think the women should be eligible for any emoluments or pensions that men are entitled to.[13]

When the Constabulary Bill was introduced in May 1922, McMordie challenged both party and government, successfully demanding that a clause dealing with women officers be introduced. Unlike McMordie, who served for only four years, Dehra Chichester (becoming Parker in 1928), during a total of thirty-five years in parliament, was able to make an impact as one of the staunchest supporters of unionist policy. She was selected as the first woman in the British Empire to present the annual address on behalf of the

Sectarianism

Elizabeth Bloxham, from a west of Ireland, Protestant background and working as a teacher in Newtownards, County Down, felt compelled to object to a sermon preached in her local Church of Ireland church. In a letter to the *Newtownards Chronicle*, under the heading of 'Politics in the Pulpit', she declared that she wished to protest

> in the strongest manner possible against the use of pulpits for political speeches . . . a pulpit does not seem to me to be a suitable place for political discussion, even if it be fair discussion, but when, as was the case, the sermon was an appeal to party prejudice, and was calculated to stir up political bitterness the thing becomes intolerable to anyone who respects either religion or fair debate. The preacher asserted that his political opponents were actuated solely by a desire to crush the Protestant religion and to take from Protestants their means of livelihood . . . Taken on the whole the sermon was the strongest appeal to party prejudice to which it has been my lot ever to listen.

Having signed her name and address to this letter, Bloxham subsequently had to be escorted by police to prevent personal injury and the abuse of shouting children.

Papers of Elizabeth Bloxham, University College Dublin, P31

House of Commons at Westminster following the King's speech at the opening of the parliamentary session of 1924, and frequently spoke out in support of highly controversial unionist legislation. Given 'the mentality of the minority,' she argued, the dissolution of those local councils that refused to recognise the authority of the new state was an acceptable response. In her abhorrence of local violence and support of special measures against terrorism, she claimed to be 'representing thousands of women in the Six Counties . . . I feel I can say that I have been shocked . . . by the terrible outrages, bloodshed and violence . . . the strongest measures are absolutely needed now . . . [to] strike the necessary fear into the hearts of criminals'.[14]

Like her male colleagues, Parker represented only the Protestant unionist constituency and would therefore have supported the abolition of proportional representation at local government elections in 1922 and at national level in 1929. These measures, together with the redrawing of electoral boundaries in 1923, ensured that in a number of councils where nationalists had a majority of electors, they were manipulated out of control.[15] Furthermore, segregated housing and voting arrangements at council level, which placed an emphasis on property, also guaranteed the maintenance of Protestant/unionist power in local areas. Parker's loyalty and her articulate defence of Unionism was rewarded. She served as the parliamentary secretary to the Ministry for Education from 1937 to 1944 and as Minister for Health and Local Government from 1949 to 1957 – the only woman cabinet minister during the entire life of the Northern Ireland parliament. In 1935, however, she made it clear that she was no representative of 'women's rights':

> Since I have been a Member of the House I have never taken up the attitude that I was here to defend, or pretend to defend the work of women who put forward the claim they should be given equal rights on every occasion. I never put that claim forward. I am not an advocate . . . that women in every case should have equal duties and equal rights with men.[16]

Arguing that the Unionist government had always 'shown the greatest sympathy in that direction', she claimed that any intervention from herself was unnecessary. Clearly, for this female politician, as for many on the opposing side, national identity was stronger than that of gender.[17]

Other politically minded women, particularly among the aristocracy, continued to play an influential role in the politics of Northern Ireland. Cecil Craig, wife of Northern Ireland's first Prime Minister and a polished speech-maker in her own right, frequently stood in for her husband James when his health failed in the mid-1930s. However, Edith of Londonderry was probably the most significant of this generation of political hostesses. Her friendship with British Labour Prime Minister Ramsay MacDonald, with whom she regularly corresponded, was believed to have been particularly influential, for example, in securing Northern Ireland's interests in the difficult boundary negotiations of the early 1920s.[18] Lady Londonderry also organised the Ulster Women's Volunteer Association, which trained women as special constables, VADs, telegraphists or telephonists, in preparation for any emergency which might threaten the new state.[19] Both Craig and Londonderry remained active in the UWUC, which underwent considerable expansion in these years. Regular speakers' classes were held, with young university graduates recruited and trained in all branches of political work. On a more popular level, women loyal to the Crown were encouraged to buy 'Home and Dominion Goods', and a 'Special Empire Shopping Week' was held in January 1927.[20] With women making up an electoral majority of 52 per cent after the passage of the Representation of the People Act in 1928, the leadership of the UUP was anxious to court their support.[21] However, the determination of women themselves to strengthen both the local unionist power base and the all-important link with Britain and the Empire should not be underestimated.

Mainstream histories of the early years of Saorstát na hÉireann are dominated by the military and high level political battles waged to secure (or overturn) the new structures. The 1921 Treaty, which had ended the War of Independence, had also served to turn Irish men and women against each other. The new state sought to assert its legitimacy against a background of considerable disruption. Nelly O'Brien described an evening in Dublin in 1922 which was typical of the early stage of the Irish Civil War:

> I have the weirdest recollection of that night – the night of Wednesday 5 July – a high narrow house, in total darkness, the din of battle outside and refugees from the streets sheltering in the corners of each landing from the stray bullets whizzing near the barricade almost under my windows.[22]

Ordinary civilians were inevitably caught up in the activities of the republican militants, which included street ambushes, sniping, destroying bridges and blocking communications. Local people in Tipperary protested against the destruction of bridges and the burning of creameries, and the resentment felt by many workers was also evident. In Dublin's Jacob's Biscuit Factory, for example, where a shortage of materials due to the 'troubles' meant a cut in employment, May Hanaphy's wage dropped by about half: 'I only got about five or six shillings. Your wages went "bang".'[23] Unlike the war fought against the British, the 'Irregulars' in the civil war could not automatically assume they had the support of the people. Instead, with the new government overwhelmingly endorsed by the population, men in search of shelter were often dependent on civilian fear. Máire Comerford despaired that, 'There was no part of Ireland now in which a column of twenty or thirty men might shelter safely, yet there had been dozens of columns, twice and three times that size, in the Tan struggle fifteen months before.'[24]

Once again, however, women played a critical role on the side of the militants. Their contributions, while risky, sometimes involved little departure from everyday life: May Dalaigh, for example, recalled putting a white cloth at the back of sheds near her home in Kiltallagh, County Kerry, to warn republicans that a raid was going on.[25] David Fitzpatrick claims that in many areas women's help was vital in keeping the IRA campaign on course.[26] During the initial bombardment of the Four Courts, for example, liaison with the outside world was entirely dependent upon 'the most energetic of the Cumann na mBan workers, and her bicycle'. Contact between the capital and the provinces again relied heavily on Cumann na mBan couriers – the organisation 'appeared to possess most of the car drivers in Republican ranks'.[27] In Cork, Mary MacSwiney 'ran what was virtually Republican headquarters' until she was arrested in October 1922, and in Limerick, Madge Daly and Nurse Guthrie plotted the escape of republican prisoners.[28] Post Office worker Siobhán Lankford passed vital information to republicans and disrupted Free State communications,[29] while Eithne Coyle played a key role in enforcing a boycott of goods from Belfast. The *Belfast Evening Telegraph* described the type of incident in which she was involved:

> The now customary burning of Belfast newspapers was again carried out, at Creeslaugh on the Derry and Lough Swilly line, on the arrival of the evening train. Three women, one of them armed with a revolver, removed all the papers from the Guard's Van and set them alight on the platform.[30]

Carrying arms and dispatches for the anti-Treaty IRA in Dublin, in addition to her work for Cumann na mBan, Coyle was one of almost four hundred republican women who were imprisoned during the civil war period. Republican links were maintained, if not reinforced, within the walls of Kilmainham Gaol. Classes in Irish language and dancing were held regularly and in 1923, for example, it was reported that Easter Week celebrations were conducted with dignity and emotion. Communication with the outside world could be more difficult, with all letters censored and the support of the Women's Prisoners' Defence League, or 'The Mothers' as they became known, was important, not only in the provision of practical necessities, but in raising public awareness of prison conditions.

Women prisoners faced the hostility of the Catholic Church, which, having had little influence over political matters under British jurisdiction, was now concerned to assert its authority and stand firm behind the Free State government. In October 1923, the Church announced the excommunication of republican 'murderers', a particularly difficult sentence for those engaged in the now traditional protest of hunger-striking, and who were denied the last rites. Madge Buckley responded with fervour:

> We had been refused the sacraments, only a week before I had tried to get Confession, but the priest, after arguing with me for an hour, did not hear my Confession. I told him I would likely be going on hunger strike, that I hoped I would die on it rather than give in, and that now I placed all my sins on him. I had done my part and he had refused to do his, as ordained by God.[31]

While there is considerable evidence that most of the female prisoners embraced orthodox Catholic teaching, they were also clearly prepared to defy episcopal authority in the interests of what they believed to be a higher mission. Oonagh Walsh comments:

> The social constraints upon women in Ireland in the early 1920s were considerable. Yet the women who became involved in militant political activity during this period acted for the most part of their own volition. Their participation in hunger-strikes, formal organisation on military lines, self-proclaimed equality with male counterparts, refusal to accept anything less than the status of political prisoners, and willingness to challenge the precepts of the Church – all these indicate their autonomy as revolutionaries.[32]

Revolutionary women also faced hostility in secular circles; a negative, sometimes hysterical, press projected images of unnatural, dangerous 'girls', 'die-hards', 'whose ecstasies at their extremest can find no outlet so satisfying as destruction'.[33] Stepping outside the boundaries of acceptable female behaviour, militant women of every generation would face similarly gendered discourse. William Cosgrave, first president of the Executive Council, argued that they 'should have rosaries in their hands or be at home with knitting needles',[34] and those working in public service, such as teacher Mary MacSwiney and civil servant Siobhán Lankford, were faced with dismissal.[35] Hanna Sheehy Skeffington lost income derived from marking papers for the Intermediate exams board.

The civil war lasted for only ten months before de Valera conceded defeat in May 1923, but it was July of the following year before the last prisoners were released, and the bitter divisions the conflict revealed were to have a more lasting impact on the course of Irish history. In April 1926 de Valera embarked on a new strategy. Recognising the need to appeal to the electorate, he broke with Sinn Féin and formed Fianna Fáil (Soldiers of Destiny). Prominent anti-Treaty women were well represented, with Countess Markievicz, Kathleen Clarke, Dorothy MacArdle, Hanna Sheehy Skeffington, Linda Kearns and Margaret Pearse on the party's first national executive. McArdle and Kearns played major roles in organising the party throughout the country and rallying support for Fianna Fáil during the election of 9 June 1927. With the Cumann na nGaedheal party considerably weakened by the loss of prominent members (Michael Collins was assassinated in 1922 and Kevin O'Higgins in July 1927), Fianna Fáil's forty-four deputies took their seats in the Dáil on 11 August, signing the book containing the 'empty formula' of allegiance to the British Crown. Further electoral gains were made in 1932, and in 1933, supported by the Labour Party, de Valera took over the leadership of the country, immediately taking steps to release republican prisoners and abolish the Oath of Allegiance.

Viewed by contemporaries as either 'adventurously romantic' or as 'people with new hope and courage', the new regime was to be as conservative as its predecessor when it considered Irish womanhood. Although women in the Free State had achieved the right to vote on the same basis as men in 1922 – six years ahead of women in the United Kingdom – 'no woman served as a government minister between 1922 and 1979'.[36] The first woman to take her seat in the parliament of the new state was school-teacher Margaret Collins-O'Driscoll, elder sister of Michael Collins, and a member of the opposition. But, as Hanna Sheehy Skeffington remarked in 1930, 'Women in Ireland still suffer from the effects of the revolution that missed and of the subsequent reaction. What was given at first with gladness has been gradually filched away. Equality has ceased to be accorded to us, save on paper.'[37] The women of Cumann na mBan were engaged in a series of realignments in the face of the changing political context. Death had taken its toll here too, with the loss of Constance Markievicz in July 1927 and Margaret Pearse in 1932. Among the rest, there was a strong sense of betrayal when Fianna Fáil abandoned its abstentionist policy and its deputies first entered the Dáil. Resignations followed from Skeffington and McArdle, while Coyle and Sheila Humphries joined the radical Saor Éire, closely linked to the IRA. In 1933 Mary MacSwiney and Caitlin and Nodlaig Brugha left Cumann na mBan to form Mná na Poblachta (Women of the Republic). A Congress of the Women's International League, held in Dublin in 1926, highlighted the complexities and tensions within Irish feminism during this period. At this, one of the first international events to be staged in the Free State, American and European delegates witnessed the debates between those Irish women who thoroughly opposed militancy and those who were prepared to use or support violent measures for the sake of what they termed 'Peace and Freedom'.[38] Female solidarity, while desirable in principle, was not yet a viable option in Ireland. The introduction of service pensions for anyone who had participated in the republican movement up to September 1923 served to further divide those still engaged in the struggle from those accepting the legitimacy of the twenty-six counties.

Although important, these militant activists represented only a small proportion of Irish men and women. The majority of people, north and south, was preoccupied with the daily anxieties of finding and keeping work, and the pleasures and pressures of courting, marrying and raising families. While such activities did not make headline news or provide the material for history textbooks, they made up the bulk of everyday experience. The new constitutional boundaries within which women worked, however, inevitably impacted upon the opportunities open to them, and the degree of personal or professional independence that they could aim to achieve.

The new constitutions did not in themselves have an immediate direct impact on the economy of the island, where working patterns were already well established. Other factors did make a difference. Northern Ireland's main industries, which had experienced a significant boost during the First World War, thereafter underwent significant decline. With a level of industrial unemployment in the early 1920s which was always higher than that in Britain, the ramifications of the Wall Street Crash in 1929 sent it soaring to 28 per cent of the insured workforce. The shipbuilding and construction industries were badly hit and families suffered as fathers, sons, brothers and husbands lost their jobs. But textile workers were also affected, with many small firms laying off their employees, and changes in industrial practice exacerbating wider economic difficulties. In Derry, for example, where over 90 per cent of the shirt-making workforce was female, a degree of deskilling resulted from the introduction of conveyor belts in the 1930s.[39] While these factors affected workers in many countries during this period, the Catholic minority in Northern Ireland carried the additional burden of religious discrimination. The determination of the government to appoint 'as far as we can manage it . . . loyal men and women', ensured that jobs in the public sector were almost entirely the reserve of Protestants.[40]

To be out of work in the inter-war period was a depressing and often degrading experience. Unemployment benefit was limited to a maximum of 150 days a year, anything after that was means tested. No benefit at all was given to under-eighteens, married women or those with another person in the household who was working. During these bleak times, many men were dependent on Outdoor Relief, their application for this meagrely paid work exposing them to the insensitivity of Boards of Guardians which were mainly concerned with keeping the rates down. One Lily Coleman, a Belfast Guardian, apparently stated that if the poor worked as hard at looking for a job as they did under the blankets there would be less of a problem.[41] This kind of attitude, coupled with anxiety and hunger, built up resentment and anger, which culminated in the Belfast Outdoor Relief strike of 1932. Although this event has gone down in history as a rare example of Protestant and Catholic working-class unity, it has probably been considerably romanticised. In reality, many of the participants were likely to have been accidentally 'caught up' in the riots which followed the strikers' march. Alice Quinn recorded:

> Me and Billy Knox from King Street, we went to see the march and were all rammed into a bar because there was shooting going on. It wasn't for the outdoor relief, like; we'd no money to go and see the pictures, so we just went to see the march.[42]

What unity there was, was both superficial and transient. With the strike broken up by a combination of police repression, concessions, and witch-hunts against republicans and communists, local sectarianism soon reappeared.

The experience of poverty, however, was very real. Long-term unemployment hit families especially hard, as Winifred Campbell explained:

> Short-term unemployment was common enough. It simply meant a tightening of the belt for a while. If essential payments fell behind they could always be cleared off at so much weekly, once work was resumed; but this was something different. As months stretched into years, people began to despair. Every possible economy became the way of life.[43]

It was commonplace to see long queues of housewives hoping to purchase stale bread and buns, cracked eggs, or the luxuries of jam and butter sold in small portions. Moneylenders were frequent visitors; items that were not currently being worn or used were dispatched to the pawnbrokers, and, as a very last resort, the mission hall could be relied upon for essential food or clothing. In the midst of such rampant poverty, infant and maternal mortality rates increased; Anne Boyle recalled that 'there was so much infant mortality that it seemed as if every week blue baby coffins were coming out of every street'.[44] She lost three brothers and a sister before they were two years old. Many such human tragedies underlay the statistical evidence of a survey carried out in Belfast in 1938, which reported that 36 per cent of the families interviewed were living in conditions classified as 'absolute poverty'.[45]

It was against this background that trade-unionist Saidie Patterson called a strike of textile workers at Ewart's factory in Belfast in support of a 'closed shop' policy in 1939. At the height of this action some 2,000 women paraded through the streets of Belfast, wearing their Sunday best and projecting a strong and positive image of female working solidarity. The strike was called off, not because of the difficulties of surviving on 12s. 6d. strike pay, but because union members were under pressure from government ministers to reach a settlement in the interests of the war effort. For example, Ernest Bevin, the Westminster Labour MP who had been strongly supportive of the union's action, joined the War Cabinet and asked leaders to wind down the strike as quickly as possible. Nonetheless, by the end of 1940, the shop steward could report wage increases of 15 per cent, holidays with pay, minimum rates for women on time work, and introduction of sickness benefit funds and accident and legal aid schemes.[46] Clearly, despite recurring political difficulties, some women at least were beginning to see the benefits of collective negotiation and bargaining. And with the Second World War bringing large numbers of women into traditionally male areas of work for the first time, the urgent necessity of their contribution during these years gave them additional leverage.

The 1920s and 1930s also saw high unemployment and economic stagnation in the Free State, where the country's new political leaders opted for 'continuity and caution in economic affairs'.[47] Agriculture remained the predominant feature of the economy, and the census recorded over one-third of women as working in this category, though if farmers' wives had been included, the total would be even higher.[48] With 'personal service' making up another 30 per cent of women's employment in 1926, change, it would seem, was slow, although by the late 1930s some upper-class families were beginning to comment on the difficulties of finding and keeping domestic servants. Mary Daly notes that in this decade young women made up a majority of those working in protected industries, mostly on the assembly line or in packaging tasks in clothing, footwear, toiletries and so forth – work which undoubtedly offered better pay and a greater degree of independence.[49] The trend in employing female clerks continued in the South as elsewhere, though the greatest increase in this sector would not be seen until the 1960s.

A marked feature of the Irish economy was the relatively low number of married women in paid employment – only 5.6 per cent in 1926 and remaining at around this level until the 1960s. This compared with around 14.5 per cent in Northern Ireland and 21 per cent in industrial Belfast. The persistence of this trend can to a large extent be explained by the introduction of legislative measures targeting working wives; in 1933 it became law for national schoolteachers to resign on marriage, and the 1935 Employment Act extended the marriage bar to all civil service posts. Similar barriers to married women's employment were common throughout Western Europe in this period, with a male job, providing a 'family wage', seen as the major social and economic priority. There is no doubt many married women contributed to the family economy through casual labour, which could be combined with housekeeping. In the Aran Islands, for example, Muriel Gahan persuaded local women to knit the distinctive off-white, woollen sweaters with Celtic patterns, that were to prove a lasting attraction to overseas tourists.[50]

The Free State's 1935 Act further restricted the participation of working-class women in paid employment by giving the Minister for Industry and Commerce powers to prohibit women from working in some industries, and to prevent employers taking on more women than men. Although Daly argues that this had little practical effect, it could certainly be seen as demoralising and as sending out a clear message about the preferred role of women in Irish society. Some women actively resisted these gendered legislative measures. Though numerically small, they were important individuals – articulate, educated, well known and respected – women such as Skeffington and Senator Jenny Wyse Power, as well as Mary Hayden and Mary Macken, both of whom held chairs at University College Dublin. Organisations as diverse as the Mothers' Union, the United Irishwomen and the IWSLGA also opposed the employment laws.

Whether under Cumann na nGaedheal or Fianna Fáil, women's role in the Free State was characterised as domestic and familial, with legislative measures progressively eroding their position in public life. For example, although under the 1922 Irish Free State Constitution women were accorded total and complete right as citizens, a Bill of 1927 proposed that, in the interests of administrative efficiency and financial savings, they should be excluded from jury service. Protests from the IWWU, the Irish Women Citizens' Association (IWCA), and the Irishwomen's International League succeeded only in securing an amendment, which enabled women to 'opt in' if they wished. Citizenship, it seemed, could be as gendered as any other social category.

The same organisations and individuals were loud in their protests over articles affecting women in de Valera's 1937 Constitution:

41(1) In particular, the State recognises that by her life within the home, woman gives to the State a support without which the common good cannot be achieved.

41(2) The State shall, therefore, endeavour to ensure that mothers shall not be obliged by economic necessity to engage in labour to the neglect of their duties in the home.

45(2) The State shall endeavour to ensure that the strength and health of workers, men and women, and the tender age of children shall not be abused and the citizens shall not be forced by economic necessity to enter avocations unsuited to their sex, age or strength.[51]

Arguing that such policies severely curtailed women's opportunities, they sent postcards to the electorate, urging them to 'vote no to the constitution', and went on to form the Women's Social and Political League to monitor legislation affecting women.[52] But feminist critiques of the Draft Constitution did not go down well at the 1937 Fianna Fáil ard fheis, and in the Dáil, Helena Concannon, National University representative, was dismissive of the arguments:

Deputies are aware that many women's societies are perturbed by certain articles in the Draft Constitution, and we have been told should this measure go through the House unamended the status of women in the State will definitely be lowered . . . It is to Irish mothers and Irish homes that we owe the fact that we have won, to the extent that we have won it, success for the long fight we have had for our faith and nationality, and I am very glad that Article 41 has recognised the services of women in the home. It does not mean – and I for one would protest most actively against it if it did mean – to close the door to work for women in any other sphere. That is not the intention at all.[53]

While it could thus be variously interpreted, Article 41 has been the focus of debate ever since, especially for feminists and for historians of women's position in Irish society. It is clear, however, that, whatever the actual intention of politicians, analysis of the discourse points to a narrow and specific view of womanhood. As Mary Mullin has argued:

The language of the Constitution illustrates, once again, the importance of struggles over definition. Not only does the Constitution assume the right to define 'Family', but it also assumes that 'Woman' can be used interchangeably with 'Mother', and that both are automatically associated with domesticity.[54]

The 1937 Constitution and the debate surrounding it need to be considered in the light of both the national and international idealisation of family, marriage and motherhood, and the fear that women's political and economic progress would undermine these so-called 'traditional' values. A warning, typical of the period, was contained in the popular publication, the *Irish Messenger of the Sacred Heart*:

> As a result of the persevering efforts of a resolute group, women have secured access to careers and positions that were hitherto closed to them, and they now vote on an equality with men. But it is a lamentable fact that during all these years there has existed a change in another direction, a gradual lessening of respect for the sanctity of marriage which leads directly to the degradation of women. 'Women have acquired the vote and have discarded the vow', is the way the situation has been summed up by a Protestant preacher in England.[55]

Modesty forbids

The conservative religious and cultural values of the Free State militated against women's participation in many areas of public life. An editorial in the *Irish Times* in May 1928 complained of female behaviour in other countries, which was deemed unacceptable in Ireland:

> In France, Germany and even in England, many girls are devoting themselves to public sports which demand violent exertion and sometimes, it would seem, a notable scantiness in clothing . . . These performances are done before crowds of male spectators. His Holiness is surely in the right when he says that they are 'irreconcilable with women's reserve'.

Such views severely limited women's sporting potential. Although a Miss Willis and Mrs Phoebe Blair-White represented Ireland at tennis in the Paris Olympics of 1924, they competed under the Union Jack. One female swimmer competed in Amsterdam four years later, but the 1932 Irish Olympic team contained no women members. Between 1934 and 1965 the National Association for Cycling and Athletics in Ireland did not hold any competitions involving women at national level.

Women fared slightly better in Northern Ireland, with the first Women's Athletic Championships held in 1949. Thelma Hopkins came fourth in the High Jump at the 1952 Helsinki Olympic Games and won silver four years later at Melbourne.

Yvonne Judge, *Chasing Gold: Sportswomen of Ireland* (Dublin, 1995)

Both Northern and Southern governments attempted to control sexual and moral behaviour through criminal law legislation which, particularly in the South, was subject to much debate, inquiry and lobbying, and which reflected the conservative nature of Church, state and mainstream society. Among the changes included in the 1923 Northern Ireland Criminal Law Amendment Act was the extension of the period for adolescents to bring charges of sexual assault from six to nine months. This was important in that it allowed time for pregnancies resulting from assault to come to full term, and thus provide critical evidence in court cases. The age of consent for sexual intercourse remained at sixteen, but in a significant reform involving cases of 'indecent assault' on under-sixteens, the defence that the victim consented to an indecent act was abolished. In an attempt to control prostitution, the penalties for keeping a brothel were raised to £100 or three months' imprisonment.

The Free State legislation of 1935 followed a similar pattern, but raised the age of consent to seventeen, and decreed that fifteen was the age of consent to indecent acts – the inconsistencies in measures which were supposedly designed to protect girls remained unexplained. In March 1935, the Joint Committee of Women's Societies and Social Workers was set up when representatives on nine voluntary organisations met to discuss the Bill. Senator Kathleen Browne advocated raising the age of consent in cases of indecent assault to at least seventeen, accusing the Free State government of 'providing less protection to our young girls than the governments of Great Britain and Northern Ireland'.[56] Louie Bennett went further, recommending that the general age of consent be raised to eighteen; others argued for an end to sexual double standards in the area of prostitution, demanding that the law treat a woman found soliciting and her client equally. A women's police force and jury service for women on the same terms as men were also demanded.[57] These arguments were echoed by a wide range of reformers concerned with 'the moral safety of the youth of the nation'. Sandra Ruth Larmour claims that the legislation was designed particularly to protect adolescent working-class girls from sexual exploitation and to regulate their behaviour, and that 'class and social control references threaded the Irish debate'.[58] Certainly, neither men nor women publicly expressed concern with, or demonstrated any understanding of, young women's own perceptions or experiences of sexuality. Undoubtedly, while the law remained focused on dealing with men in the criminal system, women continued not to report such sexual offences and to keep their own desires and activities to themselves.

Concern with sexual morality was also reflected in the area of contraception, and here Church and state seemed to work in accord with one another, adopting a censorious attitude towards sexual behaviour and stressing the importance of marriage and family life. Both the overall decline in marriage and the late age at which couples tied the knot made this a particularly relevant issue for young people and society as a whole. The 1926 census showed that 80 per cent of men and 62 per cent of women in the 25–30 age group were unmarried, and that the illegitimacy rate stood at 3.7 per cent. This compared to 53 per cent single females in the same age group in Northern Ireland and an illegitimacy rate of 4.7 per cent, though there were many local and regional variations. The Carrigan Committee, called to inquire into such matters in the South, declared that both its members and the witnesses it had called were unanswered in their view that 'the moral condition of the country has become gravely menaced by modern abuses'.[59] This type of alarmist rhetoric was very typical of the period and should be seen as a reflection of religious and conservative anxieties rather than an indication of the moral laxity of the population at large. Those holding such views were, however, powerful enough to influence the public debate.

Sections 16 and 17 of the 1929 Censorship of Publications Act in the South had already banned the printing, publishing, distribution or sale of publications advocating contraception or abortion as a means of birth control. The argument was that the sexually explicit nature of such information

Women at the Albion clothing factory in Belfast demonstrate the workings of an automatic buttonhole machine for royal visitor, the Duke of Gloucester, in May 1934.

– for example, on how to insert a cervical cap – made it unacceptable. As with the banning in 1941 of a book about the infertile period, because of a fear that spreading such knowledge could lead to indecent conduct and public immorality, this says a great deal about public assumptions around female sexual behaviour.[60] Section 17 of the Criminal Law Amendment Act 1935 prohibited the importation and sale of contraceptives, and it is important to note that prominent women's organisations raised no objection to this. In a predominantly Catholic state, the subject of contraception was, publicly at least, a taboo subject. Protestant families were in a different position. At the 1930 Lambeth Conference the Anglican Church hierarchy, while condemning the use of contraception 'for selfish or convenient motives', had argued that within marriage where there was a 'morally sound reason for avoiding complete abstinence', Christian principles should be used in choosing an appropriate method of family limitation. 'Scientific methods . . . which are thoughtfully and conscientiously adopted', were specifically recommended.[61] There was therefore a considerable ideological gap between the two major religious groupings, which had potentially difficult implications for Protestant medical practitioners and dispensary doctors working within the Free State. However, it again reflects the conservative nature of the period that even Protestant women's groupings did not protest about this legislation. Indeed, Catriona Beaumont points out

HENRY WILSON

that the Mothers' Union agreed that 'a selfish refusal of children is wrong ... all artificial checks to conception are against the laws of nature'.[62]

While there were no legal restrictions on contraception in the North, neither was there any widespread public demand for easier access. In Belfast the first Irish birth control clinic, which was opened in 1934 following a visit by birth control pioneer Marie Stopes, was soon reported to be 'languishing', and closed shortly after the end of the war. While some GPs might have been sympathetic to the needs of their female patients, birth control was not considered respectable at this time. In 1981 Moya Woodside recalled that 'In Belfast forty years ago few medical men (apart from those on the university staff) were prepared to come out publicly in support of birth control although they might privately agree with the need.'[63] It would seem that attitudes to sexual behaviour transcended religious and other cultural boundaries.

As part of the continuing campaign to control the personal morality of young people, the Free State took measures to limit the number of public houses and to reduce opening hours; film censorship was also introduced to protect young minds from corrupting influences. However, the craze for modern dancing, which provided the opportunity for young men and women to associate together in venues outside the control of the Catholic hierarchy, was a particular source of alarm. As one bishop complained in 1922:

> When the truce with England was proclaimed, our young men and women, in town and country, started dancing. One does not blame them for this, it was a natural reaction after the strain and terror of the preceding months. But when is this thing going to end? To-day, eight months after the cessation of hostilities, they are dancing away more furiously than ever. The fact is that, while the fate of our country is still in the balance, the nation is suffering from something like an epidemic of frivolity.[64]

Father Joseph Flinn, Jesuit and president of the Pioneers in Ireland, claimed that at dances, 'degenerate males plied girls and young women ... with port or "gin and it" in the expectation of sex in return'. The government responded with the 1935 Public Dance Halls Act, giving open-ended discretion to District Justices to impose restrictions and conditions in such venues, and banning both alcohol and drunken patrons. Jazz dancing and jazz music were seen to be especially dangerous, not only compromising sexual morality, but also having a 'denationalising' influence on young people. References to jazz as 'nigger music' were uncomfortably reminiscent of fascist discourse in contemporary Germany, and the call for young Irish men and women to return to 'clean and sprightly' national dance reflected a nationalist ideology similar to that being fervently expressed on the European Continent.[65]

In Ireland, as elsewhere, women were associated with traditional symbols of nationhood. They were perceived as 'the guardian of the continuity and immutability of the nation, the embodiment of its respectability'.[66] This applied even more specifically to mothers; as journalist Mary Holland was to remark over fifty years later, 'We have apostrophised the country itself as a mother. The concept of Mother Ireland has met with wholehearted national approval. The message has been unequivocal. The proper place for a woman apart from the convent is the home, preferably rearing sons for Ireland.'[67] Conversely, anxiety was frequently expressed in ecclesiastical circles about 'the danger to Irish girls' who left their rural homes for the lights of the big city in other countries. Cardinal Joseph MacRory, Catholic Archbishop of Armagh, for example, made detailed arrangements with the Catholic Protection and Rescue Society in London to contact and maintain links with young Irish female emigrants.[68] With Britain overtaking America as the most popular destination of Irish emigrants from the mid-1930s, and the proportion of females to males reaching its peak in these years, similar systems operated in most major British cities. However, Louise Ryan's insightful analysis of contemporary media discourse on this issue demonstrates how such concerns about sexual morality, together with more pragmatic anxieties about the loss of 'breeding stock', were strands in a complex web of tensions, fears and vulnerabilities around the public image of the Irish state.[69]

The upholding of motherhood as woman's primary and most natural function was an ideology by no means unique to the Free State, but a concept familiar also to Northern Ireland, many areas of Western Europe, and in America, where Betty Friedan's highly influential book *The Feminist Mystique*, published in 1963, would demonstrate the frustration felt by many middle-class housewives confined within this role.[70] Liam O'Dowd thus argues that the contraction of women's political and social role in the period between the Treaty and the Second World War can best be understood in the international context of 'emergent Fascism, Nazism, reactionary conservatism and Catholic social thought'.[71] However, while the concern to relate womanhood to national and religious identity was clearly articulated and restricted women's role in public life, Catriona Clear rightly questions the assumption that the maternal, domestic role was always experienced as oppressive, citing Joanna Bourke's argument that for at least some women, even as early as the late nineteenth century, full-time work within the home was seen as 'an investment worth making'.[72] Moreover, as Brian Fallon notes, the usual paternalistic view of the Free State in this era ignores the important part played by the female religious orders, particularly in education, and he goes on to argue that, in fact, 'the real backbone of Irish Catholicism were ordinary Irishwomen':

> It was on women that the clergy chiefly relied to maintain religious morale and to carry out most of the small, regular rituals (i.e. the family rosary) which kept Catholicism an active force in the home, and it was to the consciences of women that they appealed most frequently in their sermons and in the hushed, private, sealed-off world of the confessional.[73]

There is little doubt that historians and commentators have tended to underestimate the importance of religion in the everyday life of women. Spirituality and the strength of religious faith are, after all, concepts for which we have no reliable measuring stick. Margaret MacCurtain cites two examples of the ways in which spiritual belief could shape, determine and support the experience of individuals. The life of Peig Sayers, Irish-speaking storyteller from the Great Blasket and 'nourished by an intense sense of the presence of God and a delight in Creation', exemplified, MacCurtain suggests, traditional Celtic spirituality.[74] In contrast, Edel Quinn's urban-based, business lifestyle formed the background to her religious vocation. Joining the Sodality of the Children of Mary as a child, she went on to work with the Legion of Mary, eventually serving as a missionary in South Africa.[75] Alongside the personal, private dimensions of spiritual experience, collective expressions of religious faith were also of immense importance. The revival of the Marian shrine at Knock in County Mayo in the mid-1930s is a good example of popular religious fervour.

Such expressions of faith also fed into wider, international dimensions of Catholicism. Thus, during the 1930s, 'Lourdes became almost a national obsession among Irish Catholics', with annual pilgrimages organised in many parishes and dioceses. Franz Werfel's novel, *The Song of Bernadette*, was an Irish bestseller between 1942 and 1946, and the subsequent film (which came out in 1943) was enormously popular when shown in schools, convents and parish halls.[76] Perhaps the greatest 'manifestation of Irish Catholic nationalism' was the 31st International Eucharistic Congress, which began with the arrival of the Papal Legate in Dublin in June 1932. A mass meeting of men in Phoenix Park was followed by one for women, and at the height of the celebrations over a million people heard tenor John McCormack sing at an open-air mass. As a young Protestant Dubliner, Edith Devlin was thrilled by the colourful proceedings:

No fairy tale, no kings of the Orient, could have been half so dazzling as that procession. Flamboyant banners, fringed canopies supported on embroidered poles held up by boys in lace aprons, monks in brown habits with white rope around their waists, cardinals, bishops, priests in magnificent garments of purple and red and exotic hats flowed by underneath our fascinated eyes, wave after wave of them, while the sound of bands and choirs and songs filled the air. The smoke of countless censers rose up above the brightly hued raiment and exotic perfumes floated past our nostrils.[77]

Streets in nationalist areas of Belfast and Newry were brightly decorated for the occasion, but special trains and buses carrying thousands of Northern Catholics to participate in the event were subject to sectarian attacks on their way home. For Protestants too, north or south of the border, religion formed an integral part of personal and social experience. While Protestant theology emphasised the importance of individualism, many aspects of religious practice were collective experiences. As Sheila Bradshaw put it, 'the Church was the family's social and spiritual life, between services, Sunday school, square dances and socials'.[78] Winifred Campbell's experience was also fairly typical: 'We were preached to in the factory, at open-air meetings, lunch-time services, and by testimony bands.'[79] Sunday schools were particularly popular, attracting large numbers of the children of the respectable working class. Despite their middle-class and often patronising ethos, they were important in sustaining a Christian culture among working-class children, and providing recruits for participation in the adult church.[80] For both Catholics and Protestants, Church-based organisations formed a rich, vibrant, and eminently respectable subculture, an acceptable alternative to wider secular leisure activities and amusements. A range of activities – sporting and social – were organised within parishes, and opportunities for the sexes to mix were provided by Bible study groups, Pioneer societies, and the like. Gender-specific associations such as the Catholic Girl Guides, the Legion of Mary, the Church of Ireland Girls' Friendly Society, the Girls' Brigade and the Young Women's Christian Association were also popular, establishing branches in most small towns and villages. The training of girls and young women in Christian principles was viewed as particularly important, for, as Hugh McLeod points out,

> it was women who took the leading role in those areas of religious life that related to the home, to the upbringing of children, and to rituals connected with the annual cycle or the life-cycle. Sometimes this was a matter of an accepted division of labour – for instance, mothers taught their children their prayers, because prayers were conventionally said before going to bed, and mothers generally put the younger children to bed.[81]

Within Protestantism, women were also vitally important to the day-to-day running of the parish church and its various activities. The wives and daughters of clergy, for example, though unpaid, played a crucial role – in teaching in Sunday schools, co-ordinating and presiding over women's meetings, playing hostess for husbands or fathers, and organising bands of caterers for the many social occasions in the church calendar. Fund-raising was also particularly associated with the women of the church, with missionary work particularly benefiting from their efforts. Gospel halls, Salvation Army bands and evangelical campaigns, such as that led by W.P. Nicholson in the 1930s, were also part of this lively religious heritage, targeting the irreligious, but probably mostly engaging those on the peripheries of institutional religious life. While religion certainly helped to reinforce particular political positions in terms of the Church–state link in the South and the perception of a threatened religious heritage in the North, it would be a mistake to assume that its beliefs and rituals were simply imposed on unwilling congregations.

Nonetheless, all religious denominations were in this period beginning to acknowledge the need to compete with an increasing range of entertainment opportunities. The popularity of dancing has already been noted, and this continued right through the thirties, forties and fifties, with the jive replacing the jitterbug, and it in turn giving way to new 'fads'. The arrival of the 'talkies' in the late 1920s gave a real boost to cinema-goers, who revelled in such classics as Al Jolson's *The Jazz Singer*. The wider world was introduced directly into many homes through the medium of radio. Northern Ireland's own radio station, 2BE, began broadcasting on 15 September 1924 with a rendition of the British national anthem, and by the time of the official opening one month later, over 5,000 licences had been issued in Belfast alone.[82] Dublin's first radio station, 2RN, came on air in time for the New Year celebrations of 1926. Gramophones also became popular during the 1930s, with the recordings of John McCormack a strong favourite.

Youthful romance was encouraged by new magazines which provided tips on make-up and fashion. During the 1930s the *Modern Girl*, for example, encouraged its young, single readers with the suggestion that 'the right haircut has been known to lead to a June wedding'.[83] In contrast, within the Traveller community, as Molly Collins recalled, young women could still be 'matched' by their parents:

> Matches [were] usually made at fairs. Well the fathers an' mothers'd do that. The girls wouldn't even be aksed. Well they'd be match med 'ithin in the pubs an' then when they'd come home they wouldn't tell ya 'til the mornin'

Irish women artists

Irish women have made important contributions to art at both national and international levels. In 1902 the Dun Emer Guild, founded by Lily and Elizabeth Yeats and their English friend Evelyn Gleeson, was an important centre of Irish embroidery, printing and bookbinding. Though the partnership between the Yeats sisters and Gleeson was brief, Dun Emer trained young women in these crafts, supplied churches with vestments and banners, and contributed to the Arts and Crafts exhibitions which helped focus public attention on Ireland's Celtic heritage in the early twentieth century. The superb metal work of Mia Cranwill, and the ecclesiastical decorative work of Sister Concepta Lynch were also significant. Sarah Purser was a popular portrait painter who 'went through the British aristocracy like measles', but while this work provided income and established her reputation, she is best remembered as the founder of An Túr Gloine (the Tower of Glass), a stained glass studio which produced some memorable designs. Evie Hone, who joined the studio in 1934, painted *The Annunciation*, her first window, for St Nahil's Church in Dundrum, County Dublin. Her most famous commission was *The Crucifixion and Last Supper*, for the large East window of Eton College chapel. Hone is also remembered for her association with Mainie Jellett, the pair credited as being 'responsible for bringing Cubism to a stranglehold of classical art like Dublin', where they held a joint exhibition in 1924. Described as 'profoundly influential' in 1930s Dublin, Jellett was one of the founders of the Irish Exhibition of Living Art in 1943. She too worked at the Tower of Glass, establishing herself as 'one of the leading stained glass artists of the twentieth century'. Jellett's early work was said to reveal 'a sensibility and strength of vision which places her in a unique position in modern Irish painting, as innovator, as influence, and as a leader in the development of ideas'.

Jeanne Sheehy, *The Rediscovery of Ireland's Past: The Celtic Revival 1830–1930* (London, 1980); Anne Crookshank and The Knight of Glin, *The Painters of Ireland, c. 1660–1920* (London, 1978) you'd be gettin' married. They were told then ta get their shawl. It was a shawl you'd wear. A rug or a shawl. You'd be tould to get the shawl an' walk aan ta the church. You didn't even know, hardly know who you were even gettin' 'til you'd look an' see them beside ya.[84]

While on a visit to the Galway area in 1930, travel writer H.V. Morton noted a contrast between two generations of womanhood which was probably typical of this period:

From a primitive thatched house came a smart young girl in a fashionable felt hat, blue tailor-made costume and flesh-coloured silk stockings. Her mother . . . wore the wide red skirt of a fisher woman . . . her feet were bare . . . a grey shawl over her shoulders.[85]

Perhaps more significantly, the 1930s was for many a time of passionate political conviction, when it seemed that ideologies could reshape both national and international structures. Although sectarian strife and the issue of partition generally weakened the labour movement in Northern Ireland, the troubled thirties did give an impetus to more extreme left-wing movements. Sadie Menzies, founding member of the Revolutionary Workers' Group and Communist Party of Ireland, recalls that about thirty members of the Communist Party in east Belfast busied themselves in raising money for the republicans in Spain during the Spanish Civil War. Edwina Stewart, whose parents were also members, noted that party members were mostly from the Protestant section of the working class, although her own parents were atheists. The Soviet Union, of course, provided the supreme example of workers' solidarity and many socialist and communist women, north and south of the border, spent time there as delegates and observers. Charlotte Despard, secretary of the Friends of Soviet Russia, Hanna Sheehy Skeffington, Sheila Downing, Helena Moloney and others made an extensive tour of the Soviet Union in 1930, and were deeply influenced by all they saw. Menzies spent a month there, and Belfast woman Betty Sinclair attended the Lenin School in Moscow for eighteen months.[86] Rosamund Jacob's diary of her visit to the Soviet Union in 1931 contains fairly typical sentiments: 'We have seen with what joy we cannot here express, the freedom of women in the USSR from the economic dependence and its accompanying sense of inferiority which keeps them down in capitalist countries.'[87]

Fear of the extreme right was also a factor in support for Russia. In Ireland, right-wing ideologies were expressed by a coalition of Treatyite forces, alarmed by the release of IRA prisoners and the economic war with

Members of the Friends of the Soviet Union setting out for Russia in April 1931. One of the three women depicted is Rosamund Jacob who was in Russia between April and May of that year.

Britain. Eoin O'Duffy's National Guard – the Blueshirts – was made up of members of the Army Comrades' Association and this movement joined with Cumann na nGaedheal and the Centre Party to form Fine Gael in 1933. Fearghal McGarry is probably right to argue that the Blueshirts had more to do with internal Irish politics than with wider fascist movements, but the marching columns of disciplined uniformed men certainly suggested parallels.[88] The Blueshirt movement was also popular among women, who made up around 25 per cent of the overall membership. Mostly unmarried, these 'Blue Blouses' were mainly involved in the social and catering activities of the movement. It is difficult to ascertain precisely what motivated these young women, but many thousands of their contemporaries throughout much of Europe were similarly attracted to right-wing political ideologies.[89] With the Fianna Fáil government restricting women's employment, it was not difficult to see in contemporary Ireland a 'backlash against the modern woman and a return to conservative social values fostered by an alliance between the Catholic Church and fast spreading fascism.'[90] The IWWU warned of the possible consequences, particularly for women:

As for women: Women in the Fascist State have no status, no rights, no powers. Wherever possible their work is taken from them and their places given
to men. They must marry and breed sons to become soldiers. They must
learn 'how to buy more food on less wages'. (In Italy women working in the
fields earn 2½d. an hour.) The Fascists have no use for women except for
washing dishes and nursing children. The Fascist attitude towards women is
growing in Ireland. Already there is talk of reserving for men jobs where the
women have a fair wage and leaving only 2½d. jobs for women.[91]

In the North, too, Fascism had its supporters. A letter from the district officer of the Ulster Women's Units of British Fascists in 1927 had admonished
local women for their lack of enthusiasm, declaring that 'women fascists are
necessary everywhere, and Ulster is not being so energetic in forming new
branches as she should be'.[92] In Kilkeel, County Down, Dorothy Harnett led
a section of the British Fascists, not, like the Ulster Fascists, associated with
Oswald Mosley's British Union of Fascists, but combining extreme loyalism
with fascist ideology.[93] Lady Londonderry, like many aristocrats of the
period, believed Hitler to be the 'friend of Europe'. Having twice spent time
on the Continent, during which she met and talked with the Führer, she
published her views in an article for the *Anglo-German Review* in 1938:

I have never heard anything approach the acclamation, which he received.
Seeing a man thus idolized by the masses, the living symbol to them of a res-
urrected and united nation, I felt myself in the presence of a born leader . . .
extraordinary simplicity . . . the characteristics of dignity and humility. I am
quite convinced now that he stands for peace. The last thing Germany wants
is another war. Herr Hitler by his efforts saved Germany from Communism.
By his example he may well be called upon to save Europe. That he is the
genuine friend of Europe I have no doubt.[94]

Such faith in the intentions of the German leader would prove short-lived.

SECOND WORLD WAR

In 1939, Breege McCusker reported that when the locals, bringing in the
harvest in the summer of 1939, were told of Hitler's invasion of Poland,
'there was a real fear of Germany . . . Many old superstitions were recalled.
The absence of the robin that winter was seen as a sign that Ireland would
be invaded.'[95] At a more practical level, Gusty Spence recalled that the
morning the war broke out – 3 September 1939 – the owner of the local
pawnshop was called down to open up 'because the Territorials were in des-
peration: all their boots were in the pawn, and the pawn was open that
morning from after war was declared at 11.00 o'clock to five o'clock and

she done a flying business'.[96] In Éire, the Fianna Fáil government declared its neutrality and operated for the next five years in what was known as the 'Emergency' – a response that convinced many Northern Ireland citizens that their own special relationship with Britain could only be reinforced by their military contribution to the war. This perception prevailed despite the fact that recruitment levels in the six counties were, according to Jonathan Bardon, 'embarrassingly low'.[97]

Women in the North, meanwhile, began to organise themselves for the struggle on the home front. The UWUC adapted its regular meetings into work parties, and the founding of the Ulster Gift Fund in 1939 brought many such groups as well as individuals together to provide clothing and bandages for military hospitals and woollen garments and other 'comforts' for the forces. By 1943 it was estimated that there were 225 depots and 71 affiliated working parties attached to the fund.[98] Compared to the First World War, there was considerable expansion of the opportunities for women to serve, both at home and abroad, and in a wide range of capacities. New aircraft capabilities meant that civil defence was of particular importance, and the Women's Voluntary Services for Civil Defence enrolled and trained women to assist local authorities in the event of air raids and evacuations and with the running of canteen services, rest centres, transport and first aid. The Housewives' Section, organised on street or village basis and working under the Air-raid Precautions (ARP) wardens, maintained a membership of more than 24,000. Blue Housewives' Section cards placed in parlour windows indicated that trained women were ready to give assistance, and became a familiar sight everywhere; red cards were used to indicate a street leader.[99]

At the beginning of the war the central nursing reserve and voluntary aid detachments, supplementing trained nurses, were particularly attractive to women, but as time went on, other uniformed services seemed to offer greater opportunities for action, adventure and travel. The Wrens was perhaps the most popular, with the attractive uniform considered a significant bonus. Elaine Crowley, for example, was convinced that the glamorous uniform of the cinema advertisements would help her to catch the eye of a local young man. Unfortunately, she was greatly disappointed in the final article of 'rough, thick cloth and [with] no perky little cap'.[100] While both men and women responded to what they regarded as the romantic aspects of the situation, the fight against fascism did provide other openings. Following the fall of France in 1940, the naval base at Derry became an important strategic site and much of the administrative work there was carried out by around three hundred Wrens, with many of the recruits coming

Jews in Ireland

Ireland has had a small Jewish population since about the eleventh century, but the main influx was between 1880 and 1910 when around 2,000 Jews fled from persecution in Eastern Europe. They mostly settled in the cities of Belfast and Dublin, with smaller numbers in Cork, Limerick, Lurgan and Waterford. Only a handful came to Ireland during the Nazi period. These included seven-year-old Edith Zinn, who, together with her brother Zoltan, witnessed atrocities in Germany. The Zinns were brought to Ireland by Dr Collis, as was young Suzi Molnar and her brothers. Sabina Wizniak escaped the Warsaw ghetto and came to live in Dublin. Agnes Bernelle, actress, singer and writer, fled with her family from Berlin, and came to Castlebar, County Mayo, where her father gained employment in the local hat factory. Dancer Helen Lewis survived the horrors of Auschwitz but her husband died in a German concentration camp. After the war she married a friend who had escaped to Belfast. Making their home in the city, she recalled how she 'spent the first two years learning to understand that strange place, its language, customs and people'. Lewis was to make her own impact on her adopted homeland through her teaching of dance, culminating in the foundation of the Belfast Modern Dance Group.

Helen Lewis, *A Time to Speak* (Belfast, 1992); Dermot Keogh, *Jews in Twentieth-Century Ireland: Refugees, Anti-Semitism and the Holocaust* (Cork, 1998); Mary Rose Dooley, *Hidden Memories; The Personal Recollections of Survivors and Witnesses of the Holocaust Living in Ireland* (Dublin, 1994)

from around Lough Foyle, Derry and Donegal. Maeve Boyle was one of these local recruits, many of whom were Catholic, keen to learn new skills. Despite the slowness of processing applications, Richard Doherty claims that 'there were many strongly nationalist households which saw one or two daughters don the dark blue uniform of Britain's navy'.[101] Young women from the Free State, eager to join the British services, usually had to apply from an English base; Elizabeth Chamberlain took a job as a nursing aide in an English hospital so that she could join the Wrens. Once recruited, her Irish origins did not seem to cause her any problems:

> I hate to say it, but I enjoyed the war. You forget all the horrible parts. My time in Liverpool and Skipness was pure hell. Then there was the poverty of

Naples, seeing people eating out of dustbins. I never regretted joining the Wrens and there was no adverse reaction to my doing so at home. In fact, I remember my first day on the Via Roma in Naples. I met three people from Dublin. All through the war you were meeting Irish people in uniform, in train corridors, streets, everywhere you went, there were Irish people there.[102]

Romie Lambkin, another Dubliner keen to join the Wrens, became impatient at the delay in processing her application, and instead joined the Auxiliary Territorial Service (ATS) to train as a staff car driver. She commented that 'being a Catholic [was] quite useful in the ATS', as she was excused from participating in big church parades. Lambkin thoroughly enjoyed the freedom of life in England, drinking port and cider, jitterbugging and going to the cinema to see Marlene Dietrich's *The Blue Angel* or *White Cargo* in the company of the many available young men.[103] And for Maeve Boyle, war was a similarly liberating experience: 'I enjoyed myself during the war. You could go to the pictures and sometimes I'd make two dates in one day. It was difficult not to use the wrong name at times. But the whole experience broadened your outlook.'[104] The Women's Auxiliary Air Force (WAAF), formed in 1943, was also attractive to younger women, with the average age of recruitment estimated at twenty-two. Of the 60 officers and over 4,500 airwomen in Northern Ireland between 1943 and 1944, it was calculated that 'on actual airfields, as opposed to Headquarters and Signals stations, 40 per cent of the airwomen were from Northern Ireland or Éire'. These women were engaged in a great diversity of duties, taking over much of the male work. However, though one of the WAAF officers left in 1944 to become a pilot, most were content with 'passenger hours', and the vast majority remained on the ground.[105]

War also necessitated a change in civilian working patterns. For Dubliner Agnes Daly Oman, recruited to help out in the countryside in the South, bringing in the harvest was a novel experience:

When they were trying to get the wheat in they used to get the army lorries and we'd go off with the lorries down in the country to help take in the wheat . . . I was in the army lorries. We'd all be allocated to some farmer to help him take in his wheat . . . we loved it, being driven along. It was great for us. We just went into the fields and they showed us what to do and we just put it all in stacks. We thought that was marvellous, being brought out in a car. And it was lovely and coming back we'd have a singsong.[106]

Much female traditional work was brought to an end by war. For example, buyers could no longer be found for the lace doilies and gloves

Munitions workers see a demonstration of the deployment of their products at an artillery range in Holywood, County Down, on 20 December 1941.

produced by a farmer's wife in Ballycrory in County Mayo,[107] and Sheila Conroy, a confectioner in a family bakery in Cork city, also found herself without a job.[108] With a ban on wage increases and a steady rise in prices, it is not surprising that almost 7,000 citizens from Éire sought work in the North between February and December 1941.[109]

The production of armaments provided employment for many Northern Irish women, with patriotic considerations an additional inducement to economics. In 1942, Betty Sinclair called on Ulster women to 'answer the call of Soviet Russia', and

> man the factories of our country for increased production, for the opening of a Second Front in Europe, for the strengthening of the alliance of working women the whole world over, for a speedy victory, and the utter destruction of Hitlerism and all brands of fascism.[110]

The total number of female insured workers in the six counties rose from 111,900 in 1939 to a wartime peak of 118,600 in 1943, with increased opportunities in the aircraft industry and in rope- and twine-making. While engineering firms before the war were almost exclusively male, with only 250 women to 21,500 men, by 1943 numbers had risen to 12,300 women and 44,000 men.[111] It was, however, stressed whenever possible that much of the 'new' work for women involved what were perceived to be traditional 'feminine skills'. The *Belfast Weekly Telegraph* of December 1941, for example, pointed out that 'the feminine aptitude for sewing and patching gives the fair sex a flying start when it comes to repairing barrage balloons'.[112]

Young women from all parts of Ireland also sought work in England during this period. According to Dermot Keogh, 133,584 men and 58,776 women received permits to work outside Éire between 1940 and 1945. Catherine Corbally and Maureen Boyd were among those seeking employment as teachers, nurses, midwives, domestics in hospitals and hotels, or in munitions factories, cotton mills, transportation, or bus conducting.[113] Noreen Hill from Cork, working in an English munitions factory from 6 p.m. to 6 a.m., sent half of her £10 weekly wage back home, and was amused to find members of the Legion of Mary visiting her lodgings once a month to 'keep an eye' on her.[114]

The demand for women workers during the war highlighted the need for nursery places, and the Northern Ireland Nursery Schools Association was to the fore in lobbying for government action. The Ministry of Home Affairs responded by devolving powers to this association to open and run nursery schools in country districts outside Belfast to cater for young evacuee children. By 1941 there were 3 nursery schools and 17 nursery centres for two- to four-year-olds under their control. These were based in church halls and old schools in a number of towns. By 1943 the number of day nurseries for women engaged in war work in Belfast peaked at thirteen. Although a brief post-war boom in the linen industry encouraged further developments along these lines, with four Belfast mills running their own nurseries, almost all were closed with the decline of the industry in the 1950s, despite the campaigning efforts of mothers' clubs in Belfast to keep them open.[115] The war may well have created 'unusual' circumstances, but as Liz McShane notes, government ministers of the post-war era were very clear that 'mothers of young children should not go out to work but should stay at home and look after them'. The prevalence of such attitudes ensured that in the transition of power to local education authorities and in the absence of compelling political or economic 'need' the demands of working mothers fell on deaf ears.

With the everyday tasks of shopping and cooking drastically affected by the war, wives and mothers faced problems on other fronts too. In Northern Ireland, the immediate rationing of petrol was soon followed by that of food; according to Brian Barton,

> within twelve months of war, down-market products such as pigs' knees, feet and cheeks made their first appearance in the shopwindows of smart, city centre butchers; meat consumption overall fell sharply. Fruit – tinned and fresh – became almost unobtainable, as did dairy products such as cheese and cream.[116]

Nor did families in the neutral South escape the effects of war. With all kinds of shipping vulnerable to attack and isolated from any convoy arrangements made by the Allies, Éire suffered from shortages of motor parts, machinery and, in particular, coal, with households limited by March 1941 to a quarter of a ton a month. The smell of turf revealed the alternative, and several schemes for turf production were implemented. The use of gas was limited to three one-hour sessions a day, and children kept a close eye out for the 'glimmer man', who visited homes checking cookers to ensure there was no illegal usage. Members of the ICA made wax baths from the fat of fish and meat, setting wicks in them to provide home-made candles. Shortages of petrol meant a sharp reduction in train and bus services, and horses, carts and bicycles once more became common modes of transport. Clothes and shoes were rationed from the summer of 1942, and many young women became accomplished in the skill of painting stocking seams on their legs. Although milks, eggs, potatoes and vegetables were plentiful, some of the most common everyday items were scarce. Edith Devlin recalled that tea was made from roasted dandelion roots, coffee could be produced by roasting acorns, and the ICA recommended carrots and parsnips flavoured with vanilla essence as a substitute for dried fruit in Christmas pudding. In May 1942 it was made illegal to serve bread or sell wheaten flour in any form at dances, race meetings, whist or bridge drives, bazaars, carnivals or sales of work. A degree of cross-border enterprise was inevitable in this situation, with tea and sugar regularly smuggled down from the North in return for butter, eggs and bacon.[117]

A group of young married women in Dublin, anxious about how the Emergency was affecting the poor of the city, had been active in lobbying the government to ration essential food and keep down the prices of necessities, particularly for pregnant and nursing mothers, the poor and the unemployed. In 1941 they formed themselves into the Irish Housewives' Committee (becoming the Irish Housewives' Association [IHA] in 1946), and sought to unite housewives in the task of gaining recognition for their participation in 'all spheres of planning for the community', and in defending consumers' rights. A sister organisation to the ICA, in 1948 they also incorporated the IWCA and were affiliated to the Women's Emergency Conference 1943–6, which was made up of representatives of existing organisations to deal with war conditions especially affecting children and the underprivileged. While undertaking much valuable work during the war, the IHA is probably most significant in providing an element of continuity for the women's movement, forming an important bridge between the more public and political female activism of the twenties and the sixties.[118] Both upper and lower classes in the South did find some outlets for enjoyment during the war. Doreen Maloney, writing for wealthier readers in the *Irish Tatler and Sketch*, concluded that 'on the whole, considering the war abroad, and the increased taxation, matters are not so bad as at first expected in the hunting world'.[119] For those in the sailing fraternity, extravagant regattas continued to be held every other weekend during the season, and, in Dublin:

> You could dance in evening dress to the music of Billy Dingle or Jimmy Masson and his Orchestra in the Gresham Hotel every Saturday night from 8.00p.m. until midnight for 5s for the dance only and 9s 6d if you wished to have supper. The singer was Frankie Blowers, a Frank Sinatra imitator.[120]

Ice-skating on the pond in the zoological gardens in the city provided a winter alternative for the less wealthy, and Guinness, of course, was plentiful. The presence of military personnel on furlough also added an element of romance and danger. Indeed, Deputy Garda Commissioner Garrett Brennan suggested that during 'the Emergency years there developed a big increase in the number of loose women to be seen in the principal streets at night, attracted by visiting soldiers on leave and visitors from Northern Ireland and the provinces.'[121] Reports of dramatic increases of prostitutes, whether in the numbers or their visibility, provoked similar comments in all European capital cities during the war. While prostitutes themselves were often blamed for their 'avarice', the very real possibility of imminent death and the breakdown of normal family life and relationships were clearly important factors in stimulating the 'business of sex'. With many young people newly independent and far from home, it is also possible that sex became more available and was treated more casually. The real anxiety for the authorities was the reported rise in venereal disease, perhaps contributed to by the inaccessibility of condoms in Dublin. The manager of a cinema in Clones, County Monaghan, was so disturbed that he introduced regulations forcing young unmarried men and women to sit on opposite sides of the central aisle.

Even in the North there was enjoyment to be had despite the blackout, and members of the Belfast-based, upper-class Drawing Room Circle continued their regular literary meetings, debates and picnics, declaring that 'the writing of papers . . . proved an analgesic for the troubles of housekeeping and the stress of war work'.[122] Although young women were advised to 'arm themselves' with pepper pots and whistles when walking out alone during the blackout, Elizabeth McCullough's diary records numerous dances at the Plaza, knitting parties, trips to the cinema, skating and cycling trips and the pleasure of eating out.[123] Young people were particularly pleased when in 1943 the local authorities, trying to cater for large numbers of soldiers seeking entertainment, allowed cinemas to open to uniformed service members on Sundays. Shelia Hughes and Norma Barry, dancers at the Empire Theatre, recalled packed houses every night, even when patrons were warned of the threat of German bombs.[124]

For the first eighteen months of the war danger to the civilian population was not taken seriously, with a good deal of laxity around the observance of the blackout and the provision of air-raid shelters. Emma Duffin wondered whether the trial fittings of gas masks, or turning out on cold dark winter nights to listen to lectures on mustard gas, were futile exercises.[125] Belfast was utterly unprepared for the German air raids which began in April 1941. The first raid, on the night of 7–8 April, which killed 13 and injured 81, to some extent shattered that air of complacency, with 'everyone anxious to recount their reactions and experiences'. The night of 15–16 April, however, which saw many overcrowded residential areas receiving direct hits, was to bring a level of chaos, confusion and horror hitherto unknown. Sarah Nelson, a young civil servant watching from her home opposite the Waterworks on the Antrim Road, found that after a night of constant bombardment, her 'mouth was dry with praying and with countless repetitions of the rosary'. Newly married Nellie Bell spent most of her wedding night in an air-raid shelter, but there was little feeling of security:

> a landmine just missed the shelter and struck the police station and a row of houses in the street we were in. Well, the smoke and the debris all landed on our shelter and we thought we had had it. However, when it was realised we were all 'safe', somebody started singing 'Nearer My God to Thee' and from then on it was hymns.[126]

From under the stairs, where she shared the contents of the whiskey decanter with her husband, Moya Woodside reflected that 'this was civilisation in 1941 – sitting shivering, bored and frightened in a cubby hole at 3.30 a.m'.[127] In the Ulster Hall, despite the danger, Delia Murphy and her husband continued to sing throughout a night in which 745 people lost their lives.[128] For some time there was considerable confusion over who had died and who had escaped. Nurse Emma Duffin described the scene in Belfast's St George's Market, which was being used as a temporary morgue:

> Saturday afternoon, the fifth day after the Blitz, I went to the Market. Will I ever bring myself to buy flowers and vegetables there again? I had seen many dead, but they had died in hospital beds, their eyes had been reverently closed, their hands crossed on their breasts: death had, to a certain extent, been glossed over, made decent. It was solemn, tragic, dignified. Here it was grotesque, repulsive, horrible. No attendant nurse had soothed the last moments of these victims, no gentle reverend hands had closed those eyes nor crossed those arms. With tangled hair, staring eyes, clutching hands, contorted limbs, their grey green faces covered with dust they lay, bundled into the coffins, half-shrouded in rugs or blankets or an occasional sheet, still wearing their dirty torn twisted garments. Death should be dignified, peaceful. Hitler had made even death grotesque.[129]

In the immediate aftermath of this second raid, around 6,000 people from Belfast sought refuge in Dublin, and though official evacuation arrangements prioritised children, mothers with children, aged, infirm or blind persons and certified expectant mothers,[130] thousands were panicked into seeking accommodation in country regions of the North. The transition from urban to rural life was a considerable shock both to evacuees and those with whom they took up residence. Middle-class women, such as Moya Woodside's mother, were taken aback by the condition of their new lodgers:

> My mother telephones to say she took eight evacuees last night, two mothers and six children. Says one mother is about to have another baby any minute, but they are all filthy, the smell in the room is terrible, they refuse all food except bread and tea, the children have made puddles all over the floor etc. She is terribly sorry for them and kindliness itself but finds this revelation of how the other half live rather overpowering.[131]

Coping with skin diseases and other consequences of overcrowding and poverty were a new and often unwelcome challenge for the middle classes; Emma Duffin believed that it was 'a terrible indictment of our way of life'.

Belfast was not the only Northern area to suffer: Derry, Newtownards and Bangor also experienced devastating attacks. In his autobiography, philosopher Max Wright described how his father was killed when his Bangor home suffered a direct hit. His mother lost a leg, and after over two years in various hospitals, she remained severely crippled throughout her life.[132] Nor did the Free State escape the indiscriminate devastation of bomb raids. On 26 August 1940 bombs killed three women working in a creamery in Campile, County Wexford, and another three died in the German bombing of Carlow town in January 1941. Four months later thirty-four people lost their lives when parts of Amiens Street and North Strand in Dublin were flattened during air raids. Significant numbers of Irish men and women were also either temporary or permanent residents in British cities targeted by German bombers. Richard Doherty desribes how staff nurses Patricia Marmion, originally from Skibbereen in County Cork, and Catherine McGovern, a native of Bailieborough, County Cavan, rescued patients from the Royal Chest Hospital in London when it was struck by a bomb in January 1941. They were two of many Irish-born nurses who were awarded the George Medal for bravery.[133]

Social life in Northern Ireland livened up considerably with the arrival of some 3,900 American troops on 26 June 1942. Peaking at 37,000, this new transient population would inevitably have a major impact on the region, both socially and economically. Members of the Ulster Gift Fund offered to help host their American 'guests', but found that the US army 'had already made elaborate arrangements for their welfare and comfort', so hospitality was usually a matter of individual initiatives.[134] Dance halls, cinemas and hotels vied for the custom of these relatively well-off, dancing, smoking, poker-playing young men, and for many local women the war was transformed by the appearance of the 'Yanks'. One commentator noted an influx of women from the South anxious to secure nylon stockings, and romance – with passions heightened by wartime tensions – blossomed. The more casual and visible dimensions of lovemaking proved shocking to the conservative and matronly elements of Northern Irish society. Mrs Toner, a retired missionary, 'formed a vigilante group that patrolled the grounds of Belfast City Hall at night, torchlights in hand, spotlighting some of the intimate acts performed by the soldiers and their local pick-ups on the grass.'[135] These monitoring activities came to an abrupt end when she was attacked by a soldier. More permanent liaisons were given the seal of legitimacy; Belfast girl Thelma Smith, who married Private H.W. Cooke of Cleveland on 13 April 1942, was the first of 1,800 GI brides. Although the American government initially stated they would not finance the journey to the US of the new brides of servicemen, they relented in 1946 and sent a converted troop ship to bring 445 brides to a new life in America, to be shortly followed by a further 219.[136] Many love affairs between local women and GIs were terminated with the war, however, and those who found themselves pregnant by their departed lover found different ways of coping with the situation. Some kept their babies, others arranged for them to be adopted or brought up by other family members, some kept their secrets, and even amongst the current generation, the true stories of many wartime babies are still emerging.

The ending of the war saw mass expressions of relief and almost hysterical joy. On VE Day in Belfast, Jessie Woodger recalled that

Women's Auxiliary Air Force: preparing for the end of the war

This extract from the Cabinet archives graphically demonstrates the extent to which traditional views about women's role prevailed even while they were engaged in military duties.

In 1944–5 when it was apparent that thousands of men and women would soon be returning to civilian life, the service turned their educational services on to preparing them for that transition and it was realised that one of the most popular and necessary courses for the WAAF would be training in housecraft. In Northern Ireland already there had been many marriages between Airwomen and Airmen, Americans, and local men and very many more were 'engaged'. So the Air Force approached the College of Technology in Belfast and a two-week course in housecraft for WAAF officers and Airwomen who were married or engaged came into being. Courses of this kind were also started at such stations as Ballykelly – a hut in which a gas cooker and a kitchen sink had been installed would be taken over for a week by ten Airwomen. They would do all their own cooking and 'shopping'. This domesticity, apart from being valuable training, was a great change from their Air Force work and the Courses were always most popular. Incidentally, a very lovely white satin wedding dress was presented by the people of Toronto, Canada, to the WAAF of the Command, and this was kept at Headquarters and used by many WAAF Brides – a great asset when the expense in both money and clothing coupons would have otherwise precluded a 'White Wedding'.

Cabinet Papers, PRONI, CAB/3A/27

everyone in Belfast seemed to be around the City Hall, and everyone kissed everyone else. Sailors, Soldiers, Airmen, Policemen, everyone seemed to be off-duty. There were bands playing and singing, and a ring of people holding hands all round the Hall sang Auld Lang Syne.[137]

However, Felicity Braddell Smith recorded a very different reaction among the servants on her large farm on the borders of counties Wicklow and Wexford:

Then one wonderful day, we heard on our small battery wireless that the war was over. I ran along to the kitchen, where dinner was in progress, to announce the marvellous news, only to be met with blank stares. I might as well have said 'the rain's over', for all the interest they showed, and could have shot the lot.[138]

VE Day was more traditionally celebrated by Dublin students who hung British, Russian, American and French flags from Trinity College, though violence broke out when they went on to burn the Irish tricolour. Militant republicans had expressed anti-British feelings in sporadic campaigns during the war, and these had met with swift reprisals. IRA suspects were interned in Derry, Belfast and at the Curragh, County Kildare. These activities continued in the post-war period, which saw 256 men and one woman interned in Northern Ireland by 1957.[139] The difficulties faced by the wives and families of these prisoners went largely unacknowledged.

POST-WAR IRELAND

In the longer term, the Emergency marked the beginning of the end of the experiment in self-sufficiency for Éire. The North's contribution to the war effort, on the other hand, gave the Northern Ireland government the political and economic recognition in London it had long craved. An immediate priority for the post-war government at Stormont was the provision of housing, with a 1944 survey indicating that 39 per cent of all houses were in urgent need of replacement. Bombs had flattened much of north and east Belfast and rural areas had suffered years of neglect. In County Fermanagh, for example, no houses had been built between the formation of the state and the end of the war. Some female input into housing policy had been discernible when Belfast Corporation's housing scheme was launched in 1937. Emma Duffin fought masculine prejudice by insisting that the houses should have convenient kitchens as well as pleasing façades. The Northern Ireland Women's Advisory Council, which was chaired by Duffin, also called upon the government to take action to deal with the acute housing shortage, recommending the requisitioning of unoccupied houses as well as the erection of temporary dwellings. They also advocated the use of Nissen huts to ease the immediate problems, a suggestion eventually taken up for 1,500 families in November 1946. The task facing local authorities was a mammoth one, and the Northern Ireland Housing Trust was established in 1945 as a government-funded voluntary body to help cope with the housing crisis. The annual rate of construction rose rapidly thereafter, with 11,000 dwellings built in and around Belfast between 1945 and 1954, and the first Housing Trust estates appearing in Cregagh, Finaghy and Andersontown from early 1946.[140] Though rents of around 14 shillings a week kept the very poorest from taking advantage of them, these new houses were modern, easily cleaned, with indoor toilets, running hot water and baths. For Adree Wallace, moving from a cottage with no running water to Rathcoole housing estate, 'the house was like a palace',[141] and similar views were frequently expressed. East Belfast woman, Jacqueline O'Donnell, captured the sense of progress which such a move reflected:

COMING UP IN THE WORLD

A house with a garden
Something to view
And with a bathroom as well
That's luxury too.
THREE bedrooms to share
Even a coal shed for tools
We've come up in the world,
What more would you want.
It's a bus to school now,
With a walk after that!
And even a long haul
To the local shop.
It's hard in the winter
But we will survive.
We've come up in the world
We feel more alive![142]

With only an irregular bus service to the city, costing 2s. 6d. for a return ticket, Vicky McGibbon found the move from Belfast's Grosvenor Road to Suffolk, a small estate some four miles to the south of the city centre, a difficult adjustment. Most of the new neighbours were also from different parts of Belfast and many women missed the bustle and gossip of the familiar city streets and their convenient shops. Doctor Florence Stewart noted that her female patients who had moved to new blocks of flats on the city's outskirts, often took advantage of visits to the surgery to call on their mothers still living in the Woodvale and Shankill areas, and felt that the loss of 'the camaraderie of the streets' was no less than 'a tragedy'.[143]

There were, however, more serious underlying problems with the new housing developments. Quite simply, new homes were not always given to those most in need. Of 1,048 council houses built between 1945 and 1967 in the mainly Catholic County Fermanagh, for example, 82 per cent were allocated to Protestants.[144] Designed to ensure the return of unionist councils (tenancy of local authority housing brought with it a voting qualification), this type of discriminatory practice was one of the major factors leading to the emergence of the Northern Ireland civil rights movement of the 1960s.

The experiences of both the Blitz and evacuation had made it clear that more than housing was required to deal with the consequences of poverty, malnutrition and ignorance, and in 1948 the introduction of a comprehensive programme of welfare reforms, heavily subsidised by the British government, was widely welcomed. The reconstruction of educational facilities, which would promote change and provide new opportunities for thousands of young men and women, preceded health reform. The 1947 Education Act raised the school leaving age to fifteen, and put in place three distinct types of schools – grammar, technical and intermediate. As a result, between 1947 and 1953 the number of new school places of all kinds reached a total of over 13,000, with the number of students in teacher training courses actually doubling.[145] Although much remained to be done, by the end of the academic year 1955-6, over 20,000 pupils were attending grammar schools on state scholarships.[146] The opportunity for a full academic education was to transform the lives of thousands – male and female, Catholic and Protestant. Although the modernisation of the sector was largely at the expense of socio-religious segregation,[147] significant numbers of working-class Protestant and Catholic men and women would take advantage of the new system, the latter emerging within decades to challenge the sectarian and class-based culture of the North.

The remnants of the old Poor Law system disappeared under the new National Health Service (NHS); totally free to all, its impact can be seen retrospectively in a rapid decline in maternal and infant mortality rates. In terms of the quality of life, the availability of free dental and optical treatment, and doctors who could be called upon without dire consequences for the family budget, are almost immeasurable. However, the more positive aspects of government action were marred in Northern Ireland by damaging and prejudicial attitudes toward the minority community, such as the 1954 debate during which the UUP opposed paying allowances to Catholics with more than four children.[148] Nonetheless, and despite the flaws which feminist analysis would later bring to light, the emergence of the welfare state would transform life for subsequent generations.

The predominance of Church influence in Éire, on the other hand, meant that in the post-war period secular and religious values were more likely to clash, and this was particularly notable when proposed government policies threatened to intervene in family life. As Patricia Harkin noted, 'A striking feature of debates on social policy issues in Ireland in the 1930s, 40s and 50s is the constant preoccupation with protecting the family from "excessive" or "unwarranted" state intervention.'[149] Welfare schemes thus evolved more slowly and were introduced only after heated and protracted debate. In 1942, for example, the proposal to set up an Anti-Tuberculosis League had been quashed by the Catholic hierarchy, who considered it to be too secular. The most highly publicised and notorious aspect of health reform, however, was the debate surrounding the Mother and Child scheme proposed by Noel Browne in 1951. With tuberculosis already beginning to decline as a result of the use of new drugs and treatment, Browne, a member of Clann na Poblachta and Minister of Health in John A. Costello's coalition government, had established new regional sanatoria on coming to office in 1947, and then turned his attention to a more comprehensive programme of reforms, which would include free prenatal and postnatal services, and free medical care for children up to the age of sixteen. Such a proposal had already been aired by Fianna Fáil, but then shelved because of a range of objections. Browne revived the plan and received a good deal of support from both government and trade unions. But he also faced powerful opposition. The Catholic hierarchy has traditionally received most blame for the ensuing debate, which resulted in the loss of the Bill and the resignation of Browne. However, Evelyn Mahon argues that it was in fact the Irish Medical Association which was the main driving force in the opposition, translating medical questions into moral objections to state-controlled medicine in a way which appealed both to the Church and conservative public opinion.[150] In any case, with medics fearing a loss of control and the Church wary of any freedom of choice offered in the area of contraception, particularly to women, Browne was forced to resign in April 1951. A Health Bill introduced two years later was more successful; with references to family planning removed, it provided for free health care for expectant mothers and infants, and for free hospital and specialist care for children up to six years old. In 1956 provision for free hospital care for those on low incomes

was also made. The priority of the government of the day, perhaps unsur-
prisingly, was to create jobs for men or to supplement men's incomes so that
they could marry and support a family.[151] It was to take almost a social, sexual and cultural revolution before the needs of women were placed high on
the agenda of any government, and even then, the case for women's health
was to be severely compromised.

While the social gap between the North and the South was thus growing
in these post-war years, a widening gulf between urban and rural life was
also clearly emerging in Éire. In domestic terms this was most significantly
reflected in the processes of electrification and of bringing supplies of running water to individual homes. Electrification had made steady progress in
the early twentieth century, reaching most towns by 1931, with the vast
majority of urban homes enjoying the benefits of instant light. It was not
until the post-war period that the Electricity Supply Board began its rural
electrification campaign, but in the ten years following 1947, 63,000 consumers, over half of all rural households, had been connected.[152] Mary E.
Daly notes, however, that a 1953 survey of seventeen rural areas found more
rural households using electricity for leisure appliances such as radios, than
for labour-saving household devices such as irons or cookers.[153] We should
therefore perhaps not assume too readily that electricity brought immediate
changes to the housewife's daily tasks. The situation with water was very
different. By 1946, almost 92 per cent of urban homes had access to piped
water and 35 per cent per cent had a fixed bath. In sharp contrast, over 90
per cent of rural homes were still reliant on pumps or wells for running
water, while less than 4 per cent had a fixed bath. Although a committee on
piped water was established in 1947, it was disbanded a year later and only
16,000 households availed of a grants scheme for the installation of water in
rural homes between 1950 and 1959.[154] Despite the lobbying efforts of the
ICA, among others, it was reported as late as the 1960s that 'eighty per cent
of those living in rural areas relied on water from the roof tank or the daily
trip to the old-fashioned pressure pump with the lion's head'.[155] Similarly, a
small Northern town such as Strabane, County Tyrone, had electricity by
1936, but only 55 per cent of the population of the six counties had a piped
water supply in 1945. Four small towns had no piped supply at all, and most
rural households had neither piped supplies nor proper sewerage facilities.
Progress in this area was slow until the 1950s, but thereafter the pace of
improvement quickened, with 70 per cent of small communities enjoying a
supply of piped water by 1960.[156] There were clearly significant variations in
the supply of services, which impacted on the daily routine of women
throughout Ireland.

Unmarried motherhood in the 1950s

The majority of young women throughout Ireland who became pregnant while unmarried in the 1950s suffered profound shame and guilt, and most gave up their babies for adoption. Much of their experience remained hidden, their stories untold. It was not until the 1990s that a number of high profile publications about institutional cruelty and neglect brought to light the nature of their ordeals.

June Goulding, a young midwife in the early 1950s, went to work in a home for unmarried mothers in the Republic. She was intimidated by the rigid discipline and harsh treatment meted out to the young inmates and she later described a regime that viewed the mothers and mothers-to-be as sinners, who had to atone for their 'crime'. They were made to endure the pains of labour and childbirth without the benefit of any pain relief and in the most uncomfortable circumstances. 'More like a penitentiary than a nursing home', this institution was subsidised by the Corporation rates. The young women were usually recommended to the home by their local parish priest, and few would have realised what they faced. After giving birth, they breastfed their babies for a year, then worked for the following two years in the home and its self-supporting farm until their babies were fostered or adopted at the age of three. Few were able to return home because of the shame and stigma of their situation. Only those whose family could pay £100 were able to leave the home ten days after the birth, their babies immediately being fostered. Others underwent the heartbreak of separation from babies to whom they had inevitably become closely attached.

Mary O'Leary's mother left her home in West Cork in 1954 because she was pregnant and unmarried. The child was raised by her grandmother from the age of six weeks until she was four. Noreen Hill, who lived in England, brought up her sister's illegitimate baby, thus saving the child's mother from being stigmatised by the neighbours back home in Ireland.

A few women braved it out. For example, Gene Kerrigan's mother, helped by a younger sister, brought up her illegitimate child in Dublin 'with no resources, no support, amid an "ethos" hostile to the very existence of such a family'.

June Goulding, *The Light in The Window* (Dublin, 1998); Mary O'Leary, 'Lesbianism and Feminism: A Personal Reflection', *Irish Journal of Feminist Studies*, vol. 2, no. 1 (summer 1997), pp. 63-6; Gene Kerrigan, *Another Country, Growing up in '50s Ireland* (Dublin, 1998)

While dealing with the mass of social and economic issues generated by the post-war era, the governments north and south of the border did not neglect to consolidate their constitutional positions. The 1949 Ireland Act decreed that Northern Ireland would remain part of the United Kingdom for so long as the majority of its people wished, and de Valera fulfilled a long-held ambition on Easter Monday of the same year by declaring the establishment of the Irish Republic. Six years previously, during a St Patrick's Day radio broadcast, he had given his vision of an Ireland which

> would be the home of a people who valued material wealth only as the basis of right living, of a people who were satisfied with frugal comfort and devoted their leisure to the things of the spirit – a land whose countryside would be bright with cosy homesteads, whose fields and villages would be joyous with the sounds of industry, with the romping of sturdy children, the contests of athletic youths and the laughter of comely maidens, whose firesides would be forums for the wisdom of serene old age. It would, in a word, be the home of a people living the life that God desires that man should live.[157]

Evidence suggests, however, that this 'dream' was far from the reality of the experiences of many Irish men and women, who were leaving the country in droves. A total of 400,000 emigrated during the 1950s, with the years 1956-61 seeing the highest rate since the 1880s. Almost two-thirds of the female emigrants were domestics – hotel staff or servants – but a significant number responded to advertisements placed in the Irish press by the British National Health Service and left to train as nurses in England, where tuition was free and nursing homes provided safe and sheltered accommodation. In 1947 alone, 1,176 Irish women travelled on assisted passage to take up careers in nursing.[158]

With emigration at its strongest in the west of Ireland, Bridget Grealis-Guglich's experience was typical, as she recalled,

> going off with the little bag, that was the story of the people in and around Ballycrory, Co. Mayo where I came from. Life was hard . . . we knew at an early age that we'd have to be leaving and taking the bag. There was nothing in Ireland for us. That I had to leave my homeland was maybe the saddest thing in my lifetime.[159]

Future Irish President Mary Robinson in a speech to the Dáil in 1995, was surely right to stress that 'it takes from their humanity and dignity to consider (emigrants), merely as vicitims', but the absence of so many of these 'men and women with plans and dreams of future achievement' was a severe loss to the island of Ireland.[160] One consequence of predominantly female emigration was that by 1951 rural Ireland contained 868 women for every 1,000 men,[161] K.H. Connell has remarked that marriage was likely to be contemplated 'not when a man needed a wife, but when the land needed a woman',[162] and the importance of marriage to the rural economy was clearly recognised by contemporaries. A local parish priest in County Cork wanted to introduce a marriage bounty as an incentive to young men, and to encourage young women not to emigrate. Others believed that a major hindrance to marriage was the 'live-in' in-laws with whom a newly married rural bride had to contend. Carmel, from east Galway, explained that when she married, she 'went in with a mother-in-law, she ran the house for years after I going in. I just worked as one of the family. She minded my kids

Changes in the cost of living 1939–1951

During the early 1950s, the Communist Party of Northern Ireland was particularly concerned about rising prices. The following table is based on its comparison of pre- and post-war prices for essential items (adjusted here to the nearest penny).

	1939 £ s d	1951 £ s d
woman's coat	1 12 6	6 2 11
man's made-to-measure suit	3 15 0	14 10 10
man's ready-made suit	2 10 0	9 2 6
man's shirt	7 11 0	1 12 5
women's wool frock	1 15 0	6 2 11
woman's stockings	3 0	7 4
woman's shoes	1 1 0	2 12 6
bedroom suite	21 0 0	84 13 0
carpet	6 6 0	21 6 7

Communist Party of Northern Ireland Papers, PRONI D/2162/A/24

Women and children of the travelling community decorate their caravan with fresh flowers. Loughrea, County Donegal, 1954.

while I was out on the farm working.'[163] These older women could have considerable influence in the home, wielding power over the extended household, and de Valera at different times considered schemes for the building of dower houses to defuse the 'frustration and friction' often felt between married women and their mothers-in-law.[164] Such schemes came to nothing, however, and it was the 1960s before the tide of emigration began to turn.

Leaving had become much easier with revolutionary changes in transport facilitating faster, cheaper journeys to all parts of the world. The first Aer Lingus flight between Dublin and Belfast took place on 27 May 1936; in

1939 the two and a half hour flight from Dublin to London cost £5 10s. for a single ticket, £7 7s. for a return. With the first commercial flight between Ireland and North America taking off in 1947, visits home came within the realms of possibility for many emigrants, even if it was most usually to attend the funeral of an elderly parent. The job of air hostess – the first employed by Aer Lingus taking up her duties in 1945 – also seemed to hold out the prospect of an exciting and adventurous new career opportunity, though the position was in reality little more than that of traditional 'service', albeit with the chance to travel. But despite technological innovations, it would take time for Ireland to shake off the image of the 'dreary Eden' deserted by so many of the population.[165] Poet Mary Dorcey, asked for her memories on growing up in the 1950s and early 1960s, recalled:

> Silence. Repression. Censorship. Long dark winter. Poor food. Nuns and priests everywhere. Drab clothes. Censorship of books and films. Fear and suspicion surrounding anything to do with the body or the personal life. The near total repression of ideas and information. A Catholic state for a Catholic People.[166]

In Northern Ireland the coronation of Elizabeth II on 2 June 1953 was the cause of great celebration – for at least one section of the community – and for many an exciting introduction to the magic of television. On the day following the coronation, it was reported in the unionist press that:

> The greater part of Belfast lay amazingly still and quiet yesterday morning – no smoke from the factories; hardly any traffic in the streets; few pedestrians; the shopping centres deserted. But within a few hours a fete-like atmosphere prevailed, with bonfires lit everywhere, fancy dress, sporting events. And in the following month two nights of open-air dancing at Botanic Gardens and Belfast Castle free of charge during the coronation visit.[167]

Nationalist Belfast was not so enthusiastic however. On the day of the coronation the *Irish News and Belfast Morning News* reported on a mass meeting held in Belfast the previous evening to protest against 'the enforced association of any part of Irish national territory with the British Monarchy'. Councillor O'Sullivan claimed that the 'glamour and pomp of the Westminster celebration [could] not hide the injustices, sectarianism and discrimination done in these Six Counties in the name of the Queen of England'. In the same vein, Alderman S. Kearney added that 'the Coronation ceremony was the greatest lie that England had, for many years, tried to foist on a credulous world, but the Queen of England could claim not part or portion of Irish territory without the will and consent of the Irish people'.[168]

The voice of Ireland

R uby Murray, daughter of a civil service clerk, was hailed as the 'Voice of Ireland' during the 1950s. Born on the Donegall Road in Belfast on 29 March 1935, Murray moved to London while still in her teens and recorded her first hit record, 'Heartbeat', in December 1954, which launched her astounding wave of success. In 1955 she had five hit singles, including her most famous and best-loved 'Softly, Softly', which reached number one in the British pop charts. Murray's time at the top was short-lived, however, with her soft and simplistic style overtaken by a new craze for rock'n'roll imported from the United States in the following years. 'Goodbye, Jimmy, Goodbye' reached number ten in 1959, but was her final hit record. Nonetheless, Murray's domination of the hit parade during 1955 was an achievement matched only by Madonna thirty years later.

http://www.45-rpm.org.uk/dirr/rubymhtm; http://www.musica.co.uk
/musical/screen

The *Irish News* was also derisive about the expense involved in sending a couple of hundred Belfast children to London during Coronation week. But for the thousands of the monarchy's supporters in the North who could not make the trip, a new television set, often viewed by groups of neigh-bours, provided a very welcome alternative, enabling those who felt a strong link with Britain to participate in its cultural highlights. Regular television broadcasting from Northern Ireland began two years later, and Radio Telefís Éireann (RTÉ) went on the air on New Year's Day 1961. This new medium was highly significant in helping to bring about the end of the Republic's isolation, and to begin to dent its insular, conservative image. Also impor-tant would be the formation of the European Economic Community (EEC) in 1957, and, perhaps most dramatically, the clamour for justice and for human rights which began in America and which would ignite the sparks of discontent and resentment held by the Catholic minority in Northern Ireland, and by women on both sides of the Irish border.

4

Challenging the state(s)
we're in

In pooling our experiences of life, we
discovered the world as it was for females.[1]

The period between 1960 and 1980 was one of rapid change, with radical social, economic and political developments transforming the daily lives of men and women, not just in Ireland, but across Western Europe and North America. Innovations in the areas of communication and transport ensured that medical and scientific discoveries, new technologies, trends in fashion, music and culture were widely disseminated throughout the industrialised world. In an era that saw the landing of men on the moon, a seemingly unstoppable demand for civil and sexual rights and disillusionment with political and religious institutions, challenges to the status quo were mounted with increasing determination. For many women, the time seemed ripe to claim ownership of their bodies and control over their economic and political destinies. The fact that their demands were usually (indeed, still are) identified alongside those of other 'minorities', speaks volumes of the ideological and material barriers they faced. What has been called the 'ferment' of the sixties impacted strongly on the island of Ireland, though both the immediate and long-term effects were significantly different on either side of the border. In the South, the conservative and

Catholic values of a state not yet forty years old were challenged by new ideologies and, as it lost its insularity, by the changing economic and political climate of the wider European Community. In the North, the resurgence of political and sectarian violence meant that the call for women's rights was once more undermined by and subsumed within the bitter conflict of contesting nationalisms.

The rapidity of change and the overlapping nature of factors affecting both public and private life make this a particularly complex period to discuss. The difficulties of separating out events which happened simultaneously and of acknowledging and paying due respect to the multifaceted determinants of experience are of course applicable to every period. However, these are compounded in any discussion of the sixties and seventies by the nature of the military and political conflict in the North. Conscious and subconscious acceptance or rejection of disputed interpretations and sensitivities to terminology make this a minefield for any writer, never mind one burdened by her own baggage from the period. Following an introduction tracing general trends and issues facing women on both sides of the border, this chapter goes on to discuss the emergence of the women's movement in the Republic of Ireland, before dealing separately with the social, political, military and gendered struggles for equal rights and civil liberty in the North.

THE SWINGING SIXTIES

The decade remembered as the swinging sixties was dominated by a vibrant youth culture which challenged all aspects of conventional behaviour, questioning traditional aesthetic and moral values and posing radical new alternatives in their stead. The young of every generation have a strong and often disruptive impact on life, as they criticise or rebel against the norms and values of their elders. However, the rapidity and extent of the revolutions in communication technology and transport in this period ensured that the voices of young people were more clearly heard and their views more widely disseminated than ever before. Young Irish women were exposed to the latest trends in music and fashion by way of popular radio and television programmes, long-playing records and a proliferation of new 'teen' magazines. *Romeo* and *Jackie* both catered for and reinforced the dreams of a generation of teenage girls, with stories of romance, pictures of pop stars, and pages of advice on make-up and the very latest fashion. The miniskirts and tight jeans of young women were the visible evidence of an ever widening cultural gap between generations. Bob Dylan, Joan Baez, the

By the late 1960s female fashion reflected the bold innovation of a new and vibrant youth culture

Beatles, the Rolling Stones and Jimi Hendrix articulated the love, anger and rebellion of young people with more money to spend, and more to spend it on, than their parents could have imagined, and were hysterically worshipped in return. Images of girls screaming and fainting at the mere sight of their idols became commonplace. For example, in November 1963, when the Beatles arrived at the ABC cinema in Fisherwick Place, Belfast, by taxi from Dublin, they were greeted by a crowd of around 8,000 screaming teenagers. The *Irish News* reported on the phenomenon: 'Beatlemania hit the city with a bang last night. Ambulances rushed nearly a dozen people to hospital, many more were treated on the spot and weary police breathed a sigh of relief when the four Merseyside popsingers were safely tucked away in bed for the night'.[2] Seventeen-year-old Joan Strain, the first casualty to be carried into the cinema foyer, explained that she had been 'swept away' by the pushing crowds. Similar excitement greeted the Rolling Stones at the Adelphi cinema in Dublin in January 1965. New female stars also attracted the attention of the young; Eileen Kelly, growing up in Cork, constantly rehearsed the songs of top female singers such as Connie Francis, Brenda Lee, Sandie Shaw, Cilla Black and Dionne Warwick.[3]

The new international pop culture did not totally replace home-grown talent and the popularity of showbands during the sixties provided new opportunities for women. Dermot Keogh comments that these bands were a source of liberation for singers such as Eileen Reid, who fronted the Cadets, or line-ups like Tina and the trio Maxi, Dick and Twink, 'competing and surviving in a "man's world"'.[4] But female entertainers were not a new phenomenon, and it is probably more useful to see these acts as providing alternatives to more traditional engagements for individual women. Eileen Kelly went on to front the Music Makers in 1964 and 1965 and replaced Maisie McDaniel on the Nevada's line-up. Known throughout Ireland as the 'blonde bombshell', she remembered that she 'wanted to be Dusty Springfield. At that stage she was my idol.'[5]

Young unchaperoned women enjoyed the anonymity of the huge ballrooms so popular in this period, highly successful commercial enterprises which raised alarm bells among a religious hierarchy always on its guard against unsupervised interaction between young men and women. The Catholic Church reacted to the perceived threat to morality by issuing decrees that dances should end by midnight in winter, and 1 a.m. in summer, and in September 1960, Dr Morris, the new Archbishop of Cashel and Emly, advised dance promoters operating in his jurisdiction that

> no dances should be held on Saturday nights, eves of holy days, Christmas night, or during Lent (except for St. Patrick's night for traditional Irish dancing or where dancing has already been customary on that night) . . . Concern for the moral welfare of those who dance will surely be accepted as no more of an interference with legitimate amusement than concern for their health and physical safety.[6]

However, with the number of ballrooms reaching around 450 by the middle of the decade, it proved impossible to halt the new and vibrant youth culture, and by 1967 all Irish bishops had rescinded their prohibitions. As a teenager, Maeve Flanagan looked with envy on her young, single aunt from Galway, who went to dances and 'was very glamorous. She had all the latest clothes and a beehive hairstyle.' On visits to Dublin she 'floated around our house leaving clouds of perfume in her wake', singing

Put your sweet lips a little closer to the phone.
Let's pretend that we're together all alone.[7]

The more diverse leisure scene also accommodated fans of jazz and folk, though the move of traditional music from homes to pubs tended to marginalise women, with men predominant both as players and singers. On the other hand, Dana, alias Rosemary Brown, winning the Eurovision Song Contest in 1970, with 'All Kinds of Everything', gave an international boost to the Irish music scene and inspired many young women to emulate her success. Hollywood also provided popular idols and role models, who, like the rock stars, were not always acceptable to the more sedate establishment. The proposed appearance of Jayne Mansfield at an engagement in Tralee, County Kerry, for example, was cancelled when the local priest warned his parishioners 'to dissociate themselves from this attempt to besmirch the name of our town for the sake of filthy gain'.[8]

The younger generation was not the only one to be affected by the rapid changes of this period. Older women also felt the impact of both national and international influences, though those living in isolated rural areas without television or radio remained virtually immune from the advantages and disadvantages of modernity. For housewives in the larger suburbs, the routines of daily life underwent gradual but significant change, as the corner shop gave way to the supermarket chain. With the advent of fridges and later freezers, weekly shopping trips in the family car became more usual, and the twin-tubs, vacuum cleaners and central-heating systems advertised on television seemed to offer the prospect of a more leisurely lifestyle. Family holidays in Butlin's Holiday Camps, or even overseas, fell within the realms of possibility for the first time, and many working-class families aspiring to avail of the new opportunities were facilitated by 'easy pay' plans and local shopping clubs.

In a consumer-led society the usual employment pattern is an increase in the numbers of married women in the labour force: a dual income deemed necessary to keep up with rising standards. And, indeed, in line with employment trends in the UK, the proportion of married women in the labour market in Northern Ireland rose sharply, from just under 30 per cent in 1961 to almost 45 per cent in 1981. While this figure was always higher in the north-east than in the rest of Ireland, in this period it was more than double the rate in the Republic (20.4 per cent), where the sixties boom reflected, instead, rising male employment. Moreover, while the increase in Northern Ireland was mostly due to part-time employment, women's part-time employment in the Republic remained the lowest in the EEC.[9]

Rather than seeing an increase in working mothers, the response to rising living standards outside of the north-east was instead reflected in an increased tendency to marry, and to marry earlier than in the preceding generation. Furthermore, family size was, as Mary Daly remarks, still higher than in other parts of Europe and, given the strength of traditional family values and the importance attached to motherhood, the conditions were not encouraging for women to return to work. It would be the 1980s before a combination of factors – including the removal of the ban on married

Tourist Ireland

An annual influx of summer visitors also gave a boost to the rural economy as the Republic promoted itself as a holiday destination. Between 1961 and 1969 the income from tourism more than doubled and the number of hotel beds increased by half, bringing new jobs, many of them for women, in the hotel and catering industries.[1] Ironically, the main attraction for foreign tourists was an image of Ireland as romantic and quaint, as portrayed in films such as Disney's *Darby O'Gill and the Little People* (1959) or *The Quiet Man* (1952), John Ford's nostalgic homage to his Irish ancestry. The families of emigrants, brought up on stories of an oppressed and unique culture, wanted to see thatched cottages, pretty villages and shawled colleens – in reality this was a backward-looking perception, but one which could be catered for by a range of festivals promoting traditional music and culture.

With the Irish-American connection an important element of the tourist industry, the ancestral homesteads of American presidents proved a popular attraction, and one which was given a significant boost in 1963 by the visit of President John F. Kennedy. Arriving at Dublin airport on 27 June, he was welcomed to the capital by a crowd of around half a million, before travelling on to Wexford, where he had tea with his third cousin, Nurse Mary Ann Ryan. Cork, Galway and Limerick were also on the itinerary.

Only five months later, Mary Ann Ryan set out for Washington to attend the funeral of the assassinated President; and the crowds of Irish people, which had so enthusiastically welcomed him to their cities, formed sombre processions on their way to special masses and to sign books of condolence in the American embassies in Belfast and Dublin.

[1] Fergal Tobin, *The Best of Decades: Ireland in the 1960s* (Dublin, 1996)

women working in public service in 1973 (it was 1975 in the North), the impact of membership of the EEC on employment legislation, and a greater assertiveness among women themselves – would bring the Republic's female employment statistics more into line with those of other Western European countries. Nonetheless, a rapid rise in living standards provided the material and psychological basis for national recovery, as the Republic began to look beyond its own shores to develop its economic potential. The decision to apply for membership to the EEC was made in 1961, and in 1973 both the Republic and Northern Ireland became full members. The later broadening of this economic link would prove immensely important to the furtherance of 'women's rights' in the island of Ireland.

Changing emigration patterns also reflect significant shifts in attitudes and experience during this period. Demographic change was, for example, a major consequence of the outbreak of civil unrest in Northern Ireland at the end of the sixties. With renewed sectarian violence and a strong military presence reinforcing existing religious segregation, many Catholic families fled to the Republic or left the island altogether as a result of fear, intimidation or despair. Máire gan Ainm, opting to be nameless to preserve her family's anonymity in their new homeland, emigrated from County Armagh to Canada in 1973. She explained: 'We didn't like the idea that our children were going to be brought up in a society where you were going to be searched on the street at somebody's whim.'[10] Conversely, in the Republic, many of those who had left in the 1950s returned 'to work, settle, rear children'. Although the economic slump of the 1980s would temporarily reverse this trend, inward migration was an important indicator of the Republic's changing international image.

Mention has already been made of the importance of the media in transmitting ideas, and the emergence of women journalists in the *Irish Times* and the *Irish Press* ensured that the implications of the new international focus on women's issues would be debated in the serious national press. The content of articles by women such as Mary Kenny, Nell McCafferty, Mary Cummins and Nuala Fennell were a far cry from the homely recipes or knitting patterns which made up the Women's Pages of bygone years, and their writings would be of particular significance in the later development of a women's political movement. But most social historians stress the role played by television in transforming the expectations and aspirations of whole societies, and this is as true of the Republic as elsewhere. Even before RTÉ began transmission on New Year's Eve in 1961, it was argued that the new national broadcasting company should be used to defend traditional ideals of marriage and motherhood against the influences of British television. Thus a conference devoted to the challenge of television in Ireland called for 'programmes on married life, which would stress the vocation of motherhood, its satisfactions and trials'. Given the proliferation of popular male heroes, it was granted that

> a feminine ideal is a necessity for young girls and the absence of any regular 'heroines' on television screens was stated to be injurious to young girls, particularly teenagers. Serial features on women heroines such as Elizabeth Fry, Edel Quinn, the Angel of Dien Bien Phu, or some of the valiant women of the Old Testament could be attractively presented and should contain enough drama to satisfy even male as well as female viewers.[11]

However, it was the chat show format that became most popular with Irish viewers, and these live programmes proved much more difficult to control. Perhaps the best known was *The Late, Late Show*, hosted by Gay Byrne, which was top of the ratings for about twenty years. Described as 'lively and post-protectionist' in its style, it thrived on controversy and 'shocking' private revelations, with topics frequently generating extensive public debate. For example, when in February 1996 Eileen Fox said she could not remember the colour of her honeymoon nightdress because she might not have been wearing one, Dr Tom Ryan, Bishop of Clonfert, protested 'in the name of Christian morality'. His claim that the programme was unfit for Irish television and Irish audiences, while winning the sympathy of several establishment figures, was generally regarded as a gross overstatement. The *Catholic Standard* more accurately reflected conservative opinion in its comment that 'nothing very demoralizing or dangerous took place, but what shocking bad taste'.[12] By the end of the seventies Patrick Moriarty, the new chairman of RTÉ, was claiming that the programme 'has had a very liberalizing effect on the country'. With television sets in 83 per cent of Irish homes by 1976 (when all programmes were in colour), he was surely correct in suggesting that the impact of such shows must be considered in any future social history of Ireland. In the UK where neither the British Broadcasting Company (BBC) nor independent television companies operated under the same kind of social constraints as in the Republic of Ireland, concerns with upholding 'established morality' were highlighted by the 'Clean Up TV' campaigns of Mary Whitehouse, a right-wing secondary-school teacher. In 1965 Whitehouse formed the National Viewers' and Listeners' Association to monitor the moral quality of public broadcasting. Characterised variously as a moral crusader or a spoilsport, her voice was to be constantly raised against the portrayal of sexuality in any form.

For those reaching adolescence in the sixties, however, censorship meant that the more intimate aspects of life were a mystery, explored if at all in whispers, giggles and the surreptitious reading of illicit books. The novels of Edna O'Brien, with their explicit explorations of the unrestrained sexuality of young women, represented an exciting and forbidden world of desires and feelings regarded by many as unspeakable and all too often associated with guilt and fear. Nuala O'Faolain remembered that 'they were a catalyst for women to exchange confidences'.[13] The fact that such bodies were banned in the Republic only reinforced their attraction, and certainly Maeve Flanagan had no difficulty in acquiring a second-hand copy of *Lady Chatterley's Lover*, which 'put the finishing touch' to her research into the 'sex project'.[14]

The so-called sexual revolution of the 1960s, which undermined traditional 'taboos' involving restraints and limitations on sexual conduct, was slow to impact on the South, where family life was highly valued and where, despite the liberalising tendencies of the Second Vatican Council launched in 1962, the Catholic Church retained a tight control over moral and sexual behaviour. Contraception remained outlawed in the Republic for much of this period, and it is difficult to assess just how couples managed their sexual and reproductive lives. The advent of the contraceptive pill undoubtedly changed the lives of many; pharmaceutically available from 1961, it is estimated that around 12,000 Southern Irish women were taking it in 1967. Although usually prescribed to regulate the menstrual cycle, there is little doubt that many women were only too happy to avail of its well-publicised 'side effects' to limit or space their children. Mary Kenny claimed that

> the pill's impact was sensational; it appeared like a magical potion which seemed to provide mankind with what it had always dreamed about: sex without consequences, sex without cost and sex without strings. Within a short time it would have an impact on every aspect of interactive life between the sexes – from dancing to courtship rituals, from manners to morals.[15]

The 1968 Papal Encyclical prohibiting its use thus came as a major blow, 'offering a stone to those who asked for bread', stimulating public debate and provoking the first major challenge to the Catholic Church by women.[16] The first Family Planning Clinic opened in Dublin in 1969, circumventing the legal restriction on selling contraceptives by asking for 'voluntary' donations from clients. By 1971, when there were two centres in Dublin run by the Irish Family Planning Association, Senator Mary Robinson was claiming that they had seen 30,000 clients in that year alone.[17] Despite such evidence of their growing popularity, however, traditional, particularly religious, attitudes to birth control were still vigorously asserted in both parts of Ireland. For example, when the Northern Ireland Family Planning Association (NIFPA), which gave advice 'to the married and those about to be married', requested that notice of its first annual general meeting in November 1965 be announced in *Today's Diary* on the radio, it received a decidedly negative response. The broadcasting authorities were adamant that 'no publicity could be given to open advocacy of a controversial cause'.[18]

The consequences of continuing controversy over contraception, when combined with changing attitudes to sexual behaviour by many young people, was seen in the growing number of pregnancies occurring outside marriage. In the last three decades of the twentieth century, the numbers of non-marital births began to rise significantly in both parts of the island – from 2.6 per cent of all births in the Republic in 1970 to reach 22.5 per cent by 1995, and from 3.6 per cent to 21.8 per cent in the North in the same period.[19] Eileen Evason, author of a study of single parents in Northern Ireland published in 1980, noted that despite the extent of the problem no research in this area was carried out before 1978.[20] In the Republic, the issue was publicly discussed in 1970 and 1972, with illegitimacy the focus of major conferences held in Kilkenny. A particular area of concern was the large proportion of illegitimate children given up for adoption, around 90 per cent compared to Europe, where the highest national rate was 35 per cent. Clearly, the unmarried parent in Ireland was in need of significant support, both psychological and material.[21]

Many of those young women who did not see adoption as an option sought instead to terminate their pregnancies. In the UK in 1965, a televised docudrama in the popular Wednesday Play series drew public attention to the very real dangers of their situation. Ken Loach's *Up the Junction*, adapted from Nell Dunn's novel on the seedier side of life in London's Battersea area, portrayed casual sex resulting in unwanted pregnancy, and an illegal, back street abortion resulting in death. But, in contrast to the following decade, this is one area where little public concern was expressed in Ireland during the sixties and seventies. Since most women dealing with unwanted pregnancies in this way went 'across the water', it was not perceived to be a particularly Irish problem. Only when statistical information was gathered, analysed and publicised was the debate taken outside the confines of small, radical feminist groups. In the meantime, many like May in Maeve Binchy's short story, 'Shepherd's Bush', made the lonely, anxious trip to London: 'there were no legal abortions in Dublin, and she did not know of anyone who had ever had an illegal one. England and the ease of the system were less than an hour away by plane.'[22] Although legislation was introduced in Britain in 1967 to make abortion more accessible, no such provision was made in Northern Ireland, where the law was 'confused, inconsistent and determined by moral views and an unwillingness to bring test cases'.[23] While abortion in the North should have been an option when the mother suffered serious medical or psychological problems or severe learning difficulties or when the foetus was detected to be abnormal, the legal situation was not usually so clear-cut. In his discussion paper to the Standing Advisory Commission on Human Rights in May 1993, Simon Lee argued that, 'the law on abortion in Northern Ireland is so uncertain that it violates the standards of international human rights law. It could not withstand a challenge before the European Court of Human Rights at Strasbourg.'[24]

In other areas too, legislation in Northern Ireland lagged well behind that of the rest of the UK. For example, the 1967 liberalisation of the British law on homosexuality was not extended to Northern Ireland. And when the European Court of Human Rights recommended that this be pursued a decade later, Ian Paisley's Democratic Unionist Party (DUP) famously responded with the Save Ulster from Sodomy campaign. Kathryn Conrad comments that in Irish political discourse, North and South, throughout the course of the century homosexuality was 'regarded as a kind of foreign pollution, a threat from outside'.[25] Lesbian rights were rarely openly discussed. Writer and community arts worker Joni Crone explained that for many lesbians, theirs was 'a story of an underground minority, a subculture whose members have been unwilling or unable to court publicity, because to do so may have invited violence, rape, or even death'.[26] An Irish Gay Rights Movement was established in Dublin in 1974 in a (successful) attempt to create a space in which same-sex couples, gays and lesbians, could socialise, and one of the earliest lesbian groups, Sappho, was formed in Belfast in 1974. In the more public arena, a Woman's Conference on Lesbianism, attracting around eighty women, was held in Dublin in 1978, and a new network, Liberation for Irish Lesbians, emerged in the following year. Indeed, it could be argued that the link forged between lesbians and radical feminists greatly facilitated the confident articulation of public identity based on sexuality. For lesbian poet Mary Dorcey, for example, 'it was impossible to separate life as a lesbian from my life as a feminist . . . becoming a feminist gave me a tremendously strong self-image and a cultural context in which to be a lesbian'.[27]

Heterosexual couples in unhappy relationships also faced difficulties. A law enabling divorce on the grounds of irreconcilability was only passed in the North in 1978 (1968 in Britain), and even then the regional parliament introduced amendments which made it more costly and more time-consuming. Strongly opposed by both the Free Presbyterian and Catholic Churches, divorce was by no means an easy option. Even those without strong personal religious convictions, or who shrugged off the social stigma, could find the financial consequences of terminating a marriage an insurmountable barrier.

With the complete absence of divorce in the Republic, marriage breakdown was dealt with in other ways: desertion, for example, became increasingly common. One estimate in the 1970s put the number of deserted wives at 'between five and eight thousand, with a minimum annual increase of about five hundred'.[28] There is no doubt that in both parts of Ireland many women lived through the trials of failed marriages in varying degrees of unhappiness. One of the most common, yet least discussed, causes of marital unhappiness, and indeed of relationship problems in general, was abuse, mental or physical, usually inflicted by men on their female partners. Gwen, from New Mossley in Glengormley, County Antrim, who married at sixteen, told an all too typical story: 'I had just left school. He knocked my tooth out, broke another one, sunk his teeth in my leg, trailed me round the living room, wrecked the place. I had no money, no coal, no food.'[29] While domestic violence was not a new problem, it was one which was given increased publicity from the 1960s onwards. The rising wave of public anxiety on this issue came in response to in-depth research carried out by feminists and others concerned to highlight the serious nature and widespread prevalence of violence experienced by women within their own homes.[30]

WOMEN IN REPRESENTATIVE POLITICS

When Sheila Galvin won the by-election in Cork City for Fianna Fáil in February 1964, the *Irish Press* described her in patronising terms that were all too familiar:

> At 50 Mrs Galvin is still a very pretty woman. . . She neither drinks nor smokes. Since the sudden death of her husband four months ago she has been under great strain, but does not show it except when asked sudden and unexpected questions. Speeches do not as yet come easily to her, but she has the reputation in her district of having been an excellent worker for her husband and having a well-developed sense of politics . . .[31]

The prevalence of such attitudes meant that, in both parts of Ireland, women politicians, in any case making up only a tiny minority of political bodies, were unlikely to be taken seriously. Moreover, in the North, where constitutional politics were entering a period of protracted crisis, women's representation was not only limited, but also considered an irrelevant distraction. In 1962 women won 3 of the 52 contested seats to the regional parliament. Dinah McNabb, a member of the Orange Order, represented the UUP in North Armagh, and Elizabeth Maconachie (also UUP) and Sheelagh Murnaghan (Liberal) both represented Queen's University Belfast, which lost its franchise as a result of reforms in 1969. Murnaghan, a Catholic with a nationalist background, former president of Queen's University Literary and Debating Society and Northern Ireland's first woman barrister, was the only Liberal ever to serve in the Stormont parliament. A unionist with a small 'u', in 1965 she put forward a Bill that would have made it a criminal offence to discriminate on grounds of race, creed or colour. She also wanted to set up a human rights commission to investigate allegations of discrimination, but her proposals were firmly rejected by the Stormont government.[32] McNabb and Maconachie were unlikely to mount a challenge to their party, Ian Paisley, Jr. describing the UWUC as 'driven by the desire to be part of the team, to play their role in preserving and maintaining what was important to them. . . Feminism was seen by Unionists and Unionist women as pretentious and divisive.'[33]

Since the establishment of the regional parliament in 1921, a dozen MPs represented Northern Ireland at the Westminster House of Commons. The first woman to win one of these seats was Patricia Ford (UUP), who succeeded her father in North Down, serving only two years before her retirement in 1955. Florence McLaughlin, a member of the Executive Committee of the UWUC, sat at Westminster between 1955 and 1964. Despite the higher profile of women at Westminster more generally in the last three decades of the twentieth century, the only other woman to represent Northern Ireland there in this period was Bernadette Devlin, a 22-year-old nationalist, whose story is inextricably linked with the civil disturbances of the late 1960s, and will be discussed later.

Although there were only 3 female TDs out of a total of 144 in Dáil Éireann in 1970, positive action to increase women's participation was taken much earlier in the Republic. In that same year Margaret Waugh formed the Women's Progressive (later Political) Association (WPA), which aimed to encourage more women to join political parties, go forward for election and win seats, through a process of education and confidence-building. The association played a particularly important role in the general election of 1977, its slogan 'Why Not a Woman?' challenging traditional voting patterns. A landslide victory for Fianna Fáil, the election was seen as a

turning point for women. Although the proportion of seats held by women
rose to only 6 (4.1 per cent), there would be a continual rise from this point
on, reaching 11 (6.6 per cent) in 1981 and 14 (12 per cent) by the 1990s.
In 1979 Máire Geoghegan-Quinn became the first Irish woman to be
appointed to cabinet level since Countess Markievicz in 1919, when she was
made Minister of the Gaeltacht.[34] Given such slow progress, political
campaigner Gemma Hussey's later claim that women 'have to drag Ireland
kicking and screaming into the twentieth century' is understandable.[35] As in
earlier decades, family connections continued to determine the electoral
opportunities and ambitions of individual women, although Yvonne
Galligan observed that while twelve widows of former TDs were elected
between 1922 and 1977, the most common successor relationship after
1970 was that of daughter.[36] In order for women to make any dramatic
impact on parliament, however, the recruitment and selection policies of the
various main political parties would need to undergo substantial change.
Nonetheless, although legislation was piecemeal and *ad hoc*, some
liberalising trends could be identified in political legislation. In December
1972 the special position of the Catholic Church was removed from the
Irish Constitution after a popular referendum and with the broad support
of the Church itself – the first real indication that the rising tide of
secularisation, experienced in much of Western Europe, was beginning to
impact on the Republic. Three years later, the Supreme Court ruled that the
exemption of women was unconstitutional, and women were thereafter
liable to serve on the same basis as men.

  Individual women were also able to make a contribution to the world of
politics. For example, amongst the new voices emerging in the late sixties,
and destined to make an impact on the women of Ireland, was that of young
Catholic lawyer, Mary Bourke. When elected auditor of the Law Society at
Trinity College Dublin, she made a controversial inaugural speech, 'all about
how contraception, homosexuality and law must be kept apart',[37] and was
thereafter to continually question the role of the Church and the civil law
in enforcing personal morality. Elected to the Seanad in 1969, at only
twenty-five years of age, she used that body as a platform for debates on
human rights, and argued that Ireland needed to reject its insular Catholic
ideologies and become a more pluralist society. Progress of this nature, she
claimed, would also help heal the breach between North and South:

> We must change our legislation and be able to say to the people in the
> North of Ireland that they can come into the South of Ireland and find the
> same tolerance of different moral attitudes, the same tolerance of different

ideas, the same possibility of informing themselves on important medical and social matters and the possibility in their own privacy of following their own consciences in relation to family planning.[38]

The young senator married Protestant Nicholas Robinson in December 1970, but while she was arguing that 'the best way of overcoming prejudice against women is not to emphasise that you are a woman but to show that you can do a job efficiently and well',[39] women throughout Ireland were just beginning to organise and to assert their rights as women seeking justice in a male-dominated world.

THE WOMEN'S MOVEMENT IN THE REPUBLIC OF IRELAND

In recent years, historians have increasingly rejected the notion that Irish feminism was stagnant between the beginning of the First World War and the emergence of the Women's Liberation Movement in the 1970s. They have instead drawn attention to the different alliances and strategies employed by a range of groups concerned with highlighting gender inequalities. Thus, Linda Connolly forcefully argues that 'it was those organisations which existed for a long period before 1970 in an atmosphere hostile to feminism, which were crucial in maintaining a core cadre of feminists'.[40] One such organisation was the IHA, which in 1961 hosted the nineteenth Triennial Conference of the International Alliance of Women (IAW). With 350 women from 37 nations in attendance, the aim of the IAW – equality between the sexes – was given a high public profile in Ireland's capital city. Focusing on issues such as education, equal pay, inheritance law and women's pension rights, the IAW believed that its goals could be met through a combination of legislative reform and a more assertive and intelligent approach to problems by women themselves. Thus the president of the association, Ezlynn Deraniyagala, warned in her opening speech that individual women were all too often the major stumbling blocks to progress:

> . . . much remains to be done. We must learn to believe in ourselves and in our capacity to make fullest use of the rights we have won and are winning and to accept the responsibilities which come with them. We must realise the power we possess to make a significant contribution to the progress of the nation to which we belong.[41]

Women's lack of ambition was a constant theme at the congress, and one all too readily picked up by the media. But while the delegates' emphasis on individual responsibility and their strategy of trying to 'stretch the role of mother and housewife rather than abandon these concepts' underestimated the strength of patriarchal power structures, Amanda Lagerkvist argues that their work was nonetheless 'radical in their time and as they were situated'. By bringing gender issues into the public arena and working to raise the self-esteem of individual women, they provided a vital link between earlier campaigners for women's rights and the more impassioned activism of the following decade. Moreover, the intensive networking of the IHA, at both national and international levels, laid the foundations for further collective action. Consequently, in 1967, when the United Nations Commission on the Status of Women (CSW) issued a directive calling for research into women's situation and the setting up of national CSWs, Irish women in the Republic were in a strong position to respond. The IHA and the Association of Business and Professional Women took the initiative in forming an *ad hoc* committee comprising ten women's organisations to undertake research and lobby the government. Although the formation of the Republic's First Commission on the Status of Women in 1970 was also facilitated by the changing political climate as the country began to shed its insular image and respond to international influences, Connolly regards the 'rational, organised, active, strategic women's movement [as] pivotal in bringing about change'.[42]

The government had already overturned some of the worst injustices against women in family law. For example, an act of 1957 gave some property rights to married women, and legislation passed in 1964 recognised the equal right of a mother to educate and have custody of her children. The Succession Act of 1965 provided a widow with the statutory right to a share in the estate of her deceased husband.[43] In addition, and too often overlooked, women themselves had come out onto the streets to draw attention to 'bread and butter' issues. In November 1963, for example, 2,000 Dublin housewives marched in protest at the imposition of a tax on household necessities.[44] But the CSW, representing twenty-three women's organisations and chaired by Thekla Beere, the first woman to become a parliamentary secretary of a government department, continued to exert pressure for further progress. Recommendations in its first report, published in 1972, included the implementation of equal pay and legal mechanisms for combating sexual discrimination, the granting of maternity leave and the provision of day-care facilities for children of working mothers. The admission of the Republic into the EEC in 1973 brought external pressure to bear in at least some of these areas, and in 1974, an Anti-Discrimination (Pay) Act was passed, followed three years later by the Employment Equality

Act. The setting up of the CSW (later the Council for the Status of Women and now known as the National Women's Council) has been described as 'the epitome of liberal feminism in the women's movement', and it remains an important umbrella organisation.[45] However, from 1970, a new tradition was emerging – a clearly-defined, self-identified, feminist movement, which would provide Irish women with the analytical tools to begin to tackle the gender deficit.

The new women's movement should be seen in the wider context of the international climate of change and protest which witnessed the emergence of the civil rights movement, mass protests against the Vietnam War in America, and student demonstrations in major American and European cities.[46] Important, too, were the writings of Kate Millet and Germaine Greer, who offered an intellectual rationale to a generation of women beginning to question and revolt against their traditional social and political roles. June Levine was among those who would apply the new analyses and adopt the new strategies in Ireland. She later recalled that

> if one had been a mite more sensitive, it would have been possible to recognise the anger that was mounting under the surface as the decade [the 1960s] went on. It was female anger, subtle, veiled, but there. It was an anger the cause of which I only partly recognised or understood. It was a hang-over, an almighty international hang-over . . . I had looked with sympathy upon the oppression of the Red Indian, the American black, the Northern Ireland Catholic. Now here in Ireland I began to feel terribly, terribly angry.[47]

In 1970 Levine joined a group of like-minded women in the newly formed Irish Women's Liberation Movement (IWLM), which provided a focus for that anger and a powerful voice with which to challenge the institutions of oppression. The number of women within the new movement who had strong links to the media – Mary Maher and Mary Kenny were editors; Nell McCafferty, Mary Anderson, June Levine and Nuala Fennell were journalists; and Lelia Doolan was one of Ireland's few women television producers – guaranteed that their demands and actions were given a particularly high public profile. Early in 1971 they published a pamphlet entitled *Chains or Change? The Civil Wrongs of Irish Women*, listing six demands which it was felt were essential to break the chains of oppression: One Family, One House; Equal Rights in Law; Equal Pay Now and the Removal of the Marriage Bar; Justice for Widows, Deserted Wives, Unmarried Mothers; Equal Educational Opportunities; and finally access to contraception, which they considered a fundamental human right.[48] Kenny described the programme as 'entirely sensible, eminently reasonable and also eminently winnable', and, in retrospect, the demands do not seem particularly radical.[49] But even at this early stage, disagreement over the issue of contraception boded ill for future harmony, while the amount of publicity they received ensured that at least some of these issues raised alarm among the wider public.

The IWLM was famously launched on national television on 6 March 1971, with an entire programme of *The Late Late Show* devoted to discussing its manifesto. Despite the rather chaotic and rowdy nature of the debate which ensued, the message was successfully brought into the public domain. In the following month almost 1,000 women attended the IWLM's first public meeting in Dublin's Mansion House, and 28 branches were soon in existence. From the beginning, however, there were major tensions over both aims and strategies, and it was perhaps inevitable that the rapid increase in numbers would bring these to the surface and result in damaging rifts. The demands and actions of socialist and radical feminists tended to alienate those with more moderate ambitions for equal rights. For example, when on 22 May 1971 forty-seven women accompanied by journalists and television cameramen took the Dublin to Belfast train to buy condoms, which they distributed on their return, it was not only the customs officials who were embarrassed. Nuala Fennell later noted that 'The incident made press headlines the next day and greatly alarmed both the moderate elements within the movement and the ordinary women outside it. The outing was condemned from the pulpit by a priest who said it was "unworthy and undignified".'[50] Fennell also felt that those with other political agendas were exploiting the movement, and that one would have to be 'anti-American, anti-clergy, anti-government, anti-ICA, anti-police, anti-men' to remain within it. Liberal reformers such as Fennell began from this stage to shift their attention to the formation of self-help and single issue groups, while pressure groups focusing on contraception and abortion drew in the more radical strand.

Such groups were not, of course, new, but what was different about the agencies formed in the 1970s was their recognition and articulation of the structural problems which underlay women's oppression and their concern to give a voice, as well as opportunities, to those who were its victims. Anne McAllister, a founding member of AIM (Action, Information, Motivation) set up by Nuala Fennell when she resigned from the IWLM in 1971, described the first public meeting:

Women stood up and told their personal histories – overwhelming stories

Pictured outside Hall's chemist shop in Belfast's Great Victoria Street on 22 May 1971, these members of the IWLM made headline news by travelling to the North to buy contraceptives which they then freely distributed in the Republic, where they were banned.

about batterings, desertions, lack of maintenance, wives whose children were in the late teens and had never seen their fathers, women who had not been able to buy clothes for twenty years. For the first time women were standing and telling us that these things really did happen.[51]

The Dublin AIM group, which, among other things, offered advice on how to have a violent husband barred from the family home, went on to establish the Irish Women's Aid Committee, opening the first refuge for battered women in Ireland in April 1974. Domestic violence, long seen as something private, 'secret and unshareable'[52], was thus brought into the public domain. The emergence of Women's Aid centres in both parts of Ireland was to be critical, not only in providing an immediate escape route for women and their children, but in gathering statistical and other evidence of the degree and nature of the problem. With other highly publicised initiatives, such as the Reclaim the Night marches, Ailbhe Smyth commented that, at last, 'men's violence is being translated from the realm of the private and personal into the public arena where it is acknowledged as a major social problem'.[53] Even the traditional terminology was now rejected, as feminists argued that the word 'domestic' trivialised and privatised violence within the family. With the government also now more willing to intervene, further advances were made with the passage of the Family Home Protection Act in 1976 and the Family Law Act of 1981. The introduction of a Free Legal Aid Scheme in 1980 was also important in enabling abused women to pursue their rights. A similar combination of government action and female solidarity brought increased support to single mothers: a new national assistance benefit for deserted wives was introduced in 1970, and an Unmarried Mother's Allowance in 1973. The passage of the 1976 Family Law (Maintenance of Spouses and Children) Act was another significant step forward, and this financial and legal aid was complemented by the emergence of support groups such as ADAPT (Association for Deserted and Alone Parents) and CHERISH (Children Have Every Right In Society Here).[54]

Irishwomen United (IWU), formed in 1975, was a good example of the more radical feminist groupings. It was, explained Nell McCafferty, 'composed of trade unionists, professional women, and the unemployed, who had scarcely heard of motherhood. They insisted on self-determined sexuality and lived with women or men, as the fancy took them, with nigh a thought for marriage.'[55] Although itself fragmenting after 1977, IWU provided a forum for lesbians and radicals, and it was from the membership of this group that the Contraception Action Programme (CAP) emerged in 1979, with its members highlighting the injustice and hypocrisy of the law by handing out free contraceptives. The Women's Right to Choose group followed soon after and was successful in opening an Irish Pregnancy Counselling Centre in Dublin in 1980. The radical focus on rape and abortion, however, led to the emergence of counter-groups, such as Mná na

A papal visit

In October 1979 the Republic of Ireland witnessed massive popular excitement when Pope John Paul II arrived for a four-day visit. The greatest crowds of the century gathered to welcome him – at Drogheda, Knock, Galway, Limerick, and at Dublin's Phoenix Park, where over a million people attended mass on the morning of his arrival. The visit had been preceded by a huge clean-up of the city's graffiti and television cameras relayed events to watching millions. It was estimated that 200,000 people, nearly half of the Catholic population of Northern Ireland, journeyed to the Republic, and extra troops were drafted into border areas to ensure that these pilgrims could proceed to their destination without threat. The Pope was keen to speak specifically to the women of Ireland, reinforcing the Church's response to the changing times in which they found themselves. On the question of working mothers, for example, he urged

> Irish mothers, young women and girls, not to listen to those who tell them that working at a secular job, succeeding in a secular profession is more important than the vocation of giving life and caring for this life as a mother . . . I entrust this to Mary, bright Sun of the Irish Race.

At Limerick, he focused on the importance of 'traditional' family life:

> The Christian family has been in the past Ireland's greatest spiritual resource. Modern conditions and social changes have created new patterns and new difficulties for family life and for Christian marriage. I want to say to you; do not be discouraged, do not follow the trends where a close-knit family is seen as outdated. The Christian family is more important for the Church and for society today than ever before.

As John Paul acknowledged, however, times were changing, and while, in the aftermath of his visit, many of Ireland's women endeavoured to follow his guidance and embrace the values he extolled, the restrictions on personal freedom imposed by the Church were becoming an irrelevancy. Mary Kenny observed in retrospect that, 'from the start of the 1980s, the faith was faltering among the young Irish, and the notion of Ireland as a quintessentially Catholic country was fast receding'.

Irish Times, October 1979; Mary Kenny, *Goodbye to Catholic Ireland* (Dublin, 2000), p. 10

hÉireann, which picketed the counselling centre, and the Society for the Protection of the Unborn Child (SPUC), which gave a voice to more conservatively minded women.

Given the breadth of conflicting views, it is not surprising that when the Republic's government passed a Health (Family Planning) Act in 1979, which stated that contraceptives could be supplied to married couples on prescription 'for genuine medical reasons or bona fide family planning', this did not guarantee easy access. Many women remained constrained by their religious beliefs, while others found themselves reliant on the attitudes of individual doctors, nurses or pharmacists, who could refuse to co-operate with policies with which *they* disagreed on religious grounds. Nonetheless, despite these problems, the liberalising of the laws on contraception in the Republic marked a significant turning point in Church–state relations. Clearly, there were several different strands pushing in the same direction during this period. Pressure from the broad women's movement and from individuals such as Mary Robinson reinforced the liberalising influences of the EEC, the trade-union movement, and the UK government.

While feminism has by no means disappeared, it seemed to many people that it lost its initial impetus at an early stage. In October 1974, for example, the *Irish Times* decided to end its 'Women First' section, arguing that 'there no longer appears to be any justification to confine women's affairs to a purely women's section of the newspaper'.[56] While this was a particularly premature statement, others too felt that feminism had had its day, and wondered what it had achieved. Maeve Flanagan remembered that 'When Women's Liberation hit my home like a firecracker, long ago, it scared the living daylights out of me. It changed the country so very much and yet, in some ways, not at all.'[57] Feminists in the Republic would continue to challenge Church and state on a range of issues, but perhaps the greatest achievement of this early stage of activism was that by the end of the seventies women's issues were increasingly a matter of public discussion and debate.

NORTHERN IRELAND – A DIVIDED STATE

While Northern Ireland also witnessed the emergence of a 'women's movement', it is more difficult to separate this struggle from broader campaigns for social justice in the region in these years. The various strands were often tightly interwoven, as in the early twentieth century, and many women themselves would not have seen them as distinct or separate issues. For many activists, for example, female inequality was only one consequence of colonial oppression, while others, accepting the legitimacy of the state, saw the need for no more than gender reform in the liberal tradition. Issues of class and gender further compounded religious and political divisions. Cynthia Cockburn stresses that while both Catholic and Protestant working-class communities in Northern Ireland suffer poverty, violence and political neglect, women in these communities experience these things in distinctive, gendered ways.[58] Moreover, referring to women's inclusions in and admissions to, or exclusions from party politics (or socio-economic and cultural influence), Eilish Rooney argues that these are 'not the same for Catholic women as they are for Protestant women. They are not the same for working-class republican women as for middle-class nationalist women; for working-class loyalist women as for middle-class unionist women.'[59] These disparities and positions are reflected in the range of responses, contributions, and reactions to the constitutional, military, political and social problems of these years, and in the sensitivity to language and terminology consequent on differing interpretations. Wherever individual women stood on constitutional or gender issues, however, the ongoing political and military struggle ensured that a sense of urgency and emotion characterised all their activities.

Bob Purdie, in his aptly titled *Politics in the Streets*, traces the complex evolution of the civil rights campaign in Northern Ireland, identifying many different strands – labour, communist, republican – and demonstrating that, as with the women's movement, there was significant continuity from the earlier period of the state's foundation.[60] As we have already seen, successive unionist governments, perceiving the state to be under threat from both the South and from nationalists within its borders, survived and strengthened their position through a range of discriminatory practices. Those relating to housing particularly impacted on family life, with young Catholic couples frequently beginning their married lives with little hope of renting a place of their own. The problem was not uniform across the six counties, but was particularly bad in Derry and west of the River Bann, where unionists were numerically most vulnerable. From the early 1960s local newspapers in Dungannon, County Tyrone, were reporting on families living for years with their in-laws, or in 'rat-infested quarters and of as many as eight Catholic couples living in one house where they shared two cookers and two toilets'.[61] With such conditions drastically impacting on day-to-day life, some of these women were moved to take the initiative in demanding change in local housing policy. As one County Tyrone woman put it, of all the problems facing Catholics, discrimination in housing 'was the sorest, because it was always with you'.[62]

Poverty in Belfast

Visiting Belfast just before the onset of the conflict in 1969, sociologist Peter Townsend recorded his impression of living conditions in the poorer areas of the Northern capital:

> In my first visit to Belfast in 1968 (incidentally, just before the disorder and bloodshed that persisted right through the 1970s), I was struck not only by the evident poverty in Catholic and Protestant areas alike, but by scenes which seemed to belong more to the 1930s – of red-haired boys using scales on a cart drawn by an emaciated pony to sell coal by the pound, teenage girls in a second-hand clothing shop buying underslips and skirts, and some of the smallest 'joints' of meat in butchers' windows that I have ever seen. Here, as in the other areas, working conditions, housing and the immediate environment of the home were often raw and harsh. This is not to say, of course, that there were not also some superbly laid-out and well-kept homes, shops and workshops. But, by various of our measures, the deprivation in these areas was undeniable. Over two-thirds of families with children in the four areas had insufficient bedroom space, and over two-thirds declared that there was no safe place for their young children to play in near the home. Nearly two-thirds of all homes were said to suffer from structural defects, and as many as 86 per cent of the working men interviewed in the second stage of our surveys were found to have poor or bad working conditions (compared with 21 per cent in the United Kingdom as a whole).

> Peter Townsend, *Poverty in the United Kingdom: A Survey of Household Resources and Standards of Living* (Harmondsworth, 1979), pp. 58–9

In May 1963 a group of forty young Catholic housewives in Dungannon challenged their local council with a petition, and later took their protest onto the streets. The angry, pram-pushing women were given a significant degree of media coverage and their actions encouraged others to become involved in local politics. Within days, Conn and Patricia McCluskey formed the Homeless Citizens' League (HCL), and in the following year the Campaign for Social Justice (CSJ) was founded to encourage those who qualified to put their names on the electoral register. The importance of these new groups cannot be overstated: they injected vigour, optimism and enthusiasm into their practical leadership of a section of the community which seemed to have lost all hope of redressing the injustice of their situation. There was, however, a significant class dimension to the response of local Catholics. Conn McCluskey was a local GP; all ten male members of the CSJ were professionals, and the three female members were middle-class housewives. Patricia McCluskey, a former teacher who had invaluable experience of social work in the Glasgow slums and was first chairperson of CSJ, found it difficult to persuade her middle-class neighbours to participate in the early marches: 'I tried to get quite a few of my friends to join . . . they were right when they said that it was marching in to trouble . . . this was true as far as we were concerned.'[63] But although marching and picketing were not viewed as 'respectable' activities, they did attract more media attention than the abstentionist policies of the elected representatives of nationalism. Moreover, Jonathan Bardon argues that the HCL 'put together convincing evidence that local structures and practices were perpetuating inequality',[64] while Shannon claimed that Patricia McCluskey 'played a significant role in heightening the Catholic sense of grievance and in preparing large segments of the northern Catholic community to move beyond personal and local grievances to embrace the broader political ideology of civil rights'.[65] In May 1964, seven CSJ members stood as candidates for Dungannon District Council. Their slogan, 'Vote for Justice, Vote for the Team', won them four seats, with Patricia McCluskey one of the successful candidates.

With the formation of the Northern Ireland Civil Rights Association (NICRA) on 1 February 1967, the campaign broadened its base and its demands, calling for:

a universal franchise for local elections

'one man, one vote', instead of plural votes

the end of gerrymandering by redrawing electoral boundaries

the introduction of a compulsory points system for allocating public housing

the end of discrimination in local government employment

the repeal of the Special Powers Act

the disbanding of the Ulster Special Constabulary (B Specials)

Intense media interest and the strategy of lobbying Westminster MPs took the campaign over the heads of ministers at Stormont, to appeal to a wider and more sympathetic audience. The chair of the new organisation, left-wing veteran Betty Sinclair, claimed in an interview with the Irish Times that NICRA's programme was reformist rather than radical: 'I think it would be incorrect to put it down as revolutionary because the people concerned just want it to be a clearing house for claims over civil rights. There is nothing revolutionary about asking for civil rights.'[66] Both men and women were involved in NICRA and were keen to show how politics at this level affected the everyday lives of ordinary people, their experience and their opportunities. Derry city, which had a long history of gerrymandering as unionists sought to maintain political control over a nationalist majority, was also a city where women made up the majority of the workforce. Although known as the Maiden City, Nell McCafferty noted that, for women, it was 'all pedestal and no power':

> In Derry 5,000 families were on the waiting list for houses . . . the central demand of the civil rights movement was crucial to the quality of life for Catholic women, not that the men saw it that way. The demand of 'One Man, One Vote', designed to expose political gerrymandering, was based on housing.[67]

Given this background, it is unsurprising that it was the housing issue which brought about both an escalation in the number of protestors and a change in the strategies used. Derry Housing Action Committee, formed in September 1967, initiated numerous public protests and demonstrations, but it was the allocation of a council house in Caledon, County Tyrone, to Emily Beattie, a single, nineteen-year-old Protestant woman, secretary of a UUP candidate living in Armagh, which became the focus of real anger. Squatters led by Austin Currie, a local Nationalist MP, were evicted by police on 20 June 1968, and subsequent attacks on protesting marchers resulted in direct confrontations between nationalists and loyalists. By October, Catholics in Derry felt the need to protect themselves, and the Derry Citizens' Action Committee was formed in the home of Eileen Doherty in the middle of the Bogside. Barricades were erected in what became known as 'Free Derry', with locals holding out against the authorities for a total of nine weeks. Doherty remembers that

> the women didn't fight, but they made soup and sandwiches, gathered stones and broke up the pavements, then hauled the stones in wheelbarrows to the men in the Rosswell [Rossville] Flats, where they were holding the barricades. It was a community effort; without the women's help, the men couldn't have made it.[68]

International television coverage ensured that the problem would not go away, and parallels were drawn with the American civil rights movement. As early as 1962, Saidie Patterson had made the comparison, 'the colour bar in Ireland is between "Orange and Green" instead of "Black and White" ', and the *Dungannon Observer* had made a similar point in 1963:

> They talk about Alabama. Why don't they talk about Dungannon? Why don't they open their eyes and see what's going on here? Take the Killyman Road estate, for example . . . dozens of houses and not a Catholic to be found amongst them. It's a cut and dried case of religious discrimination.[69]

In line with other contemporary protest movements, university students took to the streets, and a new organisation, the People's Democracy (PD), was formed in Queen's University Belfast in October 1968. Its policy of mass marches, however, introduced a note of dissension into NICRA, with Betty Sinclair, in particular, anxious to avoid possible public conflict. Indeed, it became clear in the following months that the middle-aged moderates represented by Sinclair and the McCluskeys were considered by the new generation of activists to be out of touch with contemporary campaigning methods.

On 1 January 1969, PD led around eighty students on a march between Belfast and Derry. The marchers were stoned and heckled, and on the fourth day, at Burntollet Bridge outside Derry, they were attacked by a hostile crowd made up of supporters of arch-loyalist Ian Paisley and including members of the B Specials. Arguably a turning point in the history of Northern Ireland, it was undoubtedly so for many individual men and women. Dodie McGuinness, later a Sinn Féin councillor in Derry, described how she became politicised by these events: 'I was fairly open-minded then and had a lot of Protestant friends, but I saw those beaten, bloody students being brought into the hospital, and it changed my attitude. I began to get involved in the marches and protests.'[70] Trade-unionist Inez McCormack also recalls how that day fundamentally changed her life: 'I remember puzzlement and fear. Being hit.'[71] Loyalist sectarian violence had not, however, been unknown in recent years. In 1966, on the fiftieth anniversary of the Battle of the Somme, militant loyalists had reformed the UVF to combat republicanism and to topple Prime Minister Captain Terence O'Neill. In taking up office in 1963, O'Neill had expressed the view that 'bold and imaginative measures' were essential to building bridges between the two communities, and made an important symbolic gesture by inviting Taoiseach Sean Lemass to a meeting in the North two years later. But O'Neill's aspirations were not shared by more extreme representatives of Ulster unionism and the UVF expressed their opposition by throwing a petrol bomb into the UUP's party headquarters in May 1966. When a similar attack on a Catholic-owned Belfast pub went wrong two weeks later, Martha Gould, an elderly Protestant woman, was burned to death. Such violent attacks of sectarianism would become all too familiar in the years that followed, but it was a series of explosions that finally led to O'Neill's downfall. In the spring of 1969, public utilities were severely disrupted by the bombing of an electricity substation at Castlereagh and a pylon in County Armagh and the sabotaging of water pipelines in counties Antrim and Down. While it would later be proved that the attacks were the work of loyalists extremists, the authorities, as was intended, believed the IRA to be responsible, and in this rapidly deteriorating situation, the British government made the decision to send in the army.[72] On 21 April 1969, 1,500 British troops arrived in Northern Ireland, their remit to guard vital installations. A week later, O'Neill resigned and was replaced by Major James Chichester Clark. Regarded by fellow UUP members as a 'safe, compromise candidate', Chichester Clark lacked both the will and the nerve to deal with the situation, and riots continued through July and August. Derry and Belfast were particularly volatile, with many homes destroyed. It was reported that in Belfast alone during that summer, 1,820 families fled from their homes, 1,505 of them Catholic.[73] The army was first utilised in Belfast on Friday 15 August, and local Catholic residents welcomed them with cups of tea as an acceptable alternative to the armed Royal Ulster Constabulary (RUC). But this peaceful relationship was to be short-lived. When British troops began to target Catholic areas in their searches for arms and ammunition, a reinvigorated IRA came to be seen as the natural defenders of the Catholic population.

The breakdown of social, civil and political life came as a shock to many Protestant communities, particularly the middle classes who had remained unaware of or apathetic to the discontent which had been for so long simmering beneath the surface. Many Protestants had been brought up to believe that Catholics were controlled by their priests and were inherently disloyal, and as the Provisional IRA moved in to nationalist areas at first in defensive, but then in offensive mode, their fears appeared justified, the earlier actions of the UVF somehow forgotten. The Ulster Defence Association (UDA), a new militant loyalist group founded in September 1971, embarked on a murderous sectarian campaign, and with unionist politicians increasingly entrenched in their traditional positions and turning a blind eye to the actions of the loyalists, the stage was set for over thirty years of armed conflict.

One significant event in the political scenario was the rise of young Catholic nationalist Bernadette Devlin, who on 17 April 1969 won the by-election in Mid-Ulster, defeating Anna Forrest, the widow of the former UUP MP. At twenty-one years old, educated at St Bridget's Convent and

Bernadette Devlin, Britain's youngest MP, is to the forefront of this mural in Derry's Bogside, depicting opposition to British rule, c. 1969.

St Patrick's Academy, Dungannon, she had studied psychology at Queen's University for two years, and had risen to prominence among nationalists through her role in PD. In a 1969 interview with Mary Holland in the *Observer*, Devlin admitted the difficulties of the current situation: 'We're going to have a three-sided war. There will be Protestant bigots on one side, and Papist bigots on the other. And there will be a few, a very few, of us in the middle asking them to stop and they'll both hate us most of all.'[74] A passionate socialist, she believed that the war was not between Protestants and Catholics – 'It's a matter of the poorer class against the wealthy class.'[75] The impact of her new position as MP on her personal life was immediate:

> I have no private life left, because everything I do is news. Even what I eat for breakfast in the morning. Everything I say becomes worthy of note because I said it. Therefore, you've got to be perfectly sure that even in jest you don't make the kind of statement that could possibly fly to the other end of the earth and appear to mean what you didn't really want it to mean. It takes away a lot of the kind of ordinary freedoms that three weeks ago I could have enjoyed as an ordinary citizen.[76]

Both the national and the international press focused on her youth and her sex, describing her as, 'Cassandra in a mini-skirt' or 'Castro in a mini-skirt'. One UUP MP, Captain L.P.S. Orr, touring Canada and America in an attempt to scupper Devlin's fund-raising efforts for 'refugees of the Ulster crisis', referred to her as 'this wild irresponsible child who is a danger to any civilised society and who has left behind her a trail of human misery and suffering'.[77]

The discourse surrounding Devlin is remarkably reminiscent of the media response to those women involved in the Easter Rising or the Irish Civil War:

> Almost the entire British Press refused to take her seriously, ignoring her views or representing them as something of a joke. Fleet Street treated her like some kind of clockwork doll, an amusing diversion from the mainstream of parliamentary life: the general coverage of her early days as an MP combined sexism with patronising trivialisation and a refusal to see her in any other terms than 'swinging youth' and the then fashionable mini-skirt.[78]

Devlin herself was well aware that she was not being taken seriously: 'They [journalists] wanted to build me up into some sort of amiable freak, a sort of harmless grey-eyed figure of political fun, good for numerous photographs and non-political feature articles.'[79] The *Observer* on the other hand recognised her potential. When she began regularly appearing in Westminster, it was remarked that she used her position there 'with a confidence and wit which is making members of both sides of the house sit up and take notice'.[80] Devlin by no means confined herself to conventional political activities, however, and was to serve four months in Armagh Women's Prison for her part in the Battle of the Bogside in August 1969. Journalist and writer Susan McKay recalled how, when Devlin appeared on television in 1969, her grandfather would shout, 'There's one bad wee tinker', and there is no doubt that she was regarded with loathing by the loyalist community in the North.[81] Nor were they to limit their expressions of contempt to verbal abuse; Devlin and her husband would be seriously wounded in a UDA murder bid in 1981. Inez McCormack, who spent much of her time in the NICRA office, claimed that, 'apart from Bernadette, women did the typing. Feminism hadn't hit yet.'[82] This remark is disputed by Ann Hope, a former civil rights activist who relates detailed accounts of a wide range of dangerous, international and local activities carried out by women during these years.[83] Clearly, more research needs to be carried out on this turbulent period of the history of the North of Ireland.

However, women were soon to find themselves at the very centre of civil unrest. During a 34-hour-long curfew imposed by the military on Belfast's Falls Road in July 1970 and broken only by a 2-hour 'shopping' break, hundreds of women from outside the area collectively intervened. Knowing there was a shortage of food on the Falls, they marched onto the road; Marie Moore, from nearby Clonard, and later to become a Sinn Féin councillor and deputy Mayor of Belfast, was one of those involved: 'It was unbelievable the number who came. Most had a bottle of milk, bread, tins of food, nappies, whatever they had in their houses. One woman brought sticking plaster and germolene.'[84] It was also alleged that arms were concealed in some of the prams being pushed. The invasion of women's traditional domestic space by British soldiers searching for men, arms and ammunition in working-class nationalist areas also led to collective resistance. With men vulnerable to arrest or harassment when on the streets, women banded together in 'hen patrols', and took up what became a well-known strategy of banging bin lids, 'on a rota basis', to warn of army incursions into the neighbourhood. As Allen Feldman points out, such 'community-based resistance is centred on women as defenders of the neighbourhood, an expansion of their role as the defenders of the domestic space'.[85] In order to prevent the searching of homes by British soldiers, vehicles were burned and used to barricade streets. Inevitably, as the police and army treated all members of the Catholic community as potential terrorists, the communities responded with antagonism, fear and hatred, becoming even further alienated from the state.

This situation reached a climax in 9 August 1971 with the introduction of internment without trial. During dawn raids the army arrested 342 men whom they believed to be members of the IRA; no loyalists were lifted. On a day when eleven civilians were killed by lethal force, fifty-year-old Sarah Worthington, a Protestant shot by a soldier in her Ardoyne home in north Belfast, became the first woman to die in such circumstances in the current spate of violence.[86] Father Hugh Mullan, shot while administering the last rites to an injured man in west Belfast, became the first priest to be killed in the conflict. And Private Winston Donnell, shot at a road-block near Strabane, was the first member of the Ulster Defence Regiment (UDR) to be killed.[87] In the immediate aftermath of internment, 2,000 Protestants were left homeless and 2,500 Catholics left for refugee camps set up in the Republic.[88] Rather than reducing street violence, the 'distasteful weapon' of internment was counter-productive, resulting in the significantly increased recruitment of young Catholics into the IRA.[89]

The removal of so many men from their families proved life-changing for whole communities of women. Mothers were left with the sole responsibility of providing, caring for and disciplining their children, and with little choice but to battle for their economic survival: 'They were suddenly on their own, forced to cope, to become social security claimants in their own right, organising family care around prison visits, taking part in political protests.'[90] In an interview about the impact of the civil rights movement on women, Bernadette (Devlin) McAliskey later paid tribute to the contributions of 'ordinary women' to the political struggle:

> I think it got them out on the streets. I'd look not to the university movement, but to the women who were involved in the rank and file of civil rights marches and demonstrations . . . the Brigid Bonds, Mary Nelis's, Katherine Gallaghers and the women who, in fact, have no names. They were more militant than the men, more determined. They were a bigger thorn in the flesh of the local constabulary who had problems dealing maybe with the fact that they were women and that they were on the street.[91]

At least some of the wives, daughters, sisters and lovers of many internees, however, felt that they were making 'choiceless decisions'.[92] Thus, a 24-year-old mother of two small children stated that she

> didn't have much choice but to demonstrate. We were all in it together, they [friends, relatives and neighbours] would have thought I didn't care about my husband. And there was the army to remind me night and day. You couldn't forget that they had taken him away and that the government were to blame for the troubles.[93]

Prison visits became a regular part of family routine, interrupting children's schooling and stretching housekeeping budgets to their limits to provide small luxuries for the prisoners. There were other financial consequences to the conflict. While a rent and rates strike against government policies was supported at its height by more than 30,000 nationalist households, the government's response, in the shape of the 1971 Payment for Debt Act,

The Widow's Tale

Bullets don't whine
Close range
Bullets make loud flat sounds.

Jack's death sank like a stone
Into the well of yesterday's news.
A few ripples of sympathy
Marked the spot
Plus a riddled shirt.

Now he's a number on a notice board
Not my husband; kind father;
Just 3079.

And I'm left with a bullethole
In the mind
Plugged with Valium.

Margaret Curran, 'The Widow's Tale' (1987), in Angela Bourke, et al. (eds),
The Field Day Anthology of Irish Writing, vols IV and V,
Irish Women's Writing and Traditions (Cork, 2002), vol. V, p. 501

enabled benefits to be withheld from individual families. The loss of, for
example, their weekly family allowance was a severe blow to many women.
The republican network in the south of Ireland provided some financial
assistance. The records of Síghle Humphreys indicate that by February 1972
'more than two hundred and fifty families' in distress 'as a result of political
circumstances in Northern Ireland' had been sponsored.[94]

There were other pressures: women married to internees were conscious
that their actions would be observed and judged by members of their local
community; what they wore, how they dressed, where they went and with
whom, could be scrutinised for indications of disloyalty to their imprisoned
partner. The first loyalists were interned in February 1973, and the words of
a song of the period, supposedly spoken by a loyalist internee who has just
learned that his wife has been unfaithful, demonstrates that this was an issue

for partners on both sides of the community:

> I didn't think that my wife would be unfaithful,
> I always thought that she would play the game.
> But when they let me out of Long Kesh prison,
> I'll make her wish she'd never heard my name.[95]

Marilyn, wife of a loyalist internee, claimed that life was financially difficult, especially since the benefit system treated her as a single parent, despite the fact that she had to keep her husband supplied with parcels. Nonetheless, she revelled in her unexpected independence, declaring herself 'stronger than I ever was'.[96]

By 1971 disruptions to ordinary life had become almost routine in many areas, even for those whose family members were neither active nor imprisoned. Army patrols, traffic hold-ups and security searches became a daily fact of life, but there were much graver problems than the frustrations and resentment they generated. Those living in nationalist areas, in particular, lived with the dread of house raids by army or police; the wrecking of homes often accompanied by the removal of loved ones. Belfast and Derry city centres, and many rural towns and villages were subjected to destruction by car bomb or incendiary device, and with the targeting of pubs, shops, hotels and cinemas, nightlife ground to a standstill, though some communities were more vulnerable than others. By 1973, for example, 23 out of the 30 Catholic-frequented bars in north Belfast had been bombed by loyalists.[97] But 1972 was the most violent year of the conflict, with the killing of fourteen unarmed men by the Parachute Regiment in Derry on 30 January. Reaction to what became known as Bloody Sunday from local representatives of nationalism, the Catholic clergy, the Republic of Ireland and the wider international community was one of outrage. Bernadette Devlin was among those who rejected the attempts of British Home Secretary Reginald Maudling to defend the army's actions. During a debate in the House of Commons she accused him of lying, called him a 'murdering hypocrite' and slapped his face. Refusing to apologise, she later said, 'I didn't shoot him in the back, which is what they did to our people.'[98] The British government would continue to feel the repercussions of these killings for many years, but in the short term the decision was taken to transfer control of the security forces from Stormont to Westminster. The refusal of the Ulster Unionist government to accept this loss of power led to its suspension on 28 March, and the introduction of Direct Rule. Catholics welcomed the fall of the Protestant regime, and talks between republicans and constitutional nationalists took place behind the scenes. But a truce called by the Provisional IRA on 26 June was short-lived, ending on 9 July when the army clashed with Catholics in Lenadoon, a housing estate in west Belfast. Previously Lenadoon had been under threat from the UDA. A total of 81 Catholics and 40 Protestants died during the course of the year as a result of assassinations carried out by both loyalist and republican paramilitaries, and bombs continued to disrupt daily life. For civilians, a visit to relatives or a day in the office could all at once become a nightmare experience. On Friday 21 July, for example, when twenty-two bombs exploded in Belfast over a period of twenty minutes, at an average rate of one a minute, confusion and panic were rife. Rhoda Watson was working in a city centre office, 'and we, the staff, were scared and shaking. Hysteria hovered and threatened to overwhelm. Every explosion was greeted with muffled screams and sobs.'[99] In the course of the day, 7 people were killed at a bus station, 4 at a shopping centre, and 130 were injured, some severely mutilated. With the escalating violence, relations between the state and the nationalist community continued to deteriorate and attempts to find a political solution, for example at a conference held at Darlington in September, came to nothing.

For their part, the loyalist community regarded every step of even the most gradual and limited reforming programme as a concession to the 'disloyal' minority. One weapon, which they effectively employed as a form of protest, was the industrial strike, which aimed to demonstrate not only the degree of solidarity among the Protestant working class, but the extent of its control over industrial and commercial life. General strikes were called in March 1972, to protest against the dissolution of Stormont, in February 1973, when the first loyalists were interned, and in May 1974, to bring down the latest government initiative, the power-sharing Executive. Co-ordinated by various paramilitary groups, and involving roadblocks, power cuts and factory closures, many ordinary people were powerless to challenge the Ulster Workers' Council (UWC) call to strike action. Apart from direct intimidation, particularly of moderate Protestants in working-class areas, power cuts, the lack of transport and the absence of any intervention by the state forces, ensured the effectiveness of the strike. Some loyalist women made their contribution through Women's Action, a group formed to support the UDA and loyalist political prisoners. The Protestant paramilitary leadership later stated that the importance of their work had not been sufficiently acknowledged.[100]

The 1974 UWC strike impacted strongly on the entire community; Protestant Jean McMinn recalled:

That was when I realised that there was some force which was protecting the tradition I was supposed to be brought up in. There were barricades at the bottom of the road and huge rallies at Stormont, which was just around the corner from where we lived.[101]

It was mostly housewives who bore the brunt of the disruption: Sharon, in Anne Noble's short story, 'A Riot', grumbled,

We'll have to queue up to get some bread and milk when they allow the shops to open for a couple of hours after lunch . . . I bet the people who started all this don't have to queue for their stuff. I'm sure it wouldn't last long if they had to suffer.[102]

But although many Protestants resented the notion that the UWC was acting on their behalf, a newspaper photograph of loyalists celebrating the fall of the Executive showed hundreds of gleeful placard-waving women, signalling another victory on one side, another setback on the other.

Women's active involvement in the conflict was also evident in republican paramilitary circles. Cumann na mBan, still in place as the women's wing of the IRA, underwent significant expansion in these years. Young women were recruited at street barricades and moved from stone-throwing to training in surveillance and the use of weapons. 'A smaller organisation than the men's and more tightly knit', this movement attracted well-educated young women from respectable middle-class families.[103] However, many of this new generation, highly politicised by current events, demanded a more central involvement, and responded quickly when the IRA itself began to recruit women. A married woman volunteer told how this changed her lifestyle:

The home, marriage and children, although very important to me, are all incidental to my commitment to the struggle. When I first joined the movement I was in Cumann na mBan but I wasn't content with the limited contribution which I thought it offered me. I wanted to fully participate in operations. As a woman revolutionary, I believe that our liberation as women must go hand in hand alongside the armed struggle, so for me I find it somewhat contradictory to have a separate organisation solely for women when the IRA seemed the most obvious direct channel, so I joined it. But Cumann na mBan still provide an essential back-up as regards the aspects in intelligence and communications etc., and with supporting operations.[104]

Women's potential value in guerrilla warfare was undeniable, particularly in surveillance work and in transporting explosives, when they could exploit traditional sensitivity to their gender. While seemingly pregnant women or pram-pushing mothers provided an ideal cover for the movement of weapons, IRA commander Seán Mac Stiofáin claimed that, 'Some of the best shots I ever knew were women. So were the best intelligence officers in Belfast. From that time [1971] women were admitted on a basis of full equality with men, as in the Israeli, Chinese and certain other armed forces.'[105] Female sexual attraction could also be a weapon, as was graphically evident when two young republican women lured three off-duty soldiers to their deaths in March 1973.[106]

However, some female volunteers have disputed the degree of gender equality within the organisation, particularly in the lower ranks, arguing that they had to work much harder than the men in order to 'prove' themselves.[107] Although the ratio of women to men was low, women did engage in all areas of IRA activity. Maria Maguire, for example, spent a year working with the Provisionals, taking part in an important arms-buying mission.[108] Dolours and Marion Price participated in a bombing campaign in London in which 180 people were injured. There were many others, but the woman to reach the highest paramilitary rank was Maire Drumm, a mother of five whose husband had spent thirteen years in internment camps. She was deeply committed to the militant republican movement and was vice-president of Sinn Féin from October 1972 to 1976. She had replaced the imprisoned Ruairí Ó Brádaigh as president in 1971–2, and at once declared her intentions: 'We have levelled Belfast before and we will do it again if necessary. We will never stop until we get what we want and if our men are prevented from doing it the women will do it for them.'[109] Her public militancy would ensure that she too spent time behind bars.

The media responded with predictable outrage to the 'frightening cult of the violent women', labelling them as 'fanatics'.[110] Republican women prisoners held in Limerick were referred to as 'caged cats', the terror of the prison staff.[111] Drumm was compared by Secretary of State Merlyn Rees to 'the knitting harridans of the French Revolution'.[112] Bill Rolston, discussing the depiction of women in novels about the conflict since 1969, asserts that 'the explanation of women's violence is always on the emotional level'. The fictional stereotypical representations that he analyses are equally applicable in the non-fictional world. The gendered treatment of women paramilitaries ignores 'rational and committed participation in armed struggle'.[113] Marion Price, in a letter to her mother written in 1974 while she was on hunger strike in Durham prison, explained:

> Of course I hate the suffering you are all going through and I would take
> that away if I could . . . I'm not being morbid but sometimes we achieve

more by death than we could ever hope to living. We dedicated our lives to a cause that is supremely more important than they are.[114]

Women involved in such actions were particularly vulnerable to violent death. The first two female republican volunteers to die on active duty – Dorothy Maguire and her sister Maura Meehan – were shot in Belfast on 23 October 1971 by British soldiers as they travelled in the back of a car heading towards the Lower Falls while on their way to warn residents of an impending raid. They were the first of many. Others died when the explosives they were carrying or planting exploded prematurely. And in 1976 two loyalist gunmen, dressed as doctors, murdered Maire Drumm while she was recovering from an eye operation in a Belfast hospital.

Although much more difficult to trace in the records, loyalist women also participated in paramilitary activities. In 1972, Jean Moore, chairwoman of the women's department of the Loyalist Association of Workers, told *Spare Rib* that its work mainly consisted of

helping our women to learn to drive – in the case of civil war we'll need as many drivers as possible. We're really working on the same scale as the UDA and the Army . . . if a civil war comes, it doesn't mean everybody's going to run to the front line – there's going to have to be people left behind to organise children, old people, things like that.[115]

A leading official in the UDA also claimed that women's contribution was confined to 'welfare work and first aid'.[116] According to another source, however, women were engaged in moving weaponry, supplying safe houses, and 'on many occasions, were directly involved in all aspects of paramilitary activity'.[117] The most savage example of this was the killing of Ann Ogilby, beaten to death by two teenage women in a UDA club in loyalist Sandy Row in Belfast, while her child was held nearby. Lacking the structural coherence and historical lineage of Cumann na mBan,[118] the loyalist Women's Unit appears to have been largely inactive since the 1980s. Lily, a former member and deeply bitter about her experiences, claims that within the UDA 'men dominate completely'. Though much of the recent history of female loyalism remains hidden, the patriarchal nature of Protestant working-class society seems to impact on all aspects of life.

Women who supported the constitutional legitimacy of the state of Northern Ireland also had outlets for active engagement. The UDR, formed in 1970 to replace the B Specials (and quickly becoming an overwhelmingly Protestant force), began to recruit women in 1973. It was considered that women were essential, not only for clerical duties and to operate radios and telephones, but to counter the activities of female terrorists. Five hundred women joined in the first year and were trained, not in the use of arms, which they were not permitted to carry, but 'in drill, how to report incidents, map reading, driving, field craft, first-aid, anti-ambush procedures, the formation of vehicle and personnel checkpoints and procedures for searching'.[119] Although as a minority within the security forces they were likely to encounter traditional male prejudice,[120] women also joined the RUC and the RUC reserves. Directly involved in daily conflict situations, a total of ten RUC and UDR women lost their lives in the course of their work.

This is not the place to revisit the catalogue of deaths and injury, kidnappings and beatings, suffered by men, women and children.[121] Images of death and destruction dominated the news, with sobbing wives and mothers following a seemingly endless series of funeral processions. It was not only members of the security forces and paramilitary organisations who were targetted, but all who associated with them. Much of the killing was sectarian, much of it indiscriminate; many despaired, finding relief in tranquillisers or alcohol. Despite the widespread trauma and distress among the population, no attempt was made by the authorities to provide a counselling service – as Pauline Prior remarked, 'How many thousands of people in the towns and cities of Ireland have been exposed to gunfire, bombs and riots without any help in coping with the stress except for that provided by their family?'[122] Perhaps even more worrying was the extent to which the situation eventually became 'normalised', with militarisation and all its consequences accepted as part of everyday life. Fionnuala Ní Aoláin argues that this normalisation was in fact part of the government's strategy of dealing with the conflict by changing its external terms of reference: 'By criminalising the actions of those engaged in violence or subversiveness against the state . . . any legitimisation for violence was removed.'[123]

Many men and women were already imprisoned, with or without trial, as a result of their engagement, or suspected engagement, in the conflict. The first woman to be interned, on 29 December 1972, was Liz McKee, and by the end of 1973, 60 women were among the 650 republican internees. Both male and female detainees won special category status in 1972, after a thirty-day hunger strike. This status gave political prisoners the right to wear their own clothes and to free association; they were not required to work and were allowed extra visits and food parcels. These arrangements enabled the structures of paramilitary command to be maintained within the prison walls. One ex-prisoner remembered:

> Each morning at ten a.m. the OC came in and we had cell inspection and had to stand to attention. Then we did drill in the yard for fifteen to twenty minutes, and the screws left us alone and never bothered us. If we wanted anything like writing paper we would go to the OC and ask her to put in our request to the screws. It was like a holiday camp.[124]

Eileen Hickey claimed that military-style activities were 'very important in keeping the women together. It kept them aware that they were soldiers. In Armagh, you could feel so far removed from the movement, from the struggle outside.'[125] Republican volunteer Mairead Farrell confirmed that during her time in prison she 'learned a lot of self-discipline and the importance of strength and resolve',[126] and like the Price sisters, she also continued her academic education there. Those serving their time in English prisons had no such support. The fifteen years to which Áine and Eibhlín Nic Giolla Easpaig were sentenced in 1975, for example, were made much more difficult by their forced exile from family and friends. Moreover, the two sisters protested throughout their long imprisonment that they were not guilty of the charges of conspiracy to cause explosions with which they had been convicted. Eibhlín, who argued that she had 'clear proof' that she was totally innocent, claimed that the authorities, the security forces and the media made sure that their 'show trial' in Manchester determined the public lack of sympathy for their situation.[127]

As part of its policy of criminalisation, however, the government ended special category status for everyone sentenced after 1 March 1976. This meant a considerable change in prison conditions and experience in Northern Ireland; inmates were treated as common criminals, locked up at night in their cells, and ordered to go to work in the mornings. A campaign to reverse this situation, undertaken by both men and women, would culminate in the blanket protests and hunger strikes of the next decade. With internment also phased out by 1976, maintaining a high public profile on the issue of prisoners became even more critical. Four Derry women formed the Relatives' Action Committee (RAC) to support both the prisoners and each other. As Mary Nelis recalled, 'It was wonderful to get together each week, and know that you were talking to a group of women who understood what you were going through.'[128] Through street theatre, propaganda murals and public protests, members of the RAC ensured that the situation of prisoners remained under the spotlight, and became experienced political activists in the process. Women supporters of loyalist prisoners were similarly engaged in street protests on behalf of their men; their constant and noisy presence outside Crumlin Road jail and courthouse a continual reminder to the authorities of the unpopularity of their policies at grass-roots level.

In the early years of the conflict women internees had regarded themselves as being on equal standing with their male counterparts; as Theresa put it: 'There was no thought about women and feminism then; the idea then was the unity of Ireland. I never thought of myself then as being unequal with men.' For Theresa and others, this assumption was soundly shaken when in 1975 the Povisional IRA negotiated a truce with the British government without reference to or consultation with the women prisoners. 'It was then,' she said, 'that we realised we were women . . . we had been fighting and we were told to shut up.'[129] Gender continued to define power relations both inside and outside the prison walls.

THE WOMEN'S MOVEMENT IN THE NORTH

The emergence of a feminist movement in Northern Ireland, unrelated to the civil rights struggle, can be traced to 1971 when Joyce McCartan and Lynda Edgerton were among a group of women from Belfast's Ormeau Road who protested against the decision of Margaret Thatcher, then Minister of Education, to stop free school milk for children over the age of seven. Marching, picketing and lobbying were the tactics employed, with the women on one occasion borrowing two cows from the Ulster Farmers' Union for a demonstration at the city hall.[130] Despite winning the support of Belfast City Council, this campaign, which focused on the welfare of working-class families, was ultimately unsuccessful, and the introduction of internment took attention away from such purely social issues. A couple of years later, however, female staff and students from the University of Ulster at Coleraine joined local women to draw attention to the issue of domestic violence, while a weekend of feminist films organised by a group of women meeting at Queen's University resulted in the formation of the Northern Ireland Women's Rights Movement (NIWRM). Formed in 1975, the new movement aimed 'to spread a consciousness of women's oppression and mobilise the greatest possible numbers of women on feminist issues'.[131]

An immediate focus for its campaigning activities was to call for the extension of Britain's 1975 Sex Discrimination Act to Northern Ireland. This was part of wider international agitation for women's social, political and legal rights and it resulted in similar successes – the Equal Pay (NI) Act had been passed in 1970. The Sex Discrimination (NI) Order was passed in 1976 and the Equal Opportunities Commission (EOC) was set up in the North in the same year. The EOC was seen as particularly helpful by those feminists and trade unionists for whom the right of women to work, and to be given opportunities and rewards equal to those of their male colleagues, was considered a fundamental entitlement. But in a movement that encompassed a diversity of political allegiances and aspirations, which involved academics, trade-union and civil rights activists, communists, unionists and republicans, and which operated in the context of intense civil unrest, tensions were bound to surface. As Monica McWilliams recalls, the political identities of many Northern Irish women were 'born of the immediate experience of social injustice, rather than as a consequence of a pre-existing ideological belief'.[132]

The NIWRM attempted to distance itself from the wider political and military struggle, declaring itself to be non-aligned on the constitutional issue, though expressing opposition to emergency repressive legislation and condemning paramilitary violence as well as excessive use of violence by the security forces. The organisation defended itself from accusations of complicity with the state:

> We have condemned the British army on many occasions . . . we have decided to work for a women's movement independent of political parties and political positions. The refusal to take up positions on these general questions is not because we fear disunity and conflict: we believe that sticking to feminist issues is the best way to achieve feminist ends . . . the fact that . . . women prisoners are demanding political status does not make it a feminist issue any more than the fact that Cumann na mBan exists makes a United Ireland a feminist aim.[133]

Such a stance was, however, unacceptable to those nationalists for whom the women's struggle was inseparable from the overall context of colonial oppression. Debates over the extension of British legislation to Northern Ireland thus involved broader consideration than one's position on abortion or employment law and led to lengthy and heated exchanges. Support for women political prisoners, all of whom were republican in 1975, was a particularly emotive and divisive issue, which would dominate much of the 1980s.

As in the Republic, though perhaps with a greater degree of bitterness, the Northern women's movement fragmented. Those who aimed to combine their prior commitment to socialism with feminist and nationalist concerns formed the Socialist Women's Group in 1975, dissolving two years later with many members reuniting in the Belfast Women's Collective.[134] Women Against Imperialism and the RAC provided forums for campaigns more closely linked with the rights of political prisoners. As Pauline Jackson suggests, it is perhaps not surprising that given the unresolved national political issues, the Irish women's movement did not produce the same separatist and autonomous character as that elsewhere.[135] Even single issue support groups found their work affected by the wider political context. Derry Women's Aid, for example, was criticised for speaking out against the tarring and feathering of women by paramilitary groups.[136] While the European Court of Human Rights introduced protection and exclusion orders to Northern Ireland in 1980, giving women a degree of legal protection from violent partners and the right to remain in the matrimonial home, the wider context of social conflict again rendered the situation more complex and made solutions even more difficult to attain. In areas where republican paramilitaries operated, for example, calling on the state police for help was not an option. Similarly, the authorities were often reluctant to respond to calls from areas they considered hostile. In addition, as Monica McWilliams and Joan McKiernan have commented, 'Public attention emphasising the violence resulting from the 'Troubles' makes it more difficult to attract the necessary resources and public concern for the problems associated with other forms of violence.'[137] For its part, the Women's Aid movement disliked what it termed the hierarchical structure of the NIWRM, that it had a committee and a chairperson rather than a looser, more democratic grouping. Women's Aid was also more overtly radical in nature, interested in women's liberation rather than women's equality issues. Against the inclusion of men in the organisation, it eventually withdrew from the NIWRM which actively lobbied male trade unionists.

Commentators have frequently noted that nationalists and republicans dominated the women's movement in the North in this period. It is certainly true that those who came from a tradition that was vehemently opposed to the political establishment would have found in radical feminism a more coherent political agenda. Similarly, as Eilish Rooney comments, 'the historical accommodation between republicanism and feminism, and the links between feminism and opposition or liberation politics also pose a challenge to unionist ideology'.[138] 'Julie', brought up in Protestant east Belfast, explained why she found the women's movement alienating:

> I went to a Protestant church school, I was brought up with that culture. Our perceptions were different. In the women's movement it was not possible to express it. The only experience that was valued was of the down-trodden Catholic woman.[139]

Fermanagh woman Ruth Moore, discussing the need to 'transcend sect-arianism and the imposition of a one-size-fits-all identity', described how

> As a Protestant woman she experienced her identity as other to English women and the British state, other to Catholic women and Catholic domination in Ireland as a whole, and other to Protestant men in Northern Ireland.[140]

Moreover, once the conflict was under way, with religion, however simplistically, seen as determining national aspirations, it became difficult for more liberal Protestants to openly associate with those perceived to be Catholic/nationalist/republican. The sectarian nature of the conflict, particularly in the early years, also limited active co-operation across the boundaries of segregated communities. While individual women from Protestant backgrounds were undoubtedly involved in the women's movement, their lack of visibility and acceptance in their own communities, together with limited documentation of their experiences, means they are often overlooked. And according to Rooney, 'a debate over female identity within unionism or the possibility of unionism accommodating any form of feminism did not take place until the early 1990s'.[141]

It is important, too, not to underestimate the high value placed on traditional family values in both states, which would help explain the rejection of feminism among the wider population of women. Pearl, a former factory worker from north Belfast, expressed her pleasure in being able to remain at home when her first child was born:

> I was privileged enough to be able to be a housewife. People don't realise the pride you can take in having perfectly polished windows and dinner in the oven for your husband when he comes home. There is a freedom in that. It shouldn't be downgraded.[142]

The resistance of many such women indicates again the diversity of female aspirations, expectations and experiences. On the other hand, McWilliams cites as an example of Northern Irish Women from all shades of the political spectrum finding common purpose, the campaign to free Noreen Winchester in 1976. Winchester had been sentenced to seven years' imprisonment for killing her abusive father, who had repeatedly raped her since childhood. Turned down by the Court of Appeal, she was freed by royal pardon in 1977 – the case demonstrating the potential power of female solidarity.[143]

PEACE MOVEMENTS

During this protracted period of conflict the activism of a number of men and women, from different class, political and religious backgrounds in the

North, focused on campaigns for peace. But sustaining a pacifist position in an atmosphere of bitterness, anger and despair, and against a backdrop of sectarian murder, militarisation and political stalemate, proved no easy task. Most campaigners defined peace as an end to violence, either making their own assumptions about the political context of any resolution or evading the question altogether. So that while many people felt emotionally drawn to the idea of peace there was no agreed agenda to enable them to move their aspirations forward. Such activities were thus easily dismissed as unacceptable, oversimplistic or naive.

Nonetheless, even during the darkest days of the conflict, there were individuals on the ground who managed to sustain relationships across traditional sectarian boundaries. May Blood, a Protestant trade unionist working during the seventies in a Belfast mill which employed a majority of Catholics, recalled that: 'The girls in the Mill showed support for each other time after time . . . during tense periods, usually following some bad incident or whatever, the Catholic workers would have escorted us out of the Mill and up the road to safety.'[144] Though it was not easy to maintain such relationships in a climate of fear and hostility, many others had similar tales to tell. Indeed, with individuals often targeted by gunmen on their way to their place of employment, the importance of the trade-union movement, both collectively and in terms of individual efforts, in challenging both the political status quo and working–class sectarianism is a neglected area of study.

Anxiety about the safety of family members combined with anger to prompt spontaneous outbursts of protest against hijackings or murders. On 25 May 1972, for example, 400 mothers marched to the Derry office of Official Sinn Féin to protest against the Official IRA's killing of a nineteen-year-old Derry man who was a soldier in the British army. The resulting organisation – Derry Peace Women – won local support from both Catholic and Protestant women, as well as the clergy.[145] Women Together for Peace began in 1970 with a few women in east Belfast walking the peace line every evening and at weekends, eventually canvassing troubled areas such as Turf Lodge, Shankill Road and Falls Road, Ballymurphy and Ardoyne. Among the original organisers was Ruth Agnew, who had worked as a cleaner in the gasworks for thirty years and who was elected the group's first president, Monica Patterson, an English Catholic living in Ireland, and Jean Carson, who became the organisation's full-time paid organiser.[146] Over 500 women attended the first public meeting on Saturday 13 January. The Women Caring Trust was formed by Patricia Ford, Lady Fisher, in 1972; and Cecil Lenehan and Elizabeth Benton, two Catholic mothers, founded the

Women signing a peace petition in Derry's Bogside and Creggan
areas in May 1972, the bloodiest year of the conflict.

interdenominational All Children Together. Peace rallies, marches and prayer
meetings were held regularly, particularly at times of paramilitary truce.
Local peace committees were set up in many areas and International
Women's Day 1975 was given over to a peace rally. The UWUC organised a
peace petition, collecting over 95,000 signatures within a week on a
document that called for a restoration of peace, 'coupled with the assurance
that the Government maintained the democratic right of the Ulster people
to remain British Citizens'.[147]

Although most peace activists declared themselves, to be, as Women
Together put it, 'not political, just sick of violence', the religious make-up
of groups or their source of funding inevitably led to their identification
with one or other of the political/religious communities.[148] In a country

dominated by politically inspired violence, movements for peace could not be isolated from other loyalties or allegiances. When, in April 1972, around 100 women gathered in a school in Andersonstown in west Belfast to demand peace following the killing of Martha Crawford, a 39-year-old mother of ten who had been caught in a gun battle on her way to the shops, they were outnumbered by other women, young men and girls, who cheered the Provisional IRA and argued that the fight must go on. In February 1973 when women from Dublin, Killiney and Wicklow travelled to Belfast to meet with Belfast Peace Women for a conference on public welfare, a bomb was left in the Wellington Hotel, where they were to meet, and they were forced to adjourn to nearby Fisherwick Presbyterian Church.[149] The office of Women Together was bombed in 1976, and peace activists more generally were frequently castigated for not condemning the actions of the British army on Bloody Sunday.[150] As Marie Callaghan points out, a range of factors, including 'fundamental structural inequalities . . . [and] gender conditions, in an increasingly polarised and militarised society, ultimately left [women] little political power or "room to manoeuvre"'.[151]

In August 1976, however, it looked as though the cause of peace had captured popular imagination. On 10 August, housewife Anne Maguire was walking with her four children when the getaway car of a gunman shot dead by the British army crashed into them. Two of the children died instantly, and another the following day. Anne Maguire herself was seriously injured, and though she recovered, she committed suicide four years later. Her sister Mairead Corrigan,[152] and housewife Betty Williams, married to a Protestant, began a campaign for peace which became a focus for the great upsurge of anger and distress following the tragedy which touched the hearts of many because, as Betty Williams, remarked: 'We believe that what happened to the Maguire family on Monday could have happened to any one of us women out walking with our children.'[153] The response to the women's call for support took everyone by surprise. Thousands gathered to sign petitions and join the Peace People. Twenty thousand attended rallies in Belfast's Ormeau Park and on the Shankill Road during that first month. Twenty-five thousand turned up in Derry in September, and marches held every weekend in the different cities of Northern Ireland and England until the end of December continued to attract large crowds and massive media attention. Catholics and Protestants embraced each other at peace rallies, as the frustration and despair of years was channelled into a wave of hope and optimism. Marches attracting large numbers were also held in towns and villages throughout the Republic of Ireland; on this issue at least, common cause could be found.

A royal visit

Early in August 1977, Queen Elizabeth II and the Duke of Edinburgh staged a royal visit to Northern Ireland, an occasion which warranted the deployment of some 32,000 troops, 'possibly the biggest on–the–ground show of strength by the security forces ever seen in Northern Ireland'. Hardly the most encouraging of omens for the first visit by the reigning monarch in eleven years. That the visit coincided with the run–up to the anniversary of internment did not help matters. While the Queen and the Duke entertained at Hillsborough Castle, an army major was shot and seriously wounded during riots around the black flag march on Belfast's Falls Road. A bomb blast at the New University of Ulster, which the Queen had visited the previous day, also reflected republican opinion of the royal couple. On the other hand, around 30,000 loyal well–wishers watched the arrival of the Royal Yacht *Britannia*, and the *Belfast Telegraph* commented on the 'warmth, colour and spectacle' surrounding the visit.

Irish Times, 4 August 1977; *Belfast Telegraph*, 4 August 1997

The Peace People was a movement borne of emotion and, like every other organisation in Northern Ireland, was prone to attack from all sides of the religious and political divisions. The international media portrayed the Peace People as courageous, and undoubtedly played a manipulative role in determining the popular shape of the movement. But closer to home they were described as naive, irrelevant and counter-productive. Bernadette Devlin claimed they were 'dangerous', because they 'had the potential of dulling women's political consciousness'.[154] Marchers met with hostility on the Falls Road; an attempt was made to petrol bomb Betty Williams's house; and the Unionist-dominated Belfast City Council refused to honour Williams and Corrigan with a civic reception when they returned to Belfast after receiving the Nobel Prize for Peace in 1976. Damaging internal arguments, especially over how the Nobel money would be spent, divisions over organisation and direction, and growing popular disillusionment, saw the movement shrink from 136 groups at it peak to 23 by 1980. While individuals and organisations continued to work for peace in their localities, fundamental political issues had to be addressed before real progress would be possible.

Although it has often been claimed, somewhat controversially, that woman's ability to conceive and reproduce children gives her 'an innate aversion to war and violence', women are no more united on the question of peace than on any other issue. As Harriet Alonso comments, 'motherhood is only one aspect of a distinct woman's perception',[155] and, as we have seen in the Northern Ireland context,

> Passive victims of the troubles, viragos of the barricades, advocates of a messianic peace . . . none of these stereotypes reveal the true situation of women living in a socially deprived, war-torn, rigidly patriarchal society.[156]

CONCLUSION

Women on both sides of the Irish border faced similar problems during these decades, their lives constrained by a range of factors – political, legal, religious and socio-economic. International influences, liberalising policies and women's own agency were among the components pushing for change in a period that witnessed both challenges and counter-challenges to the status quo. The early seventies, in particular, were highly significant, not only in making women's position in Irish society, North and South, a live issue, but in raising the consciousness of ordinary women. Maeve Flanagan described how reading Mary Kenny's page in the *Irish Press* and watching the IWLM on *The Late Late Show* had impacted on her mother, and disrupted family life, so that 'everything was different':

> It had something to do with words. Words like 'lib' and 'liberation'. These words flew like sparks in the tense atmosphere of our home. My mother and other women were not free. Men like Daddy had stolen their freedom; and now they wanted it back.[157]

The complexity and controversy surrounding relationships between individuals and the state in Northern Ireland ensured, however, that the struggle there was of a different, more painful nature. Feminism in the North represented only one strand in a wider struggle affecting political, social and personal life, and women prioritised different aspects of their identities in different ways at different times. The diversity of the women's movement in Ireland was by no means unique, but common to left-wing movements of all kinds and in all countries. The situation in the North, in particular, provides a difficult and emotive reminder of the multiple identities and conflicting loyalties held by women everywhere.

5
Towards the millennium

Women are no longer prepared
to await their invitation.[1]

It is perhaps not surprising that the approach of the year 2000 prompted both private and public reflections on the achievements, triumphs and failures of twentieth-century life. Many commentators agreed that the position of women was one of the strongest factors in measuring the progress of society and, in addition to the usual statistical, oral and documentary evidence, a proliferation of feminist publications ensured that more information to assess their situation was available than ever before. Though what constitutes 'progress' is itself a matter of debate, it was clear that in Ireland, as elsewhere, there had been both significant gains and losses over the course of the century. Women were certainly more visible in public life: in 1979 Margaret Thatcher was elected as the first female Prime Minister of the UK, and two women became Presidents of Ireland before the year 2000. The opening or closing of opportunities for women related to the wider political, social and economic context in which they lived and worked, and the last two decades of the twentieth century brought massive shifts of political and financial fortune.

Though it was by no means a foregone conclusion at the beginning of the

THE LATE LATE SHOW HOAX BY EAMON DUNPHY

MAGILL

IRELAND'S CURRENT AFFAIRS MONTHLY MAGAZINE   OCTOBER 1997 £1.95

THE
FEMALE RACE

POLITICAL CORRUPTION BY VINCENT BROWNE

HELEN LUCY BURKE · GABRIEL BYRNE · PAT RABBITTE · NELL McCAFFERTY

SEAN McCARTHY

The front cover of *Magill* in October 1997 depicted the 'female race' for the Irish Presidency. From left to right, the candidates are Mary Banotti, Rosemary Scanlon (better known as the singer Dana), Adi Roche and the eventual successor to Mary Robinson, Mary McAleese.

1980s, by 1999 Ireland, in both its jurisdictions, and with some qualifications, 'could count itself among the twentieth century's winners'.[2] The impact of Europe was felt in progressive legislative measures, many of which challenged more traditional upholders of authority such as the Catholic Church. In Northern Ireland a flurry of political activity suggested that the beginning of the end of the conflict was perhaps in sight, while in the Republic an expanded educational system and huge inward investment brought many married women into the workplace for the first time. Also for the first time, it looked as though living standards in the South would overtake those of the North, though the widening of the gap between wealth and poverty suggested many underlying problems remained. As Carol Coulter put it, during the last twenty years of the century, social, economic, cultural and legislative changes combined 'to create a society that [was] much more urbanised, more sophisticated, much more educated, and much more economically and socially polarised, than it was in 1970'.[3]

SEX AND MARRIAGE

Paradoxically, the most publicly discussed changes in society related to the most intimate areas of women's experiences. Heated debates about many aspects of family life reflected political, religious and economic anxieties about the rights and responsibilities surrounding sexual relationships, marriage and parenthood. Statistical evidence suggested that young people were moving away from traditional practices. In Northern Ireland, for example, the institution of marriage, after reaching its peak of popularity in the 1970s, seems to have begun to lose its appeal, hitting its lowest ever recorded level in 1998. This did not necessarily mean, of course, that long-term relationships were themselves out of favour. The social stigma attached to cohabitation appeared to be declining: a *Northern Ireland Life and Times Survey* carried out in 2000 found that 52 per cent of young people either agreed or strongly agreed that it was 'all right for a couple to live together without intending to get married'.[4] But statistical changes do not explain the alternative arrangements which couples may have been making or the reasons underlying their decisions. Romantic inclination and the expectations of families and neighbours would undoubtedly play a part in influencing the plans of young couples; for example, it was probably easier to move away from tradition in towns and cities than in rural villages.

However, class, occupation and ethnicity are likely also to be relevant factors in determining such choices. After all, a high priority of most ethnic groups is to protect themselves from outside influence, and control over marriage is one way of ensuring this. So, for instance, matchmaking still takes place within many Traveller communities,[5] and similar concern with the continuity of traditions through marriage is frequently expressed by religious denominations. The most serious consequences of this are felt in Northern Ireland, where marriage or cohabitation between Catholics and Protestants can lead to not only family, but also communal, conflict. Demographic factors have heightened significance in a country where the relative numerical strengths of the two major religious groupings can impact on political power. Bernadette Devlin McAliskey has said,

> Unionists must ensure that nationalists don't outnumber them. On the other side what are we confined to? – outbreeding them? What are our choices? Either we shoot them or we outbreed them. There's no politics here. It's a numbers game.[6]

Within this context, couples in 'mixed' relationships have suffered harassment and intimidation to differing degrees. With constant fear almost as difficult to live with as physical violence, many chose to remove themselves from the threat, setting up home in America, Canada, England, or like Catherine and Declan, who left with their young daughter in the early 1990s, settling in Scotland. While these migrants and their families experienced the loss of close networks of support, the loss to the wider community was also significant. But, although recent research indicates that in the last years of the twentieth century less than 10 per cent of Northern Irish marriages are inter-religious, it also suggests that attitudes are slowly changing, with a new sense of societal tolerance accompanying the move towards peace.[7]

In common with trends throughout Western Europe, an increasing number of marriages in Northern Ireland – over 2,000 a year in the 1990s – are now ending in divorce. Again, the reasons are likely to be complex, with social and economic changes making it easier for women to follow their personal preferences. The decline of the social stigma attached to divorce, as well as the greater range of legal and financial supports open to divorced or separated women, means that mistakes can be rectified, abusive relationships left behind or new partnerships embarked upon. External tensions can also have a significant impact on family life. For women in the North, for example, the ongoing conflict has often been responsible for enforced separation from husband or partner. Married to a republican paramilitary, Róisín explained:

> I haven't seen my husband in fourteen years. He's on the run. He had to leave the North because he is wanted here and he is also wanted in the Free State. He gets me messages through his brother. He's lived in Africa, Spain and Australia. I have to stay here and raise the children. We can't all be moving round the world. The Ra [IRA] used to send him money but they just told me they can't give him any more money. If he had just gone to prison he would have been out by now. My children could have gone to visit him. He didn't want to go to prison. Said it was his duty to stay on the outside; well then, why do I feel like I'm in prison? I know its hard for him but at least he's free. I can't go anywhere because I send him all the money. They also watch me, so if I leave the country the Brits would follow me. As long as he's on the run I will always be in prison.[8]

Another woman, whose husband was serving a twelve-year sentence, expressed anger that she had never been given a choice in the direction her life had taken:

> So what are we supposed to do? Sit around and make a martyr out of him? That's what his so-called friends do. It makes me sick. This is my house now.

I make the decisions. I'm raising the kids. If I do something wrong, I take the blame . . . If he comes back, he comes back on my terms.[9]

Similarly, the wife of a loyalist prisoner, contemplating how independent she had become, declared, 'he's in for a shock, we've changed that much'.[10] Although it seems that, generally speaking, republican prisoners were held in high esteem within their communities, and that marriage breakdown was higher among loyalists, the day-to-day experiences of wives and partners in these situations are difficult to determine.[11] A great many women have undoubtedly stood by their men through years of prison visits or long, unexplained absences. In 1993, Geraldine, a woman in her seventies, commented, 'I've been going to that prison for my whole life, first to visit me da, then to visit my husband, then to see me daughter . . . now me grandson is in the Kesh.'[12] While the wives and partners of men engaged in criminal activities throughout the island underwent similar experiences, paramilitary presence in the entrenched communities in which they lived severely limited the choices of the families of many political prisoners in Northern Ireland. The stories of how husbands and wives responded to the freeing of political prisoners as part of the peace process in 1998 are yet to be told.

In the Republic the issue of divorce was not a private, but a public and political matter, subject to a constitutional ban from 1937. A referendum held on June 1986 provided those on either side of the debate with a platform to air their views on this issue. The liberal Divorce Action group was small with limited campaign funds, however, and those on the right were able to organise a coalition to mount a formidable campaign. The Catholic Church frequently reiterated its position on the matter, with one bishop drawing attention to the problems faced by children of divorced parents: 'Reliable studies indicate that children prefer even an unhappy marriage relationship to divorce of their parents. Divorce is always a disaster for children.'[13] Despite considerable evidence to the contrary, there was much support for this stance in secular society. With names such as Family Solidarity, the Irish Family League and Responsible Society, groups allied to the Anti-Divorce Campaign warned from the outset that the 'individualism' of feminists and other liberals represented a real threat to Irish morality. At a press conference in Dublin on 29 March 1995, housewife Monica Barber presented a document which severely criticised the

ill fruits of liberalism: family breakdown, urban violence, wasteful consumption, sexual irresponsibility and increasing personal unhappiness. We may realise that the worthwhile pursuit of freedom has been sidetracked by individualism. We might like to hear more talk of duties and less of rights.[14]

In the event, divorce was rejected by a majority of 61 per cent, though it is worth remembering that many liberals who would have supported divorce in principle were anxious to protect the economic and material rights of women and children, which they thought would be jeopardised by the proposed changes to the law. A Bill introduced by Fine Gael in February 1989, which allowed legal separation by the courts once it was proved that a marriage had broken down for a year, did provide an option for those in unhappy relationships. But with 33,793 women describing themselves as separated in the census of 1991, the matter could not be left. In November 1995 a second referendum was held, and although the issue had now been well aired, the campaign was fraught with bitter accusations. Alice Glenn, Fine Gael TD for Dublin Central, for example, declared that 'any women voting for divorce would be like a turkey voting for Christmas', and that supporters of divorce, among whom she included the Council for the Status of Women and all radical feminist organisations, 'can clearly be classed as enemies of the people'.[15] However, changes in the law relating to property rights and child custody, passed before 1995, helped prepare the ground for a more positive response, and on this occasion those advocating divorce won by the smallest of margins (50.5 per cent).

The constitutional ban on divorce was removed on 24 November 1995, but the conditions on which it was granted were stringent, involving a four-year period of separation to ensure that a couple had the opportunity to fully consider the implications of their actions. These constraints no doubt reflected ongoing concern with the impact of modern values and individualism on Irish family life. Moreover, a substantial proportion of the population had voted against divorce, and its legality is not likely to change the minds of those for whom it remains unacceptable. Indeed, it has been argued that by coming late and slowly to this position, and by imposing practical limitations on divorce, Ireland might escape the 'worst excesses' of modernity. Michele Dillon argues that 'Irish divorce . . . recognises individual autonomy while simultaneously protecting the social value of familial and communal obligation'.[16] However, Finola Kennedy notes that while there were only 100 divorces granted by mid-1997, the following three years saw the numbers rise to well over 6,000.[17]

Despite the existence of Women's Aid, the anger and activism of feminists, the prevalence of academic research and the introduction of legal constraints, women in late twentieth-century Ireland remained vulnerable to violence within the home. Twenty-one women were murdered in domestic

The Rape and Incest Line, now the Nexus Institute, first opened in Belfast in 1984. Offering support to both male and female victims of sexual abuse, the Institute now has nineteen outreach centres throughout the North of Ireland.

violence incidents in the six counties in 1993–4 alone, while in the Republic it has been estimated that between one-fifth and one-third of all women have been subjected to violence by a partner. These statistics only scratch the surface and by no means reflect the full extent of the problem facing so many women. Concern has been expressed about the often lenient sentencing of offenders, but even more worrying is that so many of the cases are not brought to court. A range of factors may prevent women from taking action – concern for the welfare and safety of their children, embarrassment, fear of reprisals, insecurities about finance and housing, and for many, the feeling that they themselves are to blame for their situation. But evidence suggests that even when they are willing to take action against their partners, abused women find it difficult to be taken seriously and have little confidence in the police. The Northern Irish statistics for domestic incidents attended by the police rose from 4,292 in 1997–8 to 6,751 in 1998–9, with women making up the vast majority of the victims. However, in a study involving sixty-seven women from the four Women's Aid refuges in

Northern Ireland during August and September 1986, 95 per cent reported that they did not always contact police when they felt they needed them. In terms of exclusion and protection orders, it was widely believed that police were more likely to adopt a peacekeeping rather than enforcement role.[18] While the poor relationship between community and police in many areas of Northern Ireland undoubtedly exacerbates this situation, a parallel study of women who had experienced violence in the Republic found that only one in five of those responding had reported the violence to the Garda Síochána. It was again confirmed that arrests were rare.[19] Hard-hitting poster campaigns by Women's Aid, with eye-catching slogans such as 'Home is Where the Hurt is', helped to keep this issue before the general public. But it is difficult not to agree with Eithne McLaughlin's assertion that 'comfortable ideas about "cheery" families supporting their members from evil without is an idealisation rather than an analysis of the nature of family life.[20]

In the meantime, the number of unmarried mothers in Irish society continued to increase during the last two decades of the century. Indeed, at over 28 per cent on either side of the border, Ireland's birth rate outside marriage is among the highest in Western Europe. There is no simple explanation for these statistics. In the South, everyone over sixteen has had the right to contraception since the early nineties, and with Aids making it a public health issue, condoms could be bought from machines from 1993. However, in a country undergoing rapid but uneven change, it was inevitable that experiences would differ. A national survey of women's health issues carried out in 1993 found that only half of the Irish women surveyed considered family planning advice easily accessible in their area, with rural women, unemployed students, the ill and the disabled expressing particular dissatisfaction.[21] Sociologist Pat O'Connor agrees that the reality of an accessible and comprehensive family planning service is probably still some time away,[22] a view also echoed by Ailbhe Smyth: 'Women all round the country, including in urban areas, say that there are many doctors who won't prescribe the pill. This seems unbelievable in 1997, but it is a fact.'[23] In other areas, too, freedom of choice was severely compromised. The forces of conservatism – both Catholic and Protestant – regularly picketed the Brook Clinic, which opened its doors to provide contraceptive advice to women in Northern Ireland in 1992. During its twice-weekly sessions, placard-carrying men taunted and belittled young women seeking admission. For eighteen-year-old Joanne, visits were often frightening ordeals:

> They couldn't touch you or stop you, but there were usually about ten of them, and you had to pass close to them to get to the door. One of the girls

I met there told me she had walked past about four times before she got the
courage to go inside.

Adding that she had the full backing of her mother, she went on to ask, 'If
I was frightened, what could it have been like for girls who didn't have any
family support?'[24]

Recent research also suggests a degree of ambivalence or passivity
regarding birth control among young working-class women. Abbey Hyde's
study of young pregnant Dublin women revealed a startling degree of
naivety in sexual practice – 24-year-old Norma commented, 'I Just thought
it wouldn't happen to me.' Likewise for Kim, the possibility of pregnancy
'never entered me head'.[25] Although the situation differed for individual
women, the consequences of pregnancy outside marriage were, generally
speaking, less catastrophic in the last twenty years of the twentieth century
than they had been in earlier decades. An Act of 1987 had dealt with some
of the practical implications by removing the status of 'illegitimacy' and
bringing property and maintenance rights of non-marital offspring into line
with those of the children of married parents. However, with unmarried
mothers now receiving financial assistance from the state, condemnation of
their moral values in the late 1980s was compounded by the fact that they
were also regarded as an economic drain on the country's resources.[26]
Nonetheless, the extent to which social attitudes had changed is reflected in
the growing numbers of lone mothers who chose to keep their babies rather
than give them up for adoption – only 6.7 per cent did so in 1991, compared to 56 per cent in 1961. Unmarried mothers are also increasingly less
likely to regard a husband as socially desirable. Veronica, single, unemployed
and pregnant at twenty-four, was pragmatic: 'Well, when you think of it, it's
only a ring and a piece of paper, and then he thinks he owns you. You'd
never have a social life or anything. I prefer the way I am.'[27] In 1998 only 6
per cent of Irish teenage mothers married, compared to 66.9 per cent in
1981, though this statistical information does not tell us whether or not they
were in long-term relationships – which may have made a considerable difference to their experience. There is some evidence that a mother's experience of marriage can be influential in determining her daughter's outlook,
and it is also likely that, as more children grow up in 'non-traditional' families, a single life, and even single parenthood will become more familiar and
acceptable.

Although remaining single is an option taken up by more and more
women, it does seem that in more isolated rural areas, much of Irish social
life still focuses on couples and the family unit. Anne Byrne argues that

Single parent families

In her 1980 study of single parent families in Northern Ireland, Eileen Evason drew attention to the ways in which they challenged contentious social assumptions:

> The problem is not simply that single parent families are atypical in statistical terms, but rather that in structure they flout and contradict the model of the family which is approved and propagated as the ideal. Moreover, their existence requires adjustments and special arrangements in everyday life and law and social policies which run counter to the pattern of rights, roles and opportunities which prevails in what is still essentially a patriarchal society. Single parent families are an unwelcome contradiction, an anomaly, in such a society. Lone fathers experience difficulties not simply because they are lone fathers but because they occupy a role ascribed to women if they wish to remain at home to care for their children or if in employment, because they lack the access to the unpaid services of a woman caring for the house and children which is enjoyed by married men. Lone mothers will be in difficulty in a society which, for example, channels income and property to the family through the male head of the household and assumes that the normal appropriate status of the woman is one of a dependant inside the family unit supported by a male and that women are therefore not in need, or deserving, of treatment as individuals on matters such as wages or employment opportunities.
>
> Eileen Evason, 1980, *Just Me and the Kids: A Study of Single Parent Families in Northern Ireland* (Belfast, 1980)

patriarchal pressure as exerted through this 'familist ideology', stigmatises those who remain single. Her study of thirty never-married women in the West of Ireland, carried out between 1995 and 1998, found that 'being constantly questioned about their singleness and asked for explanations for their failure to marry by family, friends, acquaintances, and strangers was a commonly reported experience'.[28] While most of these women enjoyed their independence, autonomy, and a range of social relationships, feeling 'like an outsider' was also reported. Moreover, single women over thirty, particularly those who socialised with other single women, also had to deal with assumptions about their sexual orientation, many taking pains to draw attention to their heterosexuality.

Sexuality is just one area where membership of the EU has had a major impact on national legislative measures, if not on popular attitudes. The decriminalisation of homosexuality both North and South, for example, which took place in 1982 and 1993 respectively, followed decisions of the European Court of Human Rights. Fine Gael TD Nora Owens echoed the views of liberal Ireland in the Dáil when she proclaimed, 'I do not believe that there is anything as fundamental as the right to our sexuality, which is our very essence and makes us what we are.'[29] As Kieran Rose pointed out, however, the change in the law was the result of a twenty-year campaign on many fronts.[30] Lesbians had also been active in promotion of their rights during this period, with individual women often making a considerable difference to public perceptions. In 1980, for example, a significant impact was made on public opinion when Joni Crone appeared on *The Late Late Show* to proclaim, 'I am Lesbian and I am proud.' Her aim, she said, was 'to dispel ignorance and fear about lesbian sexuality', and she certainly influenced many young Irish women.[31] Louise Walsh, from a small village in County Cork, remembered,

> although I had no ideas that I was queer myself at that time, her appearance raised questions for me regarding the negative representations of lesbians and gay men that were prevalent at the time. I'd seen one on the telly, and she was brilliant![32]

In Dublin, Liz Noonan ran as an independent lesbian feminist in the 1981 and 1982 general elections, receiving both publicity and a respectable vote, while a debate on homosexuality on *The Late Late Show* in 1989 'signified a decisive shift in public opinion'.[33] Lesbians continued to support themselves, establishing networks in the major cities of Dublin, Belfast, Cork and Galway, and in 1991 forming Lesbians Organizing Together (LOT) to co-ordinate activities and disseminate information. *Women's News* (Belfast) and *MsChief* (Dublin) both highlight lesbian issues and activities, and *Gay Community News*, a free monthly newsletter, has pages specifically for lesbians. Gay bars, discos and hostels are also becoming increasingly common.

No statistics are available for the number of lesbians in Ireland, though Angela O'Connell, working from British estimates, suggests that around 2–5% per cent of the Irish female population is lesbian, and that around one-third of lesbians are mothers.[34] This direct challenge to patriarchy, and the greater visibility of lesbians generally, undoubtedly helps to fuel homophobia and many women still fear the consequences of 'coming out'. Clearly, despite the advances, sexual identity remains a matter of difficult and delicate negotiation in all sections of society.

WOMEN'S HEALTH

There is no doubt that throughout the century motherhood was the most common experience shared by women. While class, age and other factors contributed to the diversity of that experience, demographic information points to general trends which reflect the broader nature of change. Family size is a good example of this, with women in the Republic now having smaller families (2.39 children in 1995). While this does suggest a significant shift in attitudes, it is nonetheless high by European standards. In the North, too, family size is larger than in Britain, with 35 per cent of households in 1993 consisting of four or more people. The rural nature of Irish society, North and South, the more limited participation of women in the work-force and the ethos of Catholicism are among the reasons given for these differentials.[35] An underlying concern about large family size is the way in which this adversely affects a mother's personal freedom and social and economic well-being, particularly reflected in low levels of income and educational attainment. While experiences no doubt vary considerably, inadequate family finances and frustrated ambition remain worrying features of Irish society, with women always tending to be over-represented at the bottom end of almost any scale of measurement. A recurring feature of surveys of poverty, for example, is the powerlessness of many married women when it comes to control of family budgets. Wives reported not knowing their husbands' salaries or being unable to negotiate housekeeping allowances. In a study carried out in the late 1970s, one woman observed, 'I was supposed to do everything on £20 a week, but I think his wages were about £80.'[36]

In purely medical terms, pregnancy and childbirth are now much less dangerous for both mothers and babies. The infant mortality rate is now 6.2 per cent in the Republic, and 5.6 per cent in Northern Ireland, with over half of the fatalities occurring during the first week of life. Women who wish to terminate a pregnancy, however, still face considerable difficulties.

Abortion, a personal issue for many women, was also, throughout the 1980s and 1990s, a political issue for Irish feminists. Referendums were again used in the South to gauge public opinion, with women's sexual and reproductive rights hotly debated. In 1983 it was the conservative anti-abortion group which was proactive, leading the attempt to prevent the possibility of abortion being legalised by introducing an amendment to the Constitution. The force of the amendment was clear:

> The State acknowledges the right to life of the unborn and, with due regard to the equal right to life of the mother, guarantees in its laws to respect and, as far as practicable by its laws, to defend and vindicate that right.

With voters facing a simple yes/no response on this highly complex issue, Monica Barnes, Fine Gael TD, attacked the amendment as 'a lunatic farce . . . ambiguous and downright dangerous'.[37] The SPUC headed up the Pro-Life Amendment Campaign in a highly-charged battle that divided men and women on both sides of the debate. Though some urban areas, and Dublin in particular, had majorities voting against the amendment, it was carried by a majority of two to one overall.

The consequences of such actions for young women finding themselves pregnant in difficult circumstances were tragically illustrated in Granard, County Longford, in January 1984. Although the pregnancy of teenager Ann Lovett was known about and even discussed in her neighbourhood, it appeared that no one offered her any help or advice. After giving birth, alone and unaided in the open air, she died, leaving her newborn child (who also died) on the steps of the parochial house.[38] In April of the same year a case of apparent infanticide in County Kerry highlighted the vulnerability of young women to the gender bias of the legal system. Joanne Hayes was accused and later confessed, to the murder of a baby found dead from stab wounds on Cahirciveen beach, although in fact she had given birth to a child which later died and had buried it on the farm where she lived, about fifty miles from the beach. Even when the body of her own baby was found, the Gardaí continued to investigate her involvement with the Cahirciveen baby, assuming she had given birth to twins, despite all evidence to the contrary. The focus of the investigation had been on Haye's sexual history, and the subsequent inquiry into the case, rather than exposing the erroneous reasoning and dubious actions of the Gardaí, continued in the same vein.[39] As Nell McCafferty commented in one of a series of newspaper reports:

> Policemen, psychiatrists, doctors, and lawyers, all of them male, [were] free with their comment on and speculations about this woman. Their own minds and assumptions have gone unchallenged. The men protected and respected each other right to the end.[40]

A further case in February 1992, which attracted a great deal of media attention, indicated again the anomalies of the legal and constitutional system. In this instance, known as the X case, a fourteen-year-old girl became pregnant following intercourse with a forty-one-year-old man. After reporting the matter to the police, her parents made arrangements to take her to England to have the pregnancy terminated. At this stage the Irish Attorney-General stepped in, seeking an injunction to prevent the family from travelling for this purpose. Once more, a girl's personal tragedy became a political issue as feminists, conservatives, Church, state and media made

known their opinions. In the event, when psychiatrists judged that the pregnant girl could be classed as suicidal, the Appeal Court decided that the
abortion was lawful under Article 40.3.3, which permitted the procedure if
it was clear that there was 'a real and substantial risk to the life, as distinct
from the health, of the mother'.[41] Ailbhe Smyth argued that the emotive
public debates, which followed this high-profile case, were 'Positively
healthy in obliging this society to talk to itself across differences and division about the meanings and values it (variously) considers to be important.'[42] And indeed, the tragic circumstances of this case did indicate to many
that a more liberal value system was necessary and led to the passing of subsequent referenda acknowledging the right of access to information on
abortion clinics, and the legal right to travel abroad to obtain such services.

While many feminists have commented on the link between the discourse
on female sexuality and Irish national identity, the situation in Northern
Ireland also raises concerns about individual sexual autonomy, with legislation around sexual and reproductive rights lagging well behind the rest of
the UK. The Northern Ireland Abortion Campaign (NIAC) was formed in
1980. Rejecting the claim that there was no need for abortion legislation in
Northern Ireland, the group carried out research to prove its point, and
engaged in a hard-hitting publicity campaign. Whereas the Ulster Pregnancy
Advisory Association worked quietly behind the scenes, assisting women
needing to travel to England, the new group took more direct and controversial action. For example, they sent 600 wire coat hangers to Westminster,
each with a facsimile of a British Airways ticket attached and a message to
MPs which read, 'These are the two ways in which NI women get abortions.[43] The Northern Ireland Abortion Law Reform Association was
formed in 1984 to lobby for the extension of the 1967 Act to Northern
Ireland. But despite the publication of *The Report of an International Tribunal*
on abortion in Northern Ireland in 1989, this goal had still not been
reached by the end of the century.

Those opposing abortion have also been active in the North through
organisations such as the Irish Pregnancy Care Service, LIFE and Precious
Life. The latter responded to an accusation of intimidation by the family
Planning Association with the declaration that 'there will never be any proof
connecting Precious Life with any types of violence because we oppose
violence in the womb and violence outside the womb'.[44] CURA is a
Catholic group with similar views. As in the South, the pro-life groups in
Northern Ireland receive the full support of the major Churches and many
political parties. In recent years anti-abortion groups have also maintained
a visible presence in city centres, with stalls featuring large colour

photographs of aborted foetuses. There is no doubt that such propaganda has a strong emotional impact on the general public, but it is perhaps more surprising that the UK government has not been more supportive of standardising the legal situation across its jurisdiction. In 1990, during a debate on extending abortion rights to Northern Ireland, Virginia Bottomley, the Conservative British Secretary of State for Health, argued that this position was 'Offensive to the overwhelming majority of those in the Province . . . all the soundings of opinion have made it very clear that there is no will in Northern Ireland for such change.'[45] As Audrey Simpson, manager of the Northern Ireland Association for Family Planning, commented in 1995, 'Bottomley's soundings could not have included the 54,000 women who have silently voted with their feet since 1967.'[46]

In 1998 alone, the number of women having abortions in England and Wales and giving an address from the Irish Republic was 5,892; around 1,500 women seeking similar treatment left from Northern Ireland. Research indicates that most of these women, around 80 per cent, were single, and they were most likely to be in their twenties. About one-third travelled alone to Britain, and, with a three-day stay necessary, their total costs were reckoned to be between £450 and £600. Many of the women undergoing termination do not receive counselling, and, as Pauline Jackson indicates, while they are mostly young and poor, requiring abortion for social and economic reasons, they need to cite health problems in order to procure the procedure.[47] Criminalisation is thus added to the emotion and distress of their situation. It is probably not possible to reach consensus on this most divisive of issues, but legislative procedures which enable women to make informed choices about their bodies is regarded by many as a fundamental human right.

There is no doubt that in the twenty-first century ethical concerns about the nature of motherhood will continue to be prominent in Irish society, though the focus is much less likely to be on single motherhood, and perhaps not even on abortion. The birth of Ireland's first test-tube baby occurred on 15 January 1986, and technological advances in fertility treatments generally, are fast changing the world of reproduction. Multiple births, surrogate motherhood, cloning, and the ability to give birth into (and beyond) middle age, are the results of scientific research which hold important implications for women everywhere. The extent to which women themselves will be able to control these innovations is, of course, less clear.

The process of ageing profoundly affects control over most aspects of life and, in Ireland, as across Europe, there is a steady rise in the proportion of older people in the population. With women outliving men, ageing women are only now being regarded as a significant category for research.[48] Poverty amongst the elderly has important implications in terms of health and general welfare, and the experience of elderly men and women should inform future policy provision. Despite the demographic realities, ageing, particularly for females, is overwhelmingly regarded as a negative experience, associated with physical decline and dependency. Although hip and knee replacements and heart bypasses can considerably extend the active lifespan, there is some evidence that the elderly are considered to be a low priority in terms of health service provision. Moreover, as Pat Thane points out, while women are less likely than men to experience retirement from paid employment 'as a seriously disruptive break in the life-course, partly because their places in the labour market were less secure than those of men', they are, in consequence, more likely than men to suffer poverty in old age.[49] As she concludes, this is by no means a new phenomenon. However, with the proportion of people aged between 55 and 64 set to increase by more than 45 per cent in the Republic over the next 15 years, there is little doubt that this will be a critical issue for legislators of the twenty-first century.[50]

In terms of overall health, the situation for both women and men is radically different from at the beginning of the century, with cancer replacing tuberculosis as the major killer. But while, generally speaking, people live longer and have better medical facilities, a report on all-Ireland mortality rates published in 1989 highlighted that there are regional, gender and socio-economic differences determining experience.[51]

The mortality rate for cancer, for example, one of the most common killers of men and women, at 177 per 100,000, does not compare well with the EU rate of 148 per 100,000. One in 8 women in Ireland (1 in 6 men) have a chance of dying from this disease by the age of 74. While the rates of Irish men were similar to the EU average, rates among Irish women were higher. This is an area where early detection and speedy, radical treatment

TABLE 5.1

Mortality data for all-Ireland, 1899 and 1999
Annual death rate per 1,000 persons in brackets

CAUSE OF DEATH	1889	1999
Tuberculosis	7,068 (157.3)	70 (1.3)
Cancer	3,895 (86.7)	10,968 (209.8)
Diabetes	335 (7.5)	482 (9.2)
All causes	63,838 (1,420.5)	46,481 (895.8)

seems to offer the most hopeful means of complete recovery, but this is often outside the control of individual women. Throughout the 1990s it was argued that administrative and economic rationalisation, leading to the closure of many small local hospitals, has had an adverse impact on women's health overall.

The area of health is one where class is perhaps of greater significance than gender. On both parts of the island, the mortality rate for 'all causes' of death in the lowest occupational classes was 100–200 per cent higher than the rate in the highest occupational classes – an indication of the failings of national health systems. Significantly, when looking at breast cancer (which accounts for one-fifth of cancer deaths among women), occupational class differences were not assessed because of 'general problems associated with occupation categories for women' in both jurisdictions. This suggests a worrying acceptance of issues around female employment. It was also reported that urban populations had higher rates (10 per cent for women, 15 per cent for men) for deaths from cancers as a whole. This is attributed to problems associated with smoking and with levels of poverty and deprivation in towns and cities. Those living in rural areas face risks of a different nature, apparently being more vulnerable to death from influenza and traffic accidents. Recent research also indicates that women from ethnic minority groups experience particular problems in accessing services.[52] A 1996 conference in the North highlighted the multi-layered nature of disadvantage affecting health. For example, Suneil Shaarma, chairperson of the Northern Ireland Council for Ethnic Minorities, cited a survey carried out by the University of Ulster which claimed that 23 per cent of the four major ethnic groups in the North – Chinese, Indian, Pakistani and Traveller – have difficulties in accessing health-care services.[53] Women with disabilities (around 150,000 in Ireland) are also more likely than the able-bodied citizens to be victims of abuse and discrimination. This is an area affecting women from all walks of life that merits the expenditure of considerably more resources in terms of both finance and research.

HOME

The different income levels which impacted on health were reflected in the wide range of living standards across the country, and again pointed out the diverse daily experiences of women throughout Ireland. One indicator of increased prosperity has been the ability to purchase one's own home; in this area, considerable progress seems to have been made, with couples in late twentieth-century Ireland more likely than those of previous generations to be living in a house for which they were paying mortgages rather than rent. Many former council-house tenants on both parts of the island took advantage of home-ownership schemes to buy their homes at greatly reduced prices. But while houses were also likely to be bigger than previously, the gap between rich and poor appeared to widen during the 1980s; as Mary Healy from Cork suggests:

> We hide behind this label of 'The Celtic Tiger' and pretend that everything is all right, when in fact it isn't, and it seems to be getting worse. There are real areas of deprivation and society is becoming increasingly compartmentalised. A lot of the more affluent sectors know very little of the life of the poor.[54]

Those continuing to rent local authority accommodation are most likely to experience poverty and disadvantage, particularly those living in urban areas, although there is considerable diversity in standards of housing. Tony Fahey, for example, notes that houses in the Deanrock estate in Cork are in high demand, with a low turnover of tenants and a long waiting list. Fatima Mansions in Dublin, on the other hand, is a more problematic area, with vacancies difficult to fill and almost half of the current tenants seeking alternative accommodation.[55] There is also diversity within council estates, and the more deprived environments, often generating a culture of violence and drug abuse, are a source of anxiety for many mothers. In the North, religious segregation, sectarian conflict and a pervasive paramilitary presence exacerbate these problems.

However difficult life is in some of these areas, the number on the waiting lists for local authority housing by far exceed the number of homes available. In 1996 it was estimated that there were approximately 28,000 households seeking such accommodation in the Republic. A majority of these would be lone parents or single people, who are not considered appropriate tenants for the typical local authority housing stock. They would therefore most likely face the options of long stays in hostels or inner-city flats, or highly-priced, poor-quality private accommodation. The most vulnerable of all in terms of housing are those who have been rejected, or abused, by their families – lesbians, gays, women and children, ex-prisoners and those with long-term psychiatric problems. Lack of resources or family support can lead eventually to homelessness, which, as the Simon Community points out, 'is more than just being without a roof or a house. It is about lack of shelter, lack of security, lack of belonging, and lack of safety.'[56] Women made homeless by difficult personal circumstances thus continue to be at risk. While an official count, carried out by the

Department of Environment over the course of a week in March 1999, found 5,324 homeless people throughout the Republic (over half of them in the Dublin region), the Simon Community believes this figure vastly underestimates the scale of the problem. Their own estimate is that around 10,000 people experience homelessness each year, a number which is increasing rapidly as a result of the rise in prices of both rented and bought accommodation.

There has also been recognition in recent years of the particular problems faced by rural women in terms of access to resources and facilities. In the Republic the Second Commission on the Status of Women made a series of recommendations in 1993, acknowledging the need for improved transport, mobile health centres, and a series of training and educational facilities. A study of women living in south-west Mayo confirms the need for these practical measures.[57] Again, however, it must be stressed that rural experience is by no means homogenous; while many struggle in isolated cottages with poor amenities, others enjoy the comforts of a prosperous rural idyll. Even minority groups such as Travellers can experience dramatically different living conditions, from official sites with clean running water and electricity to bleak areas of wasteland with 'one block of toilets (irregularly emptied and cleaned) and one tap of water unsuitable for drinking . . . infested with rats'.[58]

Travellers are no more economically homogenous than any other ethnic group, but they do face particular problems in attempting to maintain their nomadic culture, which, as Máirín Kenny notes, is more about a mindset than about being constantly on the move. Kenny claims that:

> The dominant sedentary group has taken nomadism – this core of traveller culture – and turned it into a key instrument of their oppression, ensuring that forced movement is the only experience of nomadism most travellers have.[59]

The failure of majority populations to legitimise or value the cultures of other minorities impacts on many other ethnic groups on the island of Ireland, the proportion of which is small, but growing. Travellers, Chinese, Indians and Pakistanis together made up only 1 per cent of the overall population in the North in the late 1990s.[60] Family structures remain strong within these communities, and they are therefore likely to have a household size larger than that of the rest of the population. They also tend to live in the same neighbourhoods, where they can support each other. As Rukhsar Ali, a lay health-worker with Craigavon Asian Women and Children's Association put it, 'when you feel isolated much of the time, it is essential to have regular opportunites to speak to other women in their own language about their difficulties and aspirations.'[61] Like many other Western European countries, Ireland in the late twentieth century has received a growing number of refugees and asylum seekers. About 1,212 Vietnamese 'boat people', for example, arrived in the Republic in 1979, and by 1996 they made up 125 family groups, over 6,000 people, of whom 148 had been born in Ireland.[62] The numbers of people seeking asylum increased dramatically as a result of the break up of Eastern Europe, and Paul Cullen claims that in 1999 there were 9,062 such people on the books of the Department of Social, Community and Family Affairs. He argues that, while they represented a very small proportion of overall immigrants, they recieved the lowest level of support available under the social welfare system. As he points out, the popular press has often been responsible for increasing tension about the situation of refugees, and racial prejudice is a growing problem within Irish society. The evidence suggests that in Ireland, North and South, many individuals and families fall through the net of social security, to become part of a growing underclass whose needs are not being met, and whose life experiences fall outside so-called societal norms. The increasing presence of women and children begging on city-centre streets is only the most visible aspect of this disturbing situation.

In more affluent sectors, access to modern, labour-saving devices has had a strong impact on women's daily lives, with almost 90 per cent of homes in both the Republic and the North now owning a washing machine, and around half (more in the North than the South) owning a microwave oven. Family meals can now be quickly and easily prepared, and even full-time housewives are generally much less isolated than in previous generations. Around 80 per cent of the population of the island has a telephone, about one-third have two televisions or more, and a substantial minority own more than one motor vehicle. As with housing standards, however, luxury goods are unevenly distributed. A study of poverty levels in the Republic, carried out Ireland in 1994, concluded that 'single-adult households, the elderly and households headed by someone engaged in domestic duties' faced greater risks of falling below half the average income level than they would have done in 1987.[63]

It has been recognised, however, that labour-saving devices do not significantly reduce the level of domestic work carried out in the home; instead standards of cleanliness and housekeeping have risen considerably. Furthermore, whether in town or countryside, it does seem that, even at the century's end, housework and childcare were still considered to be women's work. A survey carried out in Northern Ireland in the early 1990s found

that women were overwhelmingly viewed as responsible for routine household chores, with couples in only one household in four sharing housework
equally. One-third of fathers had never taken their children to school and
one-quarter had never changed a nappy. In families where both partners
worked, three-fifths of women continued to do the domestic chores, and
this was still the case when the husband was unemployed.[64] Madeleine
Leonard's 1989 study of a deprived housing community in west Belfast confirms these findings, and recent research in the Republic also reveals that
most couples have no expectation of household tasks being shared.[65] While
some young professional couples may be familiar with the concept of house
husbands, they would clearly be in a small minority.

WORK

Throughout the course of the twentieth century, feminists claimed that the
ability to earn an independent income was an important measure of
women's position in society. Access to skills, training, opportunities and
rewards in the labour market are seen as important factors in increasing a
woman's choices and enabling her to make informed decisions about her
life. We might therefore expect that the significant rise in the numbers of
employed Irish women by the end of the century reflect a substantial
improvement in their social and economic circumstances. As we have
already seen, however, the reality of both individual and collective experience belies any simplistic interpretation of numerical strength. The ideology of separate public and domestic spheres may well have lost much of its
direct impact, but gendered notions of ability and appropriateness still
impact negatively on women's working lives and carry important consequences in terms of experience and reward. It is already clear that much of
the work that most women do, particularly their domestic and caring tasks,
are not valued in monetary terms. The British Cabinet Office explicitly
acknowledged this in a report published in February 2000, in which the
'cost of being a woman' was calculated. Comparing men and women with
similar educational achievements, the research demonstrated that:

> A woman leaving school with no qualifications forgoes nearly £200,000
> over a lifetime and a woman who leaves school with GCSE qualifications
> forgoes nearly a quarter of a million pounds. Even women who have degrees
> and professional careers stand to lose £143,000 simply by being female.[66]

The battle for equality of treatment in the workplace

A s these examples indicate, the introduction of legislation to deal with sexual discrimination and harassment, while time-consuming and expensive to implement, revealed the extent to which such practices were commonplace.

An Equal Pay Case in Northern Ireland rested on the difference between carrying stock to a hotel bar (the barman's job) and stacking the shelves (Myrtle Preston's job as a barlady). A tribunal decided the work was of equal value and the Edenmore Hotel was ordered to award arrears of £454 to make up the difference over the past two years, in spite of the manager's plea that Ms Preston 'was very well paid for a woman'.

Guardian, 6 July 1983

. . . a young motor mechanic apprenticed in Belfast was forced out by male mechanics who pawed her and made lewd remarks, she made legal history with her award of £1,000 compensation.

Irish News, 31 October 1983

Ireland's Labour Court made its biggest ever individual equal pay award in 1997 when it held that four communications assistants represented by Civil and Public Services Union and employed by the Irish Aviation Authority were entitled to equal pay with two male radio officers. The Department of Public Enterprise has decided to accept the ruling, which was issued on 28 November 1997 and which means each of the four women will receive a total of IEP 100,000 on a backdated basis.

Eironline, 1998

Mandie Hall, after having progressed quickly as a machinist at Louise Products Ltd. in County Antrim, found that the atmosphere in the clothing factory 'turned sour' when she fell pregnant. Claiming to have been dismissed on unlawful grounds and assisted by the EOC, she took a case against her former employers, winning £10,000 in settlement.

23rd Annual Report of the Equal Opportunities Commission for Northern Ireland,
1 April 1998 to 31 March 1999

Job segregation, the gender pay gap and loss of, or reduced, earnings in her childbearing years are the main causes of this startling deficit. As the Minister for Women, Margaret Jay, commented:

> This research shows that women are paying a heavy economic price just for being female. They are experiencing a female forfeit. We should celebrate the fact that women have made great progress in the labour market over the last 20 years but the analysis starkly underlines there are still many barriers that need to be overcome.[67]

Numerical progress is, however, indisputable. By 1998 women made up 38.3 per cent of the workforce in the Republic, a substantial increase in the figure of 27 per cent for 1971, though still low by European standards and lagging behind the Northern Ireland figure of 50.4 per cent, which is in turn less than that of Great Britain (64.9 per cent). Moreover, much of this increase can be attributed to changes in the economy rather than to the success of feminism or equal opportunity procedures. In Northern Ireland, for example, jobs in the service sector, traditionally attracting women, were much more readily available after the introduction of Direct Rule in 1972. Public sector posts in the civil service, in central government agencies and in the legal and security services accounted for 42 per cent of all employees in 1998, and women filled 62 per cent of these positions. The last decades of the century also saw the expansion of the public sector in the Republic, again engaging women in clerical and administrative positions, particularly in the areas of health and welfare. While much of this employment was still identifiable as 'women's work', jobs in the public sector were more rewarding than those in the private sector in terms of wages and conditions. However, Rosemary Sales notes that in Northern Ireland, where the labour force is 'structured by both gender and religion', there were significant differences in the employment experiences of Catholic and Protestant women, although the Fair Employment Agency, established in 1976, was charged with narrowing this gap. Perhaps the most obvious area where religion was a factor was in the security forces, where in 1995 jobs accounted for nearly 10 per cent of Protestant female public employment. Only 300 Catholic women were employed in security-related occupations compared to 3,000 Protestant women, a situation which reflected the wider constitutional and political context.[68]

The feminisation of the service sector in Ireland as a whole follows a trend similar to that in other parts of Europe and, encompassing areas such as catering, cleaning and hairdressing, it is a sector characterised by part-time hours and low pay. It is interesting to note that some anxiety has been expressed that 'old norms are perpetuating themselves' in some new areas of work. Recent research into teleworking, for example, indicates that despite the so-called communication revolution and economic restructuring, 'traditional work patterns and the sexual division of labour have persisted'.[69]

Agriculture, formerly a traditional area of work for women, has undergone considerable decline in both parts of the island. The 1991 census in the South revealed that 6,800 women were farmers in their own right, while another 5,900 were enumerated as relatives assisting on farms. Taken together, these women made up just 10 per cent of all farm workers.[70] Experiences vary according to the size of holdings; large, more commercialised farms would tend to employ male hired help and operate as major business concerns. On small to medium-sized farms the whole family would be more likely to be engaged to some extent in the day-to-day work of the unit. Most farm wives are involved in essential, but often underestimated, aspects of the business – responsible for bookkeeping and administration, as well as cooking and cleaning. And these domestic tasks are likely to be particularly onerous in an agricultural setting, with farm hands as well as family members needing to be fed, and mud from fields and farmyard generating more than the normal washing load. One County Down farmwife complained:

> I'd say on average I wash this (kitchen) floor about six times a day. I'll just have it clean and then they just march all over it looking for something, boots and all . . . You clean and cook constantly, you can't say, there that's finished.[71]

The latest generation of farming women do, however, seem to have different aspirations and expectations from those of the past. Patricia O'Hara, in a series of interviews with sixty women, found that, particularly in the eastern counties of the Republic, there was now much more resistance to the idea of sharing a home with in-laws – something taken for granted a generation earlier.[72] Fionnuala Sweeney's research of farming women in Dungiven, north County Derry during 1992–3, revealed a range of different experiences and responses to the modern world of farming. For example, Rose Wilson, who was fonder of animals than of housework, effectively became the sole farmer when her husband took up haulage work as a sideline to supplement the farming income. Susan McKay notes that many Protestant farmers in the Northern border region responded to the opportunity of lucrative full- and part-time work in the security forces – 'one woman described the part-time UDR as "virtually a type of farm diversification"'.[73] The 1994 National Farm Survey in the Republic showed that

one-third of farm holders or spouses in the South worked off the farm.
Women would appear to be better able now to find outlets for their skills,
enabling them to have a major input into, or a means of supplementing, the
farming income, though Evelyn O'Kane was less traditional than most,
becoming a part-time painter and decorator when her husband scaled down
farmwork and took outside employment. Many farm women undoubtedly
remain constrained by the patriarchal and male nature of farming culture,
particularly the tradition of male inheritance. However, it does seem that
there is greater potential for empowerment than was hitherto thought.
Certainly, Sweeney's research brought to light women who were 'pro-active
in developing new and fulfilling roles in ways that are individual to themselves and their changing farming and family circumstances'.[74]

In the labour force more generally, and despite over twenty years of legislation designed to equalise pay rates, women's salaries are still less than
those of men doing comparable jobs. In 1998 the gap between male and
female pay across the economy in the Republic as a whole was 20 per cent,
while Northern Ireland hourly earnings for women averaged 84.7 per cent
of those of men. Even at the end of the century the concept of the male
breadwinner still carried some weight. Nonetheless, the recent influx of
married, particularly young married women into the workforce (the
increase is most noticeable in the Republic) is a significant development,
bringing Ireland more into line with European experience.

For many married women, particularly mothers, part-time work offers the
flexibility needed to balance earnings and domestic responsibilities. Female
part-time work has been an important element of the Northern Ireland
labour force since the 1970s, and is beginning to become a factor in the
South, accounting for about one-fifth of all working women. The 1997
Labour Report Survey in the South stated that 44 per cent of part-time
Irish women workers said they worked part-time because of family responsibilities, while 73 per cent of women who left work in the previous five
years did so because of the duties of family care. This so-called 'flexible
workforce' may well suit the circumstances of many women, but they are
open to exploitation and, despite recent legislation, are vulnerable to financial and career insecurity. As Irish Congress of Trade Unions (ICTU) representative Ann Hope points out, 'Part-time jobs are often not seen as "real
jobs". Women may be doing them from choice or from necessity, but they
need to be taken seriously as work.'[75] However, with neither state nor
employers (on either part of the island) willing to progress their poor record
in childcare facilities, it seems likely that mothers will continue to be marginalised in the labour force.

Motherhood is not, of course, the only factor affecting women's career potential. Recent research reveals that 'the level of women's educational achievement has the biggest single impact on their lifetime incomes and the extent to which they can overcome the female forfeit'.[76] Women with a university education are much more likely to have a job than those without, and also to continue with a full-time career following marriage and during motherhood. It is therefore encouraging to note a rise in the proportion of female students: 60 per cent of those attending further education colleges and 57 per cent of those in universities in Northern Ireland in the academic year 1997–8 were women. However, their choice of subject area – mainly in the humanities and social sciences – ultimately reaps less financial reward than the disciplines of science and technology, which continue to be dominated by male students. This pattern, it seems, has not changed.

Educational achievement is also important in determining a woman's ability to 'make it to the top' of her chosen profession, though it is only one factor among others over which she might have less control. In the Republic, the percentage of women in administrative, executive and managerial positions rose from 5 per cent in 1971 to 24 per cent in 1996. In contrast, in Northern Ireland 8.9 per cent of women were recorded as working in managerial positions in 1999. Again, however, these top positions are most likely to be in traditionally 'female' areas of work, primarily in education or health and welfare, and frequently carry a lower status than similar posts held by men. For example, women make up a significant proportion of head teachers at primary level, significantly less at secondary level, and are clustered in junior lectureship positions in universities.

The high media profile given to successful businesswomen in the commercial world reflects the fact that they are 'unusual' rather than typical. A combination of factors – institutional, cultural, structural and personal – are responsible for the undervaluing of women's talents and the limiting of their achievements. Maxine Jones, in a study of the 'tiny minority' of top business women in the Republic, published in 1992, argues that stereotypical understandings of 'feminine' characteristics are viewed as obstacles in the competitive and aggressive world of business, making it difficult for women to be accepted and make their way up the promotional ladder.[77] It would seem, too, that the breaking of the glass ceiling is often achieved at substantial costs to women's personal lives, with those succeeding in career terms likely to be single and childless. For many women, the balancing of home and a highly pressurised working life is too difficult to sustain, in sharp contrast to the successful male, for whom marriage and family life is seen as a positive bonus in terms of both emotional and practical support.

Several initiatives have been put in place to tackle the structural aspects of women's difficulties. In 1979, for example, an organisation called Network was established in the Republic to lend money to help finance prospective businesswomen. It offered access to credit and support in finding investors for those lacking the essential collateral to make a viable beginning. The University of Limerick took part in a scheme offering a women–only Diploma in Management to aid promotion prospects. European funding has also financed projects to bring more women into areas of 'non-traditional' employment. As part of the Triple Cross project, forty-six Dublin women completed and gained NVQ level 2 certificates in electronics, with many of them subsequently finding work in this industry. Twenty-three-year-old Susan, the only female maintenance electrician in a Moy Park food production company in Craigavon, County Armagh, is working under the same initiative, which encourages both women and employers to tackle the gender imbalance.[78] Progress towards equal opportunities was made in 1992 with the first all-female Fórsa Cosanta Áituíl recruits in the Republic's defence forces passing out at Sarsfield Barracks in Limerick. The 32 recruits, including 2 married women, ranged in age from 17 to 31 and were quali-fied to the rank of two-star soldiers. By 1996, a total of 179 women were serving in the Irish defence forces. In the North, another turning point was reached when women of the RUC were permitted to carry weapons. It should be noted, however, that the RUC women's demand for equality in this instance was only met following a court case against the Chief Constable, Sir John Hermon. In 1987, Hermon was found to be acting unreasonably in cutting the hours and contracts of female members of the RUC reserves because he felt it was too risky for them to carry guns. Thirty-one women received £242,000 compensation in total, and this was fol-lowed by an award of damages totalling almost £1million to a further 310 women in November 1988.[79]

Both the EU and trade unions have played important roles in bringing cases of discriminatory practice to the labour courts, North and South. In 1985 a fifteen-year-old girl from County Louth made history in the Republic by bringing the first claim for sexual harassment under the terms of the Employment Equality Act of 1977. A shop assistant who claimed that sexual advances by her employer constituted 'constructive dismissal', she was awarded a year's wages in a case which set an important precedent.[80] In another example of the success of equality legislation, Angela Ballantine, a teacher from Newtownards, County Down, was awarded the meagre sum of £300 as compensation for being discriminated against when applying for promotion alongside a male colleague in a local school.[81]

Involvement in trade-union activity is also likely to increase women's authority in the workplace. In 1998 the ICTU reported that women made up 39 per cent and 46 per cent of its total membership in the Republic and Northern Ireland respectively. Although the number of women taking up posts as full-time officials has risen from 7 per cent in 1987 to 17 per cent in 1991 and to 20 per cent in 1998, the figures remain disappointingly low. Nonetheless, John Lynch, former branch officer of the Association of University Teachers, claims that by trade-union standards this increase represents considerable progress.[82] The route to full-time posts at national level is through local committee and then regional officers, and while women are now becoming much more active locally, it will take some time for their participation to be fully reflected at the highest level. The time lag is exacerbated by the tendency for union officials to retain their positions for many years, and, in the North, by a degree of cautiousness engendered by the defeats suffered under the Conservative governments of the 1980s.

Some women, such as those working in the sex industry, are particularly vulnerable to violence and exploitation. It may be true, as Maggie O'Neill suggests, that prostitution offers 'a good enough standard of income for shorter working hours and some degree of autonomy and independence for those working for themselves'. But, she goes on, 'sex work also brings fear, violence, criminalization, stigmatization, reduced civil liberties and rights of human dignity, as well as the risk of disease and, for some, death'.[83] At risk from arrest for solicitation, prostitutes also know there are limits to their career. Lyn Madden, a prostitute working Dublin's Grand Canal, admitted in the 1970s that:

> I'm 37 and it scares me. The day will come when I walk along the street and a car will stop. In the dark he won't see me and I'll open the door and he'll say: 'Oh, you're too old.' And I'll have to shut the door and walk home. That's going to kill me.

In fact, it was witnessing the death of former prostitute Dolores Lynch, her mother Kathleen and her aunt Hannah (Madden's lover and pimp was convicted of Lynch's murder), that finally convinced her to end her twenty years 'on the game'.[84]

RELIGION AND THE NEW IRELAND

Church–state relations in the South have been a continual and important theme in Irish historiography, and one which strongly influences women's lives. The late twentieth century witnessed significant shifts in the nature of

Women writing Ireland

Women's contribution to Ireland's cultural and literary heritage has not often been acknowledged or, indeed, recognised. A 1983 survey found that 89 per cent of published Irish poetry was written by men, while *The New Oxford Book of Irish Verse*, published in 1986, included no women at all. *The New Penguin Book of Irish Poetry*, 1990, was an improvement, albeit with only a 35:4 ratio of male to female poets. The greatest outrage, however, followed the publication of the three-volume *The Field Day Anthology of Irish Writing* in 1991, which claimed to be a comprehensive collection of Irish writing from the sixth to the twentieth century. Contributions from only a very few women were represented in its 4,000 pages. Eleven years in preparation, volumes IV and V of the *Field Day Anthology*, featuring women's writing, was published in October 2002.

Given the scant recognition allowed to women in mainstream publications, it is not so surprising that much of the recovery of women's writing has been in 'women-only' collections. Ruth Hooley edited *The Female Line* in 1985, to celebrate ten years of the Northern Ireland Women's Rights Movement. Wolfhound Press published A.A. Kelly's *Pillars of The House*, the first anthology of Irish women's verse in 1987, with Ailbhe Smyth's anthology *Wildish Things*, an anthology of new women's writing, appearing in 1989.

Writers such as Eavan Boland, Eithne Strong, Eiléan Ní Chuilleanáin, and Medbh McGuckian, in finding their voices and forging their identity as Irish women poets, have made important contributions to the genre. Fiction writers such as Jennifer Johnston, Éilís Ní Dhuibhne, Maeve Kelly, Maeve Binchy, Julia O'Faolain and Mary O'Donnell attest to the continuing power of the Irish short story and novel.

Ruth Hooley (ed.), *The Female Line: Northern Irish Women Writers* (Belfast, 1985); Lorna Stevens, Stephen Brown and Pauline MacLaran, 'Gender, Nationality and Cultural Representations of Ireland: An Irishwoman's Place?', *European Journal of Women's Studies*, vol. 7 (2000), pp 405–21; Catherine Byron, 'The Room is a Kind of Travel Also: An Appreciation of the Poetry of Medbh McGuckian', *Linen Hall Review*, vol. 5, no.1. (spring 1988), pp. 16–17

this relationship and in the ways in which civil society responded to it. In the 1980s, as it fought off the calls to legalise divorce and abortion, lay groups rallied behind the Catholic hierarchy, and the Church's position in relation to social life appeared relatively strong. Moreover, the appearance of supernatural phenomena in various country areas in 1985 drew attention to the strength of popular emotional and spiritual attachment to the faith. During July, August and September of that year, at Ballinspittle, Mount Mellery, Asdee, Ballydesmond, Courtmacsherry, and over thirty small Marian shrines in different parts of the country, it was reported that statues of the Virgin Mary were moving or speaking, and that several people had seen visions of heavenly light. Various explanations were offered, but one common theory was that these experiences were somehow connected to the ongoing 'war of the womb' – a reference to contemporary public and media debates on sexuality, contraception and abortion. Margaret MacCurtain asserts that these examples of communal lay devotion should not be simply dismissed, but accepted as a spiritual response to the ongoing crisis, for, as she stresses, 'the statues that moved were of Mary, a woman, in a year that had not been kind to Irish women'.[85]

The 1983 abortion referendum had divided women among themselves, but while the women's movement battled with the strictures of the Church, women within the Church were also beginning to question and challenge their traditional roles. The ramifications of the Second Vatican Council, 1962, which sought to modernise the Catholic Church and took some time to filter through, began to be felt in monasteries and convents. MacCurtain, herself a Dominican sister, ardent feminist and internationally-recognised scholar, commented that until then

> diocesan control of religious women by bishops and priests [had] led to supervision of rising and retiring times, use of telephones, permission for egress from convents, supervision of wearing apparel, and even the length of a habit! It would be absurd if it were not so tragic in the wreckage of infantilism that it has left.[86]

Rejecting the seclusion of earlier times in favour of 'responsible obedience', nuns of the late twentieth century often work for the Church 'away from the altar'. Living in housing estates and amongst the poor they are an inspiration for lay workers and the disadvantaged people they serve. Sister Stanislaus Kennedy, for example, had been involved with Bishop Peter Birch's many social reforms in Kilkenny, becoming Director of the Kilkenny Social Services Group in 1970 and chairperson of the National Committee to Combat Poverty between 1974 and 1980. In 1982 she became the first nun to receive an honorary doctorate of law from Trinity College Dublin, and a year later undertook the first major study of the homeless in Dublin, in 1994 creating Focus Ireland, a national research, development and public awareness project.[87]

Despite the fine example of such individuals, by the 1990s the tide seemed to be turning against the Church, a combination of factors serving to reduce its status and diminish its authority. The economic transformation of the nation and greater international influence, experienced particularly in urban areas and among those who regularly travelled abroad on cheap foreign holidays, helped to secularise personal values. Most immediately damaging to the reputation of the Church, however, was a series of scandals which suggested that some of those who had set themselves up as arbiters of sexual behaviour had not followed such high moral standards in their own personal lives. The most infamous cases were those of Bishop Éamon Casey of Galway and Father Brendan Smyth. It came to light in May 1992 that Casey had a sixteen-year-old son with Annie Murphy, an American divorcee with whom he had had a long-standing affair. In 1994 an investigation was launched into child sexual abuse, resulting three years later in Smyth's extradition from Northern Ireland to the Republic, where he faced seventy-four sex abuse charges. Public anger at the hypocrisy and betrayal of trust which these cases revealed was exacerbated by the Church's attempts to cover up the crimes of Smyth, and protect him from legal punishment. The comment that the Church was 'not outside the law' was one repeatedly heard during the public outrage that followed. The press had something of a field day with clerical scandals thereafter: in 1996, no less than thirty-four stories focused on the sexuality, celibacy and misconduct of clergy and the religious.[88]

Female religious were also subject to criticism, though the scandals that surrounded them were not about their own sexuality, but about their treatment and care of 'fallen' women, and children born outside marriage who had been placed in their care in previous generations. When RTÉ broadcast Louis Lentin's documentary *Dear Daughter* in 1996, reaction was swift. The film brought to light the harsh treatment meted out to children in Dublin's Goldenbridge orphanage by the Sisters of Mercy during the 1940s and 1950s. It was alleged that this included 'beatings, scalding [and the] humiliation of bed-wetting children'.[89] Newspapers and radio shows facilitated those who wished to tell similar stories and the previously unsullied reputation of female religious orders was held to public account. Further anger followed the revelation that the babies of unmarried Irish women had been exported for adoption, mostly to the USA, in operations involving not only nuns but also the Church hierarchy and the state.[90] It would have been surprising if this rash of allegations and accusations had not impacted on the Church's public profile.

Regular weekly mass attendance had always been very high in Ireland,

North and South. In 1990 attendance figures in the Republic were the highest in the world at 85 per cent, dropping to 64 per cent in 1995. Perhaps more significant was the great decline in numbers taking monthly confession, with numbers falling from 47 per cent in 1974 to 14 per cent in 1995, suggesting an important shift in attitudes to the power and authority of the Church in moral matters.[91] Bridie Quinn-Conroy, from County Galway, remarked on the changes over the course of her own lifetime. She recalled that, in her youth,

> one of the greatest disincentives to sin was the fact that to get pardon, I'd have to tell the priest and he would surely shout and give out and everybody would hear. So, in order to make sure that we didn't get screamed at, we just didn't commit the sins.[92]

Now, she claimed, absolution and forgiveness were much more easily granted.

Also serious in terms of the Church's future prospects was the decline in the number of vocations to religious life, both male and female – a 96 per cent decrease for sisters, from 1966, when there were 592, to 19 in 1996. In 1998, for the first time, the main Catholic seminary in Dublin had no new recruits at all. While the Church has always enjoyed considerable control over primary- and secondary-level schooling, the decline in religious vocation in an expanding educational sector suggests that this influence will be much reduced in the twenty-first century. Tom Inglis concludes that 'the influence of the Church in the religious field has declined significantly and that this has links to its decline in other secular fields'.[93]

A survey carried out in Northern Ireland in 1997 revealed that both Protestant and Catholic churchgoers were most likely to be women, middle class and middle-aged or elderly.[94] The unemployed were poor attenders, as were the young, though it was reported that churchgoers under twenty-five years old were 'overwhelmingly conservative' in their religious convictions. That almost 25 per cent of marriages in Northern Ireland in 1998 were held in registry offices, compared to 14 per cent in 1994, is also a reflection of growing secularisation among the young.

Women are now able to engage more fully in the offices of Protestant churches. In June 1987, twenty-five-year-old Katherine Poulton was ordained at St Patrick's in Ballymacarret, in east Belfast, the first woman deacon in the Church of Ireland.[95] Going on to serve St Comgall's congregation in Bangor, she carried out all priestly duties except administering the sacraments. The Presbyterian Church admits women as elders, missionaries and, more recently, as ministers, though many congregations refuse to elect or accept women in the latter position, reflecting an 'innate chauvinism that has little to do with theology'. As Sarah, a young evangelical from Portadown, County Armagh, indicates, this means there are few role models for young Christian women:

> and if we're not careful then the women of my generation will repeat the patterns of the past. But I think men have suffered as well from not having women involved as they should be. Women have so much to offer and so many other dimensions they can bring to leadership, and it's not that we want to overthrow men in leadership, but that we offer a balance to them, and in this way the Church can fill out what has been missing.[96]

Despite the availability of statistical evidence, it is difficult to assess the overall state of religious faith on the island. Tom Inglis, focusing on recent legislative and attitudinal changes around sexuality, states that in modern Ireland things which were once hidden are now being told, 'they are being told in courts, in newspapers, radio and television, in counselling groups and among friends. A language has been found for what was once inarticulate'.[97] He goes on to suggest that with the separation of sexuality and childbirth, 'as well as revealing abuses and perversions which had been swept under the carpet, the new language of sexuality helped people discover the pleasures of sex . . . Desire and fantasy were liberated from the cells of sin'.[98] However, Andrew Greeley suggests that changes in attitudes on certain aspects of sexual morality should not be equated with rapid secularisation. Rather, he urges us to focus on the 'experiential, imaginative, metaphorical and narrative content of Irish religion', and to acknowledge 'that the Irish have an ancient and powerful heritage which is deeply rooted in their culture and tradition, a heritage that is unique and fascinating, and a heritage that will, as it has in the past, both change and survive'.[99] Women's place in that heritage has, as we have seen, not always been recognised, and the extent to which they will make an impact in the twenty-first century is by no means clear.

THE NORTHERN IRELAND CONFLICT

For both men and women in Northern Ireland, daily life continued to be dominated by political, military and communal violence. The statistics are easily related: the year 1980 saw 76 deaths resulting from the conflict, with some 642 shootings, 280 bomb explosions and 550 people charged with terrorist and serious public-order offences.[100] The ways in which individuals were affected by these events, however, varied considerably and, while gender can appear irrelevant against such a backdrop, the experience of men and women differed. Of the 3,601 people who died as a result of political violence during the first thirty years of the conflict, the vast majority (over 91 per cent) were men.[101] Many thousands of both sexes, however, were directly touched by the untimely deaths of loved ones, while the families of those either physically or psychologically scarred were changed forever. Official and unofficial armed forces, the convicted and imprisoned, whether driven by anger, fear, resentment or a sense of righteousness, all contributed to and were deeply affected by the ongoing political crisis.

One issue that did highlight gender issues and attracted the attention of both the media at the time and feminist commentators since was the position of female political prisoners. On Friday 7 February 1980 the escalation of the campaign for the return of special category status saw republican women in Armagh jail joining their male comrades in Long Kesh in the 'dirty protest'.[102] Having previously confined their protest to a refusal to work, this radical action was triggered by an assault by prison staff during a search. Thirty women stopped washing their bodies, brushing their teeth and hair, and emptied their chamber pots into the passages outside the cells until the blocking of windows and spy holes prevented them doing so. Thereafter, the cells, into which they were locked for twenty-three hours a day, were used as toilets. Although women had long argued for equality within the republican movement, there is no doubt that the health risks of the dirty protest, bad for all, were different for men and women. The dangers posed by infection during their menstrual periods caused particular anxiety, and the fact that there was 'blood on the walls of Armagh prison',[103] gave rise to deep concern among one section of the community, and expressions of disgust at such 'unwomanly' behaviour in the other.

In these difficult and dangerous conditions, both tight discipline and mutual support served as essential antidotes to the horrors of daily life. Thus, while each woman, in the words of Nell McCafferty, was 'constructing from their bodily waste a silent smelly cave', a strict daily routine was followed which included the nightly recital of the rosary. In December, Mary Doyle, Mairead Nugent and Mairead Farrell[104] followed the example of male prisoners and began a hunger strike. That she was risking her chance of ever becoming a mother was a very real fear expressed by Doyle. McCafferty again graphically captured the 'shocking power' of the situation in Armagh jail, when she characterised it by 'starvation, stench, stagnation and gilded sterility'.[105] The hunger strike was called off after eighteen days, with the prisoners' demands apparently agreed, though the men recommenced their protest the following March when these were not met. In a change of strategy designed to keep the political and media focus on the men's actions, the women prisoners called off their no-wash campaign and did not resume the hunger strike.

This was an emotive time, both inside and outside the prisons of Northern Ireland. Prime Minister Margaret Thatcher expressed her determination not to 'give in to terrorists', and ten men died over the course of six months, including Bobby Sands who had been elected as MP for Fermanagh–South Tyrone. Sands died on the sixty-sixth day of his hunger strike in an atmosphere of rising tension, and support for the martyred men became an even more important measure of political allegiance. But with many Protestants regarding them as unrepentant terrorists, the two major religious communities were driven yet further apart. Mairead Corrigan Maguire fully understood why so many ordinary Catholic people were anxious to honour the dead and dying prisoners:

> I watched Bobby Sands's funeral. The coffin stopped at the bottom of our garden in Andersonstown. I saw at the funeral of Bobby Sands people who had been at my sister's funeral, who marched in the peace rallies, walking by the coffin of Bobby Sands because people are entirely tied into the prisons. It's not that they support violence or the Provisional IRA. But they are all men from our community. We know how they have come to be there. And above all we don't want them suffering within the prisons.[106]

The Conservative government's refusal to take action further increased the bitterness felt by many nationalists, and the families of hunger-strikers, clear in the knowledge that death would achieve little, began to intervene to save the lives of relatives. The hunger strike thus ended in late 1982, with only partial concessions made; political prisoners had 50 per cent remission restored, were able to wear their own clothes, have free association and receive more visits.

From November 1982, there was a renewed focus on the problems facing women prisoners. This time the issue was strip-searching, the excessive use of which was regarded as a major form of sexual harassment. Characterised by Aretxaga Begoña as 'a violent technology of control aimed at breaking the political identity of prisoners', the first strip-searches (apart from those carried out on new inmates) were a result of keys being found in the possession of two remand prisoners.[107] The Secretary of State and the prison authorities claimed that this incident justified the introduction of random strip-searches, which continued even when women prisoners were moved from the old Armagh jail to a new high security prison at Maghaberry. Despite protests from feminists and human rights activists that the searches were unnecessary in terms of security (nothing was ever found) and both personally degrading and psychologically damaging to the victims, strip-searching continued into the 1990s. Nationalist and republican women in the community rallied round in support of the prisoners, mounting pickets and protests, with Women Against Imperialism especially involved in drawing attention to their situation. Loyalist Hester Dunn also contributed to the debate, pointing out in a UDA magazine in 1985 that this was not only an issue for republicans, but that 'any man who loves or respects women, be they wives, sisters, mothers or daughters, would [not] like them to be subject to these searches'. Dunn admitted that she found herself 'in argument with a lot of strange bed fellows on the subject of strip searching', but argued that it was 'morally wrong to remain silent on this issue'.[108] However, from most Protestant perspectives, the actions of the prison authorities were justified by the dangers of militant republicanism and there was little sympathy for the intimidating and humiliating treatment meted out to the prisoners. Within the women's movement, the tensions between republicans and other feminists reached new heights. With strip-searching seen as a 'site of political resentment and personal shame' by prisoners' supporters, the refusal of the NIWRM to engage in the protests ensured that 'Armagh became a metaphor for everything that has kept Irish women divided from each other'.[109]

The Stop the Strip Search campaign was supported in Britain as well as on both sides of the border, through organisations such as the London Armagh Group. Indeed, the plight of Irish women prisoners provided a focus for many London-based Irish women, as well as British radicals. An Irish Women's Centre was established and conferences held, and an Irish women's housing group and lesbian network also evolved as part of a wider network. Also providing a focus for campaigners were the numbers of convictions that were deemed to be unsafe, resulting from forced confessions or false evidence. For example, Annie Maguire, who was born in Belfast but had moved to England in 1957, was arrested along with her husband, two of her children, her brother, her husband's brother-in-law and a family friend, following a no-warning pub bomb in Guildford, Surrey. Charged with possessing explosives and running an IRA bomb factory, the Maguire Seven, as they came to be known, were sentenced to life imprisonment. They served between four and fourteen years in British prisons, during which time one of the group, Guiseppe Conlon, died, before being cleared by the Court of Appeal in London in June 1991. Annie Maguire, a mother with four children and three grandchildren, spent ten years in jail and later reflected, 'when I was released, I knew that I had lost my children. When I came out, the boys were men and Anne Marie was a young woman. I had to get to know them again. They were different people.'[110] Relatives of the Guildford Four and the Birmingham Six, who also served long terms in British prisons before being acquitted of the charges against them,[111] similarly suffered from the lengthy absence of their loved ones. Having to travel to England considerably exacerbated the difficulties of prison visiting. Reaction to the IRA's bombing campaign in Britain had other implications for the wider Irish community. Irish women living in England may not have been directly accused of terrorist activity, but some found that just to be recognised as Irish could provoke hostility. One woman in her sixties who felt the need to conceal her national origins, explained:

> When a bombing or anything like that happens I say 'Thank God, for supermarkets', because you don't have to speak, you don't have to ask for a loaf of bread. I do feel intimidated. I wouldn't want to get into a difficult situation, because I wouldn't know how I'd react. When I buy *The Irish Post* I fold it over when I am in the shop – and I like to buy it in an Indian shop. I notice myself doing all these things, very much so.[112]

Reviewing the literature on Northern Ireland over the last thirty years, E. Moxon-Brown argues that there has been a significant imbalance in the religious profile of the subjects:

> Very few researchers have seemed to feel that looking in detail at the perceptions of Protestants themselves about the conflict will augment their understanding of the situation substantially . . . research students appeared to find Catholics more sympathetic, more fashionable and more interesting subjects of study.[113]

The loyalist unionist community has thus become more isolated and defensive over the course of the conflict. This was particularly true when the search for a political solution was increasingly seen to be dependent on seeking an accommodation with nationalist aspirations. The Anglo-Irish Agreement, signed by Margaret Thatcher and Irish Taoiseach Garret FitzGerald in November 1985, provided a particular focus for loyalist anger. Although it promised that any change would only come about with the consent of a majority of the people of Northern Ireland, this agreement was interpreted as a 'backward step' within unionism. The close involvement of the government of what loyalists still declared to be a 'foreign state' was a further source of contention, and viewed as an act of betrayal by the British Prime Minister, who was labelled as 'this wicked treacherous lying woman' by an enraged Ian Paisley.[114] More usually heard speaking out in support of minorities, Mary Robinson withdrew from the Irish Labour Party in protest at what she believed to be an undemocratic process.

Against this background, it was perhaps not surprising that many middle-class, 'middle-of-the-road Protestants were having an identity crisis'.[115] Thelma Agnew, a Protestant woman from Larne, County Antrim, described how she felt totally alienated when she arrived at the University of Kent to take up undergraduate studies. When the situation of Irish women was discussed, she felt that she was 'falling through the net ... in my new enlightened environment, where Ulster Unionists were regarded as Sun-reading Ayatollahs'.[116] Hazel Gordon also commented on the perceived stereotypes that made life so difficult for Protestant women, claiming that, 'a Protestant woman standing up for herself is rocking the status quo', while to be a 'staunch' or 'strong' Protestant is to be associated with bigotry.[117] Susan McKay's study of the views of Protestants at the end of the 1990s suggests, however, that many of the stereotypes ring true. Her interviews record much denial about the nature of loyalist sectarianism – whether around gerrymandering or Bloody Sunday, or in local responses to the killing of three Catholic children during Orange protests in 1998.[118] While *Northern Protestants: An Unsettled People* does not encompass all Protestant perspectives, and is perhaps rather light on liberal views, it does reflect the mixture of ambivalence, guilt and shame felt by many. It also sheds light on the difficulty of reconciling particular views of history with the realities of the present. Many Protestants, for example, became disillusioned with the British government, and indeed, with some of the official representatives of unionism. Mina Wardell felt that:

> The protestant community just wasn't aware of the discrimination, but they are now. We were told we were God's own people. Stormont would look after us and all the rest of it. We don't believe that any longer. We haven't believed that for thirty years and we are fighting back. I don't feel discrimination is any less on the protestant side than it is on the catholic side. I think all women suffer the same discrimination whether it be by the church or by the state or whatever.[119]

For many loyalists and unionists, upholding the traditions of their own community was seen as essential. Isobel McCullough from Moneymore, County Derry, vividly described her pride and pleasure in the traditions surrounding the Twelfth of July. For her, the Lambeg drums were associated with nostalgia, nationality, and the tenacity and triumph of her culture.[120] An increasing number, however, believed that their cultural heritage was under threat. The decision of the Parades Commission, backed by the security forces, to ban a march by Orangemen down the mainly Catholic Garvaghy

Road in Portadown, County Armagh, first taken in 1998, has since come to symbolise the perceived attack on Protestant rights. Protests have been held annually at Drumcree since 1995, and, while ' "Orange Lil" is not the whole story', many of those who blocked roads and turned back traffic when the disturbances spread around the North in July 2000 were women. While nationalism, at least on the surface, appears to present 'a more elaborate ideological package', 'no totalising philosophy covers the whole coalition' of unionism, much less of Protestantism.[121]

The Provisional IRA ceasefire in August 1994, followed by a ceasefire called by the Combined Loyalist Military Command in October of that year, gave the people of Northern Ireland a respite from the years of death and destruction. The main reaction was one of overwhelming relief as people tentatively returned to more 'normal' ways of life. Only during this period of relative calm was the extent of former tensions realised. As Hazel Gordon put it:

> We dealt with the Troubles by not dealing with it. I made my son ring if he was not going to come home. Now I don't have to do it. You don't notice normality. I have always gone everywhere in Belfast, but now I notice I don't worry, the tension has gone that I did not realise was there.[122]

The peace was shattered eighteen months later when, with unionists continuing to demand decommissioning as a prerequisite to all-party talks, the Provisional IRA accused the British government of acting in bad faith and called off its ceasefire. On 9 February 1996 the Provisionals exploded a bomb in the underground car park of Canary Wharf tower in London, killing two men, injuring more than 100 and causing approximately £100 million worth of damage in the financial heart of the city. Nonetheless, a turning point had been reached, and with politicians in Dublin, Belfast and London engaged in complex and protracted negotiations, some kind of official peace process was finally under way. Following talks involving representatives of constitutional parties and paramilitary groups from both sides of the political divide, a historic agreement was signed on 10 April 1998, providing the opportunity for a cross-party local assembly to take control of the government of Northern Ireland. As part of the Good Friday Agreement, all political prisoners were released by March 1999, including eight female republicans; there were no serving female loyalist prisoners at that time.

The signing of the Agreement did not bring an end to the violence, however. In August 1998 dissident republicans exploded a 500lb car bomb in Omagh, County Tyrone, killing twenty-nine people, including a woman pregnant with twins, in the single worst atrocity since the beginning of the conflict. In March 1999 Catholic lawyer Rosemary Nelson was killed by a loyalist booby-trap car bomb near her home in Lurgan, County Armagh, and in June of the same year Elizabeth O'Neill, a Protestant married to a Catholic, died when loyalists threw a pipe bomb into her home in Portadown. The violence has continued into the twenty-first century, a sombre background to the fragile political settlement.

COMMUNITY POLITICS

One of the most interesting phenomena of the 1980s and 1990s was the development of women's role in community politics, much of it originating in local organisations where women came together to provide support, resources and leadership. Unlike the organisations associated with the women's movements of the 1970s, this strand of female activism is strongly working-class. As community activist Cathleen O'Neill put it, 'it is a different kind of feminism, it is literally bread and butter issues.'[123] Women's community groups provide, first and foremost, a safe space for local women. Christine, from north Belfast, who attended a women's centre in her housing estate, explained, 'What I liked about the centre is, you got a lot of support from each other and you could say what you liked'.[124] While Protestant groups became involved later than their Catholic counterparts, most working-class areas had vibrant women's centres by the end of the century. Like early republican political activism, the involvement of many loyalist women in such groups came out of their own experiences. Caroline in east Belfast, for example, had to learn how to fight for her legal rights when her husband was imprisoned on the word of a loyalist supergrass. She had to engage in dialogue with local politicians and educate herself in welfare and other rights. She moved on to bringing experts in to speak to other women at local meetings, their placards proclaiming, 'We are British Citizens, Give us British Law'.[125] This engagement at grass-roots level seems to have facilitated the politicisation of loyalist women in many areas. Although there is some co-operation across sectarian boundaries, most groups work within their own locality, securing European and 'peace' funding to run classes on health, politics, local environmental issues, history and creative writing. In 1989, however, Protestant women of the Shankhill Road joined the protest of those from a women's centre on the Catholic Falls Road when Belfast City Council withdrew funding from the latter – a rare example of gender issues being given priority over more entrenched identities.

Downtown Women's Centre, a neutral venue and more overtly feminist than many of the others, is the base for the Belfast Women's Support Network. This organisation helps to facilitate co-operative ventures such as the Women's Information Day, which brings women together on the first Tuesday of each month, in alternating Catholic, Protestant and neutral venues. Although the political origins and loyalties of the women involved differ widely, by focusing on common experiences of poverty and margin-alisation, they work to ensure that issues affecting working-class women are heard at government level. A host of other networks have evolved at coun-ty level, or to bring together rural women or older women, or to facilitate research and developmental activities. The wider context is often problem-atic; on International Women's Day 1993, for example, Belfast City Council excluded the Lesbian Line, the Brook clinic, and Sinn Féin women from participating in an event in the City Hall. Only grant-aided women's groups received invitations.[126]

Nonetheless, the work of local women's groups has often provided a gleam of light on dark and difficult days, and their efforts and achievements have been acknowledged by visits from successive Presidents of Ireland, Mary Robinson and Mary McAleese, and the American First Lady, Hillary Clinton. Powerful leaders in their own communities, women like the late Joyce MacCartan of Belfast's Ormeau Road, who lost thirteen family mem-bers in the course of the conflict, and trade-union and community activist May Blood, became household names and won international recognition. Indeed Blood, having received an honorary doctorate from the University of Ulster in 1998, was granted a life peerage a year later.

Women's groups also thrived in the Republic in this period. Mary Cummins noted that the

> reams of journalists coming to look for the 'real Ireland', focusing in on the
> X case, abortion, Kerry Babies etc., the sensational news and the oppressed
> woman, [failed] however to mention the conferences, women's groups, [they
> were] selling only one side of Ireland.[127]

As in the North, these groups offered a wide range of facilities and oppor-tunities: educational, environmental, political, cultural, social and personal. And here, too, they could be feminist or familist in their composition and objectives. They were particularly significant for women living in isolated rural areas, where the existence of a friendly and accessible centre and the building of networks helped to empower both individuals and their com-munities. Western Women's Link, for example, launched by Mary Robinson in July 1991, had sixty member groups by 1995, stretching from Donegal to

Clare and east to Athlone.

Eilís Ward and Orla O'Donovan, exploring the relationship between such groups and the women's movement, suggested that too many assumptions have been made about the politicising potential of the former. Previous research had indicated that it was problematic to raise the issues of Northern Ireland and abortion among women within these groups, and Ward and O'Donovan concluded that while there may be an organic link, views on feminism and politics were divided. They felt that the most significant impact made by women's groups was on women's personal and private lives. The 'combination of feminism and tradition' they highlighted confirms an earlier European comparative study which pointed out that Ireland had the highest percentage of strong feminists in Europe, but also the highest percentage of non-feminists.[128] Moreover, as a report from Democratic Dialogue in 2000 suggests, 'non-institutional or even anti-institutional activities are empowering to the individual, but the ability to exert influence and assert change, over and for others, is limited.'[129] Nonetheless, the Opsahl Commission, which consulted individuals and groups throughout Northern Ireland on the region's political future during 1992 and 1993, and also considered this issue, commented that,

> while there is no simple relationship between women's political participation and the resolution of the conflict, the experience of women's involvement in local community groups suggests that they could have an important contribution to make in the search for a political and constitutional settlement.[130]

Opportunities to become involved in politics increased rapidly following the paramilitary ceasefires of 1994. A series of events took place on both sides of the border, including the Women into Politics initiative, designed to raise the political visibility and participation of women, and a conference held in June 1995 on Women, Politics and The Way Forward was described by political scientist Elisabeth Porter as

> a historic occasion in bringing together women from diverse political backgrounds . . . The conference articulated widespread urgency to instil feminist voices not only in the peace-process, but in actual political decision-making.[131]

In the search for innovative strategies to break the political deadlock, Baroness Jean Denton, as Junior Minister of State from 1994 and the first woman minister in the Northern Ireland Office since Direct Rule, ran a series of public meetings throughout the North, providing the forum and the opportunity for women to make their voices heard. The first woman Secretary of State for Northern Ireland, Mo Mowlam, made an even greater impact, encouraging and facilitating women's political input at the highest level. On the broader political canvas, Mowlam's personality and methods, and the determination of the British Labour government, were significant factors in bringing all sides of Northern Irish political opinion to the nego-tiating table.

In America, the Clinton administration was keen to facilitate the fledgling peace initiative, and the Vital Voices seminars held on either side of the Atlantic were an important aspect of this, ensuring that women were part of the process. Ailbhe Smyth and May Blood both recalled a Boston conference in mid-November 1994, organised and financed by American women, when around fifty women from Northern Ireland and the Republic, attempting to 'reach the common ground', were instead brought face to face with their differences. The Southern contingent was made up of articulate, professional, middle-class urban women, while those from the North, Catholic and Protestant, were mostly working-class community activists[132] – clear evidence of the divergent paths taken by Irish women North and South since the emergence of this stage of the women's move-ment in the 1970s.

Early in 1996, with all the main political parties in the North failing to respond to a series of demands to facilitate women's formal inclusion, it was suggested that one way forward would be through an alternative structure – a gender-specific political party. The decision to go down this route was taken in response to forthcoming elections for a Northern Ireland Forum, and was initially discussed by Monica McWilliams, at the time a senior lecturer at the University of Ulster at Jordanstown, and Avila Kilmurray, director of the Northern Ireland Voluntary Trust.[133] The Northern Ireland Women's Coalition (NIWC) was launched on 17 April 1996, with the aim of winning two seats on the new Forum. In the six weeks remaining before the election, the coalition 'translated argument into action' and put seventy women candidates forward for election. On polling day they took almost everyone by surprise. As the *Belfast Telegraph* reported:

> The Women's Coalition had the last laugh of the polls. Critics nicknamed them the 'hen party' and called them naïve, and an election distraction. But the new cross-community female group won enough votes to be at the talks table. In doing so, they edged out more-established parties like the Ulster Tories, the Workers' Party and Democratic Left. Not bad for an organisation which was formed only six weeks ago.[134]

Members of the NIWC canvassing during the 1998 election campaign.
From left to right they are Kate Fearon, Anne Carr,
Monica McWilliams, Pearl Sagar and Annie Campbell.

Members of the NIWC had no trouble agreeing amongst themselves about matters such as health, poverty and unemployment, as reflected in the party's key principles: 'inclusion, equality and human rights'. On the more divisive constitutional issues, however, election agent May Blood stated, 'We have agreed to differ. Peace is the bottom line'.[135] She further explained:

> We are not going into these negotiations with mind-sets but with a mind set for peace. We will have our differences but we will agree to differ. We are committed to keep working until we reach an accommodation.[136]

For many women in the North, it was refreshing to have a different party to vote for, one which was not vociferously sectarian and which claimed to represent their views. Others viewed the party as a catalyst for change. Support was given by Senator Mary Henry of Group 84, a cross-party association of women deputies in the Republic, and by Kathleen Stephens, then US Consul-General in Belfast. But there was considerable unease from women inside and outside the political arena in the North, both about the party's evasion of the constitutional question and the way in which it appeared to diminish the achievements of women in other political parties.

Women's Coalition

In 1996 the election manifesto of the Northern Ireland Women's Coalition read:

Working for a solution

Offering inclusion

Making women heard

Equity for all

New thinking

Most of the key players in the Women's Coalition were already well-known activists. Whether through student politics, trade union circles, the women's movement, community groups or other areas of the voluntary sector, women such as Bronagh Hinds, Avila Kilmurray, Monica McWilliams, Pearl Sagar, Annie Campbell, Brenda Callaghan, Robin Whittaker, Kate Fearon, Jane Wilde, May Blood, Margaret Logue, Diane Greer, Lynda Edgerton Walker and Gerry Gribben, had collectively accumulated a mass of exprience and expertise. Felicity Huston and Anne Carr had been more involved in formal politics, while two women named Anne McCann had served on the Board of Visitors at Maze Prison. The insights thus gained provided the fledgling party with a strong base in a wide range of local issues.

Kate Fearon, *Women's Work: The Story of the Northern Ireland Women's Coalition* (Belfast, 1999), pp. 40–50

One Social Democratic and Labour Party (SDLP) woman was dismayed by the media attention given to the NIWC, declaring that she was

> very angry that suddenly the whole media discovered women in politics, as if women did not exist before Monica McWilliams and Pearl Sagar came forward. They didn't do one serious interview with any woman from any political party throughout the campaign; it was a trendy headline grabbing thing to do.[137]

Having won only 1.03 per cent of the overall vote, it was also felt the election of two 'women's party' representatives was undemocratic. Others voiced disbelief in the general opinion that 'women's voice would change everything, simply by virtue of their gender'.[138]

Of the 110 candidates elected to the Northern Ireland Forum, 14 were women: 4 were Sinn Féin, 3 Democratic Unionist Party (DUP), 3 SDLP, 2 NIWC, 1 Alliance Party and 1 UUP. Only the top two or three from every party were invited to be at the negotiating table when talks began, and the only women involved at this level were those from the NIWC: Monica McWilliams and Pearl Sagar, a community worker from a unionist background. The Forum was only in existence for two years, but during its lifetime women were closely involved in the frequently controversial negotiations that led to the signing of the Agreement in 1998.

All the major parties had policy statements on women's issues by that stage; and all endorsed the concept of equal rights, though only Sinn Féin and the SDLP exercised positive discrimination in their selection of their parliamentary and council candidates. Gerry Adams had admitted in 1983, that it was 'only in the last few years that we have begun to treat women's affairs in a political way and we do stand open to criticism on that issue.'[139] His party's adoption of the Women's Right to Choose position in the Republic's abortion referendum of 1985 had appeared to reflect the greater influence of feminist voices, but in 1995 republican women formed Clár na mBan in frustration and anger about women's invisibility in the new round of political negotiations, which they regarded as 'exclusive and undemocratic'.[140] Similarly, Rhonda Paisley, daughter of the leader of the DUP, stated that, within its ranks,

> the feminist message is one which is not winning its battle. During my time (short though it may be) of involvement in Unionist politics, I have witnessed no inclination to take on board feminist issues. If anything, the longer I am involved the more distasteful I find attitudes and the more superficial I believe the majority of male elected representatives are in their interests in feminist concerns.[141]

Although one of the newer parties, the Progressive Unionist Party (PUP), formed to represent the viewpoints of paramilitary loyalists, has four women on its executive, the gender balance in the party in general is not so strong. As Irene Murphy, PUP party member, feminist and community activist, pointed out, 'The party grew out of a very macho environment, and showing men their issues are not the only issues is hard.'[142] The general pattern is one of lower political representation of women within unionism and a relatively high presence of nationalist women and, particularly so, of republican women within Sinn Féin.[143]

The signing of the Good Friday Agreement proved to be a massive turning point in Northern Ireland's history, with its arrangements for devolution, decommissioning and demilitarisation endorsed by a Yes vote of over 70 per cent in a referendum held in Northern Ireland, and 95 per cent in the Republic. But, although the Agreement called for 'the right of women to full and equal political participation', only 14 of the 110 members of the new Assembly – 13 per cent – were women, as were 17 of the 110 committee places. Brid Rodgers of the SDLP was appointed Minister of Agriculture, and Bairbre de Brún, Sinn Féin, Minister of Health, Social Services and Public Safety. Rodgers was not, however, impressed, complaining, 'when they were giving out the Ministerial portfolios at the Assembly, the two women were given the two that nobody else wanted.'[144] A report by the Northern Ireland Committee of ICTU and the Equality Commission for Northern Ireland stated that the Assembly, as a key player in shaping the equality agenda, 'has the potential to transform the situation of women'. However, as debates continue to focus on constitutional and military lines, little progress has been made in this direction. Moreover, female MLAs, even if they wished to, have been unable to work together as a group because of traditional unionist–nationalist hostility.

WOMEN AND POLITICS
IN THE REPUBLIC OF IRELAND

Women in the South have made considerably more progress than their counterparts in Northern Ireland in terms of political participation. They have not only gained more parliamentary seats, but more positions of power generally. The increase was gradual, but is undoubtedly beginning to pick up pace. In 1982 women were elected to 14 of the 166 Dáil seats, but in 1992 20 (12 per cent) reached their highest level in 7 decades.[145] At one point during 1996–7 there were 23 female TDs, but this number had fallen to 20 again by 1997. While this sounds quite impressive, the proportion of elected female deputies recorded in 1992 compared poorly with 33 per cent in Denmark, 28.6 per cent in Holland and 20.5 per cent in Germany, though it was better than the UK figure of 9.2 per cent.[146] In 1997 the all-party Oireachtas Committee Report on the Constitution commented that:

> Even casual observation of the Irish political system reveals that there is marked gender imbalance among public representatives. This is another systems weakness because it means that the knowledge, experience and sensibility of women are largely absent from the process through which the state seeks to express the values of its people.[147]

It was nonetheless encouraging that women were beginning to be represented in government posts: Eileen Desmond (Labour), as Minister for

Health and Social Welfare from June 1981 to March 1982, was the first woman in a senior cabinet position since the founding of the state; after holding a range of positions, Máire Geoghegan-Quinn (Fianna Fáil) became the first woman Minister for Justice in January 1993; and Mary Harney (Progressive Democrats), Minister of State at the Department of the Environment between 1989 and 1992, became the first woman leader of a national party in 1993 and the first woman Tánaiste in the history of the state in 1997, when she was also appointed Minister for Enterprise, Employment and Trade. It was equally encouraging to see the increasingly high political profile attained by those formerly active in the women's movement: Gemma Hussey (Fine Gael), a former chairwoman of WPA and member of the CSW, was appointed Minister for Education in 1982 and Minister for Social Welfare in 1986. Nuala Fennell (Fine Gael), one of the original founders of the IWLM, was Minister of State at the Department of the Taoiseach and the Department of Justice with Responsibility for Women's Affairs and Family Law Reform, between December 1982 and February 1987.[148]

Many women, however, found it difficult to combine politics and family life. Geoghegan-Quinn, who resigned from politics in January 1997 because of media intrusion into her private life, claimed:

Once you get elected you instantly become public property. You are on call 24 hours a day, 365 days a year ... As a TD you become responsible for whatever it is that any one of your 100,000 constituents wants you to be responsible for. They will raise these issues with you when you are out shopping, relaxing in the pub on Sunday night or at any other time they happen to run into you. Alternately they might decide to, and indeed often do, call to your home to discuss their problems ...[149]

The extreme pressures of political life could impact strongly on relationships. Mary Harney commented that it took over her whole life and she 'put everything into politics in the years between twenty-four and twenty-eight ... the best years in terms of relationship development'. She therefore missed out on giving marriage serious consideration. Women TDs held different views on the role and behaviour of women in parliament. Frances Fitzgerald (Fine Gael), former chairwoman of the CSW, felt that 'Leinster House changes women, that politics de-sexes them and that they assume a style of expression that is more male in attitude.'[150] In a similar vein, Mary Harney claimed that to be successful in politics it was 'necessary to develop male habits', though there were problems with this too; she added:

> If you want to push something you're accused of being aggressive and that's not supposed to be a good thing for a woman. If you get upset and show it, in a way that a man doesn't, you're accused of being emotional. You can never win.[151]

However, Róisín Shorthall, one of Labour's four Dublin women deputies, saw 'no difference between being a female or a male politician', and argued that women's issues should be mainstreamed to avoid the danger of marginalisation. Mary O'Rourke (Fianna Fáil), also said she did not feel that 'women's affairs should be separate from all other affairs'. Fitzgerald disagreed, claiming that 'Women's issues are *all* issues and I'm proud to be associated with them.'[152] Mary Wallace (also Fianna Fáil) described herself as a conservative and was especially concerned with the 'protection of the family, women and children in particular', and took a pro-life stance on abortion.[153] Overall, it would appear that the women of the Dáil hold a range of views, reflecting the diversity of opinions and concerns held by women from all walks of life.

Women are entitled to stand for election to the European Parliament, which has fifteen members from the Republic and three from the North. Northern Ireland elected no women MEPs in the twentieth century, the Republic elected ten. Arguably the most influential Irish woman politician of the twentieth century, however, was a President, who was not only female, but also feminist.

Mary Robinson was elected President of Ireland on 9 November 1990 and her appointment injected a significant degree of optimism and energy into the final decade of the twentieth century. In a pre-vote editorial, with Brian Lenihan (Fianna Fáil) and Robinson (Labour) identified as the main contenders, the *Irish Times* suggested that voters were facing a choice between past and present, tradition and modernity. The newspaper argued that with Lenihan the people would be voting for a man who was experienced and well-liked but who had shown that he embraced 'a set of attitudes and values which ought to be consigned to history'. Robinson, on the other hand, despite the pragmatic twists and turns of the campaign, 'represents and has committed herself over the years to a vision of a future Ireland which can be open, generous, pluralist and tolerant. That is where the choice lies, where two cultures and two Irelands clash.'[154] Robinson was well known for her frequent and successful challenges to the traditional conservatism of the state. In a series of landmark legal cases she had fought for the rights of men, women and children on the issues of illegitimacy, adoption, jury service, homosexuality, contraception, and access to information on abortion.

Late in 1990, what was known as 'Robinson's Rainbow', 'left, liberal, feminist (male and female) and minorities cohesion, together with cross-party and catch-all "top-up" votes, brought victory for the left'.[155]

Like any victor, Mary Robinson was concerned to unite the whole country behind her, but she did pay particular attention to the women of Ireland:

> I must be a President for all the people. Because I was elected by men and women of all parties and none, by many with great moral courage, who stepped out from the faded flags of the Civil War and voted for a new Ireland, and above all by the women of Ireland, mná na hÉireann, who instead of rocking the cradle, rocked the system, and who came out massively to make their mark on the ballot paper and on a new Ireland.[156]

And indeed, during her time in office the presidential residence in Phoenix

Popular culture

Examples of Ireland's changing image in the wider world could be found in all aspects of popular culture. By the 1990s, Irishness no longer suggested conservative agricultural backwardness, but a vibrant, cosmopolitan society, from which originated some of the most popular performers of the times. The new breed of Irish women included singers who won international acclaim, among them The Corrs, Sinéad O'Connor, Mary Black, Mary Coughlan, Sharon Shannon, Enya and Clanaad. Actress Amanda Burton from Ballougry in the North has appeared in some of British television's best-known drama series including *Brookside* and *Peak Practice* and as Dr Samantha Ryan in *Silent Witness*. Pauline McLynn grew up in Galway and her hilarious portrayal of the priests' housekeeper in the irreverent *Father Ted* has won considerable acclaim in a programme whose popularity pointed to a significantly changed attitude towards the Church and its clergy. The icons of today's young Irish women are not necessarily local, of course, but range from Madonna to Ally McBeal. However, since the 1980s, contemporary Ireland has been the setting for popular soap operas such as the small rural community of *Glenroe* and the urban-based *Fair City*. These RTÉ productions, like their long-running British predecessors, *Emmerdale* and *Coronation Street*, have introduced a range of strong female characters whose varied lifestyles reflect at least some of the complexities facing modern Irish women.

MYRTLE HILL

During her eight years as President of Ireland, Mary Robinson
welcomed many groups and individuals to Áras an Uachtarárain who
rarely entered the formal world of politics. She is pictured here with
the editorial board of the *Irish Journal of Feminist Studies*.

Park opened its doors to women from all paths of life, North and South –
academic, community-based, professional – and from all kinds of minority
groups. These included members of the lesbian and gay community, thirty-
five representatives of which were invited to meet Robinson in December
1992. As Mary Holland commented in the *Irish Times*, 'not for the first time,
our President, effortlessly, and generously subversive of entrenched prejudice, has given a signal that cannot be ignored'.[157] Regarded by many as a
'voice for the voiceless', she did face some uncomfortable situations, and was
by no means popular with everyone. Journalist Eamon Dunphy thought her
'an attractive package' and in a patronising article he remarked, 'Most of all
we loved the glory that reflected upon Ireland when Robinson travelled
abroad. In the age of the Supermodel, Ireland possessed its own Supermodel
President.'[158] More serious was the criticism she endured during a visit to
the North in 1993, when she was pictured shaking the hand of Sinn Féin
leader Gerry Adams.

The importance of Mary Robinson cannot be overstated. Her leadership
brought a new style of openness and professionalism to the political arena,
unlike, for example, Margaret Thatcher, who

never made a single major public declaration which addressed itself princi-
pally to women's concerns, or recognised the need to release women's energies and potential. On the contrary, her policies thwarted those energies.[159]

Energising, modernising and liberal, Robinson seemed to represent all that
was best in the now-mature, newly-confident state, providing a face of modern Ireland which, in her person, was 'acceptable to near neighbours and to
the global market'. That acceptability, argues Mary Jones, 'threw significant
assumptions of "Irishness" into stark relief'.[160] By the end of her term of
office she had played a vital role in creating the new, vibrant Ireland which
was attracting tourists and investors alike. In 1997 she took up a new challenge as United Nations High Commissioner for Human Rights.

It was perhaps inevitable that with Robinson's departure women would
dominate the 1997 presidential election campaign, reflecting the popular
perception that her outstanding success in an office that had previously been
of symbolic value only, was, at least in part, due to the strengths of her sex
rather than her personality. A 'Female Race' (the one male candidate was
quickly eliminated), the campaign was described by one journalist as 'the
oddest political contest in the history of the state'.[161] Rosemary Scanlon, the
former singer Dana, who had been living in Alabama where she had a 'God
spot' on radio, was the first ever presidential hopeful to win her candidacy
through nomination from county councils; Adi Roche (Labour candidate)
was an anti-nuclear campaigner; and Mary Banotti (Fine Gael) was an MEP
and former Minister of Justice. In the event, however, the winning candidate was from the North. Mary McAleese, a Catholic lawyer and Pro-Vice
Chancellor of Queen's University Belfast, was elected President on 31
October 1997. The Building Bridges theme of her presidency reflected her
commitment to 'the longstanding challenge of finding a pathway through
the chaos to respectful partnership and peace'.[162]

As a Northern Catholic from one of the most disturbed areas of Belfast,
McAleese and her family had personally experienced prejudice, bigotry and
sectarian violence. Moreover, while working for RTÉ in Dublin during the
1970s, she had been shocked by the general level of Southern ignorance and
disinterest about the situation in the North. Her choice of theme was not
therefore surprising. However, her background did not work in her favour,
with many critics publicly questioning her relationship with Sinn Féin
(Gerry Adams had endorsed her candidacy) and deriding her as a 'loose
cannon'. Within Dublin political circles she was also resented for ousting
former Taoiseach Albert Reynolds as the government's nominee.

Largely unknown by the wider electorate, McAleese has worked hard to establish her reputation. The constraints of the office ensure that these are largely symbolic, but their importance should not be underestimated. In November 1998, for example, she joined Queen Elizabeth II to open the round tower memorial to the Irish who died in the First World War at Messines Ridge in Belgium – a long overdue acknowledgement of the Irish contribution to the Allied forces. With strong spiritual convictions, McAleese is regarded as a 'friendly critic' of the Catholic Church, but though she has advised bishops on various occasions, she can hardly be termed a conventional Catholic. She supports ecumenical endeavours, and once took communion at an Anglican Church in Dublin. She also, controversially, supports gay rights and the ordination of women. In supporting pluralism and viewing Catholicism as just one of Ireland's strengths, it could

Feminist frictions

Even within radical feminism – a small category in itself – the existence of the border, and the conflict to which it gave rise, have caused division and misunderstanding. In the last year of the century, Marie Mulholland and Ailbhe Smyth reflected on the impact of partition on their own feminist activism over a period of fifteen to twenty years. Smyth confessed that from her Dublin base in the 1970s, when she was passionately engaged in the exciting struggle for 'liberation, dignity, equality [and] rights for women', both fear and wariness contributed to her denial of the 'hard realities of the relationship between north and south'. Mulholland, on the other hand, living in west Belfast, felt that she had 'no choice' but to engage with the nationalist struggle, explaining that, 'we wanted to be feminists and we wanted feminist social change. But we also had this war to deal with and we couldn't run away from that. That just wasn't an option.' Both women recounted the difficulty of openly confronting the issue from their respective homes, citing the internal feminist conflicts in Northern Ireland, and the fear, suspicion and guilt felt by those in the Republic when considering the 'problem' of the North. They agreed, however, that the election of Mary Robinson as President had had a huge impact on helping to bridge the gap between feminists on either side of the border, reinforcing Eavan Boland's contention that, 'her presence . . . radicalised the symbolic definition of women' in Ireland.

Marie Mulholland and Ailbhe Smyth, 'A North–South Dialogue', *f/m*, no. 3 (1999), pp. 10–17 perhaps be argued that Ireland's eighth President is well placed to help the Church cope with the challenges of the twenty-first century.[163]

There is no doubt that by the end of the century women throughout the island of Ireland were becoming more visible and more vocal in the public arena. Feminism had helped push open doors which had formerly admitted 'Men Only', and a series of world conferences focused attention on the global nature of gender inequalities. Gertrude Mongella, secretary-general of the Fourth World Conference for Women at Beijing in 1995, claimed that it would be

> the biggest and I dare say the most important United Nations Conference in history, because it is not about one group or the other. This Conference affects every human being on earth. It is the chance for people, in particular women, around the world to link up and communicate, but as you all know, women make the difference in the lives of everyone.[164]

However, while events such as this, resulting in specific agendas for change, have raised hopes and influenced governments, progress should not be seen as inevitable. Economic trends, military conflicts and other political priorities all too often push demands for the rights of women to the margins of public debate. Ireland is no exception; as Yvonne Galligan observed in the final years of the century:

> Tensions remain between women's expectations of partaking in full citizenship, cultural values which seek to inhibit that role, and institutional and policy responses which offer a modest and piecemeal response to the place women are claiming in civic society.[165]

Conclusion
Reflections, revisions and peaceful possibilities

As a woman, I want women who have felt themselves outside history to be written back into history.[1]

Throughout the course of the twentieth century, Irish society underwent a series of dramatic transformations. Social and economic changes impacted on the lives of both men and women, though in different ways, and members of both sexes contributed to the emergence and development of new cultural and political forces. Like those of men, the stories of women were diverse, multifaceted and difficult to confine within the limits of a historical narrative. But it is possible to outline general trends and to identify events which, in retrospect, represented important turning points in women's collective experience.

Although Ireland was constitutionally divided for most of the century, with separate political and legal jurisdictions, there was considerable commonality of experience in many areas of women's lives. Both the rhetoric and the reality reveal that attitudes to women's work and sexual behaviour, for example, did not radically differ on either side of the border. Moreover, some developments, like the two world wars, had implications for women right across Western Europe. The First World War made widows and orphans in both parts of the island, and many women took up the new opportunities offered by the war effort, in and out of uniform, between 1939 and

1945. Recent research suggests that the world wars 'did not bring about profound changes, defined in relation to equality or difference, to women as a category', but rather that they had a more personal impact on the lives of individual women.[2] The nature of such change is difficult to trace, but it must have been variously influenced by fear, grief, loneliness, patriotic fervour or pacifist conviction. Independence and self-confidence were perhaps among the more positive 'gains' felt by those joining the workforce at home or abroad, but this was all too often a short-lived experience. Women in most European countries were similarly regarded as a reserve labour force to be utilised in times of need.

Conflict on the island of Ireland also impacted on and helped determine the experience of women, who were as divided as men in terms of party politics and in their attitudes to the constitutional issue. Women were engaged on both sides during the Easter Rising, the War of Independence and the Civil War. Republican and unionist, they formed organisations to propagandise, fight elections, carry guns and ammunition and, though much less frequently, take up arms in the furtherance of their political aspirations. Gender was therefore by no means a unifying category, and this was particularly true of the North in the second half of the century, where political debate took place against the backdrop of continuing violence and opposing views of national identity. Bernadette Devlin, Mairead Corrigan and Monica McWilliams represented different strands of a struggle that saw women in the firing line in official or unofficial military forces, in prisons, on the streets and in campaign headquarters. More usually, however, as Eilish Rooney commented, many were 'ordinary women living in extraordinary times', caught up in situations over which they had little control. Writing of her mother, Kathleen McManus, Rooney explains:

> Involvement is perhaps too strong and certain a word – suggesting choices and decisions and commitments. Quite simply, during her lifetime in the course of 'the troubles', she sometimes went on protests, attended meetings and, in deference to the range of political attitudes and aspirations of her well-loved children, she bought all of the political newspapers that different political groups sold around the door . . . When she went on rent and rates strike in the civil rights protest during internment, my mother, like thousands of others, ended up in endless debt. Repayments were withdrawn from her meagre benefits, for years and years afterwards. Her house was searched on 'umpteen' occasions . . .[3]

For many women in similar situations, and on both sides of the political divide, maintaining and supporting family and neighbourhood connections could mean sheltering men or women 'on the run' or providing emotional and material support to prisoners. Thousands of women coped with the consequences of bereavement and injury long after 'incidents' were dropped from the news headlines. The proliferation of women's groups, centres and networks during the final decades of the century reflected the extent to which women sought support from each other.

Despite the very real diversities and divisions created by competing religious and nationalist beliefs, class structures and the consequences of history,[4] women's activism has nonetheless been a powerful agent of change. The achievements of first-wave feminism, for example, have often been overlooked in mainstream histories that focused on political and constitutional developments. But through their demands for the vote, a living wage, and for the right to full citizenship, women individually and collectively provided an alternative discourse on the nature and dynamics of power. They also laid firm foundations on which later activists could build. The feminism of the 1970s was more broadly-based than that of the early twentieth century, to a much greater degree concerned with personal and sexual experience, and bringing into open debate issues such as domestic violence, divorce, birth control and abortion. In these areas, as in the more public arenas of employment and parliamentary representation, the campaigns of Irish women were given a higher public profile and increased chance of success by being aired on European as well as national platforms. The Commission on the Status of Women in the Republic, and various Equality Commissions in the North, have worked with their counterparts across Europe to bring about changes in the working environment, designed to ensure that women's increased participation in the labour market is not open to exploitation. But despite considerable success in the implementation of legislative safeguards, Pat O'Connor argues that it is difficult to envisage radical changes to the traditional gendered patterns of employment, 'unless and until women-oriented women constitute a critical mass (at least 30 per cent) of senior management within the structures of the state'.[5] The same point can be made about political institutions, where, while the elections of Mary Robinson and Mary McAleese as Presidents of Ireland reflect a growing willingness to embrace progress, only a radical overhaul of procedures and structures, from the level of local parties to that of national government, will facilitate the evolution of a system that does not equate masculinity with public power.

Overall, however, and despite its minority status, Ailbhe Smyth considered the impact of feminism in the 1980s and 1990s on socio-political, economic and cultural structures to have been transformative:

For over two decades, women have been strenuously contesting the narrow boundaries of their social location(s). No arena is 'sacred' for feminism: family life and structures, personal and sexual relationships, reproduction, safety and security, education, labour market and political participation have all been opened up to critique and in-depth actions for change.[6]

Over the course of the century as a whole, other factors have contributed to the transformation of women's lives. In 1900 agriculture provided employment for around 80 per cent of the population outside of the north-east; by the late 1990s, only 10 per cent of the population worked in this sector. Furthermore, Fintan O'Toole claims that 'those who remained were not romantic peasants but business people who spent much of their time filling out forms for EU subsidies'.[7] However, the view that Irish rural life can ever have been described as 'romantic' is no longer sustainable as anything other than one shaped by contemporary nostalgia. Nor can that image be replaced with the narrow and constricted portrayal of countrywomen constructed by some feminist historians. Catriona Clear has particularly warned of the dangers of assessing the past by the criteria of the present, and her own research offers a positive reinterpretation of women's lives in the home, whether in rural or urban Ireland. Clear argues that the realities of their experiences and their aspirations, as revealed through interviews and a wide-ranging survey of the literature, are not consistent with the historical focus on an oppressive 'domestic ideology'. While acknowledging the hostility to women expressed in much of the public discourse, Clear presents persuasive evidence that many women found their domestic tasks satisfying and fulfilling. With a majority of women, past and present, situated in the home where they are carers, mothers, and workers of all kinds, it is hard to disagree with her conclusion that 'the women whose "duties" made and remade daily life over several generations deserve to be seen in all their complexity'.[8] Nonetheless, the choices made by such women, and the positive experiences of many, does not detract from the wide range of disadvantages resulting from women's marginalisation in the public world of employment. The general underevaluation of women's work – paid and unpaid – has severe repercussions on those at the lower end of the social scale, with low pay, insufficient pension funding and social service benefits affecting the quality of both individual and family life.

With easier access to divorce and remarriage, and the gradual but growing acceptance of lone-parent families and single-sex relationships, the nature of family life for many was radically different at the century's end. This was reinforced by advances in technology and medicine and the evolution of nationwide welfare provisions that dramatically increased the lifespan of both men and women. In addition, a consumer-based culture and changing economic structures led to an expansion of the wealthier sectors of society, but their lifestyles contrast sharply with an equally growing underclass. On the day before New Year's Eve 1999, the Society of St Vincent de Paul warned:

> We are on the doorstep of the new millennium and one would hope that a brave new world was ahead of us. But the truth is that with all the developments which have enriched many lives, the poor continue to be entrapped in their poverty.[9]

The difficulties of the poor in society are often multilayered, with gender of particular significance. Joanne Templeton, for example, discusses the 'double burden' of discrimination often faced by women in Traveller communities, and their experience is paralleled in other ethnic and minority groupings.[10] Indeed, Pat O'Connor insists that 'Irish society remains highly gendered: being a woman is seen as the most important element in women's identity'.[11]

In tracing the experiences and responses of Irish women to this public social construct over the past one hundred years, it is clear that any idea of straightforward linear progression is misleading. Rather, the complex nature of progress and setbacks, successes and failures, affecting different women in different ways, demonstrates the dangers of oversimplified accounts of gains and losses, and points to the complexities and paradoxes of historical analysis.

The new millennium was ushered in with a flurry of excitement; old and young, male and female, celebrated with street and city-centre parties, fireworks and a host of festivities. In interdenominational services in churches and chapels throughout the country, prayers focused on the promise of peace. One striking image reported in the *Irish News* on New Year's Eve was that of 105-year-old Susan Quinn, a Belfast woman who had seen the calendar turn from the nineteenth, to the twentieth, to the twenty-first century. The mother of 9 children, 49 grandchildren, 129 great-grandchildren and 16 great-great-grandchildren she had witnessed the building of the ill-fated *Titanic* and shared a city's grief at its sinking; she had stripped tobacco in Gallaher's factory before leaving to get married at the age of twenty-one; and she had been widowed during the Second World War. She had no profound words of wisdom to offer the reporter, simply nostalgic reminiscences: 'there were hard times and a lot of sickness . . . we used to have wee children's parties in the street'. That the country had undergone momentous changes since her birth was of much less significance to her than the ups and downs of family life, work, courtship, marriage and motherhood.[12] But the life of the individual is inextricably interwoven with the progress of the nation. The quality of the lives of Susan Quinn's children and grandchildren, filled with so much more potential than that of their mother and grandmother, will reflect and be shaped by the overall position of women in Irish society and, like women of the twentieth century, they will help to determine the strength of that position.

Notes

INTRODUCTION

1. Deirdre Beddoe, *Discovering Women's History: A Practical Guide to Researching the Lives of Women since 1800*, 3rd ed. (Harlow, Essex, 1998), p. 3
2. Denis O'Hearn, *Inside the Celtic Tiger* (London, 1998), p. 57. The extent to which the resurgence in the Republic's economy specifically impacted on women has yet to be fully assessed.
3. Tony Fahey, quoted in Pat O'Connor, *Emerging Voices: Women in Contemporary Irish Society* (Dublin, 1998), p. 99
4. Bridie Quinn-Conroy, *Not a Word of a Lie* (Kinvara, County Galway, 1993), p. 83
5. Quoted in Yvonne Judge, *Chasing Gold: Sportswomen of Ireland* (Dublin, 1993), p. 9
6. Jeanne Sheehy, *The Rediscovery of Ireland's Past: The Celtic Revival 1830–1930* (London, 1980), pp. 158–63
7. Brian Kennedy, 'Women Artists and the Modern Movement 1943–49', in *Irish Women Artists from the Eighteenth Century to the Present Day* (Dublin, 1987), pp. 34–45, p. 41
8. Aidan Dunne, 'Contemporary Women Artists', in *ibid.*, pp. 61–70, p. 61
9. Joan Fowler, 'Contemporary Women Artists: Practices and Issues into the Future', in *ibid.*, pp. 71–8, p. 71
10. Ruth Hooley (ed.), *The Female Line: Northern Irish Women Writers* (Belfast, 1985)
11. Catherine Byron, 'The Room is a Kind of Travel Also: An Appreciation of the Poetry of Medbh McGuckian', *Linen Hall Review*, vol. 5, no. 1 (spring 1988), pp. 16–17, p. 17
12. Nuala O'Faolain, *Are You Somebody? The Life and Times of Nuala O'Faolain* (Dublin, 1996), p. 111
13. Angela Bourke, et al. (eds.), *The Field Day Anthology of Irish Writing*, vols IV and V, Irish Women's Writing and Traditions (Cork, 2002)
14. Lorna Stevens, Stephen Brown and Pauline Maclaran, 'Gender, Nationality and Cultural Representations of Ireland: An Irish Woman's Place?', *European Journal of Women's Studies*, vol. 7 (2000), pp. 405–21, p. 405
15. Mary Cullen, 'History Women and History Men: The Politics of Women's History', *History Ireland*, vol. 2, no. 2 (summer 1994), pp. 31–6
16. Published by Arlen House, The Women's Press, Dublin
17. Mary E. Daly, '"Oh Kathleen Ni Houlihan, Your Way's a Thorny Way!" The Condition of Women in Twentieth-century Ireland', in Anthony Bradley and Maryann G. Valiulis, (eds), *Gender and Sexuality in Modern Ireland* (Amherst, 1997), pp. 102–26, p. 106
18. Salma Leydesdorff, 'Politics, Identification and the Writing of Women's History', in Arena Angerman et al. (eds), *Current Issues in Women's History* (London, 1989), pp. 9–20, p. 19
19. Lynne Segal, *Is the Future Female? Troubled Thoughts on Contemporary Feminism* (London, 1987), p. xxii
20. Dervla Murphy, *A Place Apart* (London, 1978), p. 10

21 O'Hearn, *Inside the Celtic Tiger*, p. 55
22 Quoted in Elizabeth Janeway, 'Women: Their Changing Roles, Reflections on the History of Women', in Anne Stibbs (ed.), *Words of Women* (London, 1993), p. 113

CHAPTER 1

1 Mary Jones, *These Obstreperous Lassies: A History of the IWWU* (Dublin, 1988), p. 2
2 *Irish News and Belfast Morning News*, 5 April 1900
3 Janette Condon, 'The Patriotic Children's Treat: Irish Nationalism and Children's Culture at the Twilight of Empire', *Irish Studies Review*, vol. 8, no. 2 (2000), pp.167–78, p. 172
4 Margaret Ward, *In Their Own Voice: Women and Irish Nationalism* (Dublin, 1995), pp. 10–13
5 E.M. Fingall, *Seventy Years Young: Memories of Elizabeth, Countess of Fingall* (Dublin, 1995), p. 253
6 *Irish News and Belfast Morning News*, 1 January 1900
7 Fintan O'Toole, *The Irish Times Book of the Century* (Dublin, 1999), pp. 2–3
8 Quoted in Daniel Mulhall, *A New Day Dawning: A Portrait of Ireland in 1900* (Cork, 1999), p. 18
9 Stephen A. Royle, 'Industrialization, Urbanization and Urban Society in Post-Famine Ireland, c. 1850–1921', in B.J. Graham and L.J. Proudfoot (eds), *An Historical Geography of Ireland* (London, 1993), pp. 258–92, p. 279
10 K. Theodore Hoppen, *Ireland since 1800: Conflict and Conformity* (London and New York, 1989), p. 104
11 In Dublin in 1911, 98 per cent of the upper class, 71 per cent of the middle class and 23 per cent of the lower middle class had servants. Mona Hearn, *Below Stairs: Domestic Service Remembered in Dublin and Beyond, 1880–1922* (Dublin, 1993)
12 Correspondence of Duffin family, PRONI, D/2109/7/3
13 Michael McConville, *Ascendancy to Oblivion: The Story of the Anglo-Irish* (London, 1986), p. 248
14 Quoted in John Lynch, *A Tale of Three Cities: Comparative Studies in Working-Class Life* (London, 1998), p. 136
15 David Bleakley, *Saidie Patterson: Irish Peacemaker* (Belfast, 1980), p. 1
16 Lynch, *A Tale of Three Cities*, p. 112
17 Jonathan Bardon, *Belfast: A Century* (Belfast, 1999), p. 3
18 Lynch, *A Tale of Three Cities*, p. 164
19 Kevin C. Kearns, *Dublin Tenement Life: An Oral History* (Dublin, 1994), p. 12
20 Mary Daly, 'Social Structure of the Dublin Working Class, 1871–1911', *Irish Historical Studies*, vol. 23, no. 90 (November 1982), pp. 121–33
21 Edith Newman Devlin, *Speaking Volumes: A Dublin Childhood* (Belfast, 2000), p. 75
22 Quoted in Kearns, *Dublin Tenement Life*, p. 30
23 *Ibid.*, p. 33
24 Lynch, *A Tale of Three Cities*, pp. 128–9
25 Anne V. O'Connor and Susan M. Parkes, *Gladly Learn and Gladly Teach: A History of Alexandra College and School, Dublin 1866–1966* (Dublin, n.d.), pp. 69–76
26 Quoted in Jenny Beale, *Women in Ireland: Voices of Change* (Dublin, 1986), p. 21
27 Maureen Keane, *Ishbel: Lady Aberdeen in Ireland* (Newtownards, 1999), pp. 196–8
28 O'Toole, *The Irish Times Book of the Century*, p. 21

29 Anne-Marie Walsh, 'Root Them in the Land: Cottage Schemes for Agricultural Labourers', in Joost Augusteijn (ed.), *Ireland in the 1930s* (Dublin, 1999), pp. 47–66, p. 49

30 Robin Flower, *The Western Island* (Oxford, 1978), pp. 43–5

31 A.H. Fahy, 'Place and Class in Cork', in Patrick O'Flanagan and Cornelius G. Buttimer (eds), *Cork History and Society: Interdisciplinary Essays on the History of an Irish County* (Dublin, 1993), pp. 793–812, p. 808

32 Mary Kenny, *Goodbye to Catholic Ireland* (Dublin 2000), p. 36

33 Finola Kennedy, *Cottage to Crèche: Family Change in Ireland* (Dublin, 2001), pp. 208–9

34 Art Cosgrove, quoted in *ibid.*, pp. 57–8

35 K.C. Kearns, *Stoneybatter* (Dublin, 1989)

36 Nora Tynan O'Mahony, 'The Mother', *Irish Monthly*, vol. 91 (1913), quoted in Maria Luddy, *Women in Ireland 1800–1918: A Documentary History* (Cork, 1995), p. 18

37 Boole Library, Cork, BL/EP/G1365

38 Bleakley, *Saidie Patterson*, p. 12

39 Kearns, *Dublin Tenement Life*, p. 48

40 Tony Farmar, *Holles Street 1894–1994: The National Maternity Hospital: A Centenary History* (Dublin, 1994), pp. 13–62

41 Catriona Clear, *Women of the House: Women's Household Work in Ireland 1922–1961* (Dublin, 2000), p. 112

42 Robert E. Kennedy, *The Irish: Emigration, Marriage, and Fertility* (California, 1973), p. 46

43 Farmar, *Holles Street*, p. 62

44 Keane, *Ishbel*, pp. 143–4

45 *Ibid.*, p. 191

46 Janet Dunwoody, 'Child Welfare', in David Fitzpatrick (ed.), *Ireland and the First World War* (Dublin, 1986), pp. 69–75; minutes of Cork Child Welfare League, UCC Archive Collection, H7

47 J. Sandford (ed.), *Mary Carbery's West Cork Journal 1898–1901* (Dublin, 1998), p. 86

48 Joanna Bourke, ' "The Best of All Home Rulers?" The Economic Power of Women in Ireland, 1880–1914', *Irish Economic and Social History*, vol. 18 (1991), pp. 34–47

49 *Ibid.*, p.45

50 Michael Verdon, *Shawlies, Echo Boys, the Marsh and the Lanes: Old Cork Remembered* (Dublin, 1993), pp. 87–8

51 John Logan, 'The Dimensions of Gender in Nineteenth-Century Schooling', in Margaret Kelleher and James H. Murphy (eds), *Gender Perspectives in 19th Century Ireland* (Dublin, 1997), pp. 36–49

52 Florence Mary McDowell, *Other Days Around Me* (Belfast, 1972), p. 151

53 Kathleen Sheehan, 'Life in Glangevlin, County Cavan, 1900–1920', *Ulster Folklife*, vol. 32 (1985), pp. 53–8, p. 55

54 Report of the Inter-Departmental Committee on the Employment of Children during School Age, H.C. 1902, xlix [cd. 1144]

55 Nesca A. Robb, *A History of Richmond Lodge School* (n.d.), p. 7

56 Margaret Ward, *Hanna Sheehy Skeffington: A Life* (Cork, 1997), p. 9

57 Marie O'Neill, *Grace Gifford Plunkett and Irish Freedom: Tragic Bride of 1916* (Dublin, 2000), pp. 5–8

58 John Kelly and Eric Domville (eds), *The Collected Letters of W.B. Yeats*, vol. 1, 1865–1895 (Oxford, 1986), p. 161

59   Senia Paseta, *Before the Revolution: Nationalism, Social Change and Ireland's Catholic Elite, 1879–1922* (Cork, 1999), pp. 139–40

60   Reverend James Cassidy, quoted in Alex Guilbride, 'Mad or bad? Women Committing Infanticide in Ireland from 1925 to 1957' in R. Lentin (ed.), *In From the Shadows: The UL Women's Studies Collection*, vol. 2 (1996), pp. 84–92, p. 89

61   Kearns, *Dublin Tenements*, pp. 107–8; interview with author, June 2000

62   Hearn, *Below Stairs*, p. 98

63   *The Nationalist*, 17 October 1900, quoted in Luddy, *Women in Ireland*, pp. 40–1. From 1864 the Home Office adopted a policy of advising the commutation of the death penalty in cases of infanticide by mothers.

64   Quoted in R.M. Fox, *Rebel Irishwomen* (Dublin, 1935), p. 29

65   O'Connor and Parkes, *Gladly Learn and Gladly Teach*, p. 71

66   Louise Ryan, *Irish Feminism and the Vote: An Anthology of the Irish Citizen Newspaper 1912–1920* (Dublin, 1996), p. 53

67   Elizabeth Steiner-Scott, ' "To Bounce a Boot off Her Now and Then . . .": Domestic Violence in Post-Famine Ireland', in Maryann G. Valiulis and Mary O'Dowd (eds), *Women and Irish History: Essays in Honour of Margaret MacCurtain* (Dublin, 1997), pp. 125–43

68   Quoted in Catherine Rose, *The Female Experience: The Story of the Woman Movement in Ireland* (Galway, 1975), p. 17

69   Kennedy, *The Irish*, p. 13

70   Verdon, *Shawlies, Echo Boys*, p. 191

71   Ian D'Alton, 'Keeping Faith: An Evocation of the Cork Protestant Character 1820–1920', in Flanagan and Buttimer (eds), *Cork: History and Society*, pp. 759–92, p. 769

72   Maria Luddy, *Women and Philanthropy in Nineteenth-Century Ireland* (Cambridge, 1995)

73   Vivienne Draper, *The Children of Dunseverick* (Dingle, 1994), p. 18

74   See, for example, Elizabeth McCullough, *A Square Peg: An Ulster Childhood* (Dublin, 1997), George Gissing, *The Odd Women* (London, 1893), and though set at a later time, Brian Moore's *The Lonely Passion of Judith Hearne* (London, 1965)

75   Edith Somerville, *Irish Memories* (1917), cited in Angela Bourke, et al. (eds), *The Field Day Anthology of Irish Writing*, vol. IV (Cork, 2002), pp. 1105–7

76   See, for example, the works of Elizabeth Bowen, Molly Keane and Kate O'Brien.

77   Tony Fahey, 'Nuns in the Catholic Church in Ireland in the Nineteenth Century', in Mary Cullen (ed.), *Girls Don't Do Honours: Irish Women in Education in the 19th and 20th Centuries* (Dublin, 1987), pp. 7–30

78   Sue Ellen Hoy, 'The Journey Out: The Recruitment and Emigration of Irish Religious Women to the United States, 1812–1914', Joan Hoff and Moureen Coulter (eds), *Irish Women's Voices: Past and Present* (Indiana, 1995), *Journal of Women's History*, vols. 6 and 7, pp. 64–98

79   Pauric Travers, ' "There was Nothing for Me There": Irish Female Emigration, 1922–71', in Patrick O'Sullivan (ed.), *Irish Women and Irish Migration* (London, 1995), pp. 146–67, p. 148

80   *Bean na hÉireann*, 1909, quoted in Sarah McNamara, *Those Intrepid Irishwomen: Pioneers of the Irish Countrywomen's Association* (Limerick, 1995), p. 13

81   John Hutchinson and Alan O'Day, 'The Gaelic Revival in London, 1900–22: Limits of Ethnic Identity', in Roger Swift and Sheridan Gilley (eds), *The Irish in Victorian Britain: The Local Dimension* (Dublin, 1999), pp. 254–76, p. 257

82   Liam O'Flaherty, 'Going into Exile', in Frank O'Connor (ed.), *Modern Irish Short*

Stories (Oxford, 1977), pp. 133–46, p. 138

83   Lawrence J. McCaffrey, *The Irish Catholic Diaspora in America*, rev. ed. (Washington, 1997), p. 85

84   'In 1900 54% of the Irish-born women were house servants ... another 6.5% were laundresses; Irish women composed a majority of all servants in New England and 40% or more of those in New York, Philadelphia, and other eastern cities.' Kerby A. Miller, *Emigrants and Exiles: Ireland and the Irish Exodus to North America* (Oxford, 1985), pp. 499–500

85   Lawrence J. McCaffrey, *The Irish Diaspora in America* (London, 1976), p. 80

86   David Fitzpatrick, 'Emigration, 1871–1921', in W.E. Vaughan (ed.), *A New History of Ireland*, vol. VI: *Ireland under the Union (II) 1870–1921* (Oxford, 2000), pp. 606–45, p. 636

87   Quoted in Maureen Murphy, 'The Fionnuala Factor: Irish Sibling Migration at the Turn of the Century', in Anthony Bradley and Maryann G. Valiulis (eds), *Gender and Sexuality in Modern Ireland* (Amherst, 1997), pp. 85–101, p. 86

88   David Fitzpatrick, *Irish Emigration 1801–1921* (Dublin, 1984), pp. 38–40

89   Michael Turner, 'Rural Economies in Post-Famine Ireland, *c.* 1850–1914', in Graham and Proudfoot, *An Historical Geography*, pp. 293–37, p. 321

90   Walter Love, *The Times of Our Lives: Recollections from Town and Country* (Belfast, 1990), p. 38

91   Gusty Spence, *Past Discovery: Report of a Seminar Organised by Ballymacarret Arts and Cultural Society* (Belfast, 1997), p. 16

92   Kearns, *Dublin Tenement Life*, p. 28

93   Nora Connolly O'Brien, in Uinseann MacEoin (ed.), *Survivors* (Dublin, 1987) pp. 183–215, p. 185

94   Quoted in Beale, *Women in Ireland*, p. 21

95   Florence Irwin, *The Cookin' Woman: Irish Country Recipes*, 2nd ed., (Belfast, 1986)

96   *Ibid.*, pp. 2–3

97   Elizabeth Bloxham, 'Training Our Housekeepers', in W.G. Fitzgerald (ed.), *The Voice of Ireland* (n.d.), pp. 167–9, p. 168

98   McNamara, *Those Intrepid Irishwomen*, p. 22

99   Joanna Bourke, *Husbandry to Housewifery: Women, Economic Change and Housework in Ireland, 1890–1914* (Oxford, 1993), p. 215

100 Quoted in Kearns, *Dublin Tenement Life*, p. 107

101 Alison Jordan, *Who Cared? Charity in Victorian and Edwardian Belfast* (Belfast, n.d.), pp. 96–141

102 Diane Urquhart, *Women in Ulster Politics 1890–1940* (Dublin, 2000), pp. 118–49

103 Those women entitled to stand as candidates in Poor Law elections were 'occupiers or householders, rated occupiers, lodgers of premises worth £10 per annum, non-resident leaseholders for a term of sixty years with profit rent of £10 and ... non-resident freeholders with £20 yearly profit'. *Ibid.*, p. 121

104 *Ibid.*, quoted on p. 148

105 In her doctoral thesis, Gillian McClelland demonstrates the powerful network of alliances maintained amongst the middle-class congregation of Fisherwick Presbyterian Church, Belfast, 'Evangelical Philanthropy and Social Control, or Emancipatory Feminism? A Case Study of Fisherwick Presbyterian Working Women's Association 1870–1918', unpublished Ph.D. thesis, Queen's University Belfast, 1999

106 Sean Connolly, *Religion and Society in Nineteenth-Century Ireland* (Dundalk, 1985), pp. 49–51

107 Bleakley, *Saidie Patterson*, p. 18

108 Jordan, *Who Cared?*, pp. 144–6

109 Mulhall, *A New Day Dawning*, pp. 76–7

110 Jeanne Sheehy, *The Rediscovery of Ireland's Past: The Celtic Revival 1830–1930* (London, 1980), p. 147

111 Margaret Ward, '"Ulster was different?" Women, Feminism and Nationalism in the North of Ireland', in Yvonne Galligan, Eilis Ward and Rick Wilford (eds), *Contesting Politics: Women in Ireland, North and South* (Colorado and Oxford, 1999), pp. 219–39, p. 226

112 Ulick O'Connor, *Oliver St John Gogarty: A Biography* (London, 1964), p. 117

113 Verdon, *Shawlies, Echo Boys*, p. 121

114 Love, *The Times of Our Lives*, pp. 39–41

115 Tony Farmar, *Ordinary Lives: Three Generations of Irish Middle Class Experience 1907, 1932, 1963* (Dublin, 1991), p. 40

116 Delia Larkin, *Irish Worker*, 8 March 1913

117 Andrea Ebel Brozyna, *Labour, Love and Prayer: Female Piety in Ulster Religious Literature 1850–1914* (Belfast, 1999)

118 Keane, *Ishbel*, p. 127

119 Lynch, *Tale of Three Cities*, p. 14

120 Keane, Ishbel., p. 145

121 *Ibid.*, quote on p. 158

122 Ward, *Hanna Sheehy Skeffington*, p. 11

123 Quoted in *Irish Times*, 25 August 2001

124 Bleakley, *Saidie Patterson*, p. 15

125 Kennedy, *The Irish*, p. 55

126 Ruth Barrington, *Health, Medicine and Politics in Ireland 1900–1970* (Dublin, 1987), pp. 35, 60

127 Mary E. Daly, *Women and Work in Ireland* (Dundalk, 1997), p. 27

128 Marilyn Cohen, 'Working Conditions and Experiences of Work in the Linen Industry: Tullylish, County Down', *Ulster Folklife*, vol. 30 (1984), pp. 1–21, p. 16

129 *Ibid.*, p. 7

130 John Gray, *City in Revolt: James Larkin and the Belfast Dock Strike of 1907* (Belfast, 1985), p. 7

131 Patricia McCaffrey, 'Jacob's Women Workers during the 1913 Lock-out', *Saothar* (Ireland), vol. 16 (1991), pp. 118–29, p. 121

132 Maura Cronin, 'Work and Workers in Cork City and County 1800–1900', Flanagan and Buttimer (eds), *Cork: History and Society*, pp. 721–58, p. 741

133 Mona Hearn, 'Life for Domestic Servants in Dublin: 1880–1920', in Maria Luddy and Cliona Murphy (eds), *Women Surviving: Studies in Irish Women's History in the 19th and 20th Centuries* (Dublin, 1990), pp. 148–79

134 *Ibid.*, p. 164

135 Reverend Jeremiah Newman (ed.), *The Limerick Rural Survey 1958–1964* (Tipperary, 1964), p. 200

136 Vivienne L. Pollock, 'The Herring Industry in County Down 1840–1940', in L. Proudfoot (ed.), *Down: History and Society: Interdisciplinary Essays on the History of an Irish County* (Dublin, 1997), pp. 405–29, pp. 414–6

137 Daly, *Women and Work in Ireland*, p. 19

138 Love, *The Times of Our Lives*, p. 33

139 P. Beresford Ellis (ed.), *James Connolly, Selected Writings* (London, 1975), pp. 190–1

140 Unpublished paper, D.S. Johnson, 'Prostitution and Venereal Disease in Ireland during the Second Half of the Nineteenth Century', in possession of the author

141 John Finegan, *The Story of Monto: An Account of Dublin's Notorious Red Light District* (Dublin, 1978), p. 1

142 Kearns, *Dublin Tenement Life*, p. 55

143 O'Connor, *Oliver St. John Gogarty*, pp. 49–52; Sandra Ruth Larmour, 'Aspects of the State and Female Sexuality in the Irish Free State, 1922–1949', Unpublished Ph.D. thesis, University College Cork, 1998, pp. 75–128

144 Anne V. O'Connor, 'The Revolution in Girls' Secondary Education in Ireland 1860–1910', in Cullen (ed.), *Girls Don't Do Honours*, pp. 31–54

145 Logan, 'The Dimensions of Gender', in Kelleher and Murphy (eds), *Gender Perspectives*, p. 48

146 Daly, *Women and Work*, pp. 39–40

147 Myrtle Hill, 'Women in the Irish Protestant Foreign Missions, *c.* 1873–1914: Representations and Motivations', in P. Holtrop and H. McLeod (eds), *Missions and Missionaries* (Woodbridge and Rochester, NY, 2000), pp. 170–85, pp. 178–9

148 *Irish Citizen*, May 1919

149 Mary E. Daly, 'Women and Trade Unions', in Donal Evin (ed.), *Trade Union Century* (Dublin, 1994), pp. 106–16, p. 107

150 Mats Greiff, '"Marching through the Streets Singing and Shouting": Industrial Struggle and Trade Unions among Female Linen Workers in Belfast and Lurgan 1875–1910', *Saothar* (Ireland), vol. 22 (1997), pp. 29–44

151 Dermot Keogh, *The Rise of the Irish Working Class: The Dublin Trade Union Movement and Labour Leadership 1890–1914* (Belfast, 1982), pp. 67–86

152 Gray, *City in Revolt*, pp. 96–8

153 Ward, ' "Ulster was Different?" ', pp. 230–31

154 Jones, *These Obstreperous Lassies*, pp. 10–13

155 McCaffrey, 'Jacob's Women Workers during the 1913 Lock-out'

156 Greiff, ' "Marching through the Streets Singing and Shouting" '

CHAPTER 2

1 Helena Moloney (editor), *Bean na hÉireann*, vol. 1, no. 3 (January 1909)

2 Quoted in Rosemary Cullen Owens, *Smashing Times: A History of the Irish Women's Suffrage Movement 1889–1922* (Dublin, 1984), p. 74

3 Isabella Tod formed the North of Ireland Women's Suffrage Society in Belfast in 1872; Anna Haslem's Dublin Suffrage Society, formed in 1876, became the Irish Women's Suffrage and Local Government Association in 1901

4 Typed manuscript of suffrage involvement in Belfast by Marie A. Johnson, written to Andrée Skeffington, PRONI, T/3259/2/7

5 Quoted in Owens, *Smashing Times*, p. 49

6 *Ibid.*, p. 32

7 Diane Urquhart, *Women in Ulster Politics, 1890–1940* (Dublin, 2000), pp. 11–12

8 Editorial, *Irish Citizen*, 10 August 1912, quoted in Louise Ryan, *Irish Feminism and the Vote: An Anthology of the Irish Citizen Newspaper 1912–1920* (Dublin, 1996), p. 15

9 Quoted in Owens, *Smashing Times*, p. 39

10 Quoted in Ryan, *Irish Feminism and the Vote*, p. 16

11 *Irish Citizen*, 28 December 1912

12 Nora Tynan O'Mahony, 'The Mother', *The Irish Monthly*, vol. 91 (1913), quoted in Maria Luddy, *Women in Ireland: A Documentary History 1800–1918* (Cork, 1995), p. 17

13 Quoted in Owens, *Smashing Times*, p. 45

14 Margaret Ward, *Hanna Sheehy Skeffington: A Life* (Cork, 1997), p. 77. Ulster Unionists had responded violently to the introduction of the third Home Rule Bill and stated their determination to resist its imposition by force. The Ulster Volunteer Force was officially formed in January 1913, but training in arms for the possibility of civil war was already well under way. By the end of that year the Irish Volunteer Force had also been established to organise nationalists in defence of legislative independence. Jonathan Bardon, *A History of Ulster* (Belfast, 1992) pp. 439–43

15 Margaret Robinson, who ran a small private school in Whitehead, near Belfast, joined the Belfast branch of the WSPU, selling *Votes for Women* on the Belfast streets. In 1911 she set off with Dr Elizabeth Bell to present a petition to parliament with stones in her pocket, and was jailed for breaking shop windows in Piccadilly Circus. Transcript of tape-recorded interview with Margaret Robinson, Cleggan, County Galway, a former suffragette in Belfast, 1975, PRONI, Tp. 35

16 The sentences were two months for the first four women and six months for the other four.

17 Bushmills society 'deeply regretted the policy of the militant suffragettes in attacking property'. Letter from Mrs Heron in Holywood, leaving the Belfast Women's Suffrage Society to join the nonmilitant local Holywood branch, 29 April 1912, PRONI T/3259/1/6. On 16 April 1913 the Derry branch of the Irish Women's Suffrage Society resolved to 'sever the connection with the Belfast militants and become affiliated to the IWSF. Letter from Robina Gamble, Londonderry, to Mrs Robinson, 16 April 1913, PRONI, T/3259/1/7

18 Quoted in Margaret Ward, 'Nationalism, Pacifism, Internationalism: Louie Bennett, Hanna Sheehy Skeffington, and the Problems of "Defining Feminism"', in Anthony Bradley and Maryann G. Valiulis (eds), *Gender and Sexuality in Modern Ireland* (Amherst, 1997), pp. 60–84, p. 64

19 Quoted in Rosemary Cullen Owens, 'Votes for Women', *Labour History News*, vol. 9 (summer 1993), pp. 15–19, reprinted in Alan Hayes and Diane Urquhart (eds), *The Irish Women's History Reader* (London, 2001), pp. 37–43, p. 41

20 Hanna Sheehy Skeffington, 'Reminiscences of an Irish Suffragette' (Dublin, 1975), in Angela Bourke, et al., *The Field Day Anthology of Irish Writing*, vols. IV and V, Irish Women's Writing and Traditions (Cork, 2002), vol. V, p. 94

21 Ward, *Hanna Sheehy Skeffington*, pp. 102–3

22 *Irish Citizen*, 15 June 1912

23 Cliona Murphy, 'A Problematic Relationship: European Women and Nationalism 1870–1915', in Maryann G. Valiulis and Mary O'Dowd (eds), *Women and Irish History: Essays in Honour of Margaret MacCurtain* (Dublin, 1997), pp. 145–58

24 Quoted in Ryan, *Irish Feminism and the Vote*, pp. 149–50

25 Margaret Ward, *Unmanageable Revolutionaries: Women and Irish Nationalism*, 2nd ed. (London, 1995), p. 51

26 *Bean na hÉireann*, September 1909, quoted in Margaret Ward, *In Their Own Voice: Women and Irish Nationalism* (Dublin, 1995), p. 29

27 Urquhart, *Women in Ulster Politics*, p. 108

28 Editorial, *Bean na hÉireann*, vol 1, no. 4 (February 1909)

29 Ward, *Hanna Sheehy Skeffington*, p. 60

30 Quoted in Ward, *Unmaneageable Revolutionaries*, p. 93.

31 Diane Urquhart (ed.), *The Minutes of the Ulster Women's Unionist Council and Executive Committee 1911–40* (Dublin, 2001)

32 UWUC Minute Books, PRONI D/1098/1/1. 7 June 1911 Executive Committee meeting

33 *Ibid.*, 28 November 1911

34 *Ibid.*, 25 August 1911

35 Quoted in Diane Urquhart, 'In Defence of Ulster and the Empire: The Ulster Women's Unionist Council, 1911–1940', *University College Galway Women's Studies Review* (1996), pp. 31–40, p. 33

36 Quoted in Urquhart, *Women in Ulster Politics*, p. 60

37 Londonderry Letters, PRONI D/2846/1/8/23; 16 September 1913, Lady Dufferin, Clandeboye, to Lady Londonderry

38 *Irish Citizen*, 28 March 1914

39 Papers relating to Dorothy Evans, PRONI, BELF/1/1/2/45/8

40 Diane Urquhart, 'The Political Role of Women in North East Ulster, 1880–1940', unpublished MA thesis, Queen's University Belfast, 1996, p. 49

41 Suffrage Correspondence, PRONI, T/2125/32/1–32

42 Mary Spring Rice, log of the *Asgard*, 1–25 July 1914, typescript, TCD 7841

43 Urquhart, *Women in Ulster Politics*, p. 50

44 *Ibid.*, pp. 27–8

45 Rosemary Cullen Owens, 'Women and Pacifism in Ireland 1915–32', in Maryann G. Valiulis and Mary O'Dowd (eds), *Women and Irish History*, pp. 220–38, pp. 223–4

46 Quoted in Ward, 'Nationalism, Pacifism, Internationalism', in Bradley and Valiulis (eds), *Gender and Sexuality in Modern Ireland*, pp. 60–84, p. 70

47 Mary Clancy, 'The "Western Outpost": Local Government and Women's Suffrage in County Galway 1898–1918', in Gerard Moran (ed.), *Galway History & Society: Interdisciplinary Essays on the History of an Irish County* (Dublin, 1996), pp. 557–87

48 Killyleagh Women's War Work, PRONI, D/3524/2/1

49 WNHA, Omagh Branch Report 1916–19, PRONI D/1884/1/1/5

50 Margaret Downes, 'The Civilian Voluntary Aid Effort', in David Fitzpatrick (ed.), *Ireland and the First World War* (Dublin, 1986), p. 34

51 Anne V. O'Connor and Susan M. Parkes, *Gladly Learn and Gladly Teach: A History of Alexandra College and School, Dublin 1866–1966* (Dublin, n.d.), p. 93

52 Helen Jones, *Women in British Public Life, 1914–50: Gender, Power and Social Policy* (Harlow, 2000), pp. 45–6

53 Quoted in Philip Orr, *The Road to The Somme: Men of the Ulster Division Tell Their Story* (Belfast, 1987), p. 50

54 Emily Ussher, 'The True Story of a Revolution: An Account of Life at Cappagh, County Wexford, Spring 1914–Spring 1925', TCD 9269

55 Keith Jeffery, *Ireland and the Great War* (Cambridge, 2000)

56 Mary Kenny, *Goodbye to Catholic Ireland* (Dublin, 2000), pp. 68–73

57 Somme Heritage Centre, Newtownards

58 Emma Duffin, Nursing Diaries, PRONI D/2109/8–13

59 Papers of Lady Londonderry, PRONI D3099

60 Winifred Campbell, 'Down the Shankill', *Ulster Folklife*, vol. 22 (1976), pp. 1–33, p. 2

61 Quoted in Sarah McNamara, *Those Intrepid United Irishwomen: Pioneers of the Irish Countrywomen's Association* (Limerick, 1995), p. 80

62 *Seventy Years Young: Memories of Elizabeth, Countess of Fingall* (Dublin, 1995), p. 362

63 D. S. Johnson, 'The Northern Ireland Economy, 1914–39', in Liam Kennedy and Philip Ollerenshaw (eds), *An Economic History of Ulster, 1820–1939* (Manchester, 1985), pp. 184–223, p. 184

64 Jeffery, *Ireland and the Great War*, p. 32
65 Elizabeth McCullough, *A Square Peg: An Ulster Childhood* (Dublin, 1997), p. 15
66 Extract from the *Turret Lathers*, a magazine produced in Mackie's factory (December, 1916), Somme Heritage Centre, Newtownards
67 Orr, *The Road to the Somme*, p. 198
68 Peter Somerville-Large, *Irish Voices: An Informal History 1916–1966* (London, 1999), p. 15
69 *Ibid.*, p. 4
70 Ward, *Unmanageable Revolutionaries*, p. 111
71 Ruth Taillon, *When History was Made: The Women of 1916* (Belfast, 1996)
72 Quoted in *ibid.*, pp. 27–8
73 Patricia Lynch, *Women's Dreadnought*, 13 May 1916
74 Taillon, *When History was Made*, p. 56
75 Quoted in *ibid.*, p. 70
76 Ward, *Unmanageable Revolutionaries*, p. 110
77 Taillon, *When History was Made*, p. 70
78 Ward, *Unmanageable Revolutionaries*, p. 113; Nora Connolly O'Brien recalled that Margaret Skinnider, a member of Glasgow Cumann na mBan, used to regularly travel to Ireland during her school holidays: 'she would wear a "toque-ish" hat, which would be stuffed with bullets and other such supplies, and with detonators wound round and round inside the rim'. Nora Connolly O'Brien, *We shall Rise Again* (London, 1981), p. 79
79 Taillon, *When History was Made*, pp. 73–4
80 Quoted in K.C. Kearns, *Stoneybatter* (Dublin, 1989), p. 39
81 Somerville-Large, *Irish Voices: An Informal History*, pp. 6–9
82 *Irish Times*, 2 May 1916
83 Nuala O'Faolain, *Are You Somebody? The Life and Times of Nuala O'Faolain* (Dublin, 1996), p. 26
84 Máire Comerford, in Uinseann MacEoin (ed.), *Survivors* (Dublin, 1987), pp. 35–55, p. 40
85 Kathleen Clarke, *Revolutionary Woman: My Fight for Ireland's Freedom* (Dublin, 1997), p. 89
86 Daughter of Provost, Trinity College Dublin, account of the Rising, TCD274
87 Louise Ryan, '"Furies" and "Die-hards": Women and Irish Republicanism in the Early Twentieth Century', *Gender and History*, vol. 11, no. 2 (July 1999), pp. 256–75, p. 261
88 Nora Connolly, *Atlantic Monthly* (1916), quoted in Angela Bourke, et al (eds), *The Field Day Anthology of Irish Writing*, vol. V, (Cork, 2002), p. 107
89 Bridget Foley, typescript description of her prison experiences, Cork Public Museum, AQNOL 1957:24
90 Francis Sheehy Skeffington, journalist and well-known pacifist, was murdered by British soldiers while in custody, having been arrested while trying to prevent the looting of shops. Ward, *Unmanageable Revolutionaries*, p. 121
91 Ward, *Unmanageable Revolutionaries*, pp. 127–30
92 Keith Jeffrey suggests a lower estimate of around 27,500, explaining that it is impossible to be more precise, since statistics do not distinguish between men serving in Irish units who were born outside Ireland or who made up part of the Irish diaspora. *Ireland and the Great War*, p. 35
93 Bardon, *A History of Ulster*, p. 450–61. As leader of the IPP, John Redmond had called

on the Irish Volunteers to join the Allied forces, and thus unite Irish men north and south against the common Germany enemy. Around 11,000 Volunteers rejected this stance, but an estimated 27,000 of the majority, who thereafter took the name the National Volunteers, did join up.

94 Jones, *Women in British Public Life*, pp. 45–6
95 Urquhart, *Women in Ulster Politics*, pp. 65–6
96 Nancy Kinghan, *United We Stood: The Official History of the Ulster Women's Unionist Council 1911–1974* (Belfast, 1975), p. 41
97 Margaret Ward, '"Ulster was Different?" Women, Feminism and Nationalism in the North of Ireland', in Yvonne Galligan, Eilis Ward, Rick Wilford (eds.), *Contesting Politics: Women in Ireland, North and South* (Colorado and Oxford, 1999), pp. 219–39, pp. 233–4
98 Quoted in Ward, *In Their Own Voice*, p. 82
99 Benton, 'Women Disarmed'; Sinéad McCoole, *Guns and Chiffon: Women Revolutionaries and Kilmainham Gaol* (Dublin, 1997); Ryan, '"Furies" and "Die–hards"'; Louise Ryan, '"Drunken Tans": Representations of Sex and Violence in the Anglo-Irish War (1919–21)', *Feminist Review*, no. 66 (autumn 2000), pp. 73–94
100 Ryan, '"Drunken Tans"', p. 73
101 Letter outlining Nora Wallace's activities in the IRA, Cork Public Museum, Nora Wallace Collection, AQNOL 1996:111
102 Quoted in Ryan, '"Drunken Tans"', p. 73
103 Somerville-Large, *Irish Voices: An Informal History*, p. 38
104 Quoted in Benton, 'Women Disarmed', p. 64
105 Owens, 'Women and Pacifism in Ireland', p. 230
106 Ward, *Unmanageable Revolutionaries*, pp. 145–6
107 Quoted in Ward, *Unmanageable Revolutionaries*, p.149
108 Ryan, '"Drunken Tans"', p. 83
109 Somerville-Large, *Irish Voices: An Informal History*, pp. 48–9
110 *Ibid.*, p. 56
111 *Ibid.*, p. 55
112 Michael Verdon, *Shawlies, Echo Boys, the Marsh and the Lanes: Old Cork Remembered* (Dublin, 1993), p. 173
113 F.S.L. Lyons, *Ireland since the Famine* (London, 1982), p. 419
114 Bardon, *A History of Ulster*, pp. 471–2
115 Michael Laffan, *The Partition of Ireland 1911–1925* (Dublin, 1983), p. 76
116 Quoted in Alvin Jackson, *Ireland 1798–1998* (Oxford, 1999), p. 262
117 Clarke, *Revolutionary Woman*, p. 192
118 Cork Archives Institute, U192
119 Quoted in Ward, *Unmanageable Revolutionaries*, p. 168
120 *Ibid.*, pp. 174–8
121 *Ibid.*, p. 173
122 Eamon Phoenix, 'Political Violence, Diplomacy and the Catholic Minority in Northern Ireland', in John Darby (ed.), *Political Violence: Ireland in a Comparative Perspective* (Belfast, 1988), pp. 29–47, p. 45
123 Jonas Jorstad, 'Nations Once Again: Ireland's Civil War in European Context', in David Fitzpatrick (ed.), *Revolution? Ireland 1917–1923* (Dublin, 1990), pp. 59–73, p. 159
124 David Fitzpatrick, *The Two Irelands: 1912–1939* (Oxford, 1998), p. 117
125 Mary E. Daly, '"Oh, Kathleen Ni Houlihan, Your Way's a Thorny Way!" : The

Condition of Women in Twentieth-Century Ireland', in Bradley and Valiulis (eds), *Gender and Sexuality in Modern Ireland*, pp. 102–26, p. 107

CHAPTER 3

1   Irish Constitution 1937, Article 41(1), cited in Finola Kennedy, *Cottage to Crèche: Family Change in Ireland* (Dublin, 2001), p. 81
2   Diane Urquhart, *Women in Ulster Politics 1890–1940* (Dublin, 2000), pp. 67–8
3   Nancy Kinghan, *United We Stood: The Official History of the Ulster Women's Unionist Council 1911–1974* (Belfast, 1975), p. 43
4   Urquhart, *Women in Ulster Politics*, p. 72
5   *Ibid.*, p. 114
6   *Ibid.*, quoted on p. 104
7   *Ibid.*, pp. 85–117
8   Minutes of the Executive Committee of the UWUC, PRONI, D/1098/1/2, 25 January 1921
9   *Ibid.*, letters, February 1921 and April 1921
10   Winifred Campbell, 'Down the Shankill', *Ulster Folklife*, vol. 22 (1976), pp. 1–33, p. 21
11   The state opening of parliament was presided over by George V. The new Parliament Buildings at Stormont were officially opened by the Prince of Wales in 1932.
12   Maedhbh McNamara and Paschal Mooney, *Women in Parliament: Ireland 1918–2000* (Dublin, 2000), p. 223
13   Quoted in Urquhart, *Women in Ulster Politics*, pp. 178–9
14   Quoted in Diane Urquhart, 'The Political Role of Women in North-East Ulster, 1890–1940', unpublished MA thesis, Queen's University Belfast, 1996
15   John Whyte, 'How much Discrimination was there under the Unionist Regime, 1921–68?' in Tom Gallagher and James O'Connell (eds), *Contemporary Irish Studies* (Manchester, 1983), pp. 1–35, p. 7
16   Quoted in Urquhart, 'The Political Role of Women', p. 261
17   *Ibid.*, p. 265
18   Roger Sawyer, *'We are but Women': Women in Ireland's History* (London, 1993), pp. 122–4
19   Urquhart, *Women in Ulster Politics*, p. 83
20   Kinghan, *United We Stood*, p. 51
21   Urquhart, 'The Political Role of Women', p. 104
22   Nelly O'Brien, 'A Hot Corner', Dublin, 5 July 1922, TCD10343/4
23   Quoted in K.C. Kearns, *Dublin Voices: An Oral History* (Dublin, 1998), p. 145
24   Quoted in Uinseann MacEoin, *Survivors*, 2nd ed. (Dublin, 1987), p. 48
25   *Ibid.*, p. 367
26   David Fitzpatrick (ed.), *Revolution? Ireland 1917–1923* (Dublin, 1990)
27   Michael Hopkinson, *Green Against Green: The Irish Civil War* (Dublin, 1988), pp. 123, 128
28   Calton Younger, *Ireland's Civil War* (London, 1968), p. 450
29   Cork Archives Institute, Siobhán Lankford Papers, U169A
30   *Belfast Telegraph*, 12 April 1922
31   Quoted in Oonagh Walsh, 'Testimony from Imprisoned Women', in Fitzpatrick (ed.), *Revolution? Ireland 1917–1923*, pp. 69–85, p. 84
32   *Ibid.*, p. 85
33   Louise Ryan, '"Furies" and "Die-hards": Women and Irish Republicanism in the

Early Twentieth Century', *Gender and History*, vol. 11, no. 2 (July 1999), pp 256–75

34   *Ibid.*, p. 267

35   MacSwiney Papers, UCD P46A/7

36   Dermot Keogh, *Twentieth-Century Ireland: Nation and State* (Dublin, 1994), p. 279

37   Quoted in Margaret Ward, *Hanna Sheehy Skeffington: A Life* (Cork, 1997), p. 304

38   Margaret Ward, 'Nationalism, Pacifism, Internationalism: Louie Bennett, Hanna Sheehy-Skeffington, and the Problems of "Defining Feminism" ', in Anthony Bradley and Maryann G. Valiulis (eds), *Gender and Sexuality in Modern Ireland* (Amherst, 1997), pp. 60–84, pp. 77–80

39   Andrew Finlay, 'The Cutting Edge: Derry Shirtmakers', in Chris Curtin, Pauline Jackson and Barbara O'Connor (eds), *Gender in Irish Society* (Galway, 1987), pp. 87–107, p. 92

40   Bob Rowthorn and Naomi Wayne, *Northern Ireland: The Political Economy of Conflict* (Oxford, 1988), p. 33

41   Ronnie Munck and Bill Rolston, *Belfast in the Thirties: An Oral History* (Belfast, 1987), p. 25

42   *Ibid.*, quoted on p. 35

43   *Ibid.*, quoted on p. 65

44   *Ibid.*, quoted on p. 74

45   David Bleakley, *Saidie Patterson: Irish Peacemaker* (Belfast, 1980), p. 23

46   *Ibid.*, p. 43

47   Cormac O'Grada, *Ireland: A New Economic History 1780–1939* (Oxford, 1994), p. 385

48   Mary Daly, *Women and Work in Ireland* (Dundalk, 1997), p. 41

49   *Ibid.*, p. 41

50   Peter Somerville-Large, *Irish Voices: 50 Years of Irish Life 1916–1966*, (London, 1999), p. 169

51   Irish Constitution 1937, Articles 41(1), 42(2), 45(2), quoted in Kennedy, *Cottage to Crèche*, pp. 81–2

52   Hilda Tweedy, *A Link in the Chain: The Story of the Irish Housewives Association 1942–1992* (Dublin, 1992), p. 19

53   Quoted in McNamara and Mooney, *Women in Parliament*, p. 92

54   Mary Mullin, 'Representations of History, Irish Feminism, and the Politics of Difference', *Feminist Studies*, vol. 17, no. 1 (1991), pp. 29–50, p. 42

55   *Irish Messenger of the Sacred Heart*, vol. 43 (February 1930), pp. 95–6

56   Quoted in Catriona Beaumont, 'Women and the Politics of Equality: The Irish Women's Movement 1930–1943', in Maryann G. Valiulis and Mary O'Dowd (eds), *Women and Irish History* (Dublin, 1997), pp. 173–205, p. 178

57   Sandra Ruth Larmour, 'Aspects of the State and Female Sexuality in the Irish Free State, 1922–1949', Unpublished Ph.D. thesis, University College Cork, 1998, p. 34

58   *Ibid.*, p. 40

59   Quoted in Jim Smyth, 'Dancing, Depravity and all that Jazz: The Public Dance Halls Act of 1935', *History Ireland* (summer 1993), pp. 51–4, p. 52

60   Máire Mullarney, *What about Me?: A Woman For Whom One Damn Cause Led to Another* (Dublin, 1992), p. 160

61   Larmour, 'Aspects of the State', p. 172

62   Quoted in Beaumont, 'Women and the Politics of Equality', p. 179

63   Greta Jones, 'Marie Stopes in Ireland: The Mother's Clinic in Belfast, 1936–47', *Social History of Medicine*, vol. 512 (April 1992), pp. 255–77

64   Quoted in Maire Leane, 'Female Sexuality in Ireland 1920–1940: Construction and

Regulation', Unpublished Ph.D. thesis, University College Cork, 1999, p. 75

65 Smyth, 'Dancing, Depravity and all that Jazz', p. 54

66 Quoted in Ryan, '"Furies" and "Die-Hards"', pp. 256–75

67 Quoted in Monica McWilliams, 'The Church, the State and the Women's Movement in Northern Ireland', in Ailbhe Smyth (ed.), *Irish Women's Studies Reader* (Dublin, 1993), pp. 79–99

68 Cardinal Joseph MacRory Archive, Armagh Diocesan Archive

69 Louise Ryan, 'Sexualising Emigration: Discourses of Irish Female Emigration in the 1930s', *Women's Studies International Forum*, vol. 25 (January–February 2002), pp. 51–65

70 Mary E. Daly, '"Oh, Kathleen Ni Houlihan, Your Way's a Thorny Way!" The Condition of Women in Twentieth-Century Ireland', in Bradley and Valiulis (eds), *Gender and Sexuality in Modern Ireland*, pp. 102–26, 105

71 Liam O'Dowd, 'Church, State and Women: The Aftermath of Partition', in Chris Curtin, Pauline Jackson and Barbara O'Connor (eds), *Gender in Irish Society* (Galway, 1987), pp. 3–36, p. 4

72 Catriona Clear, *Women of the House: Women's Household Work in Ireland 1922–1961* (Dublin, 2000), p. 10

73 Brian Fallon, *An Age of Innocence: Irish Culture 1930–1960*: (Dublin, 1998), p. 186

74 Margaret MacCurtain, 'Fullness of Life: Defining Female Spirituality in Twentieth-Century Ireland', in Maria Luddy and Cliona Murphy (eds), *Women Surviving: Studies in Irish Women's History in the 19th and 20th Centuries* (Dublin, 1989), pp. 233–63, p. 237

75 *Ibid.*, pp. 239–61

76 James S. Donnelly, Jr. 'The Peak of Marianism in Ireland 1930–60', in Stewart J. Brown and David W. Miller (eds), *Piety and Power in Ireland 1760–1960: Essays in Honour of Emmet Larkin* (Belfast, 2000), pp. 252–83

77 Edith Newman Devlin, *Speaking Volumes: A Dublin Childhood* (Belfast, 2000), p. 143

78 Quoted in Susan McKay, *Northern Protestants: An Unsettled People* (Belfast, 2000), p. 81

79 Campbell, 'Down the Shankill', pp. 1–33

80 Thomas W. Laqueur, *Religion and Respectability: Sunday Schools and Working-Class Culture, 1780–1850* (London, 1976), p. 160

81 Hugh McLeod, *Piety and Poverty* (New York, 1996), p. 156

82 Jonathan Bardon, *Beyond the Studio: A History of BBC Northern Ireland* (Belfast, 2000), pp. 3–4

83 Peter Somerville-Large, *Irish Voices: An Informal History 1916–1966* (London, 1999), p. 180

84 *Traveller Ways Traveller Words* (Dublin, 1992), pp. 28–9

85 Quoted in Somerville-Large, *Irish Voices: An Informal History 1916–1966* (London, 1999), pp. 76–7

86 Helen Morrissey, 'Betty Sinclair: A Woman's Fight for Socialism, 1920–81', *Saothar*, vol. 9 (1983), pp. 121–32, p. 124

87 Reports of the Irish delegation, 21 May, 1931, Rosamund Jacob Papers, National Library of Ireland, MS. 33,129 (2)

88 Fearghal McGarry, *Irish Politics and the Spanish Civil War* (Cork, 1999), pp. 5–7

89 Mike Cronin, *The Blueshirts in Irish Politics* (Dublin, 1997)

90 Ward, *Hanna Sheehy Skeffington*, pp. 321–2

91 *The Wooden Horse: A Reply to Fascists* (n.d.), IWWU pamphlet held in University College Dublin archives

92   PRONI, D/3783/A/2

93   McGarry, *Irish Politics and the Spanish Civil War*, p. 21

94   Articles and Speeches by Lady Londonderry, PRONI, D/3099/3/38

95   Quoted in Brian Barton, *Northern Ireland in the Second World War* (Belfast, 1995), p. 1

96   *Past Discovery: Report of a seminar organised by Ballymacarrett Arts and Cultural Society* (1997), p. 18

97   Jonathan Bardon, *A History of Ulster* (Belfast, 1992), p. 562

98   A History of the Ulster Gift Fund, 1939–46, compiled by John W. Blake, PRONI, D/912/1/13

99   History of Women's Voluntary Services for Civil Defence in Northern Ireland, PRONI, CAB/31/64

100   Elaine Crowley, *Technical Virgins* (Dublin, 1998), p. 23

101   Richard Doherty, *Irish Men and Women in the Second World War* (Dublin, 1999), pp. 45–6

102   *Ibid.*, quoted on p. 266

103   Romie Lambkin, *My Time in the War: An Irishwoman's Diary* (Dublin, 1992)

104   Quoted in Doherty, *Irish Men and Women*, p. 268

105   Notes on the Women's Auxiliary Air Force stationed in Northern Ireland, November 1943–September 1945 (from Wing-Commander Conan-Doyle), PRONI, CAB/3A/27

106   Quoted in Kearns, *Dublin Voices*, p. 255

107   Bridget Grealis-Guglich, 'Going off with the Little Bag', in Sheelagh Conway, *The Faraway Hills are Green: Voices of Irish Women in Canada* (Ontario, 1992), pp. 123–31, p. 124

108   Marianne Heron, *Sheila Conroy: Fighting Spirit* (Dublin, 1993), p. 15

109   Robert Fisk, *In Time of War: Ireland, Ulster and the Price of Neutrality, 1939–45* (Dublin, 1996), p. 418

110   Betty Sinclair, *Ulster Women and the War* (Belfast, 1942)

111   Brian Barton, *The Blitz: Belfast in the War Years* (Belfast, 1989), pp. 261–2

112   Cited in Derek Gibson-Harries, *Life-Line to Freedom: Ulster in the Second World War* (Lurgan, 1990), p. 68

113   Keogh, *Twentieth-Century Ireland*; K.C. Kearns, *Dublin Folklore, An Oral Folk History* (Dublin, 1998), pp. 153, 173; Ann Rossiter, 'Bringing the Margins into the Centre: A Review of Aspects of Irish Women's Emigration from a British Perspective', in Smyth (ed.), *Irish Women's Studies Reader*, pp. 177–202, p. 191

114   Mary Lennon, Marie McAdam and Joanne O'Brien, *Across the Water: Irish Women's Lives in Britain* (London, 1988), pp. 92–6

115   Liz McShane, 'Day Nurseries in Northern Ireland 1941–1955: Gender Ideology in Social Policy', in Curtin, Jackson and O'Connor (eds), *Gender in Irish Society*, pp. 249–62

116   Brian Barton, *Northern Ireland in the Second World War* (Belfast, 1995), p. 5

117   Tweedy, *A Link in the Chain*; Devlin, *Speaking Volumes*

118   Tweedy, *A Link in the Chain*

119   Tony Gray, *The Lost Years: The Emergency in Ireland 1939–45* (London, 1997), p. 43

120   *Ibid.*, p. 145

121   Quoted in Larmour, 'Aspects of the State', p. 113

122   Records of the Drawing Room Circle, PRONI, D/3866/2/1

123   Elizabeth McCullough, *A Square Peg: An Ulster Childhood* (Dublin, 1997)

124   Bardon, *Beyond the Studio*, p. 81

125 Emma Duffin, Nursing Diaries, PRONI, D/2109/18/9
126 Barton, *The Blitz*
127 *Ibid.*, p. 126
128 Bardon, *Beyond the Studio*, p. 80
129 Emma Duffin, Nursing Diaries, PRONI, D/2109/8–13
130 Cabinet Papers, PRONI, CAB/31/64
131 Moya Woodside a volunteer observer for the Mass Observation Social Research organisation, typescript in PRONI, T/3808/1
132 Max Wright, *Told in Gath* (Belfast, 1990), p. ix
133 Richard Doherty, *Irish Volunteers in the Second World War* (Dublin, 2002), pp. 136–7
134 Blake, A History of the Ulster Gift Fund, 1939–46
135 McCullough, *A Square Peg*, p. 114
136 Barton, *Northern Ireland in the Second World War*, p. 106–7
137 Jessie Woodger, *Jessica's People* (Hampshire, 1998), p. 155
138 Felicity Braddell Smith, *They Were Good Days* (Durham, 1994), p. 54
139 Bardon, *Belfast: An Illustrated History*, pp. 606–8
140 *Ibid.*, p. 250
141 Quoted in McKay, *Northern Protestants*, p. 109
142 Muirhevna Mó, Short Strand, Newtownards Road Women's Group and Women's Action Group East, *Us, Them and Others* (n.d.), p. 18
143 Papers of Dr Florence Stewart, PRONI, D/3612/3/1
144 Rowthorn and Wayne, *Northern Ireland*, p. 31
145 Graham Walker, *The Politics of Frustration: Harry Midgley and the Failure of Labour in Northern Ireland* (Manchester, 1985), p. 201
146 *Ibid.*, pp. 209–10
147 Sabine Wichert, *Northern Ireland since 1945*, 2nd ed. (London, 1999), p. 47
148 McWilliams, 'The Church, the State and the Women's Movement', p. 88
149 Patricia Harkin, 'La Famille, Fruit du Passé, Germe de l'Avenir: Family Policy in Ireland and Vichy France', Unpublished MA thesis, University College Dublin, 1992, p. 55, quoted in Daly, 'Oh, Kathleen Ni Houlihan', p. 113
150 Evelyn Mahon, 'The Development of a Health Policy for Women', in Joseph Robins, (ed.), *Reflections on Health: Commemorating Fifty Years of the Department of Health 1947–97* (Dublin, 1997), pp. 77–96, p. 80
151 Daly, 'Oh, Kathleen Ni Houlihan', p. 113
152 Mary E. Daly '"Turn on the Tap": The State, Irish Women and Running Water', in Valiulis and O'Dowd (eds), *Women in Irish History*, pp. 206–19, p. 207
153 *Ibid.*, p. 208
154 *Ibid.*
155 Somerville-Large, *Irish Voices: An Informal History 1916–1966*, p. 272
156 R.H. Buchanan and B.M. Walker (eds), *Province, City and People: Belfast and Its Region* (Belfast, 1987), pp. 172–3
157 M. Moynahin (ed.), *Speeches and Statements by Eamon de Valera* (Dublin, 1980), p. 466
158 Rossiter, 'Bringing the Margins into the Centre', p. 191
159 Grealis-Guglich, 'Going off with the Little Bag', p. 123
160 Quoted in Anne Holohan, *Working Lives: The Irish in Britain* (Dublin, 1995), p. 2
161 Daly, '"Turn on the Tap"', p. 206
162 Quoted in Pauric Travers, '"There was Nothing for Me There": Irish Female Emigration, 1922–71', in Patrick O'Sullivan (ed.), *Irish Women and Irish Migration* (London, 1995), pp. 146–67, p. 153

163 Quoted in Catriona Clear, *Women of the House: Women's Household Work in Ireland 1922–1961* (Dublin, 2000), p. 176

164 Travers, "'There was Nothing for Me There'", pp. 154–8

165 Keogh, *Twentieth-Century Ireland*, p. 242

166 'Interview with Mary Dorcey', in Ide O'Caroll and Eoin Collins (eds), *Lesbian and Gay Visions of Ireland: Towards the Twenty-First Century* (London, 1995), pp. 25–44

167 Quoted in Gillian McIntosh, *The Force of Culture: Unionist Identities in Twentieth Century Ireland* (Cork, 1999), p. 122

168 *Irish News and Belfast Morning News*, 2 June 1953

CHAPTER 4

1 My title for Chapter 4 is an adaptation of Ailbhe Smyth's 'Paying Our Disrespects to the (Bloody) States We're In: Women, Culture, Violence and the State', in G. Griffin, et al. (eds), *Stirring It: Challenges for Feminism* (London, 1994), pp. 13–39. The epigraph is from June Levine (Irish Women's Liberation Movement), *Sisters: The Personal Story of an Irish Feminist* (Dublin, 1982), quoted in Lorna Siggins, *The Woman Who Took Power in the Park: Mary Robinson* (Edinburgh, 1997), p. 60

2 *Irish News and Belfast Morning News,* 9 November 1963

3 Vincent Power, *Send 'em Home Sweatin': The Showband Story* (Cork, 1990), p. 349

4 Dermot Keogh, *Twentieth-Century Ireland: Nation and State* (Dublin, 1994), pp. 260–1

5 Power, *Send 'em Home Sweatin'*, pp. 349–52

6 Quoted in Fergal Tobin, *The Best of Decades: Ireland in the 1960s* (Dublin, 1996), pp. 19–20

7 Quoted in Maeve Flanagan, *Dev, Lady Chatterley and Me: A 60s Suburban Childhood* (Dublin, 1998), p. 25

8 Quoted in Keogh, *Twentieth-Century Ireland*, pp. 259–60

9 Mary E. Daly, *Women and Work in Ireland* (Dundalk, 1997), p. 43

10 Máire gan Ainm, 'Barbed Wire and Barricades', in Sheelagh Conway, *The Faraway Hills are Green: Voices of Irish Women in Canada* (Ontario, 1996), pp. 233–42, p. 238

11 Luke Gibbons, 'From Kitchen Sink to Soap: Drama and the Serial Form on Irish Television', in McLoone and McMahon (ed.), *21 Years of Irish Television*, pp. 21–51, p. 27

12 Maurice Earls, 'The Late Late Show: Controversy and Context', in McLoone and McMahon (ed.), *21 Years of Irish Television*, pp. 107–22, p. 110

13 Nuala O'Faolain, *Are You Somebody? The Life and Times of Nuala O'Faolain* (Dublin, 1996), p. 64

14 Flanagan, *Dev, Lady Chatterley and Me*, pp. 31–8. This D.H. Lawrence novel was unpublished in England until 1960. When Penguin produced it that year it was prosecuted under the Obscene Publications Act of 1959, and was acquitted in a celebrated trial.

15 Mary Kenny, *Goodbye to Catholic Ireland* (Dublin, 2000), pp. 235–7

16 *Ibid.*

17 Finola Kennedy, *Cottage to Crèche: Family Change in Ireland* (Dublin, 2001), p. 230

18 Minute Books of NIFPA from 11 February 1965, PRONI, D/3543/2/2

19 Abbey Hyde, 'Marriage and Motherhood: The Contradictory Position of Single Mothers', *Irish Journal of Feminist Studies*, vol. 2, no. 1 (summer 1997), pp. 22–36, p. 24

20 Eileen Evason, *Just Me and the Kids: A Study of Single Parent Families in Northern Ireland* (Belfast, 1980), p. 6

21 *The Unmarried Mother in the Irish Community: A Report on the National Conference on Community Services for the Unmarried Parent* (Kilkenny, 1972)

22 Maeve Binchy, 'Shepherd's Bush', in *Central Line: Stories of Big City Life* (London, 1978), pp. 7–23, p. 9

23 Quoted in Audrey Simpson, 'Abortion in Northern Ireland: A Victorian Law', in Ann Foredi (ed.), *Human Rights and Reproductive Choice* (Belfast, 1995), pp. 6–15, p. 8

24 *Ibid.*, quoted on p. 7

25 Kathryn Conrad, 'Women Troubles, Queer Troubles: Gender, Sexuality, and the Politics of Selfhood in the Construction of the Northern Irish State', in Marilyn Cohen and Nancy J. Curtin (eds), *Reclaiming Gender: Transgressive Identities in Modern Ireland* (New York, 1999), pp. 53–68, p. 55

26 Joni Crone, 'Lesbians: The Lavender Women of Ireland', in Íde O'Carroll and Eion Collins (eds), *Lesbian and Gay Visions of Ireland: Towards the Twenty-First Century* (London, 1995), pp. 60–70, p. 61

27 Interview with Mary Dorcey, in O'Carroll and Collins (eds), *Lesbian and Gay Visions*, pp. 25–44, pp. 29–30

28 Yvonne Galligan, *Women and Politics in Contemporary Ireland: From the Margins to the Mainstream* (London, 1998), p. 93

29 Quoted in Susan McKay, *Northern Protestants: An Unsettled People* (Belfast, 2000), p. 84

30 Monica McWilliams and Joan McKiernan, *Bringing it Out in the Open: Domestic Violence in Northern Ireland* (Belfast, 1993)

31 Quoted in Maedhbh McNamara and Paschal Mooney, *Women in Parliament: Ireland 1918–2000* (Dublin, 2000), p. 107

32 Bob Purdie, *Politics in the Streets: The Origins of the Civil Rights Movement in Northern Ireland* (Belfast, 1990), p. 77

33 Quoted in Rosemary Sales, *Women Divided: Gender, Religion and Politics in Northern Ireland* (London, 1997), p. 171

34 McNamara and Mooney, *Women in Parliament*, p. 18

35 Quoted in Monica McWilliams, 'Women in Northern Ireland: An Overview', in Eamonn Hughes (ed.), *Culture and Politics in Northern Ireland 1960–1990* (Milton Keynes, 1991), pp. 81–100, p. 81

36 McNamara and Mooney, *Women in Parliament*, p. 35

37 Siggins, *The Woman Who Took Power in the Park*, pp. 41–2

38 *Ibid.*, quoted on p. 70

39 *Ibid.*, quoted on p. 57

40 Linda Connolly, 'The Women's Movement in Ireland, 1970–1995: A Social Movements Analysis', *Irish Journal of Feminist Studies*, vol. 1, no. 1 (1996), pp. 43–77, p. 49

41 Amanda Lagerkvist, '"To End Women's Night": A Resistance Discourse of the Irish Housewives' Association in the Media in 1961–62', *Irish Journal of Feminist Studies*, vol. 2, no. 2 (December 1997), pp. 18–33, p. 25

42 Connolly, 'The Women's Movement', p. 52

43 Galligan, *Women and Politics in Contemporary Ireland*, p. 92

44 *Irish News and Belfast Morning News*, 15 November 1963

45 Connolly, 'The Women's Movement', p. 53

46 Ailbhe Smyth, 'The Contemporary Women's Movement in the Republic of Ireland', *Women's Studies International Forum*, vol. 11, no. 4 (1988), pp. 331–41, p. 332

47 Levine, *Sisters: The Personal Story of an Irish Feminist*, p. 8

48 Smyth, 'The Contemporary Women's Movement', p. 333

49 Kenny, *Goodbye to Catholic Ireland*, p. 238

50 Quoted in Evelyn Mahon, 'Women's Rights and Catholicism in Ireland', *New Left Review*, no. 166 (November/December 1987), pp. 53–77, p. 60

51 Quoted in Galligan, *Women and Politics in Contemporary Ireland*, p. 95

52 Ailbhe Smyth, 'Seeing Red: Men's Violence Against Women in Ireland', *In From the Shadows: The UL Women's Studies Collection*, vol. 2 (1996), pp. 15–37, p. 15

53 *Ibid.*, pp. 17–18

54 Catherine Rose, *The Female Experience: The Story of the Woman Movement in Ireland* (Galway, 1975), p. 75

55 Quoted in Smyth, 'The Contemporary Women's Movement', p. 337

56 Rose, *The Female Experience*, p. 78

57 Flanagan, *Dev, Lady Chatterley and Me*, p. 72

58 Cynthia Cockburn, *The Space between Us: Negotiating Gender and National Identities in Conflict* (London, 1998), p. 53

59 Eilish Rooney, 'Women in Northern Irish Politics: Difference Matters', Carmel Roulston and Celia Davies (eds.), *Gender, Democracy and Inclusion in Northern Ireland* (Basingstoke, 2000), pp. 164–86, p. 166

60 Bob Purdie, *Politics in the Streets: The Origins of the Civil Rights Movement in Northern Ireland* (Belfast, 1990)

61 Catherine Shannon, 'Women in Northern Ireland', in Mary O'Dowd and Sabine Wichert (eds.), *Chattel, Servant or Citizen: Women's Status in Church, State and Society* (Belfast, 1995), pp. 238–53, p. 239

62 Fionnuala O Connor, *In Search of a State: Catholics in Northern Ireland* (Belfast, 1993), p. 182

63 Interview with Patricia McCluskey, 1993, quoted in Sarah Ward, 'The Genesis of Civil Rights in Northern Ireland', dissertation submitted in partial fulfilment of requirements for M.Sc. in Irish Poltical Studies, Queen's University Belfast, 1993

64 Jonathan Bardon, *A History of Ulster* (Belfast, 1992), p. 637

65 Shannon, 'Women in Northern Ireland', p. 241

66 Quoted in Mary Kathryn Bolster, 'Women on the March: Women in the Civil Rights Movement in Northern Ireland in the 1960s', dissertation submitted in partial fulfilment of requirements for MA, University College Dublin, 1991, p. 34

67 Quoted in Chrissie McAuley (ed.), *Women in a War Zone: Twenty Years of Resistance* (Dublin, n.d.), p. 13. The label 'Maiden City' is a reference to the failure of James II to breach Derry's walls during the siege of 1689, when the overwhelmingly Protestant population defended the city for 105 days.

68 Quoted in Elizabeth Shannon, *I am of Ireland: Women of the North Speak Out* (Philadelphia, 1989), p. 47

69 *Dungannon Observer*, 21 September 1963

70 Quoted in Shannon, *I am of Ireland*, p. 49

71 Quoted in McKay, *Northern Protestants*, p. 356

72 Bardon, *A History of Ulster*, p. 635, p. 664

73 *Ibid.*, p. 671

74 *Observer,* 27 April 1969

75 WNBC and NBC interview, *Today Show,* 7 May 1969, Northern Ireland Office press cuttings files; Bernadette Devlin, 27 April 1969 to 31 January 1971, Linen Hall Library, biographical press cuttings file

76 *Ibid.*

77 *Belfast Telegraph*, 2 September 1969

78 Quoted in Bronwen Walter, *Outsiders Inside: Whiteness, Place and Irish Women* (London and New York, 2001), p. 85

79 *Irish Times*, 29 October 1969

80 *Observer*, 30 November 1969

81 McKay, *Northern Protestants*, p. 360

82 *Ibid.*, quoted on p. 357

83 Interview with the author, May, 2002

84 Sinn Féin Women's Department, *Women in Struggle*, no. 1 (spring 1991)

85 Allen Feldman, *Formations of Violence: The Narrative of the Body and Political Terror in Northern Ireland* (London, 1991), p. 96

86 Fionnuala Ní Aoláin, *The Politics of Force: Conflict Management and State Violence in Northern Ireland* (Belfast, 2000), p. 263

87 Paul Bew and Gordon Gillespie, *Northern Ireland: A Chronology of the Troubles 1968–1999* (Dublin, 1999), pp. 36–7

88 *Ibid.*

89 Martyn Turner, 'Living with Bombs', *Fortnight*, vol. 25 (1 October 1971)

90 Margaret Ward, 'The Women's Movement in the North of Ireland: Twenty Years On', in Seán Hutton and Paul Stewart (eds), *Ireland's Histories: Aspects of State, Society and Ideology* (London, 1991), pp. 149–63, p. 151

91 Interview with Bernadette McAliskey, in Bolster, 'Women on the March', pp. 69–70

92 The phrase is used by Begoña Aretxaga, *Shattering Silence: Women, Nationalism, and Political Subjectivity in Northern Ireland* (Princeton, 1997), p. 61

93 Quoted in Lynda Edgerton, 'Public Protest, Domestic Acquiescence: Women in Northern Ireland', in Rosemary Ridd and Helen Calloway (eds), *Caught Up in Conflict: Women's Responses to Political Strife* (London, 1986), pp. 61–79

94 Síghle Humphreys Papers, University College Dublin, P106/1586

95 Quoted in Geoffery Bell, *The Protestants of Ulster* (London, 1976), p. 54

96 Carol Coulter, *Web of Punishment: An Investigation* (Dublin, 1991), pp. 96–100

97 O Connor, *In Search of a State*, p. 161

98 Quoted in Bew and Gillespie, *Northern Ireland: A Chronology*, p. 45

99 Rhoda Watson, *Along the Road to Peace: Fifteen Years with the Peace People* (Belfast, 1991), p. 33

100 Prisoners' Aid and Protestant Conflict Resettlement Group, *A Brief History of the UDA/UFF in Contemporary Conflict. Northern Ireland 1969–1995* (Belfast, 1995), p. 52

101 Quoted in Marilyn Hyndman, *Further Afield: Journeys from a Protestant Past* (Belfast, 1996), p. 15

102 Anne Noble, 'A Riot', in Ruth Hooley (ed.), *The Female Line: Northern Irish Women Writers* (Belfast, 1985), pp. 113–7, p. 114

103 Martin Dillon, *God and the Gun: The Church and Irish Terrorism* (London, 1997), p. 154

104 'Women in Struggle', *An Phoblacht/Republican News,* 20 May 1982

105 Seán Mac Stiofáin, *Memoirs of a Revolutionary* (London, 1975), p. 218

106 Martin Dillon, *The Dirty War* (London, 1988), pp. 231–47

107 Eileen Fairweather, Roisin McDonough and Melanie McFadyean, *Only the Rivers Run Free. Northern Ireland: The Women's War* (London, 1984), pp. 240–4

108 Maria Maguire, *To Take Arms: A Year in the Provisional IRA* (Bristol, 1973)

109 Maire Drumm, quoted in *Protestant Telegraph*, 17 February 1973, Maire Drumm, Linen Hall Library, biographical press cuttings file

110 *Daily Mail,* 26 March 1973

111 *Sunday World*, 30 November 1975

112 *Belfast Telegraph,* 2 April 1976

113 Bill Rolston, 'Mothers, Whores and Villains: Images of Women in Novels of the Northern Ireland Conflict', *Race and Class,* vol. 31, no. 1 (1989), pp. 41–57, p. 55

114 Quoted in Margaretta D'Arcy, *Tell them Everything: A Sojourn in the Prison of Her Majesty Queen Elizabeth II at Ard Macha (Armagh)* (London, 1981), p, 43

115 *Spare Rib* (September 1972) quoted in Bolster, 'Women on the March', p. 81

116 Quoted in Bell, *Protestants of Ulster,* p. 55

117 Prisoners, Aid . . . Group, *A Brief History of the UDA/UFF,* p. 52

118 Dillon, *God and the Gun,* p. 156

119 Chris Ryder, *The Ulster Defence Regiment: An Instrument of Peace?* (London, 1991), pp. 63–7

120 John Brewer, 'Hercules, Hippolyte and the Amazons – or Policewomen in the RUC', *British Journal of Sociology,* vol. 42, no. 2, (June 1991), pp. 233–47

121 For information on the lives lost during the conflict, see David McKittrick, Seamus Kelters, Brian Feeney and Chris Thornton (eds), *Lost Lives: The Stories of the Men, Women and Children Who Died as a Result of the Northern Ireland Troubles* (Edinburgh, 1999)

122 Pauline Prior, *Mental Health and Politics in Northern Ireland* (Belfast, 1993)

123 Ní Aoláin, *The Politics of Force,* pp. 44–5

124 Quoted in Eileen MacDonald, *Shoot the Women First* (London, 1991), p. 162

125 Eileen Hickey, *Women in Struggle* (autumn 1994), pamphlet issued by Sinn Féin Women's Department

126 *Women in Struggle,* vol. 4, interview with Mairead Farrell on 20 September 1986

127 Áine and Eibhlín Nic Giolla Easpaig, 'Sisters in Cells: Two Republican Prisoners in England' (1985), in Angela Bourke, et al. (eds), *The Field Day Anthology of Irish Writing,* vols. IV and V, Irish Women's Writing and Traditions (Cork, 2002), vol. V, pp. 1501–5

128 Quoted in Monica McWilliams, 'Struggling for Peace and Justice: Reflections on Women's Activism in Northern Ireland', in Joan Hoff and Moureen Coulter (eds.), *Irish Women's Voices: Past and Present* (Indianna, 1995), *Journal of Women's History,* vols. 6 and 7, pp. 13–39, p. 23

129 Aretxaga, *Shattering Silence,* p. 76

130 Edgerton, 'Public Protest, Domestic Acquiescence', p. 72

131 Statement by NIWRM, Political Section, Linen Hall Library, Belfast

132 McWilliams, 'Struggling for Peace and Justice', p. 21

133 Quoted in Eileen Evason, *Against the Grain: The Contemporary Women's Movement in Northern Ireland* (Dublin, 1991), p. 23

134 *Ibid.,* p. 26

135 Pauline Conroy Jackson, 'Women's Movement and Abortion: The Criminalization of Irish Women', in Drude Dahlerup (ed.), *The New Women's Movement: Feminism and Political Power in Europe and the USA* (London, 1986), pp. 48–63, p. 49

136 Carmel Roulston, 'Women on the Margin: The Women's Movement in Northern Ireland, 1973–1988', *Science and Society,* vol. 53, no. 2 (summer 1989), pp. 219–36, p. 226

137 McWilliams and McKiernan, *Bringing it Out in the Open,* p. 124

138 Rooney, 'Political Division, Practical Alliance: Problems for Women in Conflict', in Joan Hoff and Moureen Coulter (eds), *Irish Women's Voices: Past and Present,* (Indiana, 1995), *Journal of Women's History,* vols. 6 and 7, pp. 41–8, p. 44

139 Quoted in Rosemary Sales, 'Women, the Peace Makers?', in James Anderson and

James Goodman (eds), *DIS/Agreeing Ireland: Contexts, Obstacles, Hopes* (London, 1998), pp. 141–61, p. 153

140 'Proper Wives, Orange Maidens or Disloyal Subjects: Situating the Equality Concern of Protestant Women in Northern Ireland', *Women's News* (June/July 1994), p. 6

141 Rooney, 'Political Division', p. 42

142 Quoted in McKay, *Northern Protestants*, p. 74

143 Monica McWilliams, 'Struggling for Peace and Justice', p. 28

144 May Blood, 'People at Peace', in Dominic Murray (ed.), *Protestant Perceptions of the Peace Process in Northern Ireland* (Limerick, 2000), pp. 73–100, p. 75

145 Marie Hammond Callaghan, 'Surveying Politics of Peace, Gender, Conflict and Identity in Northern Ireland: The Case of the Derry Peace Women in 1972', *Women's Studies International Forum*, vol. 25 (January–February 2002), pp. 33–49

146 Women Together/Peace People, Linen Hall Library, press cuttings file, vol. 1

147 Nancy Kinghan, *United We Stood: The Official History of the Ulster Women's Unionist Council 1911–1974* (Belfast, 1975), p. 68

148 *Irish Independent,* 4 April 1972

149 *News Letter,* 5 February 1973

150 *Irish News,* 10 April 1972

151 Callaghan, 'Surveying Politics of Peace', p. 33

152 Mairead Corrigan married her widowed brother-in-law, Jackie Maguire, in September 1981

153 *Belfast Telegraph,* 12 August 1976

154 Quoted in Suzann Buckley and Pamela Lonergan, 'Women and the Troubles, 1969–1980', in Yonah Alexander and Alan O'Day (eds.), *Terrorism in Ireland* (London and Canberra, 1984), pp. 75–87, p. 83

155 Harriet H. Alonso, *Peace as a Women's Issue* (Syracuse, 1993), p. 263

156 Quoted in Bill Rolston, 'Mothers, Whores and Villains', p. 56

157 Flanagan, *Dev, Lady Chatterley and Me*, p. 59

CHAPTER 5

1 M. McGilloway, quoted in Monica McWilliams and Avila Kilmurray, 'Athene on the Loose: The Origins of the Northern Ireland Women's Coalition', *Irish Journal of Feminist Studies*, vol. 2, no. 1 (summer 1997), pp. 1–21, p. 7

2 Fintan O'Toole, *The Irish Times Book of the Century* (Dublin, 1999), p. 325

3 Carol Coulter, '"Hello Divorce, Goodbye Daddy": Women, Gender and the Divorce Debate', in Anthony Bradley and Maryann G. Valiulis (eds), *Gender and Sexuality in Modern Ireland* (Amherst, 1997), pp. 275–98, p. 276

4 Wanda Wigfall-Williams and Gillian Robinson, 'A World Apart: Mixed Marriages in Northern Ireland', *Northern Ireland Life and Times Survey*, Research Update, no. 8 (November 2001)

5 Mary O'Malley Madec, 'The Irish Travelling Woman: Mother and Mermaid', in Ailbhe Smyth (ed.), *Irish Women's Studies Reader* (1993), pp. 214–29

6 Quoted in Kathryn Conrad, 'Women's Troubles, Queer Troubles: Gender, Sexuality, and the Politics of Selfhood in the Construction of the Northern Irish State,' in Marilyn Cohen and Nancy J. Curtin (eds), *Reclaiming Gender: Transgressive Identities in Modern Ireland* (New York, 1999), pp. 53–68, p. 54

7 *Northern Ireland Life and Times Survey,* 2001

8 Quoted in Lorraine Dowler, '"And They Think I'm just a Nice Old Lady": Women

and War in Belfast, Northern Ireland', *Gender, Place and Culture*, vol. 5, no. 2 (1998), pp. 159–76, p. 165

9   Quoted in Elizabeth Shannon, *I am of Ireland: Women of the North Speak Out* (Philadelphia, 1989), pp. 217–18

10   Quoted in Eileen Fairweather, Roisin McDonough and Melanie McFadyean, *Only the Rivers Run Free. Northern Ireland: The Women's War* (London, 1984), p. 301

11   Carol Coulter, *Web of Punishment: An Investigation* (Dublin, 1991), p. 25

12   Quoted in Dowler, '"And They Think I'm Just a Nice Old Lady"', p. 165

13   Quoted in Monica McWilliams, 'The Church, the State and the Women's Movement in Northern Ireland', in Smyth (ed.), *Irish Women's Studies Reader*, pp. 79–99, p. 81

14   Quoted in Coulter, '"Hello Divorce, Goodbye Daddy"', p. 282

15   Maedhbh McNamara and Paschal Mooney, *Women in Parliament: Ireland 1918–2000* (Dublin, 2000), p. 119

16   Michele Dillon, 'Divorce and Cultural Rationality', in Michel Peillon and Eamonn Slater (eds), *Encounters with Modern Ireland: A Sociological Chronicle 1995–1996* (Dublin, 1998), pp. 127–33, p. 133

17   Finola Kennedy, *Cottage to Crèche: Family Change in Ireland* (Dublin, 2001)

18   Pamela Montgomery and V. Bell, *Police Responses to Wife Assault: A Northern Ireland Study* (1986), p. 57

19   Pat O'Connor, *Emerging Voices: Women in Contemporary Irish Society* (Dublin, 1998), p. 71

20   Eithne McLaughlin, 'Women and the Family in Northern Ireland: A Review', *Women's Studies International Forum*, vol. 16, no. 6 (1993), pp. 553–68, p. 555

21   Miriam M. Wiley and Barry Merriman, *Women and Health Care in Ireland: Knowledge, Attitudes and Behaviour* (Dublin, 1996)

22   O'Connor, *Emerging Voices* p. 51

23   Ailbhe Smyth, 'Feminism: Personal, Political, Unqualified (or Ex-Colonized Girls Know More)', *Irish Journal of Feminist Studies*, vol. 2, no. 1 (summer 1997), pp. 37–54, p. 43

24   Interview with the author, May 2001

25   Abbey Hyde, 'Unmarried Pregnant Women's Accounts of Their Contraceptive Practices: A Qualitative Analysis', *Irish Journal of Sociology*, vol. 6 (1996), pp. 179–211, p. 185

26   Abbey Hyde 'Marriage and Motherhood: The Contradictory Position of Single Mothers', *Irish Journal of Feminist Studies*, vol. 2, no. 1 (summer 1997), pp. 22–36, p. 24

27   *Ibid.*, p. 27

28   Anne Byrne, 'Familist Ideology and Difficult Identities: "Never-married" Women in Contemporary Irish Society', in Cohen and Curtin (eds), *Reclaiming Gender: Transgressive Identities in Modern Ireland*, pp. 69–90, p. 72

29   Quoted in Kieran Rose, *Diverse Communities: The Evolution of Lesbian and Gay Politics in Ireland* (Cork, 1994), p. 58

30   *Ibid.*, p. 9

31   Joni Crone, 'Lesbians: The Lavender Women of Ireland', in Íde O'Carroll and Eoin Collins (eds), *Lesbian and Gay Visions of Ireland: Towards the Twenty-First Century* (London, 1995), pp. 60–70, pp. 66–7

32   Louise Walsh, 'Artist-Activist', *Ibid.*, pp. 171–80, p. 171

33   Rose, *Diverse Communities*, pp. 13, 30

34   Angela O'Connell, 'The Other Boat to England: The Route to Pregnancy for Irish

Lesbians'. Unpublished paper presented at a conference on Theorising Sexuality, held in University College Cork, 24 March 2001

35   R.H. Buchanan (ed.), *Province, City and People: Belfast and Its Region* (Antrim, 1987), p. 252

36   Eileen Evason, *Just Me and the Kids: A Study of Single Parent Families in Northern Ireland* (Belfast, 1980), p. 73

37   Quoted in Pauline Conroy Jackson, 'Women's Movement and Abortion: The Criminalization of Irish Women', in Drude Dahlerup (ed.), *The New Women's Movement: Feminism and Political Power in Europe and the USA* (London, 1986), pp. 48–63, p. 54

38   Tim Pat Coogan, *Disillusioned Decades: Ireland 1966–87* (Dublin, 1987), p. 79

39   Paul O'Mahoney, 'The Kerry Babies: Towards a Social Psychological Analysis', *Irish Journal of Psychological Analysis*, vol. 13, no. 2 (1992), pp. 223–38

40   Nell McCafferty, 'Not Guilty Enough', *Irish Press*, 16 May 1985

41   Mary Donnelly, 'The Calm of Reasoning: Judicial Attitudes to Sentencing in Sexual Offence Cases', *Irish Journal of Feminist Studies*, vol. 1, no. 1 (March 1996), pp. 26–42, p. 29

42   Quoted in Lisa Smyth, 'Narratives of Irishness and the Problem of Abortion: The X Case 1992', *Feminist Review*, no. 60 (autumn 1998), pp. 61–83, p. 78

43   Eileen Evason, *Against the Grain: The Contemporary Women's Movement in Northern Ireland* (Dublin, 1991), p. 27

44   Bernadette Smyth, quoted in 'Pro-choice Forum, Ireland and Abortion', http://www.prochoiceforum.org.uk, 23 March 1999

45   Quoted in Audrey Simpson, 'Abortion in Northern Ireland', in Ann Furedi (ed.), *The Abortion Law in Northern Ireland: A Human Rights and Reproductive Choice* (Belfast, 1995), pp. 6–15, p. 14

46   *Ibid.*

47   Jackson, 'Women's Movement and Abortion', p. 58

48   Of the 72 centenarians who died in Northern Ireland in 1998, only 8 were male. Pat Thane, 'Old Women in 20th Century Britain', in Lynn Botelho and Pat Thane (eds), *Women and Ageing in British Society Since 1500* (London, 2001), pp. 207–31

49   *Ibid.*, p. 227

50   European Commission, *The Social Situation in the European Union 2000*, p. 23

51   All-Ireland Mortality Rates 1989–1999 "Inequalities in Mortality" 1989–1998, a Report on All-Ireland Mortality Data

52   http://cain.ulst.ac.uk/csc/reports/ethnic/htm

53   'Speaking Out', *Conference Report on Health and Social Needs of Ethnic Minorities in Northern Ireland* (Belfast, 1996), p. 19

54   Mary Healy, *For the Poor and for the Gentry: Mary Healy Remembers Her Life* (Dublin, 1989), p. 96

55   Tony Fahey (ed.), *Social Housing in Ireland: A Study of Success, Failure and Lessons Learned* (Dublin, 1999), p. 240

56   'Homeless in Ireland, What are the Facts?', pages of the Workers Solidarity Movement, http://flag. blackened.net/revolt/ws/home48html

57   Mary Owens and Anne Byrne, 'Family, Work and Community – Rural Women's Lives', *U.C.G. Women's Studies Centre Review*, vol. 4 (1996), pp. 77–94

58   Jocelyne Rigal, 'Changing Families of the Irish Travellers: The Experiences of Women', *Irish Journal of Feminist Studies*, vol. 3, no. 2 (autumn 1999), pp. 32–48, p. 35

59   Máirín Kenny, 'Final Thoughts: A Case for Celebration', in May McCann, Seamus

Ó Siochain and Joseph Ruane (eds), *Irish Travellers: Culture and Ethnicity* (Belfast, 1994), pp. 79–88, p. 80

60   http://cain.ulst.ac.uk/csc/reports/ethnic/htm

61   'Speaking Out', p. 25

62   Paul Cullen, *Refugees and Asylum Seekers in Ireland* (Cork, 2000), p. 6

63   Tim Callan, Brian Nolan, Brendan J. Whelan, Christopher T. Whelan and James Williams, *Poverty in the 1990s: Evidence from the 1994 Living in Ireland Survey* (Dublin, 1996), p. 125

64   Pamela Montgomery, 'Paid and Unpaid Work', in John Kremer and Pamela Montgomery (eds), *Women's Working Lives* (Belfast, 1993), pp. 15–41

65   Madeleine Leonard, 'Ourselves Alone: Household Work Strategies in a Deprived Community', *Irish Journal of Sociology*, vol. 2 (1992), pp. 70–84; O'Connor, *Emerging Voices*, p. 144

66   *The Female Forfeit – The Cost of Being a Woman*, Cabinet Report, CAB 79/00, 21 February 2000

67   *Ibid.*

68   Rosemary Sales, *Women Divided: Gender, Religion and Politics in Northern Ireland* (London, 1997), p. 167

69   Catherine ChiChi Aniagolu, 'Teleworking and the Sexual Division of Labour in Ireland', *Irish Journal of Feminist Studies*, vol. 2, no. 2 (winter 1997), pp. 57–75, p. 73

70   Patricia O'Hara, *Partners in Production? Women, Farm and Family in Ireland* (Oxford, 1998), p.4

71   Quoted in Deirdre Heenan and Derek Birrell, 'Farmwives in Northern Ireland and the Gendered Division of Labour', in Anne Byrne and Madeleine Leonard (eds), *Women and Irish Society: A Sociological Reader* (Belfast, 1997), pp. 377–94, p. 380

72   O'Hara, *Partners in Production*

73   Susan McKay, *Northern Protestants: An Unsettled People* (Belfast, 2000), p. 199

74   Fionnuala Sweeney, 'Women's Work is Never Done: The Changing Role and Status of Farming Women in Dungiven', *Causeway* (winter 1994), pp. 21–4

75   Sales, *Women Divided*, p. 156

76   *The Female Forfeit*

77   Maxine Jones, *Successful Irish Businesswomen* (Dublin, 1992)

78   Triple Cross Network, *Tipping the Balance: A Fresh Look at Issues Impacting on Equality for Women at the Beginning of the 21st Century* (2000)

79   *Guardian*, 10 November 1988

80   *Belfast Telegraph*, 30 October 1985

81   *Irish News*, 27 July 1983

82   Interview with author, May 2000

83   Maggie O'Neill, 'Prostitute Women Now', in Graham Scambler and Annette Scambler (eds), *Rethinking Prostitution: Purchasing Sex in the 1990s* (London, 1997), pp. 3, 328

84   June Levine and Lyn Madden, *Lyn: A Story of Prostitution* (Dublin, 1987), p. 8

85   Margaret MacCurtain, 'Moving Statues and Irish Women', in Smyth (ed.), *Irish Women's Studies Reader*, pp. 203–13, p. 207. MacCurtain cites the aftermath of the 1983 abortion referendum and the 'Kerry Babies' tribunal, which had preoccupied the media for most of the year.

86   Quoted in Catherine Rose, *The Female Experience: The Story of the Woman Movement in Ireland* (Galway, 1975), p. 73

87   Louis McRedmond (ed.), *Modern Irish Lives: Dictionary of 20th-Century Biography*

(Dublin, 1998), p. 157

88   Tom Inglis, *Moral Monopoly: The Rise and Fall of the Catholic Church in Modern Ireland*, 2nd ed. (Dublin, 1998), p. 216

89   Ruth Torode and Eoin O'Sullivan, 'The Impact of *Dear Daughter*', *Irish Journal of Feminist Studies*, vol. 3, no. 2 (autumn 1999), pp. 85–97

90   Inglis, *Moral Monopoly*, pp. 228–9

91   *Ibid.*, p. 209

92   Bridie Quinn-Conroy, *Not a Word of a Lie* (Kinvara, County Galway, 1993), p. 91

93   Inglis, *Moral Monopoly*, p. 205

94   Frederick Boal, Margaret Keane and David Livingstone, *Them and Us? Attitudinal Variations among Churchgoers in Belfast*, Insight Series no. 1, Online Research Bank (Belfast, 1997)

95   *Irish Times*, 16 June 1987

96   Glenn Jordan, *Not of this World? Evangelical Protestants in Northern Ireland* (Belfast, 2001), p. 81

97   Tom Inglis, 'From Sexual Repression to Liberation?', in Peillon and Slater (eds), *Encounters with Modern Ireland*, pp. 99–104, p. 103

98   *Ibid.*

99   Andrew M. Greeley, 'Are the Irish Really Losing the Faith?', *Doctrine and Life*, vol. 44, no. 3 (1994), pp. 132–42, p. 142

100   Paul Bew and Gordon Gillespie, *Northern Ireland: A Chronology of the Troubles, 1968–1999* (Dublin, 1999), p. 550

101   See David McKittrick, Seamus Kelters, Brian Feeney and Chris Thornton (eds), *Lost Lives: The Stories of the Men, Women and Children Who Died as a Result of the Northern Ireland Troubles* (Edinburgh, 1999)

102   Aretxaga Begoña, 'Dirty Protest: Symbolic Overdetermination and Gender in Northern Ireland Ethnic Violence', *Ethos*, vol. 23, no. 2 (1995), pp. 123–48

103   Nell McCafferty, *Irish Times*, 17 June 1980

104   Mairead Farrell and two other known republican activists, Seán Savage and Daniel McCann, were shot dead at point-blank range by the SAS in Gibraltar on 6 March 1988. Controversy surrounded the killings – none of the three were armed and witnesses testified that no warnings were given before the firing of at least twenty-seven shots; the SAS claimed that the trio was about to detonate a bomb. Bew and Gillespie, *Northern Ireland: A Chronology*, pp. 213–14

105   Nell McCafferty, *The Armagh Women* (Dublin, 1981), p. 9

106   Quoted in P. O'Malley, *The Uncivil Wars, Ireland Today* (Belfast, 1983), pp. 267–8

107   Aretxaga Begoña, 'The Sexual Games of the Body Politic: Fantasy and State Violence in Northern Ireland', *Culture, Medicine and Psychiatry*, vol. 25 (2001), pp. 1–27

108   Hester Dunn, 'Strip Searches' (1985), in Angela Bourke et al. (eds), *The Field Day Anthology of Irish Writing*, vols IV and V, Irish Women's Writing and Traditions (Cork, 2002), vol. V, pp. 1505–6

109   Margaret Ward, 'The Women's Movement in the North of Ireland: Twenty Years On', in Seán Hutton and Paul Stewart (eds), *Ireland's Histories: Aspects of State, Society and Ideology* (London, 1991), pp. 149–63, p. 156

110   Quoted in Rita Wall, *Irish Women in Britain* (Dublin, 1991), pp. 15–28

111   The Birmingham Six were convicted in July 1975, and were seriously assaulted whilst in custody. They were eventually freed in March 1991. The case against the Guildford Four, also sentenced in 1975, collapsed in 1989, although a further conviction against Paul Hill was not quashed until 1994. These cases implicated the police

and, more generally, the British legal system.

112 Quoted in Mary Lennon, Marie McAdam and Joanne O'Brien, *Across the Water: Irish Women's Lives in Britain* (London, 1988), pp. 175–6

113 E. Moxon-Brown, quoted in Rosemary Sales, 'Gender and Protestantism in Northern Ireland', in Peter Shirlow and Mark McGovern (eds), *Who are 'the People'? Unionism, Protestantism and Loyalism in Northern Ireland* (London, 1997), pp. 140–57, p. 147

114 Bew and Gillespie, *Northern Ireland: A Chronology*, p. 191

115 McKay, *Northern Protestants*, p. 22

116 Thelma Agnew, 'Through the Net', in Amanda Sebestyen (ed.), *'68, '78, '88: From Women's Liberation to Feminism* (Dorset, 1988), pp.185–90, p. 186

117 Hazel Gordon, 'Women, Protestantism and Unionism', unpublished paper given at a workshop on Women in Ireland, 4 October 1990

118 McKay, *Northern Protestants*, pp. 173–6. At the height of the Drumcreee protests loyalists blocked roads, provoked riots and attacked Catholic homes. At 4 a.m. on the morning of 12 July a petrol bomb was thrown into the Ballymoney home of Catholic woman Chrissie Quinn, whose three sons, aged from eight to ten, were burned to death.

119 Quoted in Catherine Shannon, 'Women in Northern Ireland', in Mary O'Dowd and Sabine Wichert (eds), *Chattel, Servant or Citizen: Women's Status in Church, State and Society* (Belfast, 1995), pp. 238–53, p. 249

120 Gordon Lucy and Elaine McClure (eds), *The Twelfth and What it Means to Me* (Lurgan, 1997), p. 110

121 Edna Longley, *From Cathleen to Anorexia: The Breakdown of Irelands* (Dublin, 1990), pp. 3–4

122 Quoted in Sales, *Women Divided*, p. 196

123 Quoted in Linda Connolly, 'The Women's Movement in Ireland, 1970–1995: A Social Movements Analysis', *Irish Journal of Feminist Studies*, vol. 1, no. 1 (March 1996), pp. 43–77, p. 70

124 Quoted in McKay, *Northern Protestants*, p. 86

125 Sally Belfrage, *The Crack: A Belfast Year* (London, 1987), p. 51

126 Eilish Rooney, 'Political Division, Practical Alliance: Problems for Women in Conflict', in Joan Hoff and Moureen Coulter (eds), *Irish Women's Voices: Past and Present*, (Indiana, 1995), *Journal of Women's History*, vols 6 and 7, pp. 41–8, p. 46

127 Mary Cummins, *The Best of About Women* (Dublin, 1996), p. 32

128 Eilís Ward and Orla O'Donovan, 'Networks of Women's Groups and Politics in Ireland: What (Some) Women Think', *U.C.G. Women's Studies Centre: Review*, vol. 4 (1996), pp. 1–20

129 Democratic Dialogue, *Power, Politics, Positionings: Women in Northern Ireland*, Report no. 4 (Belfast, 1996)

130 Quoted in Rachel Ward, 'The Northern Ireland Peace Process: A Gender Issue?', in Chris Gilligan and Jon Tonge (eds), *Peace or War? Understanding the Peace Process in Northern Ireland* (Aldershot, 1997), pp. 150–62, p. 152

131 Elisabeth Porter, 'Northern Ireland Women's Coalition', *Australian Feminist Studies*, vol. 11, no. 24 (1996), pp. 317–20, p. 317

132 Ailbhe Smyth, 'States of Change: Reflections on Ireland in Several Uncertain Parts', *Feminist Review*, no. 50 (summer 1995), pp. 24–43; pp. 39–40

133 Kate Fearon, *Women's Work: The Story of the Northern Ireland Women's Coalition* (Belfast, 1999), p. 4

134 *Ibid.*, quoted on p. 37

135 Porter, 'Northern Ireland Women's Coalition', p. 319

136 McWilliams and Kilmurray, 'Athene on the Loose', p. 19

137 Quoted in Ward, 'The Northern Ireland Peace Process', p. 159

138 *Ibid.*, p. 151

139 Quoted in Christina Loughran, 'Armagh and Feminist Strategy: Campaigns around Republican Women Prisoners in Armagh Jail', *Feminist Review*, no. 23 (June, 1986), pp. 59–79

140 Clara Connolly, 'Ourselves Alone? Clár na mBan Conference Report', *Feminist Review*, no. 50 (summer 1995), pp. 118–26

141 *Irish Reporter*, no. 8 (1992), p. 32

142 Quoted in Sales, *Women Divided*, p. 176

143 Eilish Rooney, 'Women in Northern Irish Politics: Difference Matters', in Carmel Roulston and Celia Davies (eds), *Gender, Democracy and Inclusion in Northern Ireland* (Basingstoke, 2000), pp. 164–86

144 See Margaret Ward, *The Northern Ireland Assembly and Women: Assessing the Gender Deficit*, Democratic Dialogue, Summary Report no. 4 (Belfast, 2000)

145 Frances Gardiner, 'Political Interest and Participation of Irish Women 1922–1992: The Unfinished Revolution', in Smyth (ed.), *Irish Women's Studies Reader*, pp. 45–78, p. 45

146 Una Claffey, *The Women Who Won: Women of the 27th Dáil* (Dublin, 1993)

147 Quoted in McNamara and Mooney, *Women in Parliament*, p. 13

148 *Ibid.*

149 *Ibid.*, p. 46

150 Claffey, *The Women Who Won*, pp. 34, 155

151 *Ibid.*, p. 155

152 *Ibid.*, p. 39

153 *Ibid.*, pp. 11, 131

154 Quoted in Lorna Siggins, *The Woman Who Took Power in the Park: Mary Robinson* (Edinburgh, 1997), p. 141

155 Gardiner, 'Political Interest and Participation of Irish Women', p. 67

156 Quoted in Ailbhe Smyth, ' "A Great Day for the Women of Ireland . . .": The Meaning of Mary Robinson's Presidency for Irish Women', *Canadian Journal of Irish Studies*, vol. 18, no. 1 (1992), pp. 61–75, p. 61

157 Quoted in Rose, *Diverse Communities*, pp. 33–4

158 Eamon Dunphy, 'The First Mary', *Magill* (November 1997), pp. 26–9, p. 29

159 Isobel Armstrong, quoted in Ailbhe Smyth, ' "A Great Day for the Women of Ireland" ', p. 71

160 Mary Jones, 'Mary Robinson: An Appreciation', *Irish Journal of Feminist Sudies*, vol. 3, no. 1 (December 1998), pp. 1–15, p. 10

161 Fintan O'Toole, quoted in *Magill* (October 1997), p. 21

162 Mary McAleese, *Love in Chaos* (New York, 1999)

163 Justine McCartney, *Mary McAleese: The Outsider: An Unauthorised Biography* (Dublin, 1999)

164 http://www.un.org/womenwatch/daw/beijing/platform

165 Yvonne Galligan, 'The Changing Role of Women', in William Crotty and David E. Schmitt (eds), *Ireland and the Politics of Change* (London, 1998), pp. 107–21, p. 21

CONCLUSION

1 President Mary Robinson, inaugural speech, quoted in Lorna Siggins, *The Woman*

Who Took Power in the Park: Mary Robinson (Edinburgh, 1997), p. 151

2   Penny Summerfield, 'Women and War in the Twentieth Century', in Jane Purvis (ed.), *Women's History: Britain, 1850–1945* (London, 1995), pp. 307–31, p. 336; Susan A. Grayzel, *Women's Identities at War: Gender, Motherhood and Politics in Britain and France during the First World War* (London, 1999)

3   Eilish Rooney, 'Women in Politics: A Northern Angle' (2000), in Angela Bourke, et al. (eds), *The Field Day Anthology of Irish Writing*, vols IV and V, Irish Women's Writing and Traditions (Cork, 2002), vol. V, pp. 448–9

4   Eilish Rooney, 'Political Division, Practical Alliance: Problems for Women in Conflict', in Joan Hoff and Moureen Coulter (eds), *Irish Women's Voices: Past and Present* (Indiana, 1995), *Journal of Women's History*, vols 6 and 7, pp. 40–48, p. 44

5   Pat O'Connor, *Emerging Voices: Women in Contemporary Irish Society* (Dublin, 1998), p. 254

6   Ailbhe Smyth, 'States of Change: Reflections on Ireland in Several Uncertain Parts', *Feminist Review*, no. 50 (summer 1995), pp. 24–43. p. 37

7   Fintan O'Toole, *The Irish Times Book of the Century* (Dublin, 1999), p. 325

8   Catriona Clear, *Women of the House: Women's Household Work in Ireland 1922–1961* (Dublin, 2000), p. 215

9   *Newtownards Chronicle*, 30 December 1999

10 Joanne Templeton, 'Sexism and Racism: The Double Burden of Irish Traveller Women', unpublished dissertation, in partial fulfilment of BSc Hons, University of Ulster, 1997

11 O'Connor, *Emerging Voices*, p. 256

12 *Irish News*, 31 December 1999

Bibliography

Books

Abbot, Marie and Hugh Frazer (eds). *Women and Community Work in Northern Ireland* (Belfast, 1985)

Akenson, Donald Harman. *The Irish Diaspora: A Primer* (Belfast, Toronto, 1993)

Alexander, Yonah and Alan O'Day (eds). *Terrorism in Ireland* (London and Canberra, 1984)

Alonso, Harriet, H. *Peace as a Women's Issue* (Syracuse, 1993)

Anderson, James and James Goodman (eds). *DIS/Agreeing Ireland: Contexts, Obstacles, Hopes* (London, 1998)

Augusteijn, Joost (ed.) *Ireland in the 1930s: New Perspectives* (Dublin, 1999)

Ballard, Linda May. *Forgetting Frolic: Marriage Traditions in Ireland* (Belfast, 1998)

Bardon, Jonathan, *Beyond the Studio: A History of BBC Northern Ireland* (Belfast, 2000)

   A History of Ulster (Belfast, 1992)

   Belfast: An Illustrated History (Belfast, 1982)

Barrington, Ruth. *Health, Medicine and Politics in Ireland 1900–1970* (Dublin, 1987)

Barton, Brian. *Northern Ireland in the Second World War* (Belfast, 1995)

   The Blitz: Belfast in the War Years (Belfast, 1989)

Beale, Jenny. *Women in Ireland: Voices of Change* (Dublin, 1986)

Beddoe, Deirdre. *Out of the Shadows: A History of Women in Twentieth-Century Wales* (Cardiff, 2001)

   Discovering Women's History: A Practical Guide to Researching the Lives of Women Since 1800, 3rd ed. (Harlow, Essex, 1998)

Begoña, Aretxaga. *Shattering Silence: Women, Nationalism, and Political Subjectivity in Northern Ireland* (Princeton, 1997)

Belfrage, Sally. *The Crack: A Belfast Year* (London, 1987)

Bell, Geoffery. *The Protestants of Ulster* (London, 1976)

Beresford Ellis, P. (ed.). *James Connolly, Selected Writings* (London, 1975)

Bew, Paul and Gordon Gillespie. *Northern Ireland: A Chronology of the Troubles, 1968–1999* (Dublin, 1999)

Binchy, Maeve, *Central Line: Stories of Big City Life* (London, 1978)

Blake, John W. *Northern Ireland in the Second World War* (Belfast, 1956)

Bleakley, David. *Saidie Patterson: Irish Peacemaker* (Belfast, 1980)

Boal, Frederick, Margaret Keane and David Livingstone. *Them and Us? Attitudinal Variations among Churchgoers in Belfast*, Insight Series no. 1, Online Research Bank (Belfast, 1997)

Boland, Eavan. *Object Lessons: The Life of the Woman and the Poet in Our Time* (Manchester, 1995)

 A Kind of Scar: The Women Poet in a National Tradition (Dublin, 1989)

Botelho, Lynn and Pat Thane (eds). *Women and Ageing in British Society since 1500* (London, 2001)

Bourke, Angela, et al. (eds). *The Field Day Anthology of Irish Writing*, vols IV and V, Irish Women's Writing and Traditions (Cork, 2002)

Bourke, Joanna. *Husbandry to Housewifery: Women, Economic Change and Housework in Ireland, 1890–1914* (Oxford, 1993)

Braddell Smith, Felicity. *They Were Good Days* (Durham, 1994)

Bradley, Anthony, and Maryann Gialanella Valiulis (eds). *Gender and Sexuality in Modern Ireland* (Amherst, 1997)

Bradley, Jim and Esmond Birnie. *Can the Celtic Tiger Cross the Irish Border?* (Cork, 2001)

Brozyna, Andrea Ebel. *Labour, Love and Prayer: Female Piety in Ulster Religious Literature 1850–1914* (Belfast, 1999)

Buchanan, R.H. (ed.). *Province, City and People: Belfast and Its Region* (Antrim, 1987)

Byrne, Anne and Madeleine Leonard (eds). *Women and Irish Society: A Sociological Reader* (Belfast, 1997)

Callan, Tim, Brian Nolan, Brendan J. Whelan, Christopher T. Whelan and James Williams. *Poverty in the 1990s: Evidence from the 1994 Living in Ireland Survey* (Dublin, 1996)

Cameron, Margaret. *The Women in Green: A History of the Royal Ulster Constabulary's Policewomen* (Belfast, 1993)

Claffey, Una. *The Women Who Won: Women of the 27th Dáil* (Dublin, 1993)

Clarke, Kathleen. *Revolutionary Woman: My Fight for Ireland's Freedom* (Dublin, 1997)

Clear, Catriona. *Women of the House: Women's Household Work in Ireland 1922–1961* (Dublin, 2000)

Cockburn, Cynthia. *The Space between Us: Negotiating Gender and National Identities in Conflict* (London, 1998)

Cohen, Marilyn and Nancy J. Curtin (eds). *Reclaiming Gender: Transgressive Identities in Modern Ireland* (New York, 1999)

Colum, Mary. *Life and the Dream* (Dublin, 1966)

Connolly, Linda. *The Irish Women's Movement: From Revolution to Devolution* (Hampshire and New York, 2002)

Connolly, Sean. *Religion and Society in Nineteenth-Century Ireland* (Dundalk, 1985)

Conway, Sheelagh. *The Faraway Hills are Green: Voices of Irish Women in Canada* (Ontario, 1992)

Coogan, Tim Pat. *Disillusioned Decades: Ireland 1966–87* (Dublin, 1987)

Coolahan, John. *Irish Education: Its History and Structure* (Dublin, 1981)

Coulter, Carol. *The Hidden Tradition: Feminism, Women and Nationalism in Ireland* (Cork, 1993)

 Web of Punishment: An Investigation (Dublin, 1991)

Coulter, Colin. *Contemporary Northern Irish Society: An Introduction* (London, 1999)

Coveney, Emer, Jo Murphy-Lawless and Sheila Sheridan. *Women, Work and Family Responsibilities* (Dublin, 1998)

Cox, Michael, Adrian Guelke and Fiona Stephen (eds). *A Farewell to Arms? From 'Long War' to Long Peace in Northern Ireland* (Manchester, 2000)

Coxhead, Elizabeth. *Daughters of Erin: Five Women of the Irish Renascence* (Dublin, 1979)

Cronin, Mike. *A History of Ireland* (Basingstoke, 2001)

 The Blueshirts in Irish Politics (Dublin, 1997)

Cronin, Mike and John M. Regan. *Ireland: The Politics of Independence, 1922–49* (London, 2000)

Crookshank, Anne and The Knight of Glin. *The Painters of Ireland, c. 1660–1920* (London, 1978)

Crowley, Elaine. *Technical Virgins* (Dublin, 1998)

Cullen, Mary (ed.). *Girls Don't Do Honours: Irish Women in Education in the 19th and 20th Centuries* (Dublin, 1987)

Cullen, Paul. *Refugees and Asylum Seekers in Ireland* (Cork, 2000)

Cummins, Mary. *The Best of About Women* (Dublin, 1996)

Curtin, Chris, Pauline Jackson and Barbara O'Connor (eds). *Gender in Irish Society* (Galway, 1987)

Curtis, Liz. *Ireland: The Propaganda War: The British Media and the 'Battle for Hearts and Minds'* (London, 1984)

Dahlerup, Drude (ed.). *The New Women's Movement: Feminism and Political Power in Europe and the USA* (London, 1986)

Daly, Mary E. *Women and Work in Ireland* (Dundalk, 1997)

D'Arcy, Margaretta. *Tell Them Everything: A Sojourn in the Prison of Her Majesty Queen Elizabeth II at Ard Macha (Armagh)* (London, 1981)

Davies, Celia and Eithne McLaughlin (eds). *Women, Employment and Social Policy in Northern Ireland: A Problem Postponed?* (Belfast, 1991)

Devaney, Fran, Marie Mulholland and Judith Willoughby. *Essays on the Irish Women's Movement* (Belfast, 1989)

Devlin, Bernadette. *The Price of My Soul* (London, 1969)

Devlin, Edith Newman. *Speaking Volumes: A Dublin Childhood* (Belfast, 2000)

Dillon, Martin. *God and the Gun: The Church and Irish Terrorism* (London, 1997)

 The Dirty War (London, 1988)

Doherty, Richard. *Irish Volunteers in the Second World War* (Dublin, 2002)

 Irish Men and Women in the Second World War (Dublin, 1999)

Donaldson, Peggy. *A History of Nurses and Nursing at the Royal Victoria Hospital, Belfast* (Belfast, 1988)

Dooley, Mary Rose. *Hidden Memories: The Personal Recollections of Survivors and*

Witnesses to the Holocaust Living in Ireland (Dublin, 1994)

Draper, Vivienne. *The Children of Dunseverick* (Dingle, 1994)

Dunn, Seamus (ed.). *Facets of the Conflict in Northern Ireland* (London, 1995)

Evason, Eileen. *Against the Grain: The Contemporary Women's Movement in Northern Ireland* (Dublin, 1991)

    On the Edge: A Study of Poverty and Long-Term Unemployment in Northern Ireland (London, 1985)

    Hidden Violence: A Study of Battered Women in Northern Ireland (Belfast, 1982)

    Just Me and the Kids: A Study of Single Parent Families in Northern Ireland (Belfast, 1980)

Fahey, Tony (ed.). *Social Housing in Ireland: A Study of Success, Failure and Lessons Learned* (Dublin, 1999)

Fairweather, Eileen, Roisin McDonough and Melanie McFadyean. *Only the Rivers Run Free. Northern Ireland: The Women's War* (London, 1984)

Fallon, Brian. *An Age of Innocence: Irish Culture 1930–1960* (Dublin, 1998)

Farmar, Tony. *Holles Street 1894–1994: The National Maternity Hospital: A Centenary History* (Dublin, 1994)

    Ordinary Lives: Three Generations of Irish Middle Class Experience 1907, 1932, 1963 (Dublin, 1991)

Farrell, Michael (ed.). *Twenty Years On* (Dingle, 1988)

Fay, Marie Thérèse, Mike Morrissey, Marie Smyth and Tracy Wong. *The Cost of the Troubles Study: Report on the Northern Ireland Survey: The Experience and Impact of the Troubles* (Derry, 1999)

Fearon, Kate. *Women's Work: The Story of the Northern Ireland Women's Coalition* (Belfast, 1999)

Feldman, Allen. *Formations of Violence: The Narrative of the Body and Political Terror in Northern Ireland* (London, 1991)

Finegan, John. *The Story of Monto: An Account of Dublin's Notorious Red Light District* (Dublin, 1978)

Fingall, E.M. *Seventy Years Young: Memories of Elizabeth, Countess of Fingall* (Dublin, 1995)

Fitz-Gerald, William G. (ed.). *The Voice of Ireland* (Dublin, n.d.)

Fitzpatrick, David. *The Two Irelands: 1912–1939* (Oxford, 1998)

    Irish Emigration, 1801–1921 (Dublin, 1984)

    (ed.). *Revolution? Ireland 1917–1923* (Dublin, 1990)

    (ed.). *Ireland and the First World War* (Dublin, 1986)

Flanagan, Maeve. *Dev, Lady Chatterley and Me: A 60s Suburban Childhood* (Dublin, 1998)

Flower, Robin. *The Western Island* (Oxford, 1978)

Gaffikin, Frank and Mike Morrissey. *Northern Ireland: The Thatcher Years* (London, 1990)

Gallagher, Tom and James O'Connell (eds). *Contemporary Irish Studies* (Manchester, 1983)

Galligan, Yvonne. *Women and Politics in Contemporary Ireland: From the Margins to the Mainstream* (London, 1998)

Galligan, Yvonne, Eilís Ward and Rick Wilford (eds). *Contesting Politics: Women in Ireland, North and South* (Colorado and Oxford, 1999)

Gilligan, Chris and Jon Tonge (eds). *Peace or War? Understanding the Peace Process in Northern Ireland* (Aldershot, 1997)

Goodman, Lizbeth. *Feminist Stages: Interviews with Women in Contemporary British Theatre* (Amsterdam, 1996)

Goulding, June. *The Light in the Window* (Dublin, 1998)

Graham, B.J. and L.J. Proudfoot (eds). *An Historical Geography of Ireland* (London, 1993)

Gray, John. *City in Revolt: James Larkin and the Belfast Dock Strike of 1907* (Belfast, 1985)

Gray, Tony. *The Lost Years: The Emergency in Ireland 1939–45* (London, 1997)

Grayzel, Susan A. *Women's Identities at War: Gender, Motherhood and Politics in Britain and France during the First World War* (London, 1999)

Green, Marion. *Mill to Millennium* (Belfast, 1996)

Haberstroh, Patricia Boyle. *Women Creating Women: Contemporary Irish Women Poets* (Dublin, 1996)

Healy, Mary. *For the Poor and for the Gentry: Mary Healy Remembers Her Life* (Dublin, 1989)

Hearn, Mona. *Below Stairs: Domestic Service Remembered in Dublin and Beyond, 1880–1922* (Dublin, 1993)

Hennessey, Thomas. *A History of Northern Ireland 1920–1996* (Dublin, 1997)

Heron, Marianne. *Sheila Conroy: Fighting Spirit* (Dublin, 1993)

Heverin, Aileen. *ICA: The Irish Countrywomen's Association* (Dublin, 2000)

Hill, Myrtle and Vivienne Pollock. *Women of Ireland: Image and Experience c. 1880–1920* (Belfast, 1999)

Hoff, Joan and Moureen Coulter (eds). *Irish Women's Voices: Past and Present* (Indiana, 1995), *Journal of Women's History*, vols. 6 and 7

Holmes, Janice and Diane Urquhart (ed.). *Coming into the Light: The Work, Politics and Religion of Women in Ulster, 1840–1940* (Belfast, 1994)

Holohan, Anne. *Working Lives: The Irish in Britain* (Dublin, 1995)

Hooley, Ruth (ed.). *The Female Line: Northern Irish Women Writers* (Belfast, 1985)

Hopkinson, Michael. *Green Against Green: The Irish Civil War* (Dublin, 1988)

Hoppen, K. Theodore. *Ireland since 1800: Conflict and Conformity* (London and New York, 1989)

Hussey, Gemma. *Ireland Today: Anatomy of a Changing State* (Dublin, 1993)

Hutton, Seán and Paul Stewart (eds). *Ireland's Histories: Aspects of State, Society and Ideology* (London, 1991)

Hyndman, Marilyn. *Further Afield: Journeys from a Protestant Past* (Belfast, 1996)

Inglis, Tom. *Lessons in Irish Sexuality* (Dublin, 1998)

　Moral Monopoly: The Rise and Fall of the Catholic Church in Modern Ireland, 2nd ed., (Dublin, 1998)

Irish Consumer Research. *The Irish Housewife: A Portrait* (Dublin, 1986)

Irwin, Florence. *The Cookin' Woman: Irish Country Recipes* (Belfast, 1986)

Jackson, Alvin. *Ireland 1798–1998* (Oxford, 1999)

Jeffery, Keith. *Ireland and the Great War* (Cambridge, 2000)

Jones, Helen. *Women in British Public Life, 1914–50: Gender, Power and Social Policy*
 (Harlow, 2000)

Jones, Mary. *These Obstreperous Lassies: A History of the IWWU* (Dublin, 1988)

Jones, Maxine. *Successful Irish Businesswomen* (Dublin, 1992)

Jordan, Alison. *Who Cared? Charity in Victorian and Edwardian Belfast* (Belfast, n.d.)

Jordan, Glenn. *Not of this World? Evangelical Protestants in Northern Ireland*
 (Belfast, 2001)

Judge, Yvonne. *Chasing Gold: Sportswomen of Ireland* (Dublin, 1995)

Keane, Maureen. *Ishbel: Lady Aberdeen in Ireland* (Newtownards, 1999)

Kearns, K.C. *Dublin Voices, An Oral Folk History* (Dublin, 1998)
 Dublin Tenement Life: An Oral History (Dublin, 1994)
 Stoneybatter (Dublin, 1989)

Kelleher, Margaret and James H. Murphy (eds). *Gender Perspectives in 19th Century
 Ireland* (Dublin, 1997)

Kelly, A.A. *Wandering Women: Two Centuries of Travel Out of Ireland* (Dublin, 1995)

Kelly, John and Eric Domville (eds). *The Collected Letters of W.B. Yeats*, vol. 1,
 1865–1895 (Oxford, 1986)

Kennedy, Finola. *Cottage to Crèche: Family Change in Ireland* (Dublin, 2001)

Kennedy, Liam and Philip Ollerenshaw (eds). *An Economic History of Ulster,
 1820–1939* (Manchester, 1985)

Kennedy, Robert E. *The Irish: Emigration, Marriage, and Fertility* (Berkeley and
 Los Angeles, 1973)

Kenny, Mary. *Goodbye to Catholic Ireland* (Dublin, 2000)
 The Best of Mary Kenny (Dublin, 1986)

Keogh, Dermot. *Jews in Twentieth-Century Ireland: Refugees, Anti-Semitism and the
 Holocaust* (Cork, 1998)
 Twentieth-Century Ireland: Nation and State (Dublin, 1994)
 *The Rise of the Irish Working Class: The Dublin Trade Union Movement and Labour
 Leadership 1890–1914* (Belfast, 1982)

Kerrigan, Gene. *Another Country: Growing up in '50s Ireland* (Dublin, 1998)

King, Sophia Hillan and Sean McMahon. *Hope and History: Eyewitness Accounts of
 Life in Twentieth-Century Ulster* (Belfast, 1996)

Kinghan, Nancy. *United We Stood: The Official History of the Ulster Women's Unionist
 Council 1911–1974* (Belfast, 1975)

Kremer, John and Pamela Montgomery (eds). *Women's Working Lives*
 (Belfast, 1993)

Lacquer, Thomas W. *Religion and Respectability: Sunday Schools and Working-Class
 Culture, 1780–1850* (London, 1976)

Laffan, Michael. *The Partition of Ireland 1911–1925* (Dublin, 1983)

Lambkin, Romie. *My Time in the War: An Irishwoman's Diary* (Dublin, 1992)

Lander, Ben. *Irish Voices: Irish Lives* (Dingle, 1997)

Lazenbatt, Bill (ed.). *America and Ulster: A Cultural Correspondence, Writing Ulster*
 no. 5 (Jordanstown, 1998)

Lee, Raymond, M. *Mixed and Matched: Interreligious Courtship and Marriage in*

Northern Ireland (London, 1994)

Lennon, Mary, Marie McAdam and Joanne O'Brien. *Across the Water: Irish Women's Lives in Britain* (London, 1988)

Lentin, Ronit (ed.). *In From the Shadows: The UL Women's Studies Collection*, 2 vols. (Limerick, 1995–8)

Levine, June. *Sisters: The Personal Story of an Irish Feminist* (Dublin, 1982)

Levine, June and Lyn Madden. *Lyn: A Story of Prostitution* (Dublin, 1987)

Lewis, Helen. *A Time to Speak* (Belfast, 1992)

Longley, Edna. *From Cathleen to Anorexia: The Breakdown of Irelands* (Dublin, 1990)

Love, Walter. *The Times of Our Lives: Recollections from Town and Country* (Belfast, 1990)

Lucy, Gordon and Elaine McClure (eds). *The Twelfth and What it Means to Me* (Lurgan, 1997)

Luddy, Maria. *Women and Philanthropy in Nineteenth-Century Ireland* (Cambridge, 1995)
Women in Ireland 1800–1918: A Documentary History (Cork, 1995)

Luddy, Maria and Cliona Murphy (eds). *Women Surviving: Studies in Irish Women's History in the 19th and 20th Centuries* (Dublin, 1989)

Lynch, John. *A Tale of Three Cities: Comparative Studies in Working-Class Life* (London, 1998)

Lyons, F.S.L. *Ireland since the Famine* (London, 1982)

McAleese, Mary. *Love in Chaos* (New York, 1999)

McAuley, Chrissie (ed.). *Women in a War Zone: Twenty Years of Resistance* (Dublin, n.d.)

McCafferty, Nell. *Goodnight Sisters* (Dublin, 1987)
The Armagh Women (Dublin, 1981)

McCaffrey, Lawrence, J. *The Irish Diaspora in America* (London, 1976; rev. ed. Washington, 1997)

McCartan, Joyce. *A Battler all My Life* (London, 1994)

McCartney, Justin. *Mary McAleese: The Outsider: An Unauthorised Biography* (Dublin, 1999)

McConville, Michael. *Ascendancy to Oblivion: The Story of the Anglo-Irish* (London, 1986)

McCullough, Elizabeth. *A Square Peg: An Ulster Childhood* (Dublin, 1997)

MacCurtain, Margaret and Donncha Ó Corráin (eds). *Women in Irish Society: The Historical Dimension* (Dublin, 1978)

MacDonald, Eileen. *Shoot the Women First* (London, 1991)

McDowell, Florence Mary. *Other Days Around Me* (Belfast, 1972)

MacEoin, Uinseann (ed.). *Survivors*, (2nd ed. Dublin, 1987)

McGarry, Fearghal. *Irish Politics and the Spanish Civil War* (Cork, 1999)

McIntosh, Gillian. *The Force of Culture: Unionist Identities in Twentieth Century Ireland* (Cork, 1999)

McKay, Susan. *Northern Protestants: An Unsettled People* (Belfast, 2000)

McKendry, Seamus. *Disappeared: The Search for Jean McConville* (Dublin, 2000)

McKittrick, David, Seamus Kelters, Brian Feeney and Chris Thornton (eds).

Lost Lives: The Stories of the Men, Women and Children Who Died as a Result of the Northern Ireland Troubles (Edinburgh, 1999)

McLeod, Hugh. *Piety and Poverty* (New York, 1996)

McLoone, Martin and John McMahon (eds). *21 Years of Irish Television* (Dublin, 1984)

McNally, Kenneth. *Achill* (Devon, 1973)

McNamara, Maedhbh and Paschal Mooney. *Women in Parliament: Ireland 1918–2000* (Dublin, 2000)

McNamara, Sarah. *Those Intrepid United Irishwomen: Pioneers of the Irish Countrywomen's Association* (Limerick, 1995)

McQuillan, Deirdre. *A President in Progress* (Dublin, 1994)

McRedmond, Louis (ed.). *Modern Irish Lives: Dictionary of 20th-Century Biography* (Dublin, 1998)

McWilliams, Monica and Joan Kiernan. *Bringing it Out in the Open: Domestic Violence in Northern Ireland* (Belfast, 1993)

Maguire, Maria. *To Take Arms: A Year in the Provisional IRA* (Bristol, 1973)

Mayer, Tamar (ed.). *Gender Ironies of Nationalism: Sexing the Nation* (London and New York, 2000)

Miller, Kerby A. *Emigrants and Exiles: Ireland and the Irish Exodus to North America* (Oxford, 1985)

Miller, Robert Lee, Rick Wilford and Freda Donaghue. *Women and Political Participation in Northern Ireland* (Aldershot, 1996)

Mitchell, Arthur. *Revolutionary Government in Ireland: Dáil Éireann 1919–22* (Dublin, 1995)

Montgomery, Pamela and V. Bell. *Police Responses to Wife Assault: A Northern Ireland Study* (Belfast, 1986)

Moran, Gerard (ed.). *Galway History and Society: Interdisciplinary Essays on the History of an Irish County* (Dublin, 1996)

Morgan, Valerie and G. Fraser. *The Company We Keep: Women, Community and Organisations* (Coleraine, 1994)

Morrow, Ann. *Picnic in a Foreign Land: The Eccentric Lives of the Anglo-Irish* (London, 1989)

Mowlam, Mo. *Momentum: The Struggle for Peace, Politics and the People* (London, 2002)

Moynahin, M. (ed.). *Speeches and Statements by Eamon de Valera* (Dublin, 1980)

Mulhall, Daniel. *A New Day Dawning: A Portrait of Ireland in 1900* (Cork, 1999)

Mullarney, Máire. *What About Me?: A Woman for Whom One Damn Cause Led to Another* (Dublin, 1992)

Munck, Ronnie and Bill Rolston. *Belfast in the Thirties: An Oral History* (Belfast, 1987)

Murphy, Dervla. *A Place Apart* (London, 1978)

Murray, Dominic (ed.). *Protestant Perceptions of the Peace Process in Northern Ireland* (Limerick, 2000)

Murray, Raymond. *Hard Time: Armagh Gaol 1971–1986* (Cork, 1998)

National Women's Committee Sinn Féin. *The Rights of Women in Ireland*
(Dublin, 1975)

Nevin, Donal (ed.). *Trade Union Century* (Dublin, 1994)

Newman, Jeremiah (ed.). *The Limerick Rural Survey 1958–1964* (Tipperary, 1964)

Ní Aoláin, Fionnuala. *The Politics of Force: Conflict Management and State Violence in
Northern Ireland* (Belfast, 2000)

Nolan, Brian and Tim Callan (eds). *Poverty and Policy in Ireland* (Dublin, 1994)

Northside Folklore Project. *Life Journeys: Living Folklore in Ireland Today*
(Cork, 1999)

O'Brien, Edna. *The Country Girls Trilogy* (London, 1988)

O'Brien, Gerard. *Derry and Londonderry: History and Society: Interdisciplinary Essays
on the History of an Irish County* (Dublin, 1999)

O'Brien, Nora Connolly. *We shall Rise Again* (London, 1981)

O'Carroll, Íde and Eoin Collins (eds). *Lesbian and Gay Visions of Ireland:
Towards the Twenty-First Century* (London, 1995)

Ó Céirín, Kit and Cyril Ó Céirín, *Women of Ireland: A Biographic Dictionary*
(Newtownlynch, 1996)

O'Connor, Anne V. and Susan M. Parkes. *Gladly Learn and Gladly Teach: A History
of Alexandra College and School, Dublin 1866–1966* (Dublin, n.d.)

O'Connor, Emmet. *A Labour History of Ireland 1824–1960* (Dublin, 1992)

O Connor, Fionnuala. *In Search of a State: Catholics in Northern Ireland*
(Belfast, 1993)

O'Connor, Pat. *Emerging Voices: Women in Contemporary Irish Society* (Dublin, 1998)

O'Connor, Ulick. *Oliver St. John Gogarty: A Biography* (London, 1964)

O'Dowd, Mary and Sabine Wichert (eds). *Chattel, Servant or Citizen: Women's
Status in Church, State and Society* (Belfast, 1995)

O'Faolain, Nuala. *Are You Somebody? The Life and Times of Nuala O'Faolain*
(Dublin, 1996)

O'Farrell, Padraic. *Who's Who in the Irish War of Independence and Civil War
1916–1923* (Dublin, 1997)

O'Flanagan, Liam. 'Going into Exile', in Frank O'Connor (ed.), *Modern Irish Short
Stories* (Oxford, 1977)

O'Flanagan, Patrick and Cornelius G. Buttimer (eds). *Cork History and Society:
Interdisciplinary Essays on the History of an Irish County* (Dublin, 1993)

O'Grada, Cormac. *Ireland: A New Economic History 1780–1939* (Oxford, 1994)

O'Hara, Bernard (ed.). *Mayo: Aspects of Its Heritage* (Galway, 1982)

O'Hara, Patricia. *Partners in Production? Women, Farm and Family in Ireland*
(Oxford, 1998)

O'Hearn, Denis. *Inside the Celtic Tiger* (London, 1998)

O'Keeffe, Phil. *Standing at the Crossroads* (Dingle, 1997)

O'Malley, P. *The Uncivil Wars, Ireland Today* (Belfast, 1983)

O'Neill, Marie. *Grace Gifford Plunkett and Irish Freedom: Tragic Bride of 1916*
(Dublin, 2000)

  From Parnell to De Valera: A Biography of Jennie Wyse Power 1858–1941
  (Dublin, 1991)

Orr, Philip. *The Road to the Somme: Men of the Ulster Division Tell Their Story* (Belfast, 1987)

O'Sullivan, Patrick (ed.). *Irish Women and Irish Migration* (London, 1995)

O'Sullivan, Valerie. *Inner Thoughts: Reflections of Contemporary Irish Women* (Dublin, 1999)

O'Toole, Fintan. *The Irish Times Book of the Century* (Dublin, 1999)

Owens, Rosemary Cullen. *Smashing Times: A History of the Irish Women's Suffrage Movement 1889–1922* (Dublin, 1984)

Paseta, Senia. *Before the Revolution: Nationalism, Social Change and Ireland's Catholic Elite, 1879–1922* (Cork, 1999)

Peillon, Michel and Eamonn Slater (eds). *Encounters with Modern Ireland: A Sociological Chronicle 1995–1996* (Dublin, 1998)

Prior, Pauline. *Mental Health and Politics in Northern Ireland* (Belfast, 1993)

Prior, Vincent. *Send 'em Home Sweatin': The Showband Story* (Cork, 1990)

Prisoners' Aid and Protestant Conflict Resettlement Group. *A Brief History of the UDA/UFF in the Contemporary Conflict. Northern Ireland 1969–1995* (Belfast, 1995)

Proudfoot, Lindsay (ed.). *Down: History and Society: Interdisciplinary Essays on the History of an Irish County* (Dublin, 1997)

Purdie, Bob. *Politics in the Streets: The Origins of the Civil Rights Movement in Northern Ireland* (Belfast, 1990)

Quinn-Conroy, Bridie. *Not a Word of a Lie* (Kinvara, County Galway, 1993)

Ridd, Rosemary and Helen Calloway (eds). *Caught Up in Conflict: Women's Responses to Political Strife* (London, 1986)

Robb, Nesca A. *A History of Richmond Lodge School* (Belfast, n.d.)

Robins, Joseph (ed.). *Reflections on Health: Commemorating Fifty Years of The Department of Health 1947–97* (Dublin, 1997)

Rose, Catherine. *The Female Experience: The Story of the Woman Movement in Ireland* (Galway, 1975)

Rose, Kieran. *Diverse Communities: The Evolution of Lesbian and Gay Politics in Ireland* (Cork, 1994)

Rowbotham, Sheila. *A Century of Women: The History of Women in Britain and the United States* (London, 1997)

Rowthorn, Bob and Naomi Wayne. *Northern Ireland: The Political Economy of Conflict* (Oxford, 1988)

Ryan, Louise. *Irish Feminism and the Vote: An Anthology of the Irish Citizen Newspaper 1912–1920* (Dublin, 1996)

Ryder, Chris. *The Ulster Defence Regiment: An Instrument of Peace?* (London, 1991)

Sales, Rosemary. *Women Divided: Gender, Religion and Politics in Northern Ireland* (London, 1997)

Sandford, J. (ed.). *Mary Carbery's West Cork Journal 1898–1901* (Dublin, 1998)

Sawyer, Roger. *'We are but Women': Women in Ireland's History* (London, 1993)

Sebestyen, Amanda (ed.). *'68, '78, '88: From Women's Liberation to Feminism* (Dorset, 1988)

Segal, Lynne. *Is the Future Female? Troubled Thoughts on Contemporary Feminism* (London, 1987)

Shanks, Amanda N. *Rural Aristocracy in Northern Ireland* (Aldershot, 1988)

Shannon, Elizabeth. *I am of Ireland: Women of the North Speak Out* (Philadelphia, 1989)

Sheehy, Jeanne. *The Rediscovery of Ireland's Past: The Celtic Revival 1830–1930* (London, 1980)

Shirlow, Peter and Mark McGovern (eds). *Who are 'the People'? Unionism, Protestantism and Loyalism in Northern Ireland* (London, 1997)

Siggins, Lorna. *The Woman Who Took Power in the Park: Mary Robinson* (Edinburgh, 1997)

Sinclair, Betty. *Ulster Women and the War* (Belfast, 1942)

Sinclair, R.J.K. and F.J.M. Scully. *Arresting Memories: Captured Moments in Constabulary Life* (Coleraine, 1982)

Smith, Felicity Braddell. *They Were Good Days* (Durham, 1994)

Smyth, Ailbhe (ed.). *Irish Women's Studies Reader* (Attic Press, Dublin, 1993)
    The Abortion Papers: Ireland (Dublin, 1992)

Smyth, Marie and Marie Thérèse Fay (eds). *Personal Accounts from Northern Ireland's Troubles: Public Conflict, Private Loss* (London, 2000)

Somerville-Large, Peter. *Irish Voices: An Informal History 1916–1966* (London, 1999)
    Irish Voices: 50 Years of Irish Life 1916–1966 (London, 1999)

Spence, Gusty. *Past Discovery: Report of a Seminar Organised by Ballymacarrett Arts and Cultural Society* (Belfast, 1997)

St Peter, Christine. *Changing Ireland: Strategies in Contemporary Women's Fiction* (London, 2000)

Stibbs, Anne (ed.). *Words of Women* (London, 1993)

Swift, Roger and Sheridan Gilley (eds). *The Irish in Victorian Britain: The Local Dimension* (Dublin, 1999)

Taillon, Ruth. *When History was Made: The Women of 1916* (Belfast, 1996)

Threlfall, Monica (ed.). *Mapping the Women's Movement: Feminist Politics and Social Transformation in the North* (London, 1996)

Tobin, Fergal. *The Best of Decades: Ireland in the 1960s* (Dublin, 1996)

Townsend, Peter. *Poverty in the United Kingdom: A Survey of Household Resources and Standards of Living* (Harmondsworth, 1979)

Tweedy, Hilda. *A Link in the Chain: The Story of the Irish Housewives Association 1942–1992* (Dublin, 1992)

Urquhart, Diane (ed.). *The Minutes of the Ulster Women's Unionist Council and Executive Committee 1911–40* (Dublin, 2001)
    Women in Ulster Politics 1890–1940 (Dublin, 2000)

Valiulis, Maryann Gialanella and Mary O'Dowd (eds). *Women and Irish History: Essays in Honour of Margaret MacCurtain* (Dublin, 1997)

Vaughan, W.E. (ed.). *A New History of Ireland, Vol. VI: Ireland Under the Union (II) 1870–1921* (Oxford, 2000)

Verdon, Michael. *Shawlies, Echo Boys, the Marsh and the Lanes: Old Cork*

Remembered (Dublin, 1993)

Walker, Graham. *The Politics of Frustration: Harry Midgley and the failure of Labour in Northern Ireland* (Manchester, 1985)

Wall, Rita. *Irish Women in Britain* (Dublin, 1991)

Walter, Bronwyn. *Outsiders Inside: Whiteness, Place and Irish Women* (London and New York, 2001)

Ward, Margaret. *Hanna Sheehy-Skeffington: A Life* (Cork, 1997)

   In Their Own Voice: Women and Irish Nationalism (Dublin, 1995)

   Unmanageable Revolutionaries: Women and Irish Nationalism, (London, 1995, 1st ed. published 1985)

   Maud Gonne: Ireland's Joan of Arc (London, 1990)

Watson, Rhoda. *Along the Road to Peace: Fifteen Years with the Peace People* (Belfast, 1991)

West, Lois A. (ed.). *Feminist Nationalism* (London, 1997)

Whelan, Bernadette (ed.). *Women and Paid Work in Ireland, 1500–1930* (Dublin, 2000)

White, Richard. *Remembering Ahanagran: Storytelling in a Family's Past* (Cork, 1999)

Wiley, Miriam M. and Barry Merriman. *Women and Health Care in Ireland: Knowledge, Attitudes and Behaviour* (Dublin, 1996)

Wilkinson, Margaret. *At BBC Corner I Remember Amy Carmichael* (Coleraine, 1996)

Wilson, Gordon, with Alf McCreary. *Marie: A Story from Enniskillen* (London, 1990)

Women's Committee of National Union of Public Employees. *Women's Voices: An Oral History of Northern Irish Women's Health 1900–1990* (Dublin, 1992)

Woodger, Jessie. *Jessica's People* (Hampshire, 1998)

Younger, Calton. *Ireland's Civil War* (London, 1968)

Yules-Davis, Nira. *Gender and Nation* (London, 1997)

Articles

Aniagolu, Catherine ChiChi. 'Teleworking and the Sexual Division of Labour in Ireland', *Irish Journal of Feminist Studies*, vol. 2, no. 2 (winter 1997), pp. 57–75

Ballard, Linda May. '"Just Whatever They had Handy": Aspects of Childbirth and Early Childcare in Northern Ireland prior to 1948', *Ulster Folklife*, vol. 31 (1985), pp. 59–72

Beaumont, Catriona. 'Women and the Politics of Equality: The Irish Women's Movement 1930–1943', in Maryann Gialanella Valiulis and Mary O'Dowd (eds), *Women and Irish History: Essays in Honour of Margaret MacCurtain* (Dublin, 1997), pp. 173–205

Begoña, Aretxaga. 'The Sexual Games of the Body Politic: Fantasy and State Violence in Northern Ireland', *Culture, Medicine and Psychiatry*, vol. 25 (2001), pp. 1–27

   'Dirty Protest: Symbolic Overdetermination and Gender in Northern Ireland

Ethnic Violence', *Ethos*, vol. 23, no. 2 (1995), pp. 123–48

Bell, Christine. 'Women, Equality and Political Participation', in James Anderson and James Goodman (eds), *DIS/Agreeing Ireland: Contexts, Obstacles, Hopes* (London, 1998), pp. 211–31

Bell, Desmond. 'Acts of Union: Youth Sub-culture and Ethnic Identity amongst Protestants in Northern Ireland', *British Journal of Sociology*, vol. 38, no. 2 (1987), pp. 158–83

Benton, Sarah. 'Women Disarmed: The Militarization of Politics in Ireland 1913–23', *Feminist Review*, no. 50 (summer 1995), pp. 148–72

Bloxham, Elizabeth. 'Training Our Housekeepers', in W.G. Fitzgerald (ed.), *The Voice of Ireland* (Dublin, n.d.), pp. 167–9

Bourke, Joanna. 'The Best of All Home Rulers? The Economic Power of Women in Ireland, 1880–1914', *Irish Economic and Social History*, vol. 18 (1991), pp. 34–47

Breathnach, Eibhlín. 'Charting New Waters: Women's Experience in Higher Education, 1878–1908', in Mary Cullen (ed.), *Girls Don't Do Honours: Irish Women in Education in the 19th and 20th Centuries* (Dublin, 1987), pp. 55–78

Brewer, John. 'Hercules, Hippolyte and the Amazons – or Policewomen in the RUC', *British Journal of Sociology*, vol. 42, no. 2 (June 1991), pp. 233–47

Buckley, Suzanne and Pamela Lonergan. 'Women and the Troubles, 1969–1980', in Yonah Alexander and Alan O'Day (eds), *Terrorism in Ireland* (London and Canberra, 1984), pp. 75–87

Byrne, Anne. 'Familist Ideology and Difficult Identities: "Never-married" Women in Contemporary Irish Society', in Marilyn Cohen and Nancy J. Curtin (eds), *Reclaiming Gender: Transgressive Identities in Modern Ireland* (New York, 1999), pp. 69–90

'Revealing Figures? Official Statistics and Irish Women', in Ailbhe Smyth (ed.), *Irish Women's Studies Reader* (Dublin, 1993), pp. 140–161

Byron, Catherine. 'The Room is a Kind of Travel Also: An Appreciation of the Poetry of Medbh McGuckian', *Linen Hall Review*, vol. 5, no. 1 (spring 1988), pp. 16–17

Callaghan, Marie Hammond. 'Surveying Politics of Peace, Gender, Conflict and Identity in Northern Ireland: The Case of the Derry Peace Women in 1972', *Women's Studies International Forum*, vol. 25 (January–February 2002), pp. 33–49

Callan, Tim. 'Poverty and Gender Inequality', in Brian Nolan and Tim Callan (eds), *Poverty and Policy in Ireland* (Dublin, 1994), pp. 178–92

Campbell, Winifred. 'Down the Shankill', *Ulster Folklife*, vol. 22 (1976), pp. 1–33

Clancy, Mary. 'Shaping the Nation: Women in the Free State Parliament, 1923–37', in Yvonne Galligan, Eilís Ward and Rick Wilford (eds), *Contesting Politics: Women in Ireland, North and South* (Colorado and Oxford, 1999), pp. 201–18

'The "Western Outpost": Local Government and Women's Suffrage in County Galway 1898–1918', in Gerard Moran (ed.), *Galway History and Society:*

Interdisciplinary Essays on the History of an Irish County (Dublin, 1996),
  pp. 557–87

Clear, Catriona. 'The Women can not be Blamed: The Commission on Vocational
  Organisation, Feminism and "Home-makers" in Independent Ireland in the
  1930s and '40s', in Mary O'Dowd and Sabine Wichert (eds), *Chattel, Servant
  or Citizen: Women's Status in Church, State and Society* (Belfast, 1995),
  pp. 179–86

Cohen, Marilyn. 'Working Conditions and Experiences of Work in the Linen
  Industry: Tullylish, County Down', *Ulster Folklife*, vol. 30 (1984), pp. 1–21

Condon, Janette. 'The Patriotic Children's Treat: Irish Nationalism and Children's
  Culture at the Twilight of Empire', *Irish Studies Review*, vol. 8, no. 2 (2000),
  pp. 167–78

Connolly, Clara. 'Ourselves Alone? Clàr na mBan Conference Report', *Feminist
  Review*, no. 50 (summer 1995), pp. 118–26

Connolly, Linda. 'The Women's Movement in Ireland, 1970–1995: A Social
  Movements Analysis', *Irish Journal of Feminist Studies*, vol. 1, no. 1
  (March 1996), pp. 43–77

Conrad, Kathryn. 'Women Troubles, Queer Troubles: Gender, Sexuality and the
  Politics of Selfhood in the Construction of the Northern Irish State', in
  Marilyn Cohen and Nancy J. Curtin (eds), *Reclaiming Gender: Transgressive
  Identities in Modern Ireland* (New York, 1999), pp. 53–68

Coulter, Carol. '"Hello Divorce, Goodbye Daddy": Women, Gender and the
  Divorce Debate', in Anthony Bradley and Maryann Gialanella Valiulis (eds),
  Gender and Sexuality in Modern Ireland (Amherst, 1997), pp. 275–98

Crone, Joni. 'Lesbians: The Lavender Women of Ireland', in Íde O'Carroll and
  Eoin Collins (eds), *Lesbian and Gay Visions of Ireland: Towards the Twenty-First
  Century* (London, 1995), pp. 60–70

Cronin, Maura. 'Work and Workers in Cork City and County 1800–1900', in
  Patrick Flanagan and Cornelius G. Buttimer (eds), *Cork: History and Society:
  Interdisciplinary Essays on the History of an Irish County* (Dublin, 1993),
  pp. 721–58

Cullen, Mary. 'History Women and History Men: The Politics of Women's
  History', *History Ireland*, vol. 2, no. 2 (summer 1994), pp. 31–6

D'Alton, Ian. 'Keeping Faith: An Evocation of the Cork Protestant Character
  1820–1920', in Patrick O'Flanagan and Cornelius G. Buttimer (eds), *Cork:
  History and Society: Interdisciplinary Essays on the History of an Irish County*
  (Dublin, 1993), pp. 755–92

Daly, Mary E. '"Oh, Kathleen Ni Houlihan, Your Way's a Thorny Way!": The
  Condition of Women in Twentieth-Century Ireland', in Anthony Bradley
  and Maryann Gialanella Valiulis (eds), *Gender and Sexuality in Modern Ireland*
  (Amherst, 1997), pp. 102–26

  '"Turn on the Tap": The State, Irish Women and Running Water', in Maryann
    Gialanella Valiulis and Mary O'Dowd (eds), *Women and Irish History*
    (Dublin, 1997), pp. 206–19

  'Women and Trade Unions', in Donal Nevin, (ed.) *Trade Union Century*

(Dublin, 1994), pp. 106–116

'The Relationship between Women's Work and Poverty', in Ailbhe Smyth
(ed.), *Irish Women's Studies Reader* (Dublin, 1993), pp. 122–39

'Social Structure of the Dublin Working Class, 1871–1911', *Irish Historical
Studies,* vol. 23, no. 90 (November 1982), pp. 121–33.

Devlin, John. 'The State of Health in Ireland', in Joseph Robins (ed.), *Reflections
on Health: Commemorating Fifty Years of the Department of Health 1947–97*
(Dublin, 1997), pp. 10–28

Dillon, Michelle, 'Perceptions of the Causes of the Troubles in Ireland', *Economic
and Social Review*, vol. 21, no. 3 (April 1999), pp. 299–310

'Divorce and Cultural Rationality', in Michel Peillon and Eamonn Slater (eds),
Encounters with Modern Ireland: A Sociological Chronicle 1995–1996
(Dublin, 1998), pp. 127–33

Donnelly, James S. 'The Peak of Marianism in Ireland 1930–60', in Stewart J.
Brown and David W. Miller (eds), *Piety and Power in Ireland: Essays in Honour
of Emmet Larkin* (Belfast, 2000), pp. 252–83

Donnelly, Mary. 'The Calm of Reasoning: Judicial Attitudes to Sentencing in
Sexual Offence Cases', *Irish Journal of Feminist Studies*, vol. 1, no. 1
(March 1996), pp. 26–42

Dowler, Lorraine. ' "And They Think I'm just a Nice Old Lady": Women and War
in Belfast, Northern Ireland', *Gender, Place and Culture*, vol. 5, no. 2 (1998),
pp. 159–76

Downes, Margaret. 'The Civilian Voluntary Effort', in David Fitzpatrick (ed.),
Ireland and the First World War (Dublin, 1986), pp. 27–37

Dunne, Aidan. 'Contemporary Women Artists', in *Irish Women Artists from the
Eighteenth Century to the Present Day* (Dublin, 1987)

Dunwoody, Janet. 'Child Welfare', in David Fitzpatrick (ed.), *Ireland and the First
World War* (Dublin, 1986), pp. 69–75

Earls, Maurice. 'The Late Late Show: Controversy and Context', in Martin
McLoone and John McMahon (ed.), *21 Years of Irish Television*
(Dublin, 1984), pp. 107–22

Edgerton, Lynda. 'Public Protest, Domestic Acquiescence: Women in Northern
Ireland', in Rosemary Ridd and Helen Calloway (eds), *Caught Up in
Conflict: Women's Responses to Political Strife* (London, 1986), pp. 61–79

Evason, Eileen. 'Women and Poverty', in Ailbhe Smyth (ed.), *Irish Women's Studies
Reader* (Dublin, 1993), pp. 162–76

Fahey, Tony. 'Nuns in the Catholic Church in Ireland in the Nineteenth Century',
in Mary Cullen (ed.), *Girls Don't Do Honours: Irish Women in Education in the
19th and 20th Centuries* (Dublin, 1987), pp. 7–30

Fahy, A.M. 'Place and Class in Cork', in Patrick O'Flanagan and Cornelius G.
Buttimer (eds), *Cork History and Society: Interdisciplinary Essays on the History
of an Irish County* (Dublin, 1993), pp. 793–812

Fawcett, Liz. 'The Recruitment of Women to Local Politics in Ireland:
A Case Study', *Irish Political Studies*, vol. 7 (1992), pp. 41–55

Fearon, Kate. 'Whatever Happened to the Women? Gender and Peace in

Northern Ireland', in Michael Cox, Adrian Guelke and Fiona Stephen (eds), *A Farewell to Arms? From 'Long War' to Long Peace in Northern Ireland* (Manchester, 2000), pp. 153–64

Finlay, Andrew. 'The Cutting Edge: Derry Shirtmakers', in Chris Curtin, Pauline Jackson and Barbara O'Connor (eds), *Gender in Irish Society* (Galway, 1987), pp. 87–107

Fitzpatrick, David. 'Emigration, 1871–1921', in W.E. Vaughan (ed.), *A New History of Ireland, vol. VI: Ireland Under the Union (II) 1870–1921* (Oxford, 2000), pp. 606–45

Fletcher, Ruth. 'Silences: Irish Women and Abortion', *Feminist Review*, no. 50 (summer 1995), pp. 44–66

Fowler, Joan. 'Contemporary Women Artists: Practices and Issues into the Future', in *Irish Women Artists from the Eighteenth Century to the Present Day* (Dublin, 1987), pp. 71–8

Galligan, Yvonne. 'The Changing Role of Women', in William Crotty and David E. Schmitt (eds), *Ireland and the Politics of Change* (London, 1998), pp. 107–21

Galligan, Yvonne and Rick Wilford. 'Gender and Party Politics in the Republic of Ireland', in Yvonne Galligan, Eilís Ward and Rick Wilford (eds), *Contesting Politics: Women in Ireland, North and South* (Colorado and Oxford. 1999), pp. 149–68

Gardiner, Frances. 'Political Interest and Participation of Irish Women 1922–1992: The Unfinished Revolution', in Ailbhe Smyth (ed.), *Irish Women's Studies Reader* (Dublin, 1993), pp. 45–78

Gibbons, Luke. 'From Kitchen Sink to Soap: Drama and the Serial Form on Irish Television', in Martin McLoone and John McMahon (eds), *21 Years of Irish Television* (Dublin, 1984), pp. 21–51

Greeley, Andrew M. 'Are the Irish Really Losing the Faith?', *Doctrine and Life*, vol. 44, no. 3 (1994), pp. 132–42

Greiff, Mats. ' "Marching through the Streets Singing and Shouting": Industrial Struggle and Trade Unions among Female Linen Workers in Belfast and Lurgan 1872–1910', *Saothar*, vol. 22, (1997), pp. 29–44

Guilbride, Alex. 'Mad or Bad? Women Committing Infanticide in Ireland from 1925 to 1957', in R. Lentin (ed.), *In from the Shadows: The UL Women's Studies Collection*, 2 vols (Limerick, 1995–8), vol. 2, pp. 84–92

Hackett, Claire. 'Self-determination: The Republican Feminist Agenda', *Feminist Review*, no. 50 (summer 1995), pp. 111–16

Hearn, Mona. 'Life for Domestic Servants in Dublin: 1880–1920', in Maria Luddy and Cliona Murphy (eds), *Women Surviving: Studies in Irish Women's History in the 19th and 20th Centuries* (Dublin, 1990), pp. 148–79

Heenan, Deirdre. 'Farmwives in Northern Ireland and the Gendered Division of Labour', in Anne Byrne and Madeleine Leonard (eds), *Women and Irish Society: A Sociological Reader* (Belfast, 1997), pp. 377–94

Hill, Myrtle. 'Women in the Irish Protestant Foreign Missions, *c.* 1873–1914: Representations and Motivations', in P. Hotrop and H. McLeod (eds),

Missions and Missionaries (New York, 2000), pp. 170–85

Holmes, Heather. 'Sanitary Inspectors and the Reform of Housing Conditions for Irish Migratory Potato Workers in Scotland from 1945 to the 1970s', *Saothar*, vol. 24 (1999), pp. 45–58

Hoy, Sue Ellen. 'The Journey Out: The Recruitment and Emigration of Irish Religious Women to the United States, 1812–1914', in Joan Hoff and Moureen Coulter (eds), *Irish Women's Voices* (Indiana, 1995), *Journal of Women's History*, vols 6 and 7, pp. 64–98

Hutchinson, John and Alan O'Day. 'The Gaelic Revival in London, 1900–22: Limits of Ethnic Identity', in Roger Swift and Sheridan Gilley (eds), *The Irish in Victorian Britain: The Local Dimension* (Dublin, 1999), pp. 254–76

Hyde, Abbey. 'Marriage and Motherhood: The Contradictory Position of Single Mothers', *Irish Journal of Feminist Studies*, vol. 2, no. 1 (summer 1997), pp. 22–36

'Unmarried Pregnant Women's Accounts of Their Contraceptive Practices: A Qualitative Analysis', *Irish Journal of Sociology*, vol. 6 (1996), pp. 179–211

Inglis, Tom. 'From Sexual Repression to Liberation?', in Michel Peillon and Eamonn Slater (eds), *Encounters with Modern Ireland: A Sociological Chronicle 1995–1996* (Dublin, 1998), pp. 99–104

Jackson, Pauline Conroy. 'Women's Movement and Abortion: The Criminalization of Irish Women', in Drude Dahlerup (ed.), *The New Women's Movement: Feminism and Political Power in Europe and the USA* (London, 1986), pp. 48–63

Johnson, D.S. 'The Northern Ireland Economy, 1914–39', in Liam Kennedy and Philip Ollerenshaw (eds), *An Economic History of Ulster 1820–1939* (Manchester, 1985), pp. 184–223

Jones, Mary. 'Mary Robinson: An Appreciation', *Irish Journal of Feminist Studies*, vol. 3, no. 1 (December 1998), pp. 1–15

Jorstad, Jonas. 'Nations Once Again: Ireland's Civil War in European Context', in David Fitzpatrick (ed.), *Revolution? Ireland 1917–1923* (Dublin, 1990), pp. 59–73,

Kennedy, Brian. 'Women's Artists and the Modern Movement 1943–49', in *Irish Women Artists from the Eighteenth Century to the Present Day* (Dublin, 1987), pp. 34–45

Kenny, Máirín. 'Final Thoughts: A Case for Celebration', in May McCann, Seamus Ó Siochain and Joseph Ruane (eds), *Irish Travellers: Culture and Ethnicity* (Belfast, 1994), pp. 179–88

Knirck, Jason. ' "Ghosts and Realities": Female TDs and the Treaty Debate', *Eire-Ireland*, vol. 32, no. 4 and vol. 33, nos. 1 and 2 (winter/spring/summer 1997–8), pp. 170–94

Lagerkvist, Amanda. ' "To End Women's Night": A Resistance Discourse of the Irish Housewive's Association in the Media in 1961–62', *Irish Journal of Feminist Studies*, vol. 2, no. 2 (December 1997), pp. 18–33

Leonard, Madeleine. 'Ourselves Alone: Household Work Strategies in a Deprived Community', *Irish Journal of Sociology*, vol. 2 (1992), pp. 70–84

Leydesdorff, Salma. 'Politics, Identification and the Writing of Women's History' in Arina Angerman et al. (eds), *Current Issues in Women's Writing* (London, 1989), pp. 9–20

Logan, John. 'The Dimensions of Gender in Nineteenth-Century Schooling', in Margaret Kelleher and James H. Murphy (eds), *Gender Perspectives in 19th Century Ireland* (Dublin, 1997), pp. 36–49

Loughran, Christina. 'Armagh and Feminist Strategy: Campaigns around Republican Women Prisoners in Armagh Jail', *Feminist Review*, no. 23 (June 1986), pp. 59–79

McAliskey, Bernadette. 'A Peasant in the Halls of the Great', in Michael Farrell (ed.), *Twenty Years On* (Dingle, 1988), pp. 75–88

McCaffrey, Patricia. 'Jacob's Women Workers During the 1913 Lock-out', *Saothar* vol. 16 (1991), pp. 118–29

McCormack, Inez. 'Faceless Men: Civil Rights and After', in Michael Farrell (ed.), *Twenty Years On* (Dingle, 1988), pp. 25–38

MacCurtain, Margaret. 'Moving Statues and Irish Women', in Ailbhe Smyth (ed.), *Irish Women's Studies Reader* (Dublin, 1993), pp. 203–13
    'Fullness of Life: Defining Female Spirituality in Twentieth-Century Ireland', in Maria Luddy and Cliona Murphy (eds), *Women Surviving: Studies in Irish Women's History in the 19th and 20th Centuries* (Dublin, 1989), pp. 233–63

McDonagh, Claire. 'Domestic Violence: The Galway Perspective', *UCG Women's Studies Centre: Review*, vol. 4 (1996), pp. 109–16

McLaughlin, Eithne. 'Women and the Family in Northern Ireland: A Review', *Women's Studies International Forum*, vol. 16, no. 6 (1993), pp. 553–68

McShane, Liz. 'Day Nurseries in Northern Ireland 1941–1955: Gender Ideology in Social Policy', in Chris Curtin, Pauline Jackson and Barbara O'Connor (eds), *Gender in Irish Society* (Galway, 1987), pp. 249–62

McWilliams, Monica. 'Struggling for Peace and Justice: Reflections on Women's Activism in Northern Ireland', in Joan Hoff and Moureen Coulter (eds), *Irish Women's Voices: Past and Present, Journal of Women's History*, vols 6 and 7 (Indiana, 1995), pp. 13–39
    'The Church, the State and the Women's Movement in Northern Ireland', in Ailbhe Smyth (ed.), *Irish Women's Studies Reader* (Dublin, 1993), pp. 79–99
    'Women in Northern Ireland: An Overview', in Eamonn Hughes (ed.), *Culture and Politics in Northern Ireland 1960–1990* (Milton Keynes, 1991), pp. 81–100

McWilliams, Monica and Avila Kilmurray. 'Athene on the Loose: The Origins of the Northern Ireland Women's Coalition', *Irish Journal of Feminist Studies*, vol. 2, no. 1 (summer 1997), pp. 1–21

Madec, Mary O'Malley. 'The Irish Travelling Woman: Mother and Mermaid', in Ailbhe Smyth (ed.), *Irish Women's Studies Reader* (Dublin, 1993), pp. 214–29

Mahon, Evelyn. 'The Development of a Health Policy for Women', in Joseph Robins (ed.), *Reflections on Health: Commemorating Fifty Years of The*

Department of Health 1947–97 (Dublin, 1997), pp. 77–96

'Women's Rights and Catholicism in Ireland', *New Left Review*, no. 166 (November–December 1987), pp. 53–77

Martin, Angela K. 'Transnationalism, Bodies and Abortion in Late Twentieth-Century Ireland', in Tamar Mayer (ed.), *Gender Ironies of Nationalism: Sexing the Nation* (London and New York, 2000), pp. 64–86

Meaney, Gerardine. 'Territory and Transgression: History, Nationality and Sexuality in Kate O'Brien's Fiction', *Irish Journal of Feminist Studies*, vol. 2, no. 2 (winter 1997), pp. 77–92

Montgomery, Pamela. 'Paid and Unpaid Work', in John Kremer and Pamela Montgomery (eds), *Women's Working Lives* (Belfast, 1993), pp. 15–41

Morgan, Valerie and Grace Fraser. 'Women and the Northern Ireland Conflict: Experiences and Responses', in Seamus Dunn (ed.), *Facets of the Conflict in Northern Ireland* (London, 1995), pp. 81–96

Morrissey, Helen. 'Betty Sinclair: A Woman's Fight for Socialism, 1920–81, *Saothar*, vol. 9 (1983), pp. 121–32

Mulholland, Marie. 'Between a Rock and a Hard Place', *Unfinished Revolution: Essays on the Irish Women's Movement* (Belfast, 1989), pp. 33–7

Mullin, Mary. 'Representations of History, Irish Feminism, and the Politics of Difference', *Feminist Studies*, vol. 17, no. 1 (1991), pp. 29–50

Murphy, Cliona. 'A Problematic Relationship: European Women and Nationalism 1870–1915', in Maryann Gialanella Valiulis and Mary O'Dowd (eds), *Women and Irish History: Essays in Honour of Margaret MacCurtain* (Dublin, 1997), pp. 145–58

Murphy, Maureen. 'The Fionnuala Factor: Irish Sibling Migration at the Turn of the Century', in Anthony Bradley and Maryann Gialanella Valiulis (eds), *Gender and Sexuality in Modern Ireland* (Amherst, 1997), pp. 85–101

O'Connor, Anne V. 'The Revolution in Girls' Secondary Education in Ireland 1860–1910', in Mary Cullen (ed.), *Girls Don't Do Honours: Irish Women in Education in the 19th and 20th Centuries* (Dublin, 1987), pp. 31–54

O'Connor, Barbara. 'Riverdance', *Feminist Review*, no. 50 (summer 1995), pp. 51–60

O'Connor, Pat. 'Defining Irish Womanhood: Dominant Discourses and Sites of Resistance', *Eire-Ireland*, vol. 30 (1995), pp. 177–87

'Understanding Continuities and Changes in Irish Marriage: Putting Women Centre Stage', *Irish Journal of Sociology*, vol. 5 (1995), pp. 135–63

O Dochartaigh, Niall. 'Housing and Conflict: Social Change and Collective Action in Derry in the 1960s', in Gerard O'Brien, *Derry and Londonderry: History and Society: Interdisciplinary Essays on the History of an Irish County* (Dublin, 1999), pp. 625–45

O'Dowd, Liam. 'Church, State and Women: The Aftermath of Partition', in Chris Curtin, Pauline Jackson and Barbara O'Connor (eds), *Gender in Irish Society* (Galway, 1987), pp. 3–36

O'Hearn, Denis. 'The Two Irish Economies: Dependencies Compared', in James Anderson and James Goodman (eds), *DIS/Agreeing Ireland: Contexts,*

Obstacles, Hopes (London, 1998), pp. 54–72

O'Leary, Mary. 'Lesbianism and Feminism: A Personal Reflection', *Irish Journal of Feminist Studies*, vol. 2, no. 1 (summer 1997), pp. 63–6

O'Mahoney, Paul. 'The Kerry Babies: Towards a Social Psychological Analysis', *Irish Journal of Psychological Analysis*, vol. 13, no. 2 (1992), pp. 223–38

O'Neill, Maggie. 'Prostitute Women Now', in Graham Scambler and Annette Scambler (eds), *Rethinking Prostitution: Purchasing Sex in the 1990s* (London, 1997)

Owens, Mary and Anne Byrne. 'Family, Work and Community – Rural Women's Lives', *UCG Women's Studies Centre Review*, vol. 4 (1996), pp. 77–94

Owens, Rosemary Cullen. 'Women and Pacifism in Ireland 1915–32', in Maryann Gialanella Valiulis and Mary O'Dowd (eds), *Women and Irish History* (Dublin, 1997), pp. 220–38

Pelan, Rebecca. 'Undoing that Other Conquest: Women's Writing from the Republic of Ireland', *Canadian Journal of Irish Studies*, vol. 25, nos 1 and 2 (July–December 1999), pp. 126–44

Phoenix, Eamon. 'Political Violence, Diplomacy and the Catholic Minority in Northern Ireland', in John Darby (ed.), *Political Violence: Ireland in a Comparative Perspective* (Belfast, 1988), pp. 29–47

Pollock, Vivienne L. 'The Herring Industry in County Down 1840–1940', in L. Proudfoot (ed.), *Down: History and Society: Interdisciplinary Essays on the History of an Irish County* (Dublin, 1997), pp. 405–29

Porter, Elisabeth. 'Identity, Location, Plurality: Women, Nationalism and Northern Ireland', in R. Wilford and R.L. Miller (eds), *Women, Ethnicity and Nationalism* (London, 1998), pp. 36–60

'Diversity and Commonality: Women, Politics and Northern Ireland', *European Journal of Women's Studies*, vol. 4 (1997), pp. 83–100

'Northern Ireland Women's Coalition', *Australian Feminist Studies*, vol. 11, no. 24 (1996), pp. 317–20

Randall, Vicky and Ailbhe Smyth. 'Bishops and Bailiwicks: Obstacles to Women's Political Participation in Ireland', *Economic and Social Review*, vol. 18, no. 3 (April 1987), pp. 189–214

Rigal, Jocelyne. 'Changing Families of the Irish Travellers: The Experiences of Women', *Irish Journal of Feminist Studies*, vol. 3, no. 2 (autumn 1999), pp. 32–48

Robinson, Hilary. 'Disruptive Women Artists: An Irigarayan Reading of Irish Visual Culture', *Irish Studies Review*, vol. 8, no. 1 (2000), pp. 57–72

Rolston, Bill. 'Mothers, Whores and Villains: Images of Women in Novels of the Northern Ireland Conflict', *Race and Class*, vol. 31, no. 1 (1989), pp. 41–57

Rooney, Eilish. 'Women in Northern Irish Politics: Difference Matters', in Carmel Roulston and Celia Davies (eds), *Gender, Democracy and Inclusion in Northern Ireland* (Basingstoke, 2000), pp. 164–86

'Women in Party Politics and Local Groups: Findings from Belfast', in Anne Byrne and Madeleine Leonard (eds), *Women and Irish Society: A Sociological Reader* (Dublin, 1997), pp. 535–51

'Political Division, Practical Alliance: Problems for Women in Conflict', Joan
 Hoff and Maureen Coulter (eds), *Irish Women's Voices: Past and Present*
 (Indiana, 1995), *Journal of Women's History*, vols 6 and 7, pp. 40–8
Rossiter, Ann. 'Bringing the Margins into the Centre: A Review of Aspects of
 Irish Women's Emigration from a British Perspective', in Ailbhe Smyth
 (ed.), *Irish Women's Studies Reader* (Dublin, 1993), pp. 177–202
Rottman, David B. 'Allocating Money within Households: Better off Poorer?',
 in Brian Nolan and Tim Callan (eds), *Poverty and Policy in Ireland*
 (Dublin, 1994), pp. 193–213
Roulston, Carmel. 'Gender, Nation, Class: The Politics of Difference in Northern
 Ireland', *Scottish Affairs*, vol. 18 (winter 1997), pp. 54–68
 'Women on the Margin: The Women's Movements in Northern Ireland,
  1973–1995', in Lois A. West (ed.), *Feminist Nationalism* (London, 1997),
  pp. 41–58
 'Women on the Margin: The Women's Movement in Northern Ireland,
  1973–1988', *Science and Society*, vol. 53, no. 2 (summer 1989), pp. 219–36
Royle, Stephen A. 'Industrialization, Urbanization and Urban Society in Post-
 Famine Ireland, *c.* 1850–1921', in B.J. Graham and L.J. Proudfoot (eds),
 An Historical Geography of Ireland (London, 1993), pp. 258–92
Russell, Elizabeth. 'Holy Crosses, Guns and Roses: Themes in Popular Reading
 Material', in Joost Augusteijn (ed.), *Ireland in the 1930s: New Perspectives*
 (Dublin, 1999), pp. 11–28
Ryan, Louise. 'Sexualising Emigration: Discourses of Irish Female Emigration in
 the 1930s', *Women's Studies International Forum*, vol. 25 (January–February
 2002), pp. 51–65
 ' "Drunken Tans": Representations of Sex and Violence in the Anglo–Irish
  War', *Feminist Review*, no. 66, (autumn 2000), pp. 73–94
 ' "Furies" and "Die-hards": Women and Irish Republicanism in the Early
  Twentieth Century', *Gender and History*, vol. 11, no. 2 (July 1999),
  pp. 256–75
 'A Question of Loyalty: War, Nation, and Feminism in Early Twentieth-
  Century Ireland', *Women's Studies International Forum*, vol. 20 (1997),
  pp. 21–32
Sales, Rosemary. 'Women, the Peace Makers?', in James Anderson and James
 Goodman (eds), *DIS/Agreeing Ireland: Contexts, Obstacles, Hopes* (London,
 1998), pp. 141–61
 'Gender and Protestantism in Northern Ireland', in Peter Shirlow and Mark
  McGovern (eds), *Who are 'the People'? Unionism, Protestantism and
  Loyalism in Northern Ireland* (London, 1997), pp. 140–57
Shannon, Catherine. 'Women in Northern Ireland', in Mary O'Dowd and Sabine
 Wichert (eds), *Chattel, Servant or Citizen: Women's Status in Church, State and
 Society* (Belfast, 1995), pp. 238–53
 'Recovering the Voices of the Women of the North', *Irish Review*
  (spring–summer 1992), pp. 27–33
Sheehan, Aideen. 'Cumann na mBan: Policies and Activities', in David Fitzpatrick,

Revolution? Ireland 1917–1923 (Dublin, 1990), pp. 88–97

Sheehan, Kathleen. 'Life in Glangevlin, County Cavan, 1900–1920', *Ulster Folklife*, vol. 32 (1985), pp. 53–8

Simpson, Audrey. 'Abortion in Northern Ireland', in Ann Furedi (ed.), *The Abortion Law in Northern Ireland: Human Rights and Reproductive Choice* (Belfast, 1995), pp. 6–15

Smyth, Ailbhe. 'Feminism: Personal, Political, Unqualified (or Ex-Colonized Girls Know More)', *Irish Journal of Feminist Studies*, vol. 2, no. 1 (summer 1997), pp. 37–54

'Seeing Red: Men's Violence against Women in Ireland', in Ronit Lentin (ed.), *In from the Shadows: The UL Women's Studies Collection*, vol. 2 (Limerick, 1996), pp. 15–37

'States of Change: Reflections on Ireland in Several Uncertain Parts', *Feminist Review*, no. 50 (summer 1995), pp. 24–43

'International Trends: Paying our Disrespects to the Bloody States We're In', *Journal of Women's History*, vol. 6, no. 4 and vol. 7, no. 1 (winter–spring 1995), pp. 190–215

'The Women's Movement in the Republic of Ireland 1970–1990', in Ailbhe Smyth (ed.), *Irish Women's Studies Reader* (Dublin, 1993), pp. 245–69

'"A Great Day for the Women of Ireland . . ." The Meaning of Mary Robinson's Presidency for Irish Women', *Canadian Journal of Irish Studies*, vol. 18, no. 1 (1992), pp. 61–75

'The Contemporary Women's Movement in the Republic of Ireland', *Women's Studies International Forum*, vol. 11, no. 4 (1988), pp. 331–41

Smyth, Jim. 'Dancing, Depravity and all that Jazz': The Public Dance Halls Act of 1935', *History Ireland* (summer 1993), pp. 51–4

Smyth, Lisa. 'Narratives of Irishness and the Problem of Abortion: The X Case 1992', *Feminist Review*, no. 60 (autumn 1998), pp. 61–83

Spray, Glenys. 'The "Backlash Boys" ', *Irish Journal of Feminist Studies*, (July 1997), pp. 106–16

Steele, Karen. 'Raising Her Voice for Justice: Maud Gonne and the *United Irishman*', *New Hibernia Review*, vol. 3. no. 2 (summer 1999), pp. 84–105

Steiner-Scott, Elizabeth. ' "To Bounce a Boot off Her Now and Then . . . ": Domestic Violence in Post-Famine Ireland', in Maryann Gialanella Valiulis and Mary O'Dowd (eds), *Women and Irish History: Essays in Honour of Margaret MacCurtain* (Dublin, 1997), pp. 125–43

Stevens, Lorna, Stephen Brown and Pauline Maclaran. 'Gender, Nationality and Cultural Representations of Ireland: An Irish Woman's Place?', *European Journal of Women's Studies*, vol. 7 (2000), pp. 405–21

Summerfield, Penny. 'Women and War in the Twentieth Century', in Jane Purvis (ed). *Women's History: Britain, 1850–1945* (London, 1995), pp. 307–332

Sweeney, Fionnuala. 'Women's Work is Never Done: The Changing Role and Status of Farming Women in Dungiven', *Causeway* (winter 1994), p. 21–4

Sweeney, George. 'Irish Hunger Strikers and the Cult of Self-Sacrifice', *Journal of Contemporary History*, vol. 28 (1993), pp. 421–37

Thane, Pat. 'Old Women in 20th Century Britain', in Lynn Botelho and Pat Thane (eds), *Women and Ageing in British Society since 1500* (London, 2001), pp. 207–31

Torode, Ruth and Eoin O'Sullivan. 'The Impact of *Dear Daughter*', *Irish Journal of Feminist Studies*, vol. 3, no. 2 (autumn 1999), pp. 85–97

Travers, Pauric. 'Emigration and Gender: The Case of Ireland, 1922–60', in Mary O'Dowd and Sabine Wichert (eds), *Chattel, Servant or Citizen: Women's Status in Church, State and Society* (Belfast, 1995), pp. 187–99

' "There was Nothing for Me There": Irish Female Emigration, 1922–71', in Patrick O'Sullivan (ed.), *Irish Women and Irish Migration* (London, 1995), pp. 146–67

Turner, Michael. 'Rural Economics in Post-Famine Ireland, *c*. 1850–1914', in B.J. Graham and L.J. Proudfoot (eds), *An Historical Geography of Ireland* (London, 1993), pp. 293–337

Urquhart, Diane. 'In Defence of Ulster and the Empire: The Ulster Women's Unionist Council, 1911–1940', *UCG Women's Studies Centre Review* (1996), pp. 31–40

Valiulis, Maryann Gialanella. 'Engendering Citizenship: Women's Relationship to the State in Ireland and the United States in the Post-Suffrage Period', in Maryann Gialanella Valiulis and Mary O'Dowd (eds), *Women and Irish History* (Dublin, 1997), pp. 159–72

'Neither Feminist nor Flapper: The Ecclesiastical Construction of the Ideal Irish Woman', in Mary O'Dowd and Sabine Wichert (eds), *Chattel, Servant or Citizen: Women's Status in Church, State and Society* (Belfast, 1995), pp. 168–78

Walsh, Anne-Marie. 'Root Them in the Land: Cottage Schemes for Agricultural Labourers', in Joost Augusteijn (ed.), *Ireland in the 1930s: New Perspectives* (Dublin, 1999), pp. 47–66

Walsh, Louise. 'Artist-Activist', in Ide O'Carroll and Eoin Collins (eds), *Lesbian and Gay Visions of Ireland: Towards the Twenty-First Century* (London, 1995), pp. 171–80

Walsh, Oonagh. 'Testimony from Imprisoned Women', in David Fitzpatrick (ed.), *Revolution? Ireland 1917–1923* (Dublin, 1990), pp. 69–85

Ward, Eilís and Orla O'Donovan. 'Networks of Women's Groups and Politics in Ireland: What (Some) Women Think', *UCG Women's Studies Centre Review*, vol. 4 (1996), pp. 1–20

Ward, Margaret. ' "Ulster was Different?" Women, Feminism and Nationalism in the North of Ireland', in Yvonne Galligan, Eilís Ward and Rick Wilford (eds), *Contesting Politics: Women in Ireland, North and South* (Colorado and Oxford, 1999), pp. 219–39

'Nationalism, Pacifism, Internationalism: Louie Bennett, Hanna Sheehy-Skeffington, and the Problems of "Defining Feminism" ', in Anthony Bradley and Maryann Gialanella Valiulis (eds), *Gender and Sexuality in Modern Ireland* (Amherst, 1997), pp. 60–84

'The Women's Movement in the North of Ireland: Twenty Years On', in Seán

Hutton and Paul Stewart (eds), *Ireland's Histories: Aspects of State, Society and Ideology* (London, 1991), pp. 149–63

'From Civil Rights to Women's Rights', in Michael Farrell (ed.), *Twenty Years On* (Dingle, 1988), pp. 122–33

Ward, Rachel. 'The Northern Ireland Peace Process: A Gender Issue?', in Chris Gilligan and Jon Tonge (eds), *Peace or War? Understanding the Peace Process in Northern Ireland* (Aldershot, 1997), pp. 150–62

Whyte, John. 'How much Discrimination was there under the Unionist Regime, 1921–68?', in Tom Gallagher and James O'Connell (eds), *Contemporary Irish Studies* (Manchester, 1983), pp. 1–35

Zwicker, Heather. 'Between Mater and Matter: Radical Novels by Republican Women', in Marilyn Cohen and Nancy J. Curtin, (eds), *Reclaiming Gender: Transgressive Identities in Modern Ireland* (New York, 1999), pp. 247–65

Journals

Australian Feminist Studies
Bean na hÉireann
Canadian Journal of Irish Studies
Economic and Social Review
Eire-Ireland
European Journal of Women's Studies
Feminist Review, Fortnight
f/m feminist magazine
Gender and History
Gender, Place and Culture
History Ireland
Irish Economic and Social History
Irish Historical Studies
Irish Journal of Feminist Studies
Irish Journal of Sociology
Irish Political Studies
Irish Review
Journal of Contemporary History
Magill
New Hibernia Review
New Left Review
Race and Class
Saothar
UCG Women's Studies Centre Review
Ulster Folklife
Women's News
Women's Studies Internal Forum

Reports

Democratic Dialogue. *Power, Politics, Positionings: Women in Northern Ireland*, Report no. 4 (Belfast, 1996)

Equal Opportunities Commission for Northern Ireland. *Women and Men in Northern Ireland* (Belfast, 1995)

European Commission, *The Social Situation in the European Union 2000* (2000)

Female Forfeit: The Cost of Being a Woman, Cabinet Report, CAB 79/00 (21 February 2000)

Kilkenny Social Services. *The Unmarried Mother in the Irish Community: A Report on the National Conference on Community Services for the Unmarried Parent* (Kilkenny, 1972)

Northern Ireland Life and Times Survey, Research Update, no. 1 (June 1999), Research Update, no. 8 (November 2001)

Pollack, A. (ed.). *A Citizens' Inquiry: The Opsahl Report on Northern Ireland* (Dublin, 1993)

Triple Cross Network. *Tipping the Balance: A Fresh Look at Issues Impacting on Equality for Women at the Beginning of the 21st Century* (2000)

Unmarried Mothers in the Irish Community: A Report on the National Conference on Community Services for the Unmarried Parent (Kilkenny, 1972)

Ward, Margaret. *The Northern Ireland Assembly and Women: Assessing the Gender Deficit*, Democratic Dialogue, Summary Report no. 4 (Belfast, 2000)

Parliamentary papers

Report of the Inter-Departmental Committee on the Employment of Children during School Age, especially in Street Trading in the Large Centres of Population in Ireland. H.C. 1902, xlix [Cd. 1144]

Theses

Berguist, Margaret I. 'Mother Ireland and the Gun: Representations of Women and Violence in the Films of Northern Ireland', unpublished thesis submitted in partial fulfilment of the requirements for MA, Queen's University Belfast, 1996

Bolster, Mary Kathryn. 'Women on the March: Women in the Civil Rights Movement in Northern Ireland in the 1960s', unpublished dissertation submitted in partial fulfilment of requirements for MA, University College Dublin, 1991

Edgerton, Lynda. 'Examination of the Role of Northern Irish Women in their Domestic, Social and Political Life, 1967–1977', unpublished dissertation submitted in partial fulfilment of the requirements for BA, Queen's University Belfast, 1977

Larmour, Sandra Ruth. 'Aspects of the State and Female Sexuality in the Irish Free State, 1922–1949', unpublished PhD. thesis, University College Cork, 1998

Leane, Maire. 'Female Sexuality in Ireland 1920–1940: Construction and Regulation', unpublished PhD. thesis, University College Cork, 1999

McClelland, Gillian. 'Evangelical Philanthropy and Social Control, or Emancipatory Feminism? A Case Study of Fisherwick Presbyterian Working Women's Association 1870–1918', unpublished PhD. thesis, Queen's University Belfast, 1999

Porter, Frances. 'Faith and Feminism: Women's Christian Faith Experience in Northern Ireland', unpublished PhD. thesis, University of Ulster, 1999

Templeton, Joanne. 'Sexism and Racism: The Double Burden of Irish Traveller Women', unpublished dissertation submitted in partial fulfilment of the requirements for BSc, university of Ulster, 1997

Urquhart, Diane. 'The Political Role of Women in North-East Ulster, 1890–1940', unpublished MA thesis, Queen's University Belfast, 1996

Ward, Sarah. 'The Genesis of Civil Rights in Northern Ireland', unpublished dissertation submitted in partial fulfilment of requirements for MSc in Irish Political Studies, Queen's University Belfast, 1993

Unpublished manuscripts

Hutchinson, Elizabeth. 'Reminiscence'

Johnson, D.S. 'Prostitution and Venereal Disease in Ireland during the Second Half of the Nineteenth Century'

Ward, Rachel. 'Unionist and Loyalist Women in Contemporary Northern Ireland', Centre for Social Research Working Paper, 2000

Archive manuscripts

Boole Library, Cork

Tadgh Ó Donnchadha, Papers of, U114/Box 56/1.14

Cork Public Museum

'A Song for Cumann na mBan', AQNOL 1974 58/48

Bridget Foley, Papers, AQNOL 1957:24

Nora Wallace Collection, AQNOL 1996:111

Linen Hall Library, Belfast

Autobiography of Reverend William Hamilton
Bernadette Devlin, Biographical Press Cuttings Files
Hazel Gordon. 'Women, Protestantism and Unionism', unpublished paper
    given at workshop on Women in Ireland, 4 October 1990
Maire Drumm, Biographical Press Cuttings File
Republican Women Prisoners
Women and the IRA
Women in Struggle, Sinn Féin's Women's Department
Women Together/Peace People

National Library of Ireland, Dublin

Rosamund Jacob Papers, MS. 33,129

Public Record Office of Northern Ireland (PRONI)

Belfast Midnight Mission, D/2072
British Fascists, correspondence, D/3783/A/2
Cabinet Papers re- Civil Defence World War II, CAB/31/64; CAB/31/64;
    CAB/3A/27
Communist Party, Northern Ireland Papers, D/2162
Dorothy Evans and Madge Muir, Court Papers, BELF/1/1/2/45/8
Drawing Room Circle, Belfast, D/3866
Emma Duffin, *Nursing Diaries*, D/2109
First women barristers, D/2481/1/1
Florence Stewart Papers, D/3612
Frank Gogarty Papers, D/3253
Irish Labour Party Papers, D/3311
Killyleagh Women's War Work, D/3524/2/1
Lady Londonderry, correspondence, D/3099; D/2846
Margaret Robinson, former suffragette, interview, Belfast, Tp. 35
Moya Woodside, Diary, T/3808
National Council for Single Woman and Her Dependants, Belfast branch, D/3370
Northern Ireland Family Planning Association Papers, D/3691; D/3543
Nursery School Association Papers
Reminiscences of Education at the Lodge, Fortwilliam Park, Belfast, D/37/12/1
Sheelagh Murnaghan, typescript article, 'The Itinerant Problem', D/3219/2/18
Suffrage correspondence, T/3259; T/2125
Ulster Gift Fund, A History of, compiled by John W. Blake, D/912/1/13
Ulster Women's Unionist Association Papers, D/1098
William Topping, memoirs of his working life, 1903–56, D/3134
Women's National Health Association Papers, D/1884

Trinity College Dublin (TCD)

Daughter of the Provost of TCD, Account of the Rising, TCD 274

Emily Ussher, 'The True Story of a Revolution: An Account of Life at Cappagh, County Waterford, Spring 1914–Spring 1925', TCD 9269

'James S. Cousins and Mrs Margaret Cousins. An Appreciation', TCD 4642/2993a.

Mary Spring Rice, log of the *Asgard*, TCD 7841

Nelly O'Brien, 'A Hot Corner, Dublin, 5 July 1922', TCD 10343/4

University College Cork, Cork Archives Collection

Cork Child Welfare League, Minute Book, H7

Siobhàn Lankford, Papers, U169A

University College Dublin

Bridget Stafford, Papers, P63

Eithne Coyle O'Donnell, Papers, P61

Elizabeth Bloxham, Papers, UCD P31

Irish Federation of University Women, P63/1

IWWU, *The Wooden Horse: A Reply to Fascists*

Mary McSwiney, Papers, P48a

Singhle Humphreys, Papers, P106

Index

Abbey Theatre (Dublin), 39
Abbeylands House (Co. Antrim), 64
ABC cinema (Belfast), 139
Aberdeen, Lady, 24, 36–7, 39, 41
abortion, 104–5, 146–7, 227, 242
    constitutional referendum (1983),
        197–8, 215
    pro-life groups, 198, 199–200
    statistics, 200
    Women's Right to Choose group, 156
    X case (1992), 198–9, 226
abuse. see domestic violence; sexual abuse
academic education, 4, 27, 28
Adams, Gerry, 231, 236, 237
Adamson, Mrs, 52
ADAPT (Association for Deserted and Alone
    Parents), 156
Adelphi cinema (Dublin), 140
adoption, 146, 194
Aer Lingus, 134–5
age of consent, 103
ageing, 200–1
Agnew, Ruth, 181
Agnew, Thelma, 223
agriculture, 70, 209
    employment, 44, 99, 209, 243
    farm children, 25–6
    farm women, 45–6, 99, 209–10
AIDS, 193
AIM (Action, Information, Motivation),
    154–6
air hostesses, 135
Air-raid Precautions (ARP) wardens, 115
air raids (1941), 122–4
air travel, 21, 134–5
airwomen, 69, 117, 125
Albion clothing factory (Belfast), 104
Alexandra College (Dublin), 27, 28, 30
    philanthropic work, 19–20, 66
Alhambra, 39
Ali, Rukhsar, 204–5
All Children Together, 182

Alliance Party, 231
Alonso, Harriet, 185
America. see United States
American money, 35
American troops
    Second World War, 124–5
Amiens Street (Dublin)
    German air raid (1941), 124
Amsterdam Olympics (1928), 102
Ancient Order of Hibernians, 89
    Ladies' Auxiliary, 89–90
    revival in Ulster (1920s), 89
Anderson, Mary, 153
Andersonstown (Belfast), 127, 183, 220
Anglican Church, 238
    Lambeth Conference (1930), 105
Anglo-German Review, 114
Anglo-Irish, 64
    social life, 17
Anglo-Irish Agreement (1985), 222
Anglo-Irish Treaty (1921), 60, 84, 86, 93,
    107
    Dáil debates, 84–6
Anglo-Irish Truce (1921), 84
Anglo-Irish War (1919–21). see War of
    Independence
anti-abortion groups, 198, 199–200
Anti-Discrimination (Pay) Act, (1974), 152
Anti-Divorce Campaign, 190
Anti-Tuberculosis League, 129
Antrim, 164
    architects, 47
Ardglass (Co. Down), 45
Ardoyne (Belfast), 167, 181
Arensberg, Conrad M., 16
Ark, The, 79
Armagh, 162, 164
Armagh Suffrage Society, 58
Armagh women's prison, 166, 219, 220, 221
Army Comrades' Association, 113
Arranmore Island (Co. Donegal), 23
Arria, Cissie, 39

artists, 7–8, 111
arts, 7–8, 39, 111
Arts and Crafts exhibitions, 7
Asdee, 215
Asgard, 64
Asquith, H., 52, 57
Association for Deserted and Alone Parents
    (ADAPT), 156
Association of Business and Professional
    Women, 152
Association of University Teachers, 213
asylum seekers, 205
athletics, 7
Athlone (Co. Westmeath), 17
Auschwitz concentration camp, 116
Australia, 33
Auxiliary Territorial Service (ATS), 117
Aylesbury prison (England), 30

B Specials, 163, 174
Baez, Joan, 138
Baker, Molly, 74
Balieborough (Co. Cavan), 124
Ballantine, Angela, 212
Ballantine, Miss, 66
Ballincollig, 83
Ballinspittle, 215
ballrooms, 140
Ballycastle (Co. Antrim), 61
Ballycrory (Co. Mayo), 118
Ballydesmond, 215
Ballyheigue, 38
Ballykelly, 125
Ballymacarret (Belfast), 217
Ballymurphy (Belfast), 181
Ballyvally, Down, 40
Bangor (Co. Down), 45, 217
    German air raids, 123
    railway station, 56
Bangor Home of Rest, 38
Bann River, 159
Banotti, Mary, *187*, 237
Barber, Monica, 190
Bardon, Jonathan, 18, 83, 115, 161
Barnes, Monica, 198
Barry, Maisie, 25
Barry, Norma, 122
Barton, Brian, 120
Bates, Dawson, 62
Bates, Mr, 63
Battle of the Bogside (1969), 166

Battle of the Somme (1916), 71, 163
2BE radio (Northern Ireland), 110
Bean na hÉireann, 33, 60
Beatles, 139–40
Beattie, Emily, 162
Beaumont, Catriona, 105–6
Beere, Thekla, 152
Begoña, Aretxaga, 220
Beijing (China)
    Fourth World Conference for Women
        (1995), 239
Belfast, 2, 14, 15, 16, 17, 18, 26, 29, 35, 38,
        39, 67, 86, 98, 106, 109, 119, 181, 217,
        244. *see also* Andersonstown; Ardoyne;
        Falls Road; Shankill Road
    Albion clothing factory, 104
    Antrim Road (Belfast), 122
    Beatlemania (1963), 139–40
    Blitz (1941), 122–3
    Bloody Friday (1972), 171
    car bombs, 170
    children street-traders, 26
    College of Technology, 125
    Communist Party, 112
    community politics, 225
    conflict, 83–4, 167–8, 170, 171
    coronation celebrations (1953), 135
    Donegall Road (Belfast), 136
    Drawing Room Circle, 122
    employment, 17
    Hall's Chemist, 155
    housing, 17–8, 126–8
    internment (Second World War), 126
    Jewish population, 116
    lesbian networks, 196
    linen workers, 48
    mill workers' strike (1911), 48
    mother and baby clubs, 24
    New Year's Day (1900), 15
    outdoor relief strike (1932), 98
    peace movements, 181, 183
    population (1911), 16
    poverty, 160
    riots, 164
    St Anne's Cathedral, *9*
    St George's Market, 123
    sectarianism, 18
    strikes, 48, 98, 99
    suffrage campaign, 52, 55, 56
    textile industry, 42, 99
    tuberculosis, 40

Ulster Hall, 123
VE Day (1945), 125–6
Belfast Agreement, 1998 (Good Friday
    Agreement), 224, 231–2
Belfast City Council, 177, 184, 225, 226
Belfast City Hall, 90, 124
Belfast Corporation, 90, 126
Belfast Evening Telegraph, 62
Belfast Girls' Club Union, 38
Belfast Modern Dance Group, 116
Belfast Peace Women, 183
Belfast Technical College, 58
Belfast Telegraph, 94, 184, 228
Belfast Weekly Telegraph, 119
Belfast Women's Advisory Council, 90
Belfast Women's Citizens' Union, 90
Belfast Women's Collective, 178
Belfast Women's Support Network, 226
Belgian military, 68
Belgium, 66
    Messines war memorial, 238
Bell, Dr, 52
Bell, Nellie, 122
Bennett, Louie, 50, 54, 57, 65, 103
Bennett, Mrs, 52
Benton, Elizabeth, 181–2
Berlin (Germany), 116
Bernelle, Agnes, 116
Bevin, Ernest, 99
Bible study groups, 109
bicycles, 39–40
Biddy Doyle's corner (Ballyvally,
    Co. Down), 40
Binchy, Maeve, 146, 214
Birch, Dr Peter, 215
Birmingham Six, 222
birth control. *see* abortion; contraception;
    family planning
Black, Cilla, 140
Black, Mary, 235
Black and Tans, 82, 83, 84, 94
Black Sea, 67
Blair-White, Phoebe, 102
blind persons
    workshops, 37
Blood, May, 181, 226, 228, 229, 230
Bloody Sunday (Derry, 1972), 170, 183
Bloody Sunday (Dublin, 1920), 83
Blowers, Frankie, 121
Bloxham, Elizabeth, 36, 91
Blue Blouses, 113

Blueshirts (National Guard), 113
Boards of Guardians, 98
Boer War, 14, 16, 68
Bogside (Derry), 162, 166, 182
Boland, Eavan, 8, 214, 238
Boland's mill, 73
Bookline (RTÉ), 8
Bottomley, Virginia, 200
Bourke, Joanna, 44, 107
Bourke, Mary. *see* Robinson, Mary
Boyd, Maureen, 119
Boylan, Misses, 52
Boyle, Anne, 98
Boyle, Jeannie, 83
Boyle, Maeve, 116, 117
Bradshaw, Sheila, 109
Bray (Co. Wicklow), 83
breast cancer, 202
Bree (Co. Wexford), 36, 70
Brennan, Garrett, 121
Britain, 147
    fascists, 114
    television, 235
Britannia (royal yacht), 184
British army, 164, 167, 168, 178, 181, 183,
    184
    Bloody Sunday (Derry, 1972), 170, 183
    First World War, 67, 71
British Broadcasting Company (BBC), 144
British Cabinet Office, 206
British Empire, 39, 79
British forces. *see also* British army
    women auxiliaries (First World War),
        68–9
    Women's Royal Air Force, 69
    Women's Royal Naval Service, 69,
        115–17
British government, 170
British Ladies Open Championship, 38–9
British Medical Association, 41
British Union of Fascists, 114
British Women's Amalgamated Unionist and
    Tariff Association, 61
Brook Clinic, 193, 226
Brookside, 235
brothels, 46
Brown, Rosemary. *see* Dana
Brown, Stephen, 214
Browne, Kathleen, 103
Browne, Dr Noel, 129
Brugha, Caitlín, 96

Brugha, Nodlaig, 96
Bryon, Catherine, 8
Buckley, Madge, 95
Budapest Congress, 65
Bundoran (Co. Donegal), 45
Burntollet Bridge (Derry), 163
Burton, Amanda, 235
business women, 211, 212
Butlin's Holiday Camps, 141
Byrne, Anne, 194–5
Byrne, Gay, 144
Byrne, Maggie, 19
Byrne, Margaret, 29
Byron, Catherine, 214

Cadets (showband), 140
Cadogan, Lady, 39
Caffrey, Chris, 74
Cahirciveen (Co. Kerry), 198
Caledon (Co. Tyrone), 162
Callaghan, Brenda, 230
Callaghan, Marie, 183
Campaign for Social Justice (CSJ), 160, 161
Campbell, Annie, *229*, 230
Campbell, Winifred, 67, 70, 90, 98, 109
Campile (Co. Wexford), 124
Canada, 33
Canary Wharf (London), 224
cancer, 201–2
Cappagh (Co. Waterford), 67
car ownership, 205
Carlow (town), 124
Carna (Co. Galway), 34
Carney, Winifred, 52, 79, 80
Carr, Anne, *229*, 230
Carrigan Committee, 104
Carson, Sir Edward, 56, 64
Carson, Jean, 181
Casey, Eamon, bishop of Galway, 216
Cassidy, Revd James, 29
Castle House (Lisburn), 64
Castle Townshend (Co. Cork), 31
Castlebar (Co. Mayo), 116
Castlereagh (Belfast), 164
casual labour, 46
Catholic Church, 5, 29, 63, 107, 113, 140, 187, 238. *see also* Catholics
    church-state relations (southern Ireland), 5, 110, 129, 150, 213–14
    contraception, attitude to, 105, 145
    dances, prohibitions on, 140
    decline in power of, 5, 216–17
    discipline of girls, and, 30
    divorce, and, 148, 190
    Dublin lockout (1913), and, 49
    Eucharistic Congress (1932), 108–9
    female religious. *see* religious sisters
    lay devotion, 215
    mass attendance, 216–17
    'modern woman', opposition to, 27
    Mother and Child scheme, and, 129
    moving statues phenomenon (1985), 215
    Ne temere decree (1907), 61, 63
    papal visit to Ireland (1979), 157
    religious vocations, decline in, 217
    republicans, and, 95
    scandals, 216
    Second Vatican Council, 145, 215
    sex abuse cases, 216
    sexual morality, concerns with, 5, 103–4
    special constitutional status, removal of, 150
    sportswomen, and, 7
    suffrage movement, and, 57
    supernatural phenomena, 215
    women, importance of, 108, 217
Catholic Girl Guides, 109
Catholic nationalism, 108
Catholic organisations, 109
Catholic Protection and Rescue Society, 107
Catholic schools, 47
Catholic Standard, 144
Catholics, 18, 22, 28, 29, 61, 108
    British services, in, 116, 117
    daily life (early 20th century), 38
    discrimination against, 83–4, 159–62.
        see also civil rights movement
    First World War casualties, 79
    Northern Ireland, 83–4, 86, 88, 97, 109, 136, 157, 159–62, 164
    pilgrimages to Lourdes, 108
    religious faith and practice, 108–9, 216–17
Cavan (county), 26, 89
Celtic heritage, 7, 111
Celtic Revival, 39, 59
Celtic spirituality, 108
Celtic Tiger, 5, 203
censorship, 104–5, 106, 144–5
Central Europe, 6
Centre Party, 113

Chamberlain, Elizabeth, 116
charitable institutions, 37
charitable work. *see* philanthropic work
Chenevix, Helen, 50, 54
CHERISH (Children Have Every Right in
    Society Here), 156
Chichester, Dehra (*later* Parker), 90, 91–2
Chichester Clark, Major James, 164
childbirth, 22–3, 197
childcare, 119, 152, 205, 206, 210
Childers, Molly, 64
children
    domestic and farm tasks, 26
    education, 25–7
    employment, 26
    illegitimate, 29, 104, 146, 194
    infant mortality, 23, 24, 25, 98, 197
    infanticide, 29–30, 198
    street-traders, 26
Chinese community (NI), 202, 204
Church-based organisations, 109
Church League for Women's Suffrage, 52
Church of Ireland, 91
    women priests and deacons, 217
Church of Ireland Girls' Friendly Society,
    109
church–state relations (southern Ireland), 5,
    150, 213–14
Church Street (Dublin), 19
cinema, 39, 110, 122
Civil and Public Services Union, 207
civil rights movement, 6, 153, 159–67
    Burntollet Bridge (1969), 163
    formation of NICRA (1967), 161–2
    housing protests, 160–2
civil service, 47
Civil War (1922–23), 86, 93–6, 166, 235,
    241
Clann na Poblachta, 129
Clannad, 235
Clar na mBan, 231
Clarke, Kathleen, 73, 76, 77, 84, 96
class. *see* social class
Clear, Catriona, 22, 107, 243
clerical employment, 47, 99
Clifden (Co. Galway), 21
Clinton, Hillary, 226
Clinton administration (USA), 228
Clonard (Belfast), 167
Clonbrock, Lady, 66
Clonbrook House (Co. Galway), iii

Clones (Co. Monaghan), 121–2
cloning, 2, 200
Clonmel (Co. Tipperary), 17
Cloughjordan (Co. Tipperary), 29
co-operative movement, 36
Cockburn, Cynthia, 159
cohabitation, 188
Coleman, Lily, 98
College of Surgeons, 74, 75
Collins, Michael, 84, 96
Collins, Molly, 110
Collins-O'Driscoll, Margaret, 96
Collis, Dr, 116
Combe Barbours (Belfast), 84
Combined Loyalist Military Command, 224
Comerford, Máire, 75, 83, 94
Commission on the Status of Women, 152,
    242
communications, 4, 21, 138
communism, 112, 114
Communist Party of Ireland, 112
Communist Party of Northern Ireland, 133
community politics, 6–7, 225
    Northern Ireland, 225–32
    Republic of Ireland, 226–7
    Vital Voices seminars, 228
Concannon, Helena, 101
conflict, 241. *see also* Civil War; Easter
        Rising (1916); First World War;
        Northern conflict; Second World War;
        War of Independence
Congested Districts Board, 20, 37
Conlon, Giuseppi, 221
Connell, K.H., 133
Connolly, James, 46, 48, 72, 76
Connolly, Linda, 151, 152
Connolly, Nora, 76, 77
Connolly, Sean, 38
Conrad, Kathryn, 147
Conroy, Sheila, 118
conscription, 77
Conservative and Unionist Women's
        Franchise Association, 52
Conservative governments, 213, 220
Constabulary Bill (1922), 91
Constitution of Ireland, 1937
    anti-abortion amendment (1983),
        197–8
    Catholic Church's special position,
        removal of, 150
    divorce ban, removal of, 190–1

women, articles affecting, 101–2
Constitution of the Irish Free State (1922), 100
consumer-based culture, 141, 244
contraception, 13, 103–6, 129, 145, 150, 151, 153, 154, 155, 193. *see also* family planning
  Catholic attitudes, 105, 145
  IWLM train trip to Belfast (1971), 154, 155
  liberalisation of laws, 158
  papal encylical (1968), 145
  prohibition and censorship, 104–5, 145
  Protestant attitudes, 105–6
Contraception Action Programme (CAP), 156
Cooke, H.W., 124
Coombe Hospital (Dublin), 131
Cope, M.E., 58
Corbally, Catherine, 119
Corbally, Mary, 46
Cork, 16, 17, 25, 26, 31, 38, 43, 44, 81, 83, 94, 118, 131, 133, 148
  children street-traders, 26
  Deanrock estate, 203
  electric tramway system, 21
  Jewish population, 116
  lesbian networks, 196
Cork Child Welfare League, 24
Cork Examiner, 30
Coronation Street, 235
Corrigan Maguire, Mairead, 183, 184, 220, 241
Corrs, the, 235
Cosgrave, William, 95
cost of living
  prices, 1939 and 1951, 133
Costello, John A., 129
Coughlan, Mary, 235
Coulter, Carol, 187
Council for the Status of Women (CSW), 153, 191, 233
Courtmacsherry, 215
Cousins, Margaret, 54
Coyle, Eithne, 94, 96
Craig, Cecil, 92, 93
Craig, James, 61, 92
Craigavon (Co. Armagh), 212
Craigavon Asian Women and Children's Association, 204
Cranwill, Mia, 111

Crawford, Martha, 183
Creeslaugh, 94
Cregagh, 127
Creggan (Derry), 182
Criminal Law Amendment Act (1923), 103
Criminal Law Amendment Act (1935), 103, 105
Croke Park (Dublin)
  Bloody Sunday (1920), 83
Crone, Joni, 147, 196
Cronin, Maura, 43
Crookshank, Anne, 111
Crooksling (Co. Wicklow), 40
crossroads dancing, 40
Crowley, Elaine, 115
Crumlin Road jail (Belfast), 176
cubism, 7, 111
Cullen, Mary, 10
Cullen, Paul, 205
cultural heritage
  loyalists, 223–4
  women's contribution, 214
cultural renaissance, 39
Cumann na mBan, 33, 79, 80, 82, 89, 94, 96, 174, 178
  Easter Rising, involvement in, 72, 73, 77
  formation (1914), 60
  outlawing of, by Northern Parliament (1922), 90
  recruitment, 172
  'A song for Cumann na mBan, June 1916', 78
  suffrage movement, and, 60
  Treaty (1921), opposition to, 86
Cumann na nGaedheal, 96, 100, 113
Cumann na Saoirse (Society of Freedom), 86
Cummins, Mary, 143, 226
CURA, 199
Curragh (Co. Kildare)
  internment, 126
Curran, Margaret, 169
Currie, Austin, 162
cycling clubs, 39–40

Dáil Éireann, 2, 6, 86, 96, 101
  First Dáil, 80
  Second Dáil, 84, 85
  Treaty debates (1921–22), 84–6
  women deputies, 6, 80, 84, 96, 149–50, 232–4

women's franchise, 86
daily life
early 20th century, 21–42
First World War, during, 69–70
Dalaigh, May, 94
Daly, Madge, 94
Daly, Mary, 10, 42, 44, 47, 87, 99, 130, 142
Dana (Rosemary Scanlon), 141, *187*, 237
dancing, 38, 106–7, 110
Catholic Church attitudes, 140
dance halls legislation, 106–7
Darby O'Gill and the Little People (film, 1959), 142
Darlington, 171
De Brún, Bairbre, 232
De Valera, Eamon, 73, 95, 96, 134
Constitution of Ireland (1937), and, 101
declaration of Irish Republic (1949), 132
Deane, Seamus, 8
Dear Daughter (RTÉ documentary, 1996), 216
death rates, 42, 201
class factors, 202
infant mortality, 3, 23–4, 25, 98, 197
tuberculosis, 40, 41
Democratic Dialogue, 227
Democratic Left, 228
Democratic Unionist Party (DUP), 147, 231
demographic change, 143
Denton, Baroness Jean, 227
Department of Agriculture and Technical Instruction, 36, 47
Department of Public Enterprise, 207
Department of Social, Community and Family Affairs, 205
Department of the Environment, 204
Deraniyagala, Ezlynn, 151
Derry, 2, 44, 116, 181
Battle of the Bogside (1969), 166
Bloody Sunday (1972), 170
car bombs, 170
'Free Derry', 162
German air raids, 123
housing problems, 159, 162
internment (Second World War), 126
naval base, 115–17
peace petition (1972), 182
peace rallies, 183
riots, 164
Rossville Flats, 162
shirt–making, 42, 97

Derry Citizens' Action Committee, 162
Derry Housing Action Committee, 162
Derry Peace Women, 181
Derry Women's Aid, 179
deserted wives, 148, 153, 156
Desmond, Eileen, 232–3
Despard, Charlotte, 112
Devlin, Bernadette (*later* McAliskey), 149, 164–7, 168, 170, 184, 188, 241
Devlin, Edith, 108–9, 120
Devlin, Joseph, 90
diabetes, 201
Dietrich, Marlene, 117
Dillon, Lady Augusta Caroline, *ii*
Dillon, Edith, *ii*
Dillon, Ethel, *ii*
Dillon, Michele, 191
Dingle, Billy, 121
disabilities, women with, 202
discrimination. *see also* religious discrimination; sexual discrimination
Travelling community, 244
diseases
AIDS, 193
cancer, 201–2
tuberculosis, 40–1, 129
Disney, Walt, 142
dissident republicans, 224–5
divorce, 147–148, 189, 243
constitutional ban, removal of, 190–1
Divorce Action group, 190
doctors, 47
Doherty, Eileen, 162
Doherty, Richard, 116, 124
domestic economy, 25–6, 36
itinerant teachers, 36
domestic servants, 16–17, 29, 44–5, 99
domestic violence, 30, 148, 155, 156, 179, 191–3, 242
Women's Aid centres, 156, 179
domestic work. *see* housework
Donegal (county), 67, 89, 116
herring industry, 45
outworkers, 42–3
Donegall Place (Belfast), 53
Donnell, Winston, 168
Doolan, Lelia, 153
Dooley, Mary Rose, 116
Dorcey, Mary, 135, 147
Down (county), 36, 164, 209
Downing, Sheila, 112

Downtown Women's Centre (Belfast), 226
Doyle, Mary, 219
drama, 39
Drapers' Assistants Association, 48
Dreaper, Florrie, 83
drinking, 40
Dripsey, 83
Drogheda (Co. Louth)
  papal visit (1979), 157
Dromore, 43
Drumcree (Portadown)
  parade dispute, 224
Drumm, Maire, 173, 174
drunkenness, 40
Dublin, 16, 26, 35, 38, 44, 57, 60, 71, 86, 93,
    146, 183. *see also* Alexandra College;
    Phoenix Park; Trinity College Dublin
  AIM group, 156
  Bloody Sunday (1920), 83
  Coombe Hospital, 131
  Easter Rising (1916), 72–7
  Emergency period, 121
  Eucharistic Congress (1932), 108–9
  family planning clinics, 145
  Fatima Mansions, 203
  General Post Office, 73
  German air raids, 124
  homelessness, 204, 215
  housing, 18–20, 35
  Hugh Lane Municipal Art Gallery, 7, 39
  infant mortality, 19
  Irish Pregnancy Counselling Centre, 156
  Jewish population, 116
  lesbian networks, 196
  Liberties, 131
  lockout (1913), 49–50, 60
  Monto area, 46
  mother and baby clubs, 24
  New Year's Day (1900), 15–16
  papal visit (1979), 157
  population (1911), 16
  poverty, 18–19, 19
  prostitution, 46, 213
  royal visit (1900), 14–15
  street traders, 19, 26
  suffrage campaign, 52, 65
  tenements, 18, 19, 35
  VE Day (1945), 126
Dublin Corporation, 15
Dublin Fusiliers, 71
Dublin Metropolitan School of Art, 27

Dublin United Arts Club, 39
Dudley, Lady, 39
Dufferin and Ava, Dowager Marchioness of,
    62–3
Duffin, Emma, 17, 68, 69, 122, 123, 126
Duffin, Ruth, 17
Dun Emer Guild, 111
Duncan, Ellen, 39
Dungannon (Co. Tyrone), 39
  housing protest, 159, 160–1
Dungannon District Council, 161
Dungannon Observer, 163
Dungiven (Co. Derry), 209
Dunn, Hester, 221
Dunn, Nell, 146
Dunphy, Eamon, 236
Durham prison, 173
Dylan, Bob, 138

Easter Rising (1916), 67, 71, 72–9, 85, 166,
    241
  aftermath, 77–9
  civilian life, 74–5
  execution of leaders, 76
  prisoners, 76, 77
  women's involvement, 72–5
Eastern Europe, 6, 205
Eccles Street (Dublin)
  Dominican convent, 27
Edgerton, Lynda, 177
Edinburgh, Duke of
  visit to Northern Ireland (1977), 184
education, 4, 25–7, 36, 38, 108, 211
  academic and university, 4, 27, 28
  domestic economy, 25, 36
  farm demonstrations, 36
  health issues, 41
  itinerant teachers, 36
  ladies' seminaries, 26
  Northern Ireland, 128
  Sunday schools, 38, 109, 110
  vocational, 25
Egypt, 67, 68
Éire. *see* Irish Free State; Republic of Ireland
Eironline, 207
elderly, 200–1
  pensions, 42
elections (1918), 79–80
electric tramways, 21
Electricity Supply Board, 130
electrification, 130

Elizabeth II, 238
coronation celebrations (1953), 135–6
visit to Northern Ireland (1977), 184
Emergency (1939–45), 115, 120–2, 124, 126
German air raids, 124
Emergency Council of Suffragists, 65
emigration, 3, 33–5, 107, 132, 135, 143, 189
American money, 35
religious sisters, 33
'self-dowered returners', 34
Emmerdale, 235
Empire Theatre (Belfast), 122
employment, 4–5, 42–50, 141, 202, 206–13
agriculture, 45–6, 99, 209–10, 243
businesswomen, 211, 212
casual labour, 46
civil service, 47
clerical work, 47, 99
conditions of work, 43–5
domestic service, 44–5, 99
educational achievement, and, 211
equal opportunities, 212
equal treatment, 152–3, 177, 207, 208,
212
factory work, 42–3, 71
farm workers, 45, 209–10
First World War, during, 67–71
fishing industry, 45
flexible workforce, 210
linen industry, 43, 70
married women, 5, 50, 99–100, 141–3,
210
medical doctors, 47
nursing, 44
opportunities for women, 5, 17, 44–5,
47, 70
outdoor relief, 98
outworkers, 42–3
part-time working, 141–2, 210
professions, 44, 47–8
promotion prospects, 211, 212
prostitution, 46, 103, 121, 213
religious discrimination, 208
retail trade, 45, 48
seaside resorts, 45
Second World War, during, 115–19
service sector, 208–9
sexual discrimination, 152, 207, 212
street traders, 19, 26
teaching, 44
teleworking, 209

textile industry, 42–3
trade union organisation, 48, 213
unemployment, 97–9
war work, 67–9, 115–19
women's work, underevaluation of, 243
Employment Act (1935), 100
England, 61
Irish immigrants, 33
peace rallies, 183
English, James, 67
entertainment, 38, 39–40, 121, 122. *see also*
arts; cinema; dancing; literature;
television
opera, 39
radio, 110
Enya, 235
equal opportunities, 177, 212
Equal Opportunities Commission for
Northern Ireland (EOC), 177–8, 207
equal pay, 152, 153, 177, 210
Northern Ireland, 177, 207
equal rights, 153. *see also* civil rights
movement
Equality Commission for Northern Ireland,
232
equality legislation
Northern Ireland, 207
Republic of Ireland, 152–3
ethnic minorities, 6, 204–5, 244. *see also*
Traveller communities
health-care services, access to, 202
Eton College (England), 111
Eucharistic Congress (Dublin, 1932),
108–9
European Commission, 2
European Court of Human Rights, 147,
179, 196
European Economic Community (EEC),
136, 141, 143, 152. *see also* European
Union
Ireland's membership of, 143
European Parliament, 234
European Union (EU), 243
effects of membership, 4
sexual attitudes, effects on, 195–6
Eurovision Song Contest (1970), 141
Evans, Dorothy, 56, 64
Evason, Eileen, 146, 195
evictions, 15
Ewart's factory (Belfast), 99
excursions, 38

Fair City (RTÉ), 235
Fair Employment Agency, 208
Fairyhouse (Co. Meath), 72
Fallon, Brian, 108
Falls Road (Belfast), 38, 48, 167, 181, 184, 225
family budget, control of, 197
family holidays, 141
Family Home Protection Act (1976), 156
family law, 156
family meals, 205
family planning, 103–6, 145–6, 158, 242. *see also* abortion; contraception
    advice clinics, 106, 145–6, 193–4
    ambivalence or passivity, 194
    Catholic attitudes, 105, 145
    Health (Family Planning) Act (1979), 158
    Protestant attitudes, 105–6
family size, 3, 22, 197
Family Solidarity, 190
farm children, 25–6
farm education, 36
farm ownership, 21
farm servants, 44–5
farm women, 45–6, 99, 209–10
farm workers, 45, 209, 210
Farmar, Tony, 23
Farrell, Mairead, 176, 219
fascism, 107, 113, 114, 115
fashion, 138
Father Ted, 235
Fearon, Kate, *229*, 230
Feeney, Mary, 33
Feldman, Allen, 167
female activism. *see* political activism; public activism; suffrage campaigns
female drunkenness, 40
female employment. *see* employment
female entertainers, 140, 235
female graduates, 27
female journalists, 143
The Female Line (1985), 214
female philanthropy, 37
female political organisations
    nationalist, 59–60
    unionist, 60–64
female religious. *see* religious sisters
female suffrage. *see* suffrage campaigns
feminism, 158, 242. *see also* women's history; women's movement
    community politics, 225, 227

First World War, and, 65–6
    frictions, 238
    international co-operation, 65
    partition, and, 238
    political activism. *see* political activism; representative politics; suffrage campaigns
    republicanism, and, 179
    second-wave feminists, 1–2, 8, 242
    unionism, and, 179–80
The Feminist Mystique (Friedan, 1963), 107
Fennell, Nuala, 143, 153, 154, 233
Fermanagh (county), 126
    housing allocations, 128
Fermoy (Co. Cork), 17
fertility treatments, 200
Fianna Éireann, 85
Fianna Fáil, 96, 100, 113, 115, 129, 148, 233, 234
    ard fheis (1937), 101
    general elections (1977), 149–50
    outlawing of, by Northern Parliament (1922), 90
Field Day Anthology of Irish Writing (1991), 8, 214
films, 39, 142
    censorship, 106
    film stars, 141
Finaghy, 127
Fine Gael, 191, 198, 233
    formation (1933), 113
Fingall, Elizabeth, Countess of, 15, 70
First Aid Nursing Yeomanry (FANY), 68
first-wave feminism, 242
First World War (1914–18), 6, 26, 31, 65, 77, 97, 115, 151, 240
    Battle of the Somme (1916), 71
    casualties, 71, 79
    civilian life, 69–70
    conscription attempts, 77
    female employment, 67–71
    female suffrage campaign, and, 65–6
    Messines war memorial, 238
    nurses, 67–8, 69
    recruitment from Ulster, 67
    war relief work, 66
    women's auxiliary services, 68–9
Fisherwick Presbyterian Church (Belfast), 183
fishing industry, 45
Fitzgerald, Frances, 233

FitzGerald, Garret, 222
Fitzpatrick, David, 94
Flanagan, Maeve, 140, 145, 158, 185
flexible workforce, 210
Flinn, Fr Joseph, SJ, 106
Focus Ireland, 215
Foley, Bridget, 72, 76
folk music, 141
Ford, John, 142
Ford, Patricia, 149, 181
Forrest, Anna, 164
Fórsa Cosanta Áituíl (FCA), 212
Four Courts (Dublin), 94
Fourth World Conference for Women
    (Beijing, 1995), 239
Fowler, Joan, 8
Fox, Eileen, 144
Foynes (Wexford), 70
France, 17, 66, 67, 68, 71, 115
franchise
    municipal, 54
    parliamentary. see suffrage campaigns
Francis, Connie, 140
'Free Derry', 162
Free Legal Aid Scheme, 156
Free Presbyterian Church, 148
Free State. see Irish Free State
freezers, 141
fridges, 141
Friedan, Betty
    The Feminist Mystique (1963), 107
Friends of Soviet Russia, 112
Friends of the Soviet Union, 113
Fry, Elizabeth, 144

Gaelic League, 39, 76, 80
Gallaher's factory (Belfast), 244
Galligan, Yvonne, 150, 239
Gallipoli, 71, 75
Galvin, Sheila, 148
Galway, 16, 20, 21, 30, 35, 112, 140, 217
    lesbian networks, 196
    papal visit (1979), 157
Galway, Mary, 48
Galway County Temperance Association, 66
Garda Síochána, 193
    Kerry babies case (1984), 198
Garvaghy Road (Portadown), 223–4
Gavan, Tish, 39
Gay Community News, 196
gay rights, 147, 196

The General's Daughter (film), 39
Geoghegan-Quinn, Máire, 150, 233
George Medal, 124
Germany, 17, 106. see also Second World
    War
    Adolf Hitler, 114
    air raids, 122–4
    Belfast blitz (1941), 122–3
    concentration camps, 116
    female deputies, 232
    First World War (1914–18), 65
    Nazism, 116
GI brides, 124
Gifford, Grace, 27, 76
Gifford, Nellie, 77
Girls' Brigade, 109
Glasgow (Scotland), 29
glass ceiling, 211
Gleeson, Evelyn, 111
Glenn, Alice, 191
Glenroe (RTÉ), 235
Glin, Knight of, 111
Gloucester, Duke of, 104
Goldenbridge orphanage (Dublin), 216
golf, 38
Gonne, Maud, 14–15, 59, 85
Good Friday Agreement (1998), 224,
    231–2
Gordon, Hazel, 223, 224
Gore-Knapp, Helga, 31
Gospel halls, 110
Gould, Martha, 163
Goulding, June, 131
Government of Ireland Bill, 1920, 80
Grafton Street (Dublin), 74
gramophones, 110
Granard (Co. Longford), 198
Grand Opera House (Belfast), 39
Gray, John, 43
Grealis-Guglich, Bridget, 132
Great Blasket Island (Co. Kerry), 20, 108
Great War (1914–18). see First World War
Greeley, Andrew, 218
Greer, Diane, 230
Greer, Germaine, 153
Gregory, Lady, 39
Grehan, Cecily, 22
Grenan, Julia, 73
Gresham Hotel (Dublin), 121
Gribben, Gerry, 230
Griffith, Arthur, 86

Grosvenor Road (Belfast), 127
Group 84, 229
Guardian, 207
Guildford Four, 222
Guildford (Surrey), 221
Guinness Brewery, 47
Guthrie, Nurse (Limerick), 94

Hague Conference, 65
Hall, Mandie, 207
Hamill, Mr, 62
Hanaphy, May, 93
Hardy's School, 26–7
Harkin, Patricia, 129
Harnett, Dorothy, 114
Harney, Mary, 233
Hartney, Sarah, 21–2
Hawkin, Chrissie, 18
Hayden, Mary, 27, 100
Hayes, Joanne, 198
health. *see also* diseases; family planning
    access difficulties, 202
    ageing, 200–1
    childbirth, 22–3, 197
    class factors, 202
    disabilities, women with, 202
    education, 23–4, 41
    hazards, 40–1
    insurance, 42
    mortality rates. *see* death rates
    National Health Service (NHS), 128
    post-Second World War reforms, 128–9
    reforms, 158
    visitors, 23
    women's health, 193, 197–202
    Women's National Health Association,
        23–4
Healy, Mary, 203
Healy, Mrs, 24
Healy, T. M., 56
Hearn, Mona, 29
Heatherside (Cork), 40
Heathfield (England), 17
Helsinki Olympics (1952), 102
Hendrix, Jimi, 139
Henry, Mary, 229
Hermon, Sir John, 212
herring industry, 45
Hibernian Journal, 89–90
Hibernians, 89–90
Hickey, Eileen, 176

Hill, Noreen, 119, 131
Hillsborough (Co. Down), 21, 184
Hinds, Bronagh, 230
history. *see* women's history
Hitler, Adolf, 114
Hitlerism, 118
holidays, 38, 99, 141
Holland
    female deputies, 232
Holland, Mary, 107, 165, 236
Hollywood (California), 39, 141
Holywood (Co. Down), 118
Holy Year (1900), 15
home environment, 16–21, 202–6. *see also*
    housing
home ownership, 16, 202–3
Home Rule, 3, 53, 54, 57, 58, 59, 60, 61, 62,
    63, 67, 79
Homeless Citizens' League (HCL), 160, 161
homelessness, 203–4, 215
homophobia, 196
homosexuality, 147, 150
    decriminalisation, 195–6
Hone, Evie, 7, 111
Hooley, Ruth, 8, 214
Hope, Ann, 167, 210
Hopkins, Thelma, 102
House of Commons (Westminster), 80, 149,
    170
    women members, 92, 149
housework, 35–6, 107–8, 205–6, 209, 243
    education in, 36–7
    labour–saving devices, 141, 205
    washing, 35–6
housewives, 141, 197
housing, 17–21
    Belfast, 17–18, 126–8
    discrimination, 159–62
    Dublin, 18–20
    health, and, 42
    Northern Ireland, 17–18, 126–8,
        159–62
    post-Second World War, 126–8
    rural areas, 20–21
    standards, 17–21, 203
Housing Act (1908), 18
Howth (Co. Dublin)
    gun-running (1914), 64
Hoy, Sue Ellen, 33
Hugh Lane Municipal Art Gallery (Dublin),
    7, 39

Hughes, Sheila, 122
Humphreys, Síghle, 169
Humphries, Sheila, 96
hunger strikes
  republicans, 84, 219–20
  suffragettes, 56, 58
Hussey, Gemma, 150, 233
Huston, Felicity, 230
Hutchinson, Elizabeth, 53
Hyde, Abbey, 194
hygiene, 35

ICA. see Irish Countrywomen's Association
ICTU. see Irish Congress of Trade Unions
IHA. see Irish Housewives' Association
illegitimate children, 29, 104, 146
  removal of 'illegitimacy' status, 194
illiteracy, 4
immigration, 205
India, 17
Indian community, 202, 204
industrial disputes. see trade disputes
Industries Association, 39
infant mortality, 3, 23–4, 25, 98–9, 197
infanticide, 29–30, 198
Inghinidhe na hÉireann (Daughters of
  Ireland), 59–60, 85
Inglis, Tom, 217, 218
inter-church marriages, 188–9
  Ne temere decree (1907), 61, 63
International Alliance of Women (IAW),
  151–2
International Committee of Women for
  Permanent Peace, 65
International Congress of Women for Peace
  and Freedom, 82
International Eucharistic Congress (Dublin,
  1932), 108–9
International Women's Day
  1975, 182
  1993, 226
International Women's Suffrage Alliance, 65
internment, 126, 167–9, 175, 176, 177
Intoxicating Liquors (Ireland) Act (1902), 40
IPP. see Irish Parliamentary Party
IRA (Irish Republican Army), 80, 94, 96,
  112, 164, 189. see also Northern conflict;
  Official IRA; Provisional IRA;
  republican movement
  bombing campaigns, 171, 222
  female volunteers, 172–4

internment, 126, 167
  outlawing of, by Northern Parliament
    (1922), 90
  War of Independence (1919–21), 80, 81,
    83
IRB (Irish Republican Brotherhood), 77
Ireland Act (1949), 132
Irish-Americans, 34, 77, 142
Irish Association of Women Graduates and
  Candidate Graduates, 27
Irish Aviation Authority, 207
Irish Catholic Women's Suffrage Society, 52
Irish Citizen, 30, 47, 54, 55, 56
Irish Citizen Army, 60, 72, 79, 85
Irish Congress of Trade Unions (ICTU),
  210, 213
  Northern Ireland Committee, 232
Irish Countrywomen's Association (ICA),
  36, 73, 79, 120, 121, 154
Irish Exhibition of Living Art, 111
Irish Family League, 190
Irish Family Planning Association, 145
Irish Free State, 6, 7, 84, 88, 93, 96, 99, 106,
  108, 118, 120
  abortion, 104–5
  age of consent, 103
  Catholic Church influence, 129
  censorship, 104–5, 106
  Civil War (1922–23), 86, 93–6
  conservatism, 102
  Constitution (1922), 100
  Constitution (1937), 100–2
  contraception and family planning,
    103–6, 129
  Criminal Law Amendment Act (1935),
    103, 105
  dance halls legislation, 106
  economic stagnation, 99
  Emergency period (1939–45), 115,
    120–2, 124, 126
  employment legislation, 100
  establishment of state (1922), 86
  female employment, 99–100
  health reforms, 129
  political parties, 96
  Protestants, 86
  radio (2RN), 110
  religious and cultural values, 102
  sexual assault legislation, 103
  sportswomen, 102
  unemployment, 99

women in politics, 96
women's role, 100–2
Irish Gay Rights Movement, 147
Irish Housewives' Association (IHA),
    120–1, 151, 152
Irish Housewives' Committee, 120–1
Irish Journal of Feminist Studies, 236
Irish language, 39, 59
Irish Medical Association, 129
Irish Messenger of the Sacred Heart, 102
Irish Monthly, 22
Irish News, 136, 139, 207, 244
Irish News and Belfast Morning News, 14, 30,
    135
Irish Parliamentary Party (IPP), 53, 63, 80
Irish Post, 222
Irish Pregnancy Care Service, 199
Irish Pregnancy Counselling Centre
    (Dublin), 156
Irish Press, 143, 148, 185
Irish Republic. *see* Republic of Ireland
Irish Republican Army. *see* IRA
Irish Republican Brotherhood (IRB), 73
Irish Suffrage Societies, 56
Irish Tatler and Sketch, 121
Irish Times, 14, 16, 30, 102, 143, 157, 161,
    184, 234, 236
    'Women First' section, 158
Irish Tommies, 67
Irish Trade Union Congress, 77
Irish Transport and General Workers' Union
    (ITGWU), 49
Irish Volunteers, 60, 72, 73
Irish Women Citizens' Association (IWCA),
    100, 121
Irish Women Workers' Union (IWWU),
    48–9, 50, 77, 100, 113–14
Irish Women's Aid Committee, 156
Irish Women's Centre (London), 221
Irish Women's Civic Federation, 89
Irish Women's Franchise League (IWFL), 54,
    55, 57, 79
Irish Women's Liberation Movement
    (IWLM), 151, 153–4, 158, 185, 233
    contraceptives protest, 155
    launch (1971), 154
Irish Women's Suffrage and Local
    Government Association (IWSLGA), 52,
    55, 100
Irish Women's Suffrage Federation (IWSF),
    54, 65

Irish Worker, 50
Irishwomen United (IWU), 156
Irishwomen's International League, 100
Irregulars, 93–4
Irwin, Florence, 36
itinerant teachers, 36
IWCA. *see* Irish Women Citizens' Association
IWFL. *see* Irish Women's Franchise League
IWLM. *see* Irish Women's Liberation
    Movement
IWSF. *see* Irish Women's Suffrage Federation
IWSLGA. *see* Irish Women's Suffrage and
    Local Government Association

Jackie, 138
Jackson, Pauline, 178–9, 200
Jacob, Rosamund, 112, 113
Jacob's Biscuit Factory (Dublin), 43, 93
Janeway, Elizabeth, 13
Jay, Margaret, 208
jazz, 106, 141
The Jazz Singer (film), 110
jeans, 138
Jeffery, Keith, 67
Jellett, Mainie, 7, 111
Jews, 116
John Paul II, Pope
    visit to Ireland (1979), 157
Johnson, Marie A., 52
Johnson, Miss, 61
Johnston, Jennifer, 214
Joint Committee of Women's Societies and
    Social Workers, 103
Jolson, Al
    The Jazz Singer, 110
Jones, Mary, 237
Jones, Maxine, 211
Jordan, Alison, 37
Jordanstown, 228
journalists, 143
Judge, Yvonne, 102
jury service, 103

Kavanagh, Hannah, 29
Kavanagh, Mrs, 52
Kearney, S., 135
Kearns, Linda, 96
Kelly, A.A.
    Pillars of the House, 214
Kelly, Eileen, 140
Kelly, Maeve, 214

Kennedy, Brian, 7–8
Kennedy, Finola, 191
Kennedy, John F., 142
Kennedy, Robert, 31, 42
Kennedy, Robert E., Jr., 31
Kennedy, Sr Stanislaus, 215
Kenny, Máirín, 204
Kenny, Mary, 21, 143, 145, 153–4, 157, 185
Keogh, Dermot, 116, 119, 140
Keogh, Margaretta, 73
Kerrigan, Gene, 131
Kerry, 20
Kerry babies case (1984), 198, 226
Kilkeel (Co. Down), 114
Kilkenny Social Services Group, 215
Killiney (Co. Dublin), 183
Killyleagh (Co. Down), 66
Kilmainham Gaol (Dublin), 94
Kilmurray, Avila, 228, 230
Kiltallagh (Co. Kerry), 94
Kimball, Solon T., 16
Kingstown (Dublin), 14
Knock (Co. Mayo)
    marian shrine, 108
    papal visit (1979), 157
Knox, Billy, 98

Labour Court, 207
labour force, 44. see also employment
labour movement, 48–50, 52, 112. see also
    trade unions
Labour Party (Ireland), 53, 96, 222, 232,
    234, 237
Labour Party (UK), 228
Labour Report Survey (1997), 210
labour-saving devices, 141, 205
Ladies Cheltenham College (England), 27
ladies' seminaries, 26
Lady Chatterley's Lover, 145
Lagerkvist, Amanda, 152
Lambeg drums, 223
Lambeth Conference (1930), 105
Lambkin, Romie, 117
Land Acts, 21
Lankford, Siobhán, 80, 81, 94, 95
Larkin, Delia, 40, 49, 50
Larkin, Jim, 48
Larmour, Sandra Ruth, 103
Larne (Co. Antrim), 64, 223
The Late Late Show (RTÉ), 144, 185, 196
    homosexuality debate (1989), 196

launch of IWLM (1971), 154
Laurencetown (Co. Wexford), 70
lawyers, 47
Lee, Brenda, 140
Lee, Simon, 147
left-wing movements, 112, 185. see also
    communism; labour movement
legal aid, 156
legal profession, 47
Legion of Mary, 108, 109, 119
Leinster House (Dublin), 233
leisure and social activities, 38–40, 138–41.
    see also cinema; dancing; music; radio;
    sporting activities; television
    church-based activities, 108, 109–10
    cultural interests, 39
    cycling clubs, 39–40
    drinking, 40
    entertainment, 39, 40
    excursions and holidays, 38, 141
    Second World War, during, 121–2,
        124–5
    social élite, 17, 38–9
    wakes and weddings, 40
Leitrim (Mourne country, Co. Down), 45
Lemass, Sean, 163
Lenadoon (Belfast), 171
Lenehan, Cecil, 181–2
Lenihan, Brian, 234
Lenin School (Moscow), 112
Lentin, Louis, 216
Leo VIII, Pope, 15
Leonard, Madeleine, 206
Lesbian Line, 226
lesbians, 32, 147, 156, 196
Lesbians Organizing Together (LOT), 196
Lett, Anita, 36
Levine, June, 153
Lewis, Helen, 116
Leydesdorff, Salma, 10
Liberal government, 42, 53
Liberal Party, 52, 53, 56, 149
Liberation for Irish Lesbians, 147
Liberties (Dublin), 29, 131
LIFE, 199
life expectancy, 3, 4, 25, 42. see also death
    rates
Limerick, 16, 29, 44, 58, 94, 212
    Jewish population, 116
    papal visit (1979), 157
    prison, 173

Lindsay, Mrs, 83
linen industry, 43, 48, 70, 119
Lisburn Poor Law Union, 37
Lisburn Suffrage Society, 54
literature, 8, 39
    women's writing, 8, 10, 214
Living Art Exhibition (1940s), 7–8
living standards, 13, 17–21, 202–6
Loach, Ken
    Up the Junction, 146
local authority housing, 203
local government
    female representation, 54
Logue, Margaret, 230
London, 57, 107, 146
    coronation celebrations (1953), 136
    German air raids, 124
    IRA bombing, 224
London Armagh Group, 221
Londonderry, Lady Edith, 39, 68, 79, 92–3,
    114
Long Kesh prison, 219
Longford Street (Dublin), 74
Lough Foyle, 116
Loughrea (Co. Donegal), 134
Louise Products Ltd (Co. Antrim), 207
Lourdes (France), 108
Louth (county), 212
Lovett, Ann, 198
Loyalist Association of Workers, 174
loyalists, 6, 14, 35, 61, 64–5, 222–3. see also
    Northern conflict; Progressive
    Unionist Party; Ulster Defence
    Association; Ulster Volunteer Force
    Anglo-Irish Agreement, and, 222
    assassinations, 171
    car bombs, 170
    ceasefire (1994), 224
    community politics, 225–6
    cultural heritage, defence of, 223–4
    gun-running, 64–5
    identity crisis, 223
    prisoners' families, 190
    sectarianism, 223
    UWC strike (1974), 171–2
    women volunteers, 171, 174
Lurgan (Co. Armagh), 43, 225
    Jewish population, 116
    Orangeman, 71
Lurgan Women's Unionist Association, 61
luxury goods, 205

Lynch, Sr Concepta, 111
Lynch, Dolores, 213
Lynch, John, 17–18, 40, 213
Lynch, Patricia, 73

McAleese, Mary, 187, 226, 237–9, 242
    Building Bridges theme, 237
    election as president (1997), 237
McAliskey, Bernadette Devlin. see Devlin,
    Bernadette
McAllister, Anne, 154–5
MacArdle, Dorothy, 96
McBeal, Ally, 235
McCafferty, Nell, 143, 153, 156, 162, 219
    and Kerry babies case (1984), 198
McCaffery, Lawrence, 34
McCann, Anne, 230
McCartan, Joyce, 177, 226
McCluskey, Conn, 160, 161, 163
McCluskey, Patricia, 160, 161, 163
McCormack, Inez, 163, 167
McCormack, John, 108, 110
McCracken, L.A.M. Priestly, 64
McCracken, Mrs, 52
McCullough, Elizabeth, 71, 122
McCullough, Isobel, 223
MacCurtain, Margaret, 10, 108, 215
McCusker, Breege, 114
McDaniel, Maisie, 140
MacDonald, Ramsay, 93
McDowell, Florence Mary, 26
Macedonia, 68
McGarry, Fearghal, 113
McGibbon, Vicky, 127
McGovern, Catherine, 124
McGuckian, Medbh, 8, 214
McGuinness, Dodie, 163
McKay, Susan, 166, 209
    Northern Protestants: An Unsettled People,
    223
McKee, Liz, 175
Macken, Mary, 100
McKiernan, Joan, 179
Mackie's Foundry (Belfast), 71, 83
MacLaran, Pauline, 214
McLaughlin, Eithne, 193
McLaughlin, Florence, 149
McLaughlin & Harvey's (Belfast), 84
McLeod, Hugh, 109
McLynn, Pauline, 235
McManus, Kathleen, 241

McMinn, Jean, 171–2
McMordie, Julia, 90–1
McNabb, Dinah, 149
McNamara, Sarah, 70
Maconachie, Elizabeth, 149
MacRory, Cardinal Joseph, Archbishop of
    Armagh, 107
McShane, Liz, 119
Mac Stiofáin, Sean, 173
MacSwiney, Mary, 59, 82, 84, 85, 94, 95, 96
MacSwiney, Terence, 84
McWilliams, Monica, 178, 179, 180, 228,
    229, 230, 231, 241
Madden, Kathleen, 213
Madden, Lyn, 213
Madonna, 235
magazines, 110, 138
Maghaberry prison, 220
Magill, 187
Maguire, Anne, 183
Maguire, Annie, 221–2
Maguire, Dorothy, 174
Maguire, Maria, 173
Maguire Seven, 221
Maher, Mary, 153
Mahon, Evelyn, 129
Mallow (Co. Cork), 81
Maloney, Doreen, 121
Malta, 67
Manchester (England), 176
Manning, Georgina, 58
Mansfield, Jayne, 141
Mansion House (Dublin), 154
Marconi, 21
Marian shrines, 108, 215
Markievicz, Countess (Constance Gore-
    Booth), 29–30, 50, 52, 80, 85, 96, 150
    Anglo-Irish Treaty, and, 84
    death (1927), 96
    Easter Rising (1916), 73, 75
    election (1918), 79
Marmion, Patricia, 124
marriage, 3, 21–2, 29, 30, 31, 102, 133–4,
    142, 143, 144
    dowries, 34
    inter-church marriages, 61, 188–9
    matchmaking, 21, 110
    sex and, 188–96
    Traveller community, 188
marriage bar, 153
marriage breakdown, 147–8, 189. see also

divorce
    Anti-Divorce Campaign, 190–1
    legal separation, 191
married women
    employment of, 5, 50, 99–100, 141–3,
        210
    family budget, control of, 197
Martin, Violet, 31, 32
Martindale, Hilda, 17
Masson, Jimmy, 121
matchmaking, 21, 110, 188
maternity hospitals, 22
maternity leave, 152
Matthew, Kitty, 45
Maudling, Reginald, 170
Maxi, Dick and Twink, 140
Maze Prison, 230
media, 143, 153
Medical Society of France, 41
Meehan, Maura, 174
Menzies, Sadie, 112
Mercer Street (Dublin), 74
Messines (Belgium), 238
microwave ovens, 205
middle-classes
    childbirth, 22
    education, 27
    home environment, 16–17
    philanthropic work, 31–2, 37
    suffrage campaign, 55
Midwives (Ireland) Act (1918), 22
migration, 33
Mikado, 39
millennium celebrations, 244
Miller, Kerby, 34
Millet, Kate, 153
Milligan, Alice, 41
miniskirts, 138
Ministry of Home Affairs (Northern
    Ireland), 119
miscarriages of justice, 221–2
missionaries, 33, 110
Mistress America stove, 36
Mná na hÉireann, 156, 158
Mná na Poblachta, 96
Modern Girl, 110
modernisation, 21
Modernist art, 7
modesty, 7, 102
Molnar, Suzi, 116
Moloney, Helena, 50, 60, 112

Monaghan (county), 89
Moneymore (Co. Derry), 223
Mongella, Gertrude, 239
Monteagle, Lord, 64
Montenotte (Cork), 25
Montgomery Street (Dublin), 19
Monto area (Dublin), 46
Moore, Jean, 174
Moore, Marie, 167
Moore, Ruth, 179–80
Moriarty, Patrick, 144
Morris, Dr, Archbishop of Cashel and
    Emly, 140
mortality. see death rates
Morton, H.V., 112
Moscow (Russia), 112
Mosley, Oswald, 114
mother and baby clubs, 24
Mother and Child Scheme, 129
Mother Ireland, 107
motherhood, 22–4, 25, 30, 102, 107, 143,
    144, 197. see also unmarried mothers
    ethical concerns, 200
Mothers' Union, 100, 106
Mount Melleray (Co. Waterford), 215
Mountjoy prison (Dublin), 56
Mountstewart (Co. Down), 79
moving statues, 215
Mowlam, Mo, 6, 228
Moxon-Brown, E., 222
Moy Park (Co. Armagh), 212
MsChief (Dublin), 196
Muir, Madge, 56, 64
Muldoon, Paul, 8
Mulholland, Marie, 238
Mullan, Fr Hugh, 167–8
Mullin, Mary, 101
Mullingar (Co. Westmeath), 24
Munster Fusiliers, 71
Munster Suffrage Society, 59
Munster Women's Franchise League, 52
Murnaghan, Sheila, 149
Murphy, Annie, 216
Murphy, Cliona, 59
Murphy, Delia, 123
Murphy, Dervla, 12–13
Murphy, Irene, 231
Murray, Ruby, 136
Musgrave's (Belfast), 84
music, 39, 110, 138, 140
    jazz, 106–7

pop culture, 139, 140
Music Makers, 140

Naples (Italy), 117
National Association for Cycling and
    Athletics in Ireland, 102
National Committee to Combat Poverty,
    215
National Farm Survey (1994), 209–10
National Guard (Blueshirts), 113
National Health Service (NHS), 128, 132
National University, 101
National Women's Council, 153
Nationalist Party, 90
nationalists, 6, 41, 52, 58, 59–60. see also
Easter Rising; republican movement;
    republican women; War of
    Independence
    all-female organisations, 59–60, 89. see
    also Cumann na mBan
    Celtic Revival, 59
    Coronation celebrations (1953), and,
    135–6
    feminists, 60
    Hibernian movement, 89–90
    suffrage campaign, and, 58–60, 65
nationhood
    women as symbols of, 107
Nazism, 107, 116
Ne temere decree (1907), 61, 63
Needlework Guild (West Cork), 25
Nelis, Mary, 176
Nelson, Rosemary, 225
Nelson, Sarah, 122
Network, 212
Nevada (showband), 140
New Mossley (Glengormley, Co. Antrim),
    148
The New Oxford Book of Irish Verse (1986),
    214
The New Penguin Book of Irish Poetry (1990),
    214
New University of Ulster, 184
Newcastle, 45
Newry (Co. Down), 109
newspapers, 143
Newtownards Chronicle, 91
Newtownards (Co. Down), 91, 212
    German air raids, 123
Ní Aoláin, Fionnuala, 175
Ní Chuilleanáin, Eiléan, 214

Ní Dhuibhne, Éilís, 214
Nic Giolla Easpaig, Áine, 176
Nic Giolla Easpaig, Eibhlín, 176
Nicholson, W.P., 110
Nissen huts, 127
NIWRM. see Northern Ireland Women's
  Rights Movement
Nobel Prize for Peace (1976), 184
Noble, Anne, 172
non-marital children. see illegitimate
  children
Noonan, Liz, 196
North Strand (Dublin)
  German air raid (1941), 124
Northern conflict, 2, 5–6, 12, 13, 138, 143,
  158–77, 179, 218–25, 241
  Bloody Friday (1972), 171
  Bloody Sunday (1972), 170
  British army, 164, 170, 178, 183
  car bombs, 170, 224–5
  civil rights movement, 6, 159–67
  community politics, 225–32
  deaths and injuries, 170–1, 173, 175,
    218–19, 224–5
  demographic change, 143
  Direct Rule, 170–1
  dirty protest, 219
  family life, effects on, 189–90
  gender issues, 218–19
  Good Friday Agreement (1998), 224,
    231–2
  hunger strikes, 219–20
  internment without trial, 167–9, 175,
    176, 177
  Omagh bomb (1998), 224–5
  Opsahl Commission, 227
  parading disputes, 223–4
  paramilitary ceasefires (1994), 224
  peace movements, 180–5
  peace rallies, 183
  police and security forces, women in,
    174–5
  power-sharing executive (1974), 171
  prisoners, 167, 173–4, 175–7, 178,
    219–22
  Protestant identity crisis, 223–4
  religious identity, 5
  UWC strike (1974), 171–2
  Vital Voices seminars, 228
  women paramilitaries, 171–4
Northern Ireland, 6, 13, 86, 88, 89, 97, 100,
  106, 107. see also Northern conflict
abortion, 147, 199–200
age of consent, 103
Ancient Order of Hibernians, 89–90
2BE (radio station), 110
birth control, 106
boundary negotiations, 93
Catholics, 83–4, 86, 88, 97, 109, 136,
  157, 164
civil rights campaign, 128, 159–67
community politics, 225–6, 225–32
constitutional position, 132
coronation celebrations (1953), 135–6
Criminal Law Amendment Act (1923),
  103
Direct Rule, 6, 170–1, 208, 227
divorce legislation, 148
domestic violence, 191–2, 192–3
education reforms, 128
EEC membership, 143
elections, 89–90, 149, 228, 231, 232
electoral boundaries, redrawing of, 92
equal pay and equality legislation, 207
Equality Commissions, 242
establishment of state, 80, 84, 88
ethnic minorities, 202, 204–5
Fair Employment Agency, 208
fascism, supporters of, 114
German air raids, 122–4
GI brides, 124
Good Friday Agreement (1998), 224,
  231–2
health reforms, 128–9
homosexuality legislation, 147
housing, 17–18, 126–8, 159–62
infant mortality, 98, 197
inter-church marriages, 188–9
internment, 126, 167
left-wing movements, 112
linen industry, 43
marriage, institution of, 188
married women in employment, 141
National Health Service, 128
petrol rationing, 120
post-War period (1945–), 126–9,
  135–6
poverty, 159, 160
prostitution, 103
'Protestant State for a Protestant People',
  6
Protestants, 97

religious discrimination, 86, 88, 97, 128, 159–62
religious practice, 217
Representation of the People Act (1928), 93
school milk protest (1971), 177
Second World War, 115–19, 122–6. *see also* Second World War
sectarianism, 83–4, 91, 109, 112, 143, 223
sex discrimination legislation, 177–8
sexual assault legislation, 103
single parent families, 195
sportswomen, 7, 102
unemployment, 97–9
VE Day (1945), 125–6
vulnerability of new state, 89, 90
welfare reforms, 128–9
women in politics, 60–4, 89, 90–3, 149. *see also* nationalists; representative politics; republican women; unionist women
Women's Aid movement, 179
Women's Athletic Championships (1949), 102
women's movement, 12, 158–9, 177–80
women's writing, 8
Northern Ireland Abortion Campaign (NIAC), 199
Northern Ireland Abortion Law Reform Association, 199
Northern Ireland Assembly (1998), 232
Northern Ireland Association for Family Planning, 200
Northern Ireland Civil Rights Association (NICRA), 161, 163, 167
formation (1967), 161–2
Northern Ireland Council for Ethnic Minorities, 202
Northern Ireland Family Planning Association (NIFPA), 146
Northern Ireland Forum, 228
women members, 231
Northern Ireland government, 170
Northern Ireland Housing Trust, 127
Northern Ireland Life and Times Survey (2000), 188
Northern Ireland Nursery Schools Association, 119
Northern Ireland Office, 227

Northern Ireland Parliament
dissolution (1972), 170, 171
opening (1921), 90
women members, 90–2, 149
Northern Ireland Voluntary Trust, 228
Northern Ireland Women's Advisory Council, 126–7
Northern Ireland Women's Coalition (NIWC), 228–30, 231
election manifesto (1996), 230
Northern Ireland Women's Rights Movement, 8, 214
Northern Ireland Women's Rights Movement (NIWRM), 177, 178, 221
Nugent, Mairead, 219
nuns. *see* religious sisters
nursery schools, 119
nurses, 44, 115
First World War, 67–8, 69

Oath of Allegiance, 96
Ó Brádaigh, Ruairí, 173
O'Brennan, Lily, 72–3
O'Brian, Nora Connolly, 35
O'Brien, Edna, 145
O'Brien, Nelly, 93
Observer, 165, 166
O'Callaghan, Kate, 84, 86
O'Callaghan, Michael, 84
occupational class. *see* social class
O'Connell, Angela, 196
O'Connor, Pat, 193, 242, 244
O'Connor, Sinéad, 235
Ó Corráin, Donncha, 10
O'Doherty, Dr, 30
O'Donnell, Jacqueline, 127
O'Donnell, Mary, 214
O'Donovan, Margaret, 83
O'Donovan, Orla, 227
O'Dowd, Liam, 107
O'Duffy, Eoin, 113
O'Faolain, Julia, 214
O'Faolain, Nuala, 8, 75, 145
O'Farrell, Elizabeth, 73, 75
O'Farrelly, Agnes, 60
Official IRA, 181
Official Sinn Féin, 181
O'Flaherty, Liam
Going into Exile, 33
Ogilby, Ann, 174
O'Higgins, Kevin, 96

Oireachtas Committee Report on the
    Constitution, 232
O'Kane, Evelyn, 210
old age pension, 42
Oldham, Alice, 27
O'Leary, Mary, 131
Olympic Games, 7, 102
Omagh (Co. Tyrone)
    car bomb (1998), 224–5
Omagh (Tyrone), 66
O'Mahony, Nora Tynan, 22
Oman, Agnes Daly, 117
O'Neill, Cathleen, 225
O'Neill, Elizabeth, 225
O'Neill, Maggie, 213
O'Neill, Terence (Prime Minister of NI),
    163, 164
opera, 39
Opsahl Commission (1992–93), 227
Orange Lil, 224
Orange Order, 62, 71, 149
    female lodges, 61–2, 79
Orange parades, 223
Ormeau Park (Belfast), 183
Ormeau Road (Belfast), 177, 226
O'Rourke, Mary, 234
Orr, Captain L.P.S., 166
Osborne, Rosabelle, 67, 68
O'Sullivan, Councillor (Belfast), 135
O'Toole, Fintan, 243
Outdoor Relief, 98
outworkers, 42–3
Owens, Nora, 196
Owens, Rosemary Cullen, 54

pacifism, 6, 65. see also peace movements
Paisley, Ian, 147, 163, 222
Paisley, Ian, Jr., 149
Paisley, Rhonda, 231
Pakistani community (NI), 202, 204
pantomime, 39
papal encyclicals
    birth control (1968), 145
papal visit (1979), 157
Parachute Regiment
    Bloody Sunday (1972), 170
Parades Commission, 223
parading disputes, 223–4
Paris Olympics (1924), 102
Parker, Dehra (née Chichester), 90, 91–2
parliamentary franchise. see suffrage

campaigns
parliamentary representation. see
    representative politics
part-time employment, 141–2, 210
partition, 80, 88–9, 238
Patterns, 38
Patterson, Henry, 17
Patterson, Monica, 181
Patterson, Saidie, 17, 22, 42, 99, 162
Pau (south-west France), 66
Payment for Debt Act, 1971 [NI], 168–9
peace movements, 6, 65, 82, 180–5
    All Children Together, 181–2
    Belfast Peace Women, 182
    Derry Peace Women, 181
    Peace People, 183–4
    Women Caring Trust, 181
    Women Together for Peace, 181, 182, 183
    Women's International League for Peace
        and Freedom, 82, 96–7
Peace People, 183–4
Peak Practice, 235
Pearse, Margaret, 84, 96
Pearse, Patrick, 72, 85
pensions, 42
People's Democracy (PD), 163
philanthropic work, 23, 24–5, 31–2, 37–8
    formalisation, 37
    health education, 41
    health visitors, 23–5
    housework, education in, 36–7
    housing, 19–20
    Poor Law work, 37
    religion as motivating factor, 37–8
    war relief, 66, 115
Phoenix Park (Dublin)
    Áras an Uachtárain, 235–6
    Eucharistic Congress (1932), 108–9
    papal visit (1979), 157
Pigeon-House Fort (Dublin), 29
Pim, Mrs, 37
Pioneer societies, 109
Pioneers, 106
Pius VI, Pope, 7
Plaza (Belfast), 122
Plunkett, James, 27
Plunkett, Joseph, 76
pluralism, 150
poetry, 8
    women's contribution, 8, 214
Poland

invasion by Hitler (1939), 114
police forces, women in, 174–5, 208
political activism (women), 51–87. see also
   nationalists; republican women; suffrage
   campaigns; unionist women
   Irish Free State, 96
   Northern Ireland, 60–4, 89, 90–3, 149
   parliamentary representatives. see
   representative politics
   party politics, 159
   Republic of Ireland, 149–50, 232–9
political parties. see Alliance Party; Centre
   Party; Communist Party; Cumann na
   nGaedheal; Democratic Unionist Party;
   Fianna Fail; Fine Gael; Irish
   Parliamentary Party; Labour Party;
   Liberal Party; Northern Ireland
   Women's Coalition; Progressive
   Unionist Party; Sinn Féin; Social
   Democratic and Labour Party; Ulster
   Unionist Party; Workers' Party
political prisoners. see prisoners; republican
   prisoners
political violence. see Civil War; Easter
   Rising; Northern conflict; War of
   Independence
politics. see political activism; representative
   politics
Poor Law, 37, 90, 98, 128
   women Guardians, 37, 54
pop culture, 139, 140
   Beatlemania, 139–40
popular culture, 235
Portadown (Co. Armagh), 43, 218, 225
   Garvaghy Road parade, 223–4
Porter, Elizabeth, 227
Portrush, 45
post-Famine period, 31
Post Office, 47
post-war period
   1918–19, 77–80
   1945–, 126–36
post–War period (1945–)
   Éire, 129–35
   Northern Ireland, 126–9, 135–6
Poulton, Katherine, 217
poverty, 18, 19, 22, 35, 37, 98–9, 128, 197,
   203, 205, 244
   Belfast, 160
   elderly, amongst, 201
   health, and, 42

philanthropic intervention. see
   philanthropic work
Power, Jenny Wyse (Senator), 100
Power's whiskey, 22
Precious Life, 199
pregnancy, 22, 197
   counselling, 156
   outside marriage, 146, 194. see also
   unmarried mothers
   termination. see abortion
Presbyterian Church
   women ministers, 217–18
President of Ireland
   elections (1997), 237
   female Presidents, 6, 234–9, 242
   Mary Robinson, 234–7
   Mary McAleese, 237–9
Preston, Ellen, 18–19
Price, Dolours, 173, 175, 176
Price, Marion, 173–4, 175, 176
prices
   cost of living changes, 1939 and 1951,
   133
Princess Pauline (comedienne), 39
Prior, Pauline, 175
prisoners, 178. see also republican prisoners
   criminalisation, 176
   dirty protest, 219
   female political prisoners, 76, 82–3,
   94–5, 173–4, 175–7, 219–22
   hunger strikes, 84, 219–20
   internment, 126, 167–9, 175, 176, 177
   miscarriages of justice, 221–2
   strip-searching, 220–1
   wives and partners, effects on, 83, 189–90
Pro-Life Amendment Campaign, 198
professions
   women's participation, 44, 47–8
Progressive Democrats, 233
Progressive Unionist Party (PUP), 231
property rights, 21
Proportional Representation, 89, 92
prosperity, 202
prostitution, 46, 103, 121, 213
Protestant Churches, 5, 62, 148. see also
   Anglican Church;
   Church of Ireland; Presbyterian Church
   women's involvement, 217–8
   women's role, 110
Protestant Textile Operatives' Union, 48
Protestants, 15, 29, 31, 49, 61, 164, 223

Church-based organisations, 109
contraception, attitudes to, 105
daily life, 38
identity crisis, 223
Irish Free State, 86
Northern Ireland, 97
religious practice, 38, 109, 110
Sunday schools, 109, 110
women's movement in Northern Ireland,
   and, 179–80
Provisional IRA, 164, 171, 173, 177, 183,
   220
   Canary Wharf bomb (1996), 224
   ceasefire (1994), 224
public activism, 51–2. *see also* civil rights
   movement; peace movements; political
   activism; suffrage campaigns
Public Dance Halls Act (1935), 106
Purdie, Bob
   Politics in the Streets, 159
Purdon Street (Dublin), 19
Purser, Sarah, 39, 111

Quakers, 43
Queen Alexandra Imperial Nursing Service
   (QAINS), 67, 71
Queen's College Belfast, 28
   women students, 27
Queen's University Belfast, 149, 163, 165,
   177, 237
Queen's University Literary and Debating
   Society, 149
The Quiet Man (1952), 142
Quinn, Alice, 98
Quinn, Edel, 108, 144
Quinn, Susan, 244–5
Quinn-Conroy, Bridie, 5, 217

RAC *see* Relatives' Action Committee
racial prejudice, 205
radio, 4, 110
Radio Telefís Éireann (RTÉ), 136, 143–4,
   237
   Bookline, 8
   Dear Daughter (1996), 216
   Fair City, 235
   Glenroe, 235
   The Late Late Show, 144, 154, 185, 196
railways, 21, 45
   excursions, 38
rape, 156, 192

Rape and Incest Line, 192
Rathcoole (Belfast), 127
Rathmines (Dublin)
   College of Commerce, 58
rationing, 120
Rebellion (1916), 72
Reclaim the Night marches, 156
recreation. *see* leisure and social activities
Red Cross (Wexford), 66
Redmond, John, 79
Rees, Merlyn, 173
refugees, 205
Reid, Eileen, 140
Relatives' Action Committee (RAC), 176,
   178
religion, 5, 38, 108, 109, 213–18. *see also*
   Anglican Church; Catholic Church;
   Catholics; Protestant Churches;
   Protestants
   importance of, 5, 108–9
   missionaries, 33, 110
   philanthropic work, and, 37–8
   practice of, 38, 108–10, 216–17
   women's role, 108–10, 217–18
religious discrimination, 88
   civil rights campaign. *see* civil rights
      movement
   employment, 208
   housing, in, 159–62
   Northern Ireland, 86, 88, 97, 128, 159
religious orders, female. *see* religious sisters
religious sisters, 32–3, 47, 108
   decline in vocations, 217
   disadvantaged, service with, 215
   'responsible obedience', 215
   scandals, 216
religious vocations
   decline in, 217
Report of an International Tribunal on Abortion
   (1989), 199
Report of the Labour Commission to Ireland
   (1920), 82
*Report on the Cost of Living of the Working
   Classes* (1908), 43
Representation of the People Act (1928), 93
representative politics, women in, 148–51,
   186, 231, 232–9
   Dáil Éireann deputies, 6, 79–80, 84, 96,
      149–50, 232–4
   female Presidents, 186, 234–9
   local government, 54

Northern Ireland Assembly elections (1998), 232
Northern Ireland Forum elections (1996), 228, 231
Northern Ireland parliament, 90–91
Westminster House of Commons, 92, 149, 164
reproductive treatments, 200
Republic of Ireland, 6, 72, 75
abortion, 197–199, 200
church–state relations, 5, 129, 213–14
Commission on the Status of Women, 242
contraception and family planning, 145, 154, 155, 158
Council for the Status of Women, 153
declaration of Republic (1949), 132
divorce, 190–1
domestic violence, 192, 193
EEC membership, 143
elections 1977, 149–50
emigration, 132–3, 135, 143
equality legislation, 152–3, 212
family home protection, 156
family legislation, 156
female employment, 141–3
Fórsa Cosanta Áituíl, 212
Free Legal Aid Scheme, 156
health reforms, 129–30
homelessness, 203–4
infant mortality, 197
Kerry babies case (1984), 198, 226
marriage breakdown, 148
Mother and Child Scheme, 129
National Farm Survey (1994), 209–10
part-time employment, 141
peace rallies, 183
Presidents. see President of Ireland
religion, 5, 129, 213–18
rural electrification, 130
Succession Act (1965), 152
television, 143–4
Traveller community, 202
unmarried mothers, 131, 156, 194
urban and rural divide, 130
women in politics, 6, 80, 84, 149–50, 232–9
women's community groups, 226–7
women's movement, 151–8
X case (1992), 198–9, 226
republican movement, 79, 88, 171, 189. see
also IRA; Northern conflict; republican prisoners; republican women
dissidents, 224–5
Easter Rising (1916), 72–7
War of Independence (1919–21), 80–7
republican prisoners, 82–3, 112, 126
Civil War, 94–5
dirty protest, 219
Easter Rising (1916), 76, 77
hunger strikes, 84, 219–20
internment without trial, 167–9
strip-searching, 220–1
War of Independence (1919–21), 82–3
wives and partners, effects on, 83, 189–90
women prisoners, 76, 82–3, 94–5, 173–4, 175–7, 219, 220–1
republican women. see also Cumann na mBan
Catholic Church hostility, 95
Civil War, involvement in, 94–5
Easter Rising (1916), involvement in, 72–5
elections (1918), 79–80
feminism, and, 179
Howth gun-running (1914), 64
prisoners. see republican prisoners
Treaty (1921), and, 84–5, 86, 94, 96
volunteers, 72, 172–3
War of Independence, and, 80–2
wives and partners of prisoners, 83, 189–90
Responsible Society, 190
retail trade, 45, 48
retirement, 201
Revolutionary Workers' Group, 112
Reynolds, Albert, 237
Rice, Mary Spring, 64
Richmond Lodge School for Girls, 26–7
right-wing movements, 112–13
2RN radio (Dublin), 110
Robertson, Nora, 17
Robinson, Mary (née Bourke), 132–3, 145–6, 150–1, 158, 187, 226, 236, 238, 242
Anglo-Irish Agreement (1985), and, 222–3
leadership, 236
President of Ireland (1990–97), 234–7
UN High Commissioner for Human Rights, 237

Robinson, Nicholas, 151
Roche, Adi, *187*, 237
Rodgers, Brid, 232
Rolling Stones, 139, 140
Rolston, Bill, 173
Romeo, 138
Rooney, Eilish, 159, 179, 180, 241
Roscommon, 34
Roscrea (Co. Tipperary)
   slum housing, 20
Rose, Kieran, 196
Ross, Florence, 71
Rotunda Lying-In Hospital (Dublin), 23
Royal Chest Hospital (London), 124
Royal Hibernian Academy, 7
Royal Institute of Public Health (Dublin),
   41
Royal Irish Constabulary, 82
Royal Ulster Constabulary (RUC), 164,
   175, 212
Royal University of Ireland, 4, 27
royal visits
   Elizabeth II (1977), 184
   Victoria (1900), 14
RTÉ. *see* Radio Telefís Éireann
RUC. *see* Royal Ulster Constabulary
rural economy
   tourism, 142
rural education, 36
rural electrification, 130
rural life, 16, 130, 243
   access to resources and facilities, 203
   conservatism, 16
   crossroads dancing, 40
   housing conditions, 20–21
   marriage, 21, 133
   water supply, 130
Russia, 112, 113, 118
Ryan, Louise, 75, 107
Ryan, Mary Anne, 142
Ryan, Min, 72, 77
Ryan, Dr Tom, Bishop of Clonfert, 144
Sagar, Pearl, *229*, 230, 231
St Anne's Cathedral (Belfast), 71
   mosaic roof, *9*
St Comgall's church, Bangor, 217
St Nahil's Church, Dundrum (Co. Dublin),
   111
St Patrick's Academy, Dungannon, 165
St Patrick's Church, Ballymacarret, 217
St Vincent de Paul Society, 37, 244

Sales, Rosemary, 208
Salonika, 67
Salvation Army, 110
same-sex relationships, 32, 147, 243
sanatoria, 40–41
Sands, Bobby, 220
Sandy Row (Belfast), 174
Saor Éire, 96
Sáorstat Éireann. *see* Irish Free State
Sappho, 147
Sarsfield Barracks (Limerick), 212
Save the Kiddies Project, 49
Save Ulster from Sodomy Campaign, 147
Sayers, Peig, 108
Scanlon, Rosemary (Dana), 141, *187*, 237
schools, 25, 26–7, 128
   school milk protest (1971), 177
   teachers, 47, 128
Scotland, 33, 45, 61
Seanad Éireann, 2
seaside resorts, 38, 45
Second Commission on the Status of
   Women, 204
Second Dáil, 84, 85
Second Vatican Council, 145, 215
second-wave feminists, 1–2, 8, 242
Second World War (1939–45), 12, 107,
   114–26, 244
   air-raid precautions, 115, 122
   air raids, 122–4
   airwomen, 117, 125
   American troops, 124
   British services, recruitment to, 115–17
   civil defence, 115
   civilian work, 117–19
   gas masks, 122
   leisure and social life, 121–2, 124–5
   rationing, 120
   shortages, 120
   VE Day (1945), 125–6
   war relief efforts, 115, 120–1
   war work, 115–19
   women's involvement, 115–19
sectarianism, 83–4, 88, 91, 109, 112, 143,
   223
secularisation, 217, 218
security forces, women in, 174–5, 208
Segal, Lynne, 11
self-help, 37
servants, 16–17, 29, 44–5, 99
service sector, feminisation of, 208–9

sewerage, 130
sex industry, 213. *see also* prostitution
sexual abuse, 192
sexual autonomy, 199
sexual discrimination, 152, 207, 212
    legislation, 177
sexual exploitation, 103
sexual harassment, 212
sexual identity. *see* homosexuality; lesbians
sexual morality, 46, 103–6, 107, 121, 124,
    144–5, 218
sexual offences, 103, 156, 192
sexual relationships, 188
    age of consent, 103
sexual revolution, 145
sexuality, 5, 188–96
    EU membership and, 195–6
    naivety, 22, 194
    religious influences, 5
Shaarma, Suneil, 202
Shankill Picturedrome, 39
Shankill Road (Belfast), 38, 128, 181, 183,
    225
Shannon, Catherine, 161
Shannon, Sharon, 235
Shaw, Sandie, 140
Sheehan, Kathleen, 26
Sheehy, Jeanne, 111
Sheehy Skeffington, Hanna. *see* Skeffington,
    Hanna Sheehy
shifting perspectives, 11
shopping, 141
shopworkers, 45, 48
Shortall, Róisín, 234
showbands, 140
Silent Witness, 235
Simon Community, 203, 204
Simpson, Audrey, 200
Sinatra, Frank, 121
Sinclair, Betty, 112, 118, 161, 163
Sinclair, Miss, 66
Sinclair, Mrs, 61
single mothers. *see* unmarried mothers
single parent families, 3, 146, 194, 195, 243.
    see also unmarried mothers
single women, 30–2, 194–5
Sinn Féin, 52, 77, 80, 85, 89, 90, 96, 163,
    167, 173, 181, 226, 231, 236, 237
    1918 elections, 79
Sirocco works (Belfast), 83
Sisters of Mercy, 29, 216

Skeffington, Francis, 77
Skeffington, Hanna Sheehy, 27, 41, 50, 54,
    55, 56, 57, 58, 65, 77, 95, 96, 100, 112
skibbereen (Co. Cork), 124
Skine, Molly, 83
Skinnider, Margaret, 74
Small, Mabel, 56, 58
Smith, Felicity Braddell, 126
Smith, Thelma, 124
smoking, 202
Smyth, Ailbhe, 156, 193, 199, 228, 238, 242
    Wildish Things (1989), 214
Smyth, Fr Brendan, 216
social activities. *see* leisure and social
    activities
social class. *see also* middle classes; social
    élite; working classes
    childbirth, and, 22–3
    death rates, and, 202
    health, and, 202
    housing conditions, 16–20
    suffrage campaign, and, 55
Social Democratic and Labour Party (SDLP),
    230, 231, 232
social élite
    leisure activities, 17, 38–9
Socialist Women's Group, 178
Society for the Protection of the Unborn
    Child (SPUC), 158, 198
Society of St Vincent de Paul, 37, 244
Sodality of the Children of Mary, 108
Solemn League and Convenant, 1912, 62
Somerville, Edith, 31, 32
The Song of Bernadette (film), 108
South, the. *see* Irish Free State; Republic of
    Ireland
South Africa, 108
South Belfast Ulster Women's Association,
    66
South Berks Conservative Association, 61
South Dublin Union, 73
Soviet Russia, 118
Soviet Union, 112
Spanish Civil War, 112
Spare Rib, 174
Special Constabulary. *see* B Specials; Black
    and Tans
Spence, Gusty, 35, 114–15
Spillane, Mary, 25
sporting activities, 7, 38
    Olympic Games, 7, 102

Springfield, Dusty, 140
SPUC. *see* Society for the Protection of the
    Unborn Child
stained glass, 111
standard of living. *see* living standards
Standing Advisory Commission on Human
    Rights, 147
Stannus, Louise, 37
Starkie, Enid, 71
Steiner-Scott, Liz, 30
Stephens, Kathleen, 229
Stevens, Lorna, 214
Stewart, Edwina, 112
Stoneybatter (Dublin), 74
Stop the Strip Search campaign, 221
Stopes, Marie, 106
Stormont Parliament. *see* Northern Ireland
    Parliament
Strabane (Co. Tyrone), 61, 66, 130
Strain, Joan, 139
street traders, 19, 26
strikes. *see* trade disputes
strip-searching, 220–1
Strong, Eithne, 214
Succession Act (1965), 152
Suffolk (Belfast), 127
suffrage campaigns, 2, 6, 52–66, 242
    class background, 55
    co-ordination of activities, 54
    First World War, and, 65–6
    gender differences, 55, 57
    grant of vote to women over 30
        (1918), 79
    hunger-strikes, 56, 58
    local government reform, 54
    militant action, 56, 57–8, 64, 65
    municipal franchise, 54
    nationalism, and, 58–60, 65
    'suffrage catechism', 55
    unionism, and, 60–64
Sunday opening, ban on, 40
Sunday schools, 38, 109, 110
supermarkets, 141
supernatural phenomena, 215
surrogate motherhood, 200
Sweeney, Fionnuala, 209, 210
swimming, 102
swinging sixties, 138–48
Switzerland, 17
Synge, John Millington, 34

Taillon, Ruth, 72
Tariff Association, 61
teachers, 47
    itinerant teachers, 36
    training of, 128
technological developments, 2, 137, 243
teenage magazines, 138
telegrams, 21
telephones, 205
television, 4, 143–4, 144, 205. *see also*
        Radio Telefís Éireann
teleworking, 209
Templeton, Joanne, 244
tenant purchase, 21
tennis, 102
test-tube babies, 200
textile industry, 42–3, 48, 99
Textile Workers' Union, 48
Thatcher, Margaret, 6, 177, 186, 220, 222,
        236–7
theatre, 39
Theatre Royal (Dublin), 57
Thane, Pat, 201
Tina, 140
Tipperary (county), 93
Titanic, 244
Tobin, Fergal, 142
Today's Diary, 146
Toner, Mrs, 124
tourism, 142
Townsend, Peter, 160
Townsend Street (Dublin), 19
trade disputes, 48, 99
    Belfast, 48, 98, 99
    Dublin lockout (1913), 49–50, 60
trade unions, 48–50, 99, 212, 213
    all-female unions, 48–9, 50
Tralee (Co. Kerry), 141
trams, 21
travel and transport, 138
    air travel, 21, 134–5
    cycling clubs, 39–40
    electric tramways, 21
    railways, 21, 38
Traveller communities, 4, *134*, 204
    discrimination against, 244
    living conditions, 204
    matchmaking, 110, 188
    nomadism, 204
    Northern Ireland, 202, 204
    Republic of Ireland, 202

Treaty (1921). *see* Anglo-Irish Treaty
Trinity College Dublin, 215
  Law Society, 150
  VE Day (1945), 126
Triple Cross project, 212
Troubles (1969–98). *see* Northern conflict
tuberculosis, 40–41, 129, 201
An Túr Gloine (The Tower of Glass), 111
Turf Lodge (Belfast), 181
Twelfth of July, 223
Tyrone Nursing Corps, 66

UDR. *see* Ulster Defence Regiment
Ulster, 79. *see also* Northern Ireland
  Ancient Order of Hibernians, 89
Ulster Defence Association (UDA), 164, 171,
  174, 221
Ulster Defence Regiment (UDR), 168, 174,
  175, 209
Ulster Farmers' Union, 177
Ulster Fascists, 114
Ulster Gift Fund, 115, 124
Ulster Hall (Belfast), 123
Ulster Literary Theatre, 39
Ulster Militants, 56
Ulster Pregnancy Advisory Association, 199
Ulster Tories, 228
Ulster Unionist Council (UUC), 62, 79, 89
Ulster Unionist Party (UUP), 53, 61, 79, 80,
  90, 93, 149, 162, 163, 164, 166, 170,
  223, 231
Ulster Volunteer Force (UVF), 64–5
  re-formation (1966), 163
Ulster Women's Gift Fund, 66
Ulster Women's Suffrage Centre, 52
Ulster Women's Unionist Council (UWUC),
  60, 61, 79, 149
  anti–Home Rule campaign, 61, 63
  elections (1921), and, 89, 90
  expansion, 93
  female suffrage, and, 62–4
  peace petition (1975), 182
  war relief efforts, 66, 115
Ulster Women's Units of British Fascists,
  114
Ulster Women's Volunteer Association, 93
Ulster Workers' Council (UWC)
  strike (1974), 171–2
unemployment, 97–9
Union of Soviet Socialist Republics, 112
Union with Britain, 60, 89

unionist women
  communications network, 79
  elections (1921), 89, 90
  feminism, 180
  gun-running, 64
  Home Rule, opposition to, 61, 63
  members of parliament, 90–2
  Orangewomen, 61–2, 79
  political organisations, 60–64. *see also*
    Ulster Women's Unionist Council
  Solemn League and Covenant (1912), 62
  suffrage campaign, and, 62–4
  UVF membership, 64
  war relief work, 66, 115
unionists, 6, 11, 52, 53, 60, 83, 90–2, 163,
  222–3. *see also* unionist women
  cultural heritage, 223
  female suffrage, and, 58, 60–3
  identity crisis, 223
  Solemn League and Covenant (1912), 62
United Irishman, 15
United Irishwomen, 36, 66, 67, 70, 100
United Kingdom
  'Clean Up TV' campaigns, 144
  female deputies, 232
  homosexuality legislation, 146
  Wednesday Play series, 146
United Nations
  Commission on the Status of Women
    (CSW), 152
  Fourth World Conference for Women
    (Beijing, 1995), 239
United States, 107, 136
  anti-Vietnam War protests, 153
  civil rights movement, 162
  Clinton administration, 228
  female employment, 34
  GI brides (Second World War), 124–5
  Irish immigrants, 33–5
University College Dublin, 28, 100
university education, 4, 27, 28, 211
university graduates
  support networks, 27
University of Kent, 223
University of Limerick, 212
University of Ulster, 177, 226, 228
unmarried mothers, 29–30, 131, 146, 153,
  156, 193–4, 195
urban children
  domestic tasks, 26
  employment, 26

urban growth, 16
urban life
  health risks, 42
  housing conditions, 17–20
Urquhart, Diane, 37, 59, 79, 89
UUC see Ulster Unionist Council
UUP see Ulster Unionist Party
UWUC see Ulster Women's Unionist
  Council

vacuum cleaners, 141
Vatican II. see Second Vatican Council
Verdun, 71
Victoria, Queen, 2, 14, 15, 16
Victoria College, Belfast, 27
Vietnam War, 153
Vietnamese 'boat people', 205
violence. see also domestic violence;
  infanticide
  Northern Ireland. see Northern conflict
  suffrage militancy, 56, 57–8
visual arts, 7, 111
Vital Voices seminars, 228
vocational education, 25
Voice of Ireland (Ruby Murray), 136
Volta cinema (Dublin), 39
Voluntary Auxilary Detachment nurses
  (VADs), 68, 69

WAAF. see Women's Auxiliary Air Force
wages, 26, 42, 43, 70–71, 99, 207, 210. see
  also equal pay
wakes and weddings, 40
Wales
  emigration to, 33
Walker, Lynda Edgerton, 230
Wall Street Crash (1929), 97
Wallace, Adree, 127
Wallace, Mary, 234
Wallace, Nora, 81
Wallace, Sheila, 81
Walsh, Louise, 196
Walsh, Oonagh, 95
War Cabinet, 99
War Club, 66
War Guild, 66
War of Independence (1919–21), 6, 80–7,
  93, 241
  Black and Tans, 82, 83, 84
  Bloody Sunday (1920), 83
  intimidation and attacks, 83

IRA campaign, 80, 83
  prisoners, 82–3
  Treaty (1921). see Anglo-Irish Treaty
  truce (1921), 84
  Ulster unionism, reactions of, 83–4
  women's involvement, 80–3
war relief, 66, 115, 120–1
war work, 67–9, 115–19
Ward, Eilís, 227
Ward, Margaret, 60, 72, 79–80, 86
Wardell, Mina, 223
wars. see Civil War; First World War; Second
  World War; War of Independence
Warsaw ghetto, 116
Warwick, Dionne, 140
washing, 35–6
washing machines, 205
Washington (USA), 142
water supply, 130
Waterford, 16
  Jewish population, 116
Watson, Rhoda, 171
Waugh, Margaret, 149
Webb, Dr E., 24–5
Wellington Hotel (Belfast), 183
Werfel, Franz
  The Song of Bernadette, 108
West Carbery Hunt, 31
West Cork, 35
Western Women's Link, 226–7
Westminster. see House of Commons
Wetherall, Mrs, 61
Wexford, 67, 70, 126
  Kennedy visit (1963), 142
Wexford Farmers' Association, 36
Whitehouse, Mary, 144
Whittaker, Robin, 230
Wicklow, 126, 183
widows, 25, 153
Wilde, Jane, 230
Williams, Betty, 183, 184
Willis, Miss, 102
Wilson, Rose, 209
Winchester, Noreen, 180
wireless telegraph, 21
Wizniak, Sabina, 116
WNHA. see Women's National Health
  Association
Wolfhound Press, 214
Woman's Conference on Lesbianism, 147
Woman's Royal Naval Service (WRNS), 69

Women Against Imperialism, 178, 221
women artists, 7–8, 111
Women Caring Trust, 181
Women in Irish Society: The Historical
    Dimension, 10
Women into Politics initiative, 227
women poets, 8, 214
women prisoners. see prisoners; republican
    prisoners
Women Together for Peace, 181, 182, 183
Women's Action, 171
Women's Aid, 156, 179, 191, 192–3
Women's Army Auxiliary Corps (WAAC),
    69
Women's Athletic Championships
    (Northern Ireland, 1949), 102
Women's Auxiliary Air Force (WAAF), 117,
    125
Women's Coalition. see Northern Ireland
    Women's Coalition
women's community groups, 6–7, 225–32
Women's Emergency Conference
    (1943–46), 121
women's experiences
    shifting perspectives, 11–12
women's health, 22–3, 193, 197–202
women's history, 10–11, 13
Women's Information Day, 226
Women's Institute, 36
Women's International League for Peace
    and Freedom, 82, 96–7
Women's Legion, 68
Women's Legion Motor Drivers, 68
Women's Liberation Movement. see Irish
    Women's Liberation Movement
women's lives, 11
women's movement, 52
    AIM, 154–6
    Commission on the Status of Women,
        152, 153
    community groups, and, 227
    International Alliance of Women,
        151–2
    Irish Women's Liberation Movement,
        153–4, 158
    legislative changes, 152
    media links, 143, 153
    Northern Ireland, 177–80
    Protestants and, 179–80
    radical feminists, 156, 158
    Republic of Ireland, 151–8

women's aid centres, 156
Women's National Health Association, 23,
    24, 36–7, 41, 66
Women's News (Belfast), 196
women's political activism. see political
    activism; representative politics
Women's Political Association (WPA), 149,
    233
Women's Prisoners' Defence League, 94–5
Women's Progressive Association, 149
Women's Right to Choose, 156, 231
Women's Royal Air Force (WRAF), 69
Women's Royal Naval Service (WRNS), 69,
    115–17
Women's Social and Political League, 101
Women's Social and Political Union
    (WSPU), 53, 54, 56, 63, 64
women's studies, 11
women's suffrage. see suffrage campaigns
Women's Unit, 174
Women's Voluntary Services for Civil
Defence, 115
women's work
    underevaluation of, 243
women's writing, 8, 10, 214
Woodside, Moya, 106, 122–3, 123
Woodvale Street (Belfast), 17, 128
work. see domestic servants; employment;
    house work; trade disputes; trade
    unions; wages
Workers' Party, 228
workers' solidarity, 112
workhouse, 25, 29
working classes, 43–4
    excursions, 38
    holidays, 38
    home environment, 17–20
Workshops for the Blind, 37
World War One (1914–18). see First World
    War
World War Two (1939–45). see Second
    World War
worldwide web, 4
Worthington, Sarah, 167
WRAF. see Women's Royal Air Force
Wright, Max, 123
writing. see women's writing
WRNS (Wrens). see Women's Royal Naval
    Service
WSPU see Women's Social and Political
    Union

Wyndham Act, 21

X case (1992), 198–9, 226

Yeats, Elizabeth, 111
Yeats, Lily, 111
Yeats, William Butler, 27

Young Women's Christian Association
    (YWCA), 109
youth culture, 138–40

Zinn, Edith, 116
Zinn, Zoltan, 116
Zurich (Switzerland), 82